CHILDHOOD and ADOLESCENCE in CANADA

McGraw-Hill Ryerson
**INTERDISCIPLINARY STUDIES IN FAMILY
AND MARRIAGE.**
General Editor — Dr. K. Ishwaran
Department of Sociology
York University

FAMILY, KINSHIP AND COMMUNITY: Dr. K. Ishwaran

Forthcoming:

MARRIAGE AND DIVORCE IN CANADA: Dr. K. Ishwaran
CANADIAN FAMILIES: ETHNIC VARIATIONS: Dr. K. Ishwaran

CHILDHOOD AND ADOLESCENCE in CANADA

Edited and with an Introduction by **Dr. K. ISHWARAN**
Professor of Sociology, York University

MCGRAW-HILL RYERSON LIMITED
Toronto Montreal London New York St. Louis San Francisco Auckland
Beirut Bogota Düsseldorf Johannesburg Lisbon Lucerne Madrid Mexico
New Delhi Panama Paris San Juan São Paulo Singapore Sydney Tokyo

Canadian Cataloguing in Publication Data

Main entry under title:

Childhood and adolescence in Canada

(McGraw-Hill Ryerson interdisciplinary studies in family and marriage)

ISBN 0-07-082935-7

1. Children in Canada - Addresses, essays, lectures.   2. Child development - Canada - Addresses, essays, lectures.   3. Youth - Canada - Addresses, essays, lectures.   I. Ishwaran, Karigoudar, date.

HQ792.C3C45   301.43'1'0971   C78-001639-4

Contents

Preface

This is the first of a set of three volumes in which an attempt has been made to display fairly comprehensively the range of current research interests in the family processes and patterns in Canada. The other two volumes—*Canadian Families: Ethnic Diversities* and *Marriage and Divorce in Canada* are being prepared for publication by McGraw-Hill Ryerson and will soon follow this volume.

Within the social scientific perspective, the general orientation of these volumes is interdisciplinary. Family as a complex social unit, with a high degree of criss-crossing connections with the wider society requires a proper understanding of all the resources—theoretical, methodological and empirical—that the various social scientific disciplines have to offer. The three volumes, together with the material available in an earlier volume—*The Canadian Family*—not only give us a fair sample of on-going original research but also provide a useful basis for identification of the problems on which future research may be focused. Most importantly, the detailed research reports embodied in these volumes are needed as source-base for a genuine development of macrosociology of the family processes and patterns in Canada.

Thanks are due, first to the authors whose contributions are included in this volume. Editorial assistance of Prof. Kwok Chan of Concordia University, and of Panchu Ganguly and Lawrence Lam of York University is acknowledged with thanks. I am grateful to Mrs. Jan Rife for her excellent secretarial services. Thanks are due also to York University and Canada Council.

K. Ishwaran
York University

To
Frederick Elkin
my esteemed colleague

CHILDHOOD AND ADOLESCENCE IN CANADA:
An overview of Theory and Research*

*I am indebted to Kwok B. Chan for his comments and helpful assistance in the preparation of this Introduction.

Introduction

EARLY STUDIES ON CHILD AND ADOLESCENT SOCIALIZATION*

Historically, the study on child and adolescent socialization has been the outcome of serious intellectual interest generated separately but simultaneously in several disciplines. Thus it has been the focal point of a genuinely interdisciplinary interest and effort. The first discipline to become systematically interested in the problem was sociology. The pioneers in the field have been Simmel and Giddings in the nineteenth century, and Park and Burgess in the first decades of this century. Psychology developed serious interest in the area in the early 1900s when Hall attempted to situate the problem of socialization within an evolutionary framework. Anthropology became involved, with the emergence of a comparative approach in the study of both primitive and contemporary social systems. It was Malinowski who first attempted to broaden the perspective of the field by going beyond its earlier exclusive preoccupation with psychoanalytic-psychological aspect. Within each of these disciplines, the study has undergone changes in focus as well as perspective. The following survey aims at a concise summary of the basic patterns, perspectives and directions that characterize the development of the study in the different disciplines. The underlying framework of this survey is interdisciplinary.

Psychology

The emergence of intellectual interest in the area of child socialization among the psychologists did not really start until the beginning of the twentieth century. While not specifically concerned with the processes of socialization, early psychologists dealt with the notion of social control within the context of socialization by proposing that an individual's mental content derives from social interaction with others. Hall (1904) adopted an evolutionary perspective in theorizing child development: an individual is destined to go through the same stages of

---

*For an excellent discussion on the subject see, Clausen J. (Ed.), Socialization and Society, Little Brown & Co., 1968.

biological and psychic development that *Homo sapien* had gone through in the course of evolution.

By 1930, empirical studies of child socialization were guided and shaped by the emergence of personality theory which also reflected the intellectual impact of learning theory and psychoanalytic theory. It was only then that studies in child and socialization were embedded within some conceptual frameworks. Considerable attention was focused on the nature of relationships between socialization practices and child behaviour.

Bronfenbrenner (1963) articulated a concise summation of the major themes and areas of research and theoretical concerns that emerged after almost five decades of intensive psychological research. The psychoanalytic framework identifies the affective quality of the parent-child relationship as the necessary condition for the development of a specific mode of behaviour. The fusion of psychoanalytic and learning theories has resulted in a theoretical emphasis on the impact of parental rewards and punishments on various modes of child behaviour. The development and formulation of the concepts of modelling and identification then direct research attention to the conditions and processes of parents providing appropriate role models for the child in the family. The field theory analyzes within and without the total and cumulative impact of all environmental forces of the family on the child. Another important theoretical contribution of psychologists stems from the various studies on the relationship between acquisition of language ability and child socialization. Their primary theoretical interest is thus focused on how the psychological and social environment exerts influence on the cognitive development of the child. Then, finally, the onset of the systematic theory witnesses the gradual emergence of research sophistication in measurements and data quantification, the application of the experimental method, and the adoption and development of multivariate analysis.

Anthropology
Anthropologists made their contribution to our cumulative understanding of the processes of child socialization by making comparative studies of both contemporary and primitive cultures. Under the influence of psychoanalytic psychology, Malinowski (1921) studied the manifestations of the oedipus complex among the Trobriand Islanders. In an attempt to go beyond the concept of psychosocial development, Malinowski traced the development process of education, specifically in teaching children basic manual skills and techniques in the arts and crafts, language and knowledge of the moral culture, and the folk mores, manners and customs which make up the social organization of the society. Sharing her interest in education with Malinowski, Mead (1928) studied the ways in which children are socialized and prepared

for the activities they would engage in and the roles they would play within their society. She also focused specific attention on the education of the Samoan child in terms of maternal care, obligations of older siblings to the younger ones, and various rights and responsibilities of social participants in the society. She anticipated the modern underpinnings of the concept of socialization by conceptualizing the term education as "the whole process by which a newborn infant becomes a member of society, a member of his particular society, and an individual in his own right." In an attempt to explore the nature of interrelationships between socialization, culture and personality, Benedict (1934) argued that the personalities of individuals who share a common culture necessarily reflect the cultural configurations that are embodied in the wider society. The process of socialization is thus seen as the mediating process responsible for the interfacing of personality and culture. Sapir's (1934) study of language converged on the analysis of patterned cultural behaviour in terms of the configuration of linguistic forms, gestures, value orientations, and other culture forms and symbols.

Sociology
Having reviewed a few sociological writings prior to 1930 on the concept of socialization (Simmel, 1895; Giddings, 1897; Burgess, 1910; Park and Burgess, 1920), Clausen (1968) suggested that the earliest sociological concern with child development and child socialization adopted an essentially deterministic framework: an individual is moulded and shaped such that he or she may become an effective, functioning member of his or her group or society. According to Giddings, socialization is understood in terms of the development, maintenance and enactment of consciousness of the kind. To Park and Burgess, socialization denotes the shaping and transforming of individuals into functioning human beings.

Although the theory of symbolic interactionism has never been specifically concerned with an articulation of the concept of socialization, it seems sensible to argue that it is the symbolic interactionists who have provided the major impetus of the sociological enthusiasm with child development or "development of human nature." By identifying the group context as the functional and situational requisite for the development of language, intelligence, and human nature, the symbolic interactionists have foreshadowed the later, modern perspective of studying child development within a social context (Chan, 1975).

That an organic, indissoluble link exists between self and society remains a dominant theme in Cooley's writings and the development of human organization and human nature. In his conception of the "looking-glass self," Cooley (1964) rejects any attempts to pose the disjunction between the knower and the world to be known; between the actor, the knowing process, and the environment. Objects in the social world, to Cooley, are not only out there, but also become the essential parts of the self. The self is ultimately social, in the sense that the self becomes self by interacting with others. Cooley's stress on the sociality and reflexiveness of the self has great impact on the modern sociological conception of personality, which is immediately apparent in the works of Dewey and Mead, and the later symbolic interactionists. Dewey (1949), the pragmatist-philosopher, sees the human mind not as a fixed and predetermined structure, but as a mental faculty to be analyzed in terms of an on-going and ever-changing activity. The dynamics of the organism-environment link are to be understood as two subsystems of a larger whole engaged in continual social interaction with one another. With this explicit recognition of interaction within a social context, language, through which meanings of objects are mediated and shared, begins to take on significant theoretical importance. While highlighting interaction as a unit of analysis by itself, Dewey's stress on the pre-eminence of the group for a proper understanding of human nature completes his final theoretical link with George H. Mead's interactionist philosophy and social psychology.

Mead (1934) sees an actor in constant interaction with himself and his immediate social psychological environment. An actor becomes capable of interacting with himself due to his conception of own self both as object and as subject. An individual interacts and communicates with himself *via* similar processes in which he interacts with whatever is external to him. An actor becomes self-reflexive and self-indicative in the sense that he reflects upon himself regarding the appropriate meanings of objects, the correct courses of action, and the probable consequences and implications of each of these actions. He talks to himself, feeds back information into his mental faculty in decision-making, indicates to himself the pros and cons, strengths and weaknesses of the divergent, and sometimes, incompatible choices, and reflects upon his own self-image in connection with *how he is being looked upon by others*. This simultaneous awareness by an organism of oneself as an active subject in relentless transactions with an external environment, and also as an object constituting a legitimate and concrete entity and structure in relation with which interaction, indication and reflexion are not only possible but also necessary, is what Mead (1934: 169) meant by self-consciousness.

In his attempt to underscore the importance of subject-object and organism-environment interaction, Mead has made two things explicit: that interaction is social, and that interaction depends on the involved parties' sharing of and manipulating a specific set of symbols and their underlying meanings (Chan, 1975). The recognition of interaction as essentially social negates the possibility, and therefore, desirability, of treating organism and environment as separate entities, and upholds the necessity of locating and identifying consciousness in the field of the environment, not in the brain, the site in which physiological mechanisms are activated and regulated (Mead, 1934: 112). To Mead, thinking processes are never the monopoly of the brain; thought is never properly understood when it is completely divorced from the environmental context in which it takes place. The analytical distinction between the inside and the outside is indeed flimsy, and sometimes, exceedingly misleading.

One crucial concept in Meadian symbolic interactionism is role-taking, understood as the actor's readiness to assume the position and perspectives of his observers, and to imagine their conceptions and evaluations of himself at the moment of contemplating and reflecting upon himself and his act. This ability to look upon himself objectively from an outsider's perspective, that is, to take into account others' thoughts and feelings, enables the gradual internalization of norms and expectations of both the significant and the generalized others such that they become part of the personality parcel. The role-taking operation thus bridges the gap between the organism and the environment, and is responsible for the generation of a one-to-one correspondence and interplay between social processes and individual, autonomic functioning. It is indeed hard to visualize an individual engaging in play or game, who is either unwilling or unable to take the reactions and intentions of others into account.

Blumer (1969) has made considerable contributions to both amplifying and intensifying symbolic interactionism by attempting a systematic interpretation and reformulation of some of the most important thoughts and premises of Cooley, Dewey and Mead. Blumer sees the development of human nature as a long and developmental process of acquiring abilities of self-interaction, self-reflexion, and self-indication. The end-point of the development of the self is one in which the person has acquired the ability to indicate to himself relevant objects in the environment and to understand their underlying meanings, such that a complex decision-making process can be initiated until an optimal solution is ultimately arrived at. Blumer sees the human organism as both an active and reactive agent, one who is ready and willing to engage in appraisal and reappraisal, interpretation, and choice. Human action should then be understood as a product of an emergent process of purposive construction, not as mechanistic release or autonomic response. However, Blumer has not failed to add that self-indication takes place in a social context, and that actor's own contemplation of projects of action is influenced by his interpretation of intentions and inclinations of others, as well as his interpretations of the situation. An accurate assessment of the many situational contingencies informs the actor of the limits under which one project of action instead of another can derive maximum profits.

Blumer (1969: 108) also attempts to alert social psychologists to what their proper focus of attention should be on: the interactional links between individuals in group settings. Only in a group context will the sociologist be able to observe how actors display covert and overt gestures, how a full-blown and smooth conversation of gesture operates, how an actor decides to adopt certain symbols which are attached to certain objects, and how one indicates to oneself as well as others the intended meanings of the immediately pertinent things. Only in a group setting does an individual begin to develop and possess a self and a mind, and to take into account the other's feelings, inclinations, intentions, and idiosyncracies on the one hand, and the myriad of situational factors on the other (Chan, 1975). A human group, in which individuals are linked to each other in terms of positions and roles, duties and rights, is exactly the kind of analytical unit sociologists interested in human development can utilize to probe into the intensity and intricacy of human interaction. Attributes of individuals by themselves never constitute a group, nor do they contribute to a proper understanding of the actual nature of the group. While the legitimate concern of sociology, according to Blumer, is the manifold operational dynamics within the group, interaction between the participants in joint action should be given the most theoretical and empirical attention.

In sum, the contributions of the whole theoretical tradition of symbolic interactionism to theory and research in child development and child socialization are four fold: first, interactionists view all actors, the child included, as both object and subject at the same time, capable of making responses to external stimuli, and perhaps, more importantly, eliciting responses from objects with which they interact. The child, contrary to what most psychologists contend, is not merely a passive recipient of external forces, but is capable of reaction and counteraction. Second, interactionists locate the development of human nature in a group context within which the child is gradually initiated into the processes of self/other interaction; the child then learns to identify the meanings of objects and situations by interacting first with the significant others in the primary group, and then the generalized others in the secondary group. The existence of the primary social group makes interaction and role-taking possible, which then contribute to the gradual development of the human nature. Third, the strong emphasis placed by interactionists on the group context is thus responsible for the increase of theoretical and research interest in the family, especially the mother-child and father-child dyads, and the peer groups as the primary agents of socialization of the child. Fourth, the fact that symbolic interactionists have concerned themselves primarily with the appraisal and interpretation of the meanings of objects and situations, has resulted in a great deal of research in the past few decades on the cognitive and evaluative aspects of child development (e.g., language, intelligence, mental and conceptual abilities, etc.).

THEORIES OF SOCIALIZATION: CHILDHOOD AND ADOLESCENCE

The study of socialization draws on a variety of theoretical perspectives generated by several disciplines. Such an interdisciplinary theoretical framework includes Erikson's psycho-social approach, Piaget's cognitive approach, Sears' learning approach, to name the most dominant perspectives. However, in terms of theoretical understanding, child socialization has stimulated a larger and more diversified body of literature than adolescent socialization. While the concept of childhood can be traced back to earliest study of men, the concept of adolescence has been an almost wholly modern development.

Erikson: The Psycho-social Approach

Though theoretically embedded in the original works of Freud and the tradition of psychoanalysis, Erikson's theory (1940, 1943, 1950, 1955, 1956, 1959, 1968) of child development and personality strives to go beyond the psychoanalytic framework by formulating three important theoretical positions. First, with the shift of theoretical attention from the id to the ego, Erikson manages to emphasize the functional significance of an individual's innate ability to adjust to cope with the normal, routine and predictable environment. Second, the child-mother-father triad of familial interaction as a unit of analysis for the psychoanalysts is placed by Erikson within the context of the social environment of which the family is only a part. Third, in contrast to Freud, Erikson views the psychological hazards as normal, developmental crises providing the growing individual with opportunities for the development of adaptability and coping resources. The occurrence of developmental crises thus provides unique chances of personality growth and development, of emotional maturity, and normality. In an attempt to come to terms with life crises, the individual is thrown to his own resources and all other resources accessible in the social networks. During the process of coping, the individual unfolds and develops into a more complex and adaptable organism.

An infant is seen by Erikson as a simple organism in the beginning, gradually changing in terms of complexity and adaptability as a result of concomitant and interrelated fulfilment of biological, physiological and psychological needs and potentials. The acquisition of human nature is thus seen in the context of the individual mediating and interacting with the culture of the society, and the more immediate social psychological environment in which he finds himself. In the process of striking a strategic balance between the three affective processes of id, ego and superego, an individual operates to organize and structure the forces of his inner life in accordance with those of the external world.

In agreement with psychoanalysis, Erikson attaches central theoretical importance to the role of early experiences in later personality development. An individual's experiences and conceptions of the external world are largely determined by his first bodily contacts, which become the most meaningful life events and experiences, and form the foundation of the patterns of his later social and psychological behaviour. Then, in the later stages of personality development, such social structural variables as class, ethnicity and religion, the impact of which are transmitted by the significant others and the generalized others, function to locate the individual within a social milieu.

Erikson's stage concept of personality development owes its conceptual and theoretical origins to Freud in that all the proposed eight psychological developmental stages follow an epigenetic sequence. The eight stages are conceptualized as periods in which the individual is to acquire (1) trust (2) autonomy (3) initiative (4) industry (5) identity (6) intimacy (7) and (8) integrity. Of these eight stages, the first five are acquired during infancy, childhood and adolescence, and the last three during adulthood. For Erikson, the acquisition of a basic sense of trust and a sense of identity is integral to the development of normal and healthy personality. It is important to note that these eight stages, instead of being regarded as compartmentalized phases exclusive and independent of each other, should be appropriately seen as parts of the dynamic and developmental continuum in that the probability of coping with or adapting to the developmental crisis inherent in every given stage is determined by how well he has been able to resolve the crises in early psycho-social stages.

Piaget: The Cognitive Approach

As a theorist and an ego psychologist, Piaget (1926, 1929, 1930, 1937, 1951, 1952, 1954, 1955, 1958) is primarily concerned with the cognitive aspect of human behaviour and its development. His fundamental tenet is, then, that of conceiving learning as a function of development. Learning cannot explain development, whereas a conceptual reconstruction of the stages of development can provide a partial explanation of the learning behaviour. In an attempt to explain the development of cognition, Piaget identifies the combination of four major mechanisms: first, maturation in terms of differentiation of the nervous system; second, experience in terms of interaction with the physical environment; third, social transmission via child care and education; fourth, equilibrium in terms of self-regulation of cognitive adaptation.

A newborn human is then seen by Piaget as a biological organism with a psychological make-up possessing three types of phylogenetic drives (or instinctual behaviour): a drive for hunger, a drive to acquire a sense of balance, and, perhaps, most importantly, a drive for independence from environment and an adjustment to it. Piaget locates the child's development within a social, physical, cultural, and ideational environment, which, altogether, provides the total forces of field, the impact of which can facilitate or retard the process of growth though the sequence of the developmental phases remain essentially unaltered.

Piaget's conceptualization of the stage of cognitive development consists of three phases, which are further subdivided into several other phases: the Sensorimotor Phase, the second phase which is comprised of the Preconceptual, Intuitive and the Concrete Operational Phases, and lastly, the Formal Operations Phase. The newborn organism is thus seen by Piaget as starting out to acquire sensori and body-motor skills and techniques which enable him to construct a realistic physical world with which he can appropriately relate and interact. With the gradual acquisition of abilities in retention, experimentation, generalization and differentiation, the child proceeds to construct a rudimentary classification of events, situations and episodes. These events, in turn, contribute to learning the ability to exercise intelligent reasoning. In the first half of the second year, the infant is beginning to replace assimilative behaviour with accommodative behaviour, and to attempt various modes of imitation and identification with the characteristics of the objects he has encountered. The acquisition of the language ability, however rudimentary it is, provides the child with an important tool of intuitive thought, a vehicle of egocentric communication, and a device and mechanism to comprehend the meanings of the external environment, and to adapt to them accordingly. With the onset of the Phase of Concrete Operations, the child has gradually learnt to conduct cognitive thinking in the sense that he is capable of comprehending the functional relationship between the whole and their parts, and also of establishing corresponding systems of classification of events and objects. The child is then able to impose order and structure on a cluster of seemingly unrelated and diverse objects or experiences. Emerging from inductive into a deductive mode of thinking, the child has learnt to theorize, to explain, to acquire the qualitative comprehension of objects and events, and proficiency in complex mental operations with symbols. His dominant intellectual interests thus consist of classifying, assessing, and weighing different ideas and perspectives, and their relationships to symbols and abstracts. At the end of the Formal Operations, the youth is finally able to view his social world as an organic unit with its attendant laws, roles and functions, to dissolve his sense of egocentricity by a sense of moral solidarity, to engage in diverse social interaction and communication, and to relate to adult authority with a sense of equality and justice.

Sears: The Learning Approach
To Sears (1948, 1951, 1953, 1957, 1961, 1965), child development is to be studied and comprehended through the learning effects of the sequence

of stimulus and response; each effect of a specific action in turn becomes a learned cause of future behaviour. The stimulus-response paradigm is then understood in terms of a stimulus not only activating the individual, but also determining the nature and timing of the response which essentially consists of an action configuration geared toward the attainment of an intended goal. While Sears views man on the basis of his behaviour only, he sees behaviour as the cause and effect of other behaviour motivated by tension reduction and reinforced as a consequence of goal achievement. The concept of development, therefore, pertains to a continuous chain of events, some of which add to or replace previous acquisitions.

According to Maier (1969), Sears' theory of child development consists of three phases: first, the phase of rudimentary behaviour, which is based upon native needs and learning in early infancy; second, the phase of secondary motivational systems which is based upon family-centred learning; third, the phase of secondary motivational systems which is based upon learnings beyond the family. In the phase of learning rudimentary behaviour, the child is primarily concerned with gratifying his innate needs, which in turn produces the primary drives and cues for action. The mechanisms and processes underlying need gratification provide the child with opportunities for environmental learning experiences. From now on his actions are no longer simply caused by innate drives; they originate from his learning. Fulfilled responses then bring to the child rewarding experiences. In the context of manipulating the environment in terms of resorting to the environment to gratify his needs and, concomitantly, perceiving that the environment provides him with a range of satisfactions, the child learns not only to manipulate, but also to be manipulated. The onset of socialization commences when the child begins to develop the skills and techniques in cooperating with those providing care and need satisfaction, and in manipulating them to ensure the continued provisions of these rewards. During the phase of secondary motivation system, the child's primary needs continue to motivate him, though, simultaneously, some of these primary needs begin to be transformed into continually reinforced social learning or secondary drives.

Theoretically, Sears is less interested in the role of punishment than that of reward as a factor in the process of child socialization. To Sears, learning takes place in a context of novel and original experiences acquiring or attempting to acquire satisfactions, not in that of fear of negative and undesirable consequences. Given his emphasis on the mother-child dyad, Sears indicates that the child's early development depends heavily upon the affectional and learned dependency on the mother. It is in this phase that Sears identifies the prime theoretical importance of studying the various child rearing practices and their role in development, and focuses upon the nature of interrelations between feeding and dependency needs, and the development of the motivational systems. It is also in this phase that the important processes of identification, imitation and sex-typing emerge. The child then learns to gain control over his or her needs and impulses, and progresses from parental control to partial self-control with the continuation of parental guidance. The responsibility of the parents is to strike an appropriate balance between the provision of too much and too little dependency. By the time the child moves into the phase of motivational system, one witnesses the gradual transition from intra-familial to extra-familial learning. In the course of participation in the world external to the family, other agents of socialization such as teachers, peers and mass media take the place of the parents in exercising influence on the child's operant dependency behaviour. Sears underscores the maintenance of early socialization experiences by suggesting that the child's previous mode of upbringing affects his quality and manner of dependency upon the nonfamilial members. One may observe patterns of positive and negative attention-seeking (e.g., teasing, joking, etc.) in the child's interaction with the extrafamilial members of his immediate social world. The development of the child in this phase may then be seen as the gradual shrinkage and constriction of the field of permissiveness, and the expansion of definition and reinforcement of the spheres of control and authority imposed on the child by adults both within and without the family.

Adolescence

It seems fair to suggest that there is a much larger and more diverse body of literature both in theory and research on child than adolescence development. Only in the last thirty to forty years has adolescence been recognized as a phase of socialization, with peculiarities that are distinct and unique enough to merit the special attention of researchers in the area of socialization.

If socialization is conceptualized as an on-going, life-long process of acquiring values, beliefs and skills such that a person is able to maximally participate in social interaction, then, the most appropriate question at this juncture is: what is next after childhood? or, where does a person who has emerged out of childhood go prior to assuming fully adult responsibilities and taking on adult obligations? Any attempt to answer this question requires a firm grip, both theoretically and empirically, on the transitional period between childhood and adulthood, that is, adolescence.

Muus (1968) argues that the concept of adolescence did not come into existence and common usage until the fifteenth century. Prior to this there was a sharp, almost mutually exclusive distinction between childhood, stressing subordination of the wishes and needs of the child to his elders, and adulthood granting the adult rights and responsibilities to the growing person. The modern creation of a trichotomy — child, adolescent and adult — then replaces the older long-established dichotomy between childhood and adulthood. As indicated by Koller and Richie (1978: 274), "Adolescence, from this perspective then, is neither a child nor an adult, but in 'between' being a child and an adult." The adolescent is then cast into a social status, the important role of which consists primarily of relinquishing the system of behaviour, values and beliefs according to which one functions and operates in the past, and, perhaps more importantly, anticipates the future acquisition of an immensely different behavioural and attitudinal system *without* the simultaneous opportunity to practice on it. In distinguishing the sociological conception of adolescence from that of the psychologists, physiologists and educationists, Hollingshead (1940) defines adolescence as "The period in life of a person when the society in which he functions ceases to regard him (male or female) as a child and does not accord to him full adult status, roles, and functions." Accordingly, Koller and Richie (1978: 274) characterize this newly granted status of adolescence as marginality that stems from the absence of a careful articulation of the standards and procedures of the transitional period. As a marginal person who belongs and is expected to belong to neither worlds that precede and follow their present state of livelihood and existence, the adolescent is tempted to be both child and adult, but is prohibited from being both.

Perhaps, a more comprehensive understanding of our conceptualization of adolescence as marginality is contingent upon yet another way of viewing adolescence: adolescence as discontinuity. Benedict (1954: 142-148) distinguishes the kind of society in which the primary task of socializing the child is to prepare him to continuously and gradually achieve adulthood from another kind of society in which to be an adolescent is to undergo a discontinuous and disruptive process of relinquishing the acquired behavioural and attitudinal set. Mead (1950) marshalled impressive anthropological data indicating how the Samoan society has avoided the "discontinuity of cultural conditioning," prevalent in the North American society, by training Samoan boys and girls for a diverse range of adult responsibilities early in the socialization process. Initiation into the adult world, including training in expression of sexuality, has thus become a spontaneous and continuous facet of cultural conditioning and training. Anthropological studies done by Mead and Benedict have thus made considerable contributions to our cumulative understanding of the immediate consequences of society placing too much emphasis on anticipatory socialization in terms of encouraging submission, control of domination and self-assertiveness, repression of sexuality and delay of gratification, without, at the same time, indicating firstly what these cultural premises and values in regard to adolescence eventually lead to, and secondly, establishing proper guidelines and procedures according to which the adolescent is to undergo the transitional period without experiencing too much storm and stress.

In a classic paper, entitled, "The Sociology of Parent-Youth Conflict", Davis (1940) identifies some of the 'universal' sources of tension and conflict between parents and youth: the basic or birthcycle differential between parent and child, the decelerating rate of socialization with advancing age, and the resulting intrinsic differences between the old and the young as the physiological, psycho-social, and sociological planes. While these universal constants underlying parent-child interactions contribute to the onset of parent-youth conflicts, there are also other variable sources, unique to the modern culture of our society, that render the generation of antagonisms possible. Davis' list of variables includes the rapid social change in modern civilizations which establish a hiatus between the generations, the problems and difficulties in enforcing parental authority as a result of conflicting norms operating within different generations, education, and other institutions competing with the parents for authority, lack of explicit institutionalization of steps in parental authority, concentration within the small family, open competition for socio-economic position, and sex tension. Davis is inclined to conceptualize parent-youth conflict as a historical inevitability by concluding the paper on the following pessimistic note: "Hence, the presence of parent-youth conflict in our civilization is one more specific manifestation of the incompatibility between an urban-industrial mobile social system and the familial type of reproductive institutions."

Winch (1971) in basic agreement with Davis' (1940) notions of 'competing authorities and conflicting norms' examines parent-youth conflict from the perspective of the adolescent craving for social acceptance by the peer groups whose values and behaviour are exactly those forbidden and opposed by the parents. To the extent that the adolescents' commitment to his peer group is high, the parents become an "outgroup," sometimes almost an opposing group. The nature of attitudinal and behavioural discrepancy between the adolescent and the parents is best illustrated by the following statement of Winch (1971: 433).

> "One technique of obtaining the approval of peers is conformity to group standards. As would be expected, therefore, there is great emphasis among middle-class adolescents upon conformity to group standards in dress, speech, and manner, and other forms of behaviour. Adolescent behaviour that is strange, bizarre and unintelligible in parental eyes may only be conformity to the expectations of the peer culture."

It is one thing to recognize and identify the various sources of conflict and antagonisms between the parents and the youth, as Davis and Winch have done; it is yet another thing to see adolescence as necessarily and inevitably a period of "storm and stress." Anthropological research by Mead (1939) has carefully delineated the significance of the nature of social organization as a determinant of whether or not adolescence is going to be a stressful period of life. Winch (1971: 455) has enumerated the following conditions under which adolescence is likely to be under stress: first, the society designates clearly which adult position the adolescent will fill and permits no alternative; second, that position and its constituent roles are seen as attainable and highly rewarding; thirdly, the course of preparation for that position is not believed as either too long or too costly relative to the prospective rewards; fourth, the culture provides a means for the individual to be aware of the time when he passes into adulthood.

In an attempt to challenge and to correct the general conception in sociology and psychology that adolescence is a period of storm and stress, Westley and Elkin's (1957) intensive study of the twenty adolescents and their families in a suburban town in Montreal, has marshalled data indicating a variant picture of the adolescents. They found "a continuity in socialization between adolescence and adulthood, a continuity evidenced in the congruence of attitudes of adolescents and parents, not discrepancy, towards heterosexual relationships, career aspirations and economic matters. In contrast to current beliefs, the peer groups do not compete with parents for authority, support, and confirmation, neither do they present to the adolescents norms which are conflicting with those of parents. Instead, the peer groups are committed to the values of the parent, and further a continuity in socialization."

Westley and Elkin attribute the continuity of adolescent socialization and congruence of parent-youth norms and values to the protectiveness of the environment of the community which strategically provides a type of social organization based on socio-structural isolation. However, the study of the adolescents in a rural Dutch Canadian community in Ontario by Ishwaran and Chan (1978) indicates a similar pattern of social organization which is conducive to the continuity of adolescence socialization in the first place, and immunity from "storm and stress" in the second. The moral fabric of the rural Dutch community is deeply embedded in a religious context, which in turn, supplies the community with the ideology, the behavioural scripts, and the normative system in guiding and regulating parent-adolescent interactions, and in giving the entire child socialization process goals, objectives, and directions. While the impact of the religious doctrine is felt in familial and marital interactions, it also makes in-roads into the school system, the social organization of leisure, sports and individual-peer group relationships. Guided by a dominant and prevalent ideology based on religious doctrines and scripts, the socialization experience of the child is then seen by Ishwaran and Chan as one of congruence, direction and harmony held within bounds and limits by religion as an integrative, all encompassing and unifying force. The absence of discontinuity of the adolescent socialization can thus be attributed to the phenomenon of social integration and social cohesion made possible by a high level of functional interdependence prevailing among such crucial social institutions as the church, the school, and the community which altogether form an "intact unity of interlocking institutions."

Agencies of Socialization

Our earlier account of the history of the systematic study of the child and the process of personality development indicated that socialization occurs within a specific group context, involving human and symbolic interaction. As a result, the development of the child is perceived as primarily a process of his or her interaction with the key personnel of the group. Elkin (1978: 114), for instance, identifies distinctive socialization roles for the different groupings, which constitute the context of the child's social existence. In sociological literature, such groups have been designated the *agencies of socialization*. Notable among such groups which exert significant impact on the developing behavioural patterns of the child are: the family, the school, peer groups, mass media, political structures and the church. However, such impact does not always manifest itself as the result of any conscious purpose. It is not as if society assigns consciously any specific roles to these agencies in the overall process of child socialization. It is because of the absence of any overall, integrated system of roles and functions for such agencies that there is a potential, as well as actual possibility, of overlap between their historically evolved functions. This occasionally leads to conflict. No less important is the fact that each of these agencies tend to develop considerable institutional autonomy of their own, and this makes the ultimate product of the socialization process complex and problematic, subject to a variety of group pressures.

The internal pressures of the different agencies make it virtually impossible to socialize the child to order, according to any preconceived plan. A study of Kassof (1965) of the socialization effectiveness of highly controlled youth programs in the USSR demonstrates that such programs have failed to produce coherent and uniform attitudes among the Soviet youth. Such studies underscore the fact that the socialization patterns to which a child is subject are determined significantly by the wider historical changes on the level of the cultural system. Because of the fact that the socialization cannot be a wholly controlled or conscious process, its consequences cannot be wholly anticipated, and, in fact, it might produce latent effects. A specific act of socialization such as, for instance, the punishment for the violation of a norm, may result in the eventual assimilation of the more generalized societal values such as respect for property. Thus socialization emerges in such studies as a complex and cumulative process in which the child internalizes the wider societal norms by being first attuned to the norms of his immediate context.

The Family

The family constitutes the first among the foremost social agencies that systematically mould the normative-behavioural patterns of the child. Indeed, as the example of Johnny Rocco (Jean Evans, 1950) illustrates, the family's serious role starts even before the child is actually born, for it already determines the child's status in the community system. This role continues till the termination of the time span of the individual person. It determines the occupational priorities and preferences of the person (John Porter, 1965). Blau and Duncan (1967: 330) further clarify the situation by suggesting that this determination does not take place directly but through the type of education the child receives, which depends significantly on the family. Therefore, the family socializes the child not simply in regard to the cultural values of the general society or community but it provides a more or less continuous system of screening in and screening out behavioural patterns which the child imbibes and identifies himself with (Handel, 1972). Thus, the structure and role of the family within the society become decisive factors in selective behavioural patterns that the child develops in interaction with his environment.

It has been well documented by research that, within the family, the interaction between the siblings in their search for parental affection, approval, attention and love, results in a variety of patterns and forms. The siblings are also known to organize within themselves in order to set up "defense mechanisms" to deal with parental authority (Davis and Havinghurst, 1947; Martin and Stendler, 1953). The length of childhood in relatively larger families varies in relation to class context. For instance, it is known to be comparatively shorter in lower-class families than in families with middle-class and upper-class backgrounds (Schulz, 1969). The eldest child, more particularly a girl, is assigned greater responsibility in the running of the household. It is normal practice for her to undertake such chores as grocery shopping and cooking. In families with both parents working, she is even called upon to function as a surrogate of parental authority over the younger children. Belonging to a lower-class family entails a definite social cost for a girl. It has been shown that it very often leads to early motherhood, blocking options of developing and pursuing more self-satisfying life-goals than that of being a mother (Rainwater, 1966). These illustrations underscore the constraints on the child's developmental opportunities, imposed by the precise location of his family in social space. As a consequence, the child's original location in social space is among the most significant determinants of his or her later role and status. The precise process underlying this development, is triggered off by socialization in the immediate family context of the child.

The specific nature of the family as an interactional system, its internal structure and relationships, provide the earliest and probably the most important context in which the child develops its self-images. It is within the context of interactions with other members of the family that the child systematically lays down the foundations for its later resources and ability to establish social communicational linkages with people outside the narrow confines of the family. It is here that the child first acquires the ability to develop trust, confidence, autonomy and companionship. For instance, the sharing of toys and games with siblings in the family enables the child to forge ahead with the skills to handle the problems of balancing self-needs with the needs of others. In the family, the child begins to develop the ability to evaluate and compare, and in this he uses the family as its basic reference model. The child learns to evaluate his own behaviour and to appreciate the significance of the family as a group whose membership confers a unique status (Parsons and Bales, 1955). Three clear-cut patterns of interaction emerge within the context of family life: first, an adult-centred, predominantly working-class family pattern in which the child is expected to conform to adult career goals; second, a child-centred, predominantly lower-middle class pattern in which a child is allowed to equal and even surpass the father in occupational status; and, third, an adult-directed, predominantly upper-middle class pattern in which the child is permitted to develop its own individuality and learn to be self-dependent (Gans, 1962). These, however, are predominant patterns, and they do not rule out intra-class variations in pattern. Such variations are attributable to specific situational variables associated with individual families. This explains why working families with disturbed children possess a significantly higher potential for internal conflicts than working families without such children. In the upshot, this situation renders the pattern of interaction between the child and others, considerably problematic (Bell, 1962).

Within the family, the mother occupies a crucial position in the international process. Undoubtedly, she is the first "significant other" with whom the child identifies himself. It is only later that the child comes to shift its identification with the mother away from her and towards the father as the latter's role as the representative of the family in its external transactions becomes increasingly relevant (Benson, 1968 and Parsons, 1964). While the father represents the symbol of masculinity for both boys and girls, the precise extent to which the role situation is internalized by children of either sex depends on their comparative evaluation of the two parents (Rosen, 1964). In this process, the status of the father in the outside world has a clear impact on the child's parental images. Findings have been reported to suggest that middle-class boys tend to perceive their fathers as competent, ambitious, successful in the world and considerate in their dealings with their children, whereas lower-class boys tend to regard their fathers as shy, worried and over-anxious (Rosen, 1964).

A child's socialization process is also significantly related to the type of regimentation prevailing in the family in regard to the system of differential job allocation to children of different ages (Bossard and Boll, 1966). In larger families, the elder children play a supportive and protective role in relation to the younger children. In the case of smaller families, the child is not saddled with household tasks, and the parents are able to devote their attention to such crucial aspects as the child's education. As a result, the child finds himself in a family climate favourable to the development of his individual personality. This is the reason why children from small families tend to rely more on their parents for emotional and material security, while those from larger families tend to organize their own groups in order to seek such security.

The sex-role learning process in early years constitutes an important and inseparable part of the overall socialization process. It has been found that a girl with a brother living at home shows "high masculinity traits" while a boy with a girl living at home shows "high femininity traits" (Brim, 1958, in his reanalysis of data in Koch, 1954, 1955a, 1955b, 1956a, 1956b, 1956c and 1956d).

Family forms exert significant and systematic influence on the socialization process. A study of the 1970 U.S. census shows that as many as thirty percent of school children lived with a father and mother in a continuous first marriage (Glick, 1975). Using the same source, it has been found that 44 percent of the entire U.S. population lived in nuclear families, 15 percent in "reconstituted families," 13 percent in single parent families, and 8 percent in a variety of unconventional marital and family situations (Cogswell and Sussman, 1972). No comparable data exist for Canada, but one estimate identifies around 8.9 percent of Canadian families as one-parent type, of which nearly two-thirds have dependent children (Schlesinger, 1973). In regard to the impact of family form on socialization process, there is evidence that children belonging to "reconstituted" families experience a unique process of socialization, and that a natural parent living away from the household tends not to shoulder the responsibility for maintaining child discipline in the household (Duberman, 1975). Another relevant finding is that there exists a social norm against a step-parent assuming the role of discipline-maintenance in the family (Fast and Cain, 1971). All such evidence points to the fact that a "reconstituted" family involves parents who are disciplined to satisfy fully the role expectations associated with them.

The single most important cause for the changes in the modern nuclear family has been the phenomenal increase in the proportion of women in the labour force. There is overwhelming statistical evidence to support such a conclusion. In 1940, only 8.6 percent of women with children were involved in outside employment, but, by 1972, thirty percent of women with children age five and fifty percent of women with children age six to seventeen took employment outside the home (Hoffman and Nye, 1974). Similar data for Canadian women have been compiled by the Canadian Women's Bureau. In 1967, 19 percent of Canadian women with children under six and 28 percent with children age six to fourteen, constituted part of the labour force. By 1973, 24 percent of women with children age two and under, 30 percent with children age two to five, and 43 percent with children age six to thirteen, were involved in work away from home.

It has been claimed on the basis of an empirical study that daughters with working mothers tend to be more independent and achievement-oriented (Hoffman, 1974). In this connection, there is need to investigate if there exists any systematic relationship between father's approval of a working mother (itself an index to male acceptance of female competence) and likelihood of a daughter becoming oriented towards a strong sense of individuality. Also there is need to examine more closely the impact on preschool children of a family situation, lacking in intimate, face-to-face contacts with maternal figures. On all these issues, the existing literature contains very little hard and incontrovertible data.

The School
As one of the key agents in the socialization process, the school has the general function of weakening the child's personal dependence on his or her ties with the home — parents and siblings. Exposure to teachers and schoolmates from divergent family situations has the inevitable effect of widening the perspective and horizon of the child. Thus, the school provides the crucial transitional passage for the child's introduction to the social world at large. The interactions in the school tend to cut across the more restricted contacts with kin and neighbourhood groups.

The school plays a significant role in political socialization insofar as it inculcates in the young the appropriate political attitudes, views and beliefs, whose center of reference is the supposed working of the political system in the received tradition (Hess and Torney, 1967: 217). In fact, this is a reinforcement and refinement of vaguer and more primal loyalty and attachment to the country into which a child is socialized in the family. There is consensus in the relevant literature that primary thrust of socialization in the school is conservative and traditionalistic. It has been shown to be antithetical to attitudes and beliefs implying social change (King, 1966). The school has been mostly seen as an agent for the preservation of the status quo. The critics of this role of the school have argued for the promotion and development of alternative and radical perspectives in the young (Goslin, 1965). The demands that the school encourage attitudes and belief favourable to social change and the counterdemand that it functions primarily as a reinforcing mechanism for preserving the existing social order, lead to dilemmas in the institutional operation of the school as an agent of socialization. It has been noted that such dilemmas result in a compromising role in which the school tends to respond relatively more slowly than other social institutions to the challenge of change (Reiss, 1965). The ability of the school to change depends on the appropriate pressures which the community may exert on it, but it is more likely that the community expectation tends to be tilted in favour of socialization for the maintenance of the status quo than the other way. Therefore, the actual functioning of the school as an agent of socialization relates to the nature of the families prevalent within the community and the family socialization experienced by the children.

American schools are stated to be strengthening the family-ascribed status of the child. As a result, districts dominated by poor families get far less educational input than those dominated by upper-class and higher income families (Sexton, 1965). In Britain, on the other hand, children from poor families get no better educational deal since, irrespective of abilities, they are likely to be admitted into lower academic groups than are comparable middle-class children (Eggleston, 1967). Children from larger families tend to be assigned the lower stream. A Canadian empirical study, using reports from the Toronto Board of Education, shows that the Asian immigrants are comparatively over-represented in the academic stream in relation to the other ethnic groups (Lanphier, 1977). Considerable evidence exists to support the view that children from larger and poorer families, for whatever reasons, have to make up at school for the inadequacies of their socialization experience at home. Clearly this places them in a position of disadvantage compared to others at the time they go to school (Rist, 1973; Bossio, 1971; Fleude, 1973).

In the school, the teachers provide the role models as the most important source of influence outside the home. The behavioural and attitudinal patterns of the teachers constitute, in consequence, important factors in the process of socialization within the school. Studies have shown that most teachers prefer to serve in districts where schools are attended by children from a predominantly middle-class family background, and they are not generally anxious to remain in poor family districts (Herriot and St. John, 1966). A basic component in the preparatory stage of school learning is the language skill of the pupil. But the level of such skill depends on family socialization. It has been noted that some children do not enter the school system with adequate language proficiency (Deutsch, 1967). It has been explicitly observed that a poor family background is a positive handicap for a child in the acquisition of a language acceptable in the school and later in his occupational career (Bossio, 1971). There is further evidence of correlation between language inadequacy and mother-child relationship (Hess and Shipman, 1965). There is a more complex explanation of language inadequacy, according to which, middle-class children are more able to use language with fineness, in trying to achieve their objectives. Children from poor families, largely dominated by single-parent households, cannot receive the necessary stimulation because they have to deal with the relatively simpler role model implied in a single-parent household. The underlying assumption in this explanation is that a less complex family interactional context makes it less necessary to handle interpersonal relationships on the level of language. An additional factor is that these children are further handicapped by the fact that they have virtually no opportunity to exercise independent thinking and make personal choices (Strodtbock, 1967).

The socialization process in the school occurs within a given and specific socio-psychological ecology and it accounts for a substantial proportion of the child's time. It has been computed that a child spends approximately 7000 hours in all in schooling from Kindergarten to grade six (Rogoff, 1961). The school involves a complex system of total environment in which the child learns to pick up patiently the ability to express himself or herself, gets opportunities for satisfying through cooperative behaviour, understands and assimilates the need to control and postpone gratification till the appropriate time, and learns to accept other-evaluation of the self via the assessment of teachers and peers (Jackson, 1968). It is in the school that the child becomes involved in the set of interactions out of which emerge his skill to manipulate language and a relatively crystallized notion of the self — both essential in the long run to the successful management of life (Rist, 1973). The importance of early teacher assessment of the child's socialization into specific adult roles has been recognized (Parsons, 1950). The crucial part played by teacher-pupil interaction in the overall socialization process has received considerable emphasis in relevant literature. Teacher expectation has been found to perform the function of a self-fulfilling prophecy in the pupil's intellectual development. For instance, those evaluated as "bloom" did well, scholastically while those identified early in teacher assessment as "spurt" failed to do so (Rosenthal and Jacobson, 1968). The teacher's response to pupils has been shown to depend on the pupils' location in social space. Teachers appear to expect less from lower income pupils, and hence seem to be less prepared to spend their time and energy in assisting them in the learning process, than they do for pupils hailing from middle income families. Further, the teachers concerned seem to be ready to blame the failure of lower income pupils on their individual incapacities and their lack of personal responsibility (Leacock, 1964). While the teachers themselves may be apparently unconscious of such attitudes and dispositions and quite honestly claim to be treating all children equally, actual evidence suggests that their predominantly middle-class background generates prejudices which enter, though subsconsciously, into their evaluation of the children. Therefore, they tend to attribute the success of their middle-class pupils to genuine self-effort, while blaming the failure of working-class pupils on their individual incapacity for serious scholastic involvement (Nash, 1973). Also teachers have low expectations of success for lower-class pupils, whatever the latter's own aspirations because they are inclined to disbelieve that later opportunities in life depended on satisfactory scholastic achievement (Ogber, 1974). The situation, however, should not be exaggerated, and the fact that, in its overall thrust, the school provides opportunities for the development of flexible and versatile personalities. In fact, there is considerable empirical evidence that the school provides for the child "alternative models of life styles and occupations" (Crysdale and Beattie, 1977, p. 126). In the face of such conflicting evidence, it is perhaps not to project any definitive theory about the relationship between the school and the socialization process.

The key issue in the conflicting evidence on the socializing role of the school is class. However, sufficient data has accumulated to show that 'class' deprivation, associated with the class background of the child's family, affects significantly the child's school experience (White, 1977). Specifically, it tends to generate a sense of alienation on the part of the pupil, arising out of a subjectively perceived gap between home experience and what is taught in school. This is most acutely true for children from poor families. The situation becomes compounded by two further dimensions. Firstly, the teachers complicate the matter by showing differential attitudes and treatment. Secondly, the parents do not possess the necessary resources and attitudes to become seriously and meaningfully involved in the child's scholastic activities. A situation thus emerges in which the pupil fails to find his school performance perceptibly rewarding. It turns out, actually, to be a vicious circle: they are handicapped at the time of entering the school due to inadequate family socialization; their parents, because of their school work; the teachers themselves, admittedly without being aware in most cases, do not entertain any expectation of success for them. It all adds up to a situation where children from lower-class families are doomed from the start to gain substantially from school socialization.

In the case of children from immigrant families or Native People families, the school can produce traumatic experiences involving a process of radical resocialization. West Indian children, for instance, are assigned lower streams because they lack adequate language facility, and also perhaps because the parents occupy the lower rungs of the occupational structure (Lanphier, 1977). It must, however, be cautioned that the data relating to these issues are fragmentary and the relationship between the relevant variables unclear. It has been observed in the case of young Cree children schooling from ages six to sixteen that their schooling time coincides with the time their parents engaged in their major occupations of hunting and trapping (Sindell, 1962: 92). Such children tend to be independent, responsible and cooperative, and they expect to be given opportunities for exercising initiative and responsibility. In the school, however, they encounter a diametrically opposite situation in which the values of obedience, dependence and competition are systematically stressed. Moreover they do not feel related to their home environment because the school curricula do not relate to their normal life needs — for the boys, trapping and hunting skills, and, for the girls, the skill of cleaning and preparing pelts. On the contrary, the new skills, values and needs they acquire in school can have little use or relevance for the trapline.

Peer Group

The family and the school are primarily adult-based agencies of socialization. But children have their own informal groups of equals at every age. These are organized by the children themselves, and they involve activities developed around the idea of play, which enables the children to evolve their individual personalities and acquire skills of leadership. The basic structural principle of these groups is intense loyalty to the group, which invariably relegates adults to a peripheral position. Though no formally articulated rules, rights and duties are generated, there are nonetheless clearly recognized and accepted norms and customs, which must be implicitly followed. A central norm binding the group is "equalitarianism." A child can enroll in more than one such group at one time. Constituted by children of approximately the same age, a normal peer group is essentially oriented to a realization of its psychological-developmental needs. This is usually achieved through a system of bestowing prestige and status according to demonstrated skill and strength. Therefore, the long-range socialization impact upon the peer group is unintentional and transcends the conscious and immediate goals of the peer group.

Group commitment in the context of a peer group derives from sports activities, and it sets at work a process in which, through stages, the child finds himself committed to new social norms and roles, specific to a concrete situation and setting (Helenko, 1963; Loy and Ingham, 1973). It has been noted that children between 6 and 12 display a pronounced approval or disapproval of certain roles involved in playing games, even though there may be significant variations in the pattern of initiating the games (Iona and Opie, 1969). This tendency towards the development of game situations into systems of rules and roles has been confirmed by Elkin (1978: 153) who states, ". . . on street and playground, children sustain a subculture which consists of rules, traditions, languages, interests and activities, and ways of making and breaking peer relationships that somewhat apart from, and sometimes in opposition to, the subcultures the children are simultaneously absorbing from adult models and institutions. . . ." There is also the opposite direction and form which a peer group may take if it finds itself in serious conflict with adult authority system. As a result it may provide an alternate model of deviant and criminal behaviour, motivated by sheer excitement and adventurism (Cloward and Ohlin, 1960; Vaz, 1976). In the upshot, the play setting in a peer group may result in a significant degree of "professionalization of children's attitudes, the substitution of skill for fairness as the paramount factor in play activity and the increasing importance of victory" (Harry Webb, 1969: 164). Socialization into such values as fair play, success and achievement through play-acting in the peer group, lays down the foundations upon which will be built a full-fledged code of business conduct in later adult life. Such a code underlies the way in which a business adversary may be handled. The peer group participation may also open up new channels for mobility, as demonstrated in a study of soccer in Brazil (Lever, 1972). The peer group may also provide the basis for more lasting interpersonal relationships, involving 'chumming' (Sullivan, 1953).

Mass Media
Mass media play an important role in the socialization of the child. The collective impact on the child of the conflicting and even disjointed messages and ideas conveyed through a bewildering array of mass media — the press, radio, TV, magazines, comics and movies — is cognitive dissonance. For children, the highly commercialized process of salesmanship raises some very real dilemmas. Should "Mom" use this or that brand of diapers for her baby? Or should children demand Kentucky Fried Chicken or MacDonald's for today's dinner? Fortunately, considerable evidence exists to suggest that the mass media are far less dictatorial, since those exposed to them develop mechanisms to shift the flow of messages in such a way that only those elements are absorbed and assimilated which are in harmony with the values, desires, and expectations already in evidence among the exposed (Maccoby, 1964; McQuail, 1969).

Mass media, especially the TV, are oriented towards a systematic dissemination of norms, values and attitudes, dominant normally in the society, both among adults and children. To take a specific example from the TV shows, the feature entitled *Kojak* develops in the viewers an idea of how a detective behaves. The systematic display of sports celebrities or the legendary figures from the world of entertainment present powerful role models of successful careers. Features such as *Happy Days* and *James at 16* present detailed pictures of the dating games of the adolescents, which later on tend to provide models for behaviour in similar situations for viewers. The popular TV feature, *All in the Family*, may create in some viewers the impression that it represents ideal and typical behaviour within the family. Popular TV shows focus on themes, strategems and characters, whose ultimate thrust is to provide the viewers with a set of norms, status ideals, desirable roles and institutional goals, to be accepted, emulated and followed (DeFleur, 1964, 1967). Children carry such cognitive and normative equipment over into later life, and model their adult behaviour, conforming to them.

Of all the available mass media, the TV occupies a position of supremacy because it can be watched by children before they can read and write. It has been estimated that 99.9 percent of the entire population in the U.S., and some 97 percent of the entire population in Canada, are exposed to the TV. A San Francisco study, conducted in the 1950s, showed that, by the age of five, 82 percent of the children studied had watched some TV program but none of them had read a newspaper. Only 9 percent of them had had newspapers read to them on a limited scale (Schram, 1960). A more recent study found that, in a sample of 138 children aged three to six, 98 percent stated that they enjoyed watching TV shows. The first graders watched it 22 to 24 hours a week; the sixth graders from 30 to 31 hours; and the tenth graders, from 27 to 28 hours. This study also found that the TV was increasingly used in the period from 1959 to 1970 (Lyle and Hoffman, 1972). An even more recent study revealed that the average sixth graders spent about 85 to 88 hours watching TV every week (Stein and Friederich, 1975).

However, such findings on the impact of the TV on the process of child socialization merely in terms of average time spent in viewing it, may not help us much in mapping the total socialization process. It tells us nothing about the way ethnic or class differences affect the quantum of time spent in watching the TV. There is evidence that such differences are inversely related to the time so spent (Lyle and Hoffman, 1972; Greenberg and Dervine, 1970). The blue-collar children have been found to watch more TV than white-collar children. But such findings raise further difficulties for an adequate understanding of the specific involvement of the mass media in the socialization process. They fail to take into account the fact that children, while watching the TV, are also engaged simultaneously in other activities, and consequently fail to focus on the mechanisms of incidental learning. It has also been claimed that the positive advantages of the TV outweigh its drawbacks in the sense that it contributes to the educational process of the child while at the same time keeping him out of mischief (Steiner, 1963).

The foregoing discussion makes it clear that the precise nature of the impact of mass media on the socialization process is a problematic issue. It is likely that children tend to learn more from entertainment programs than from programs formally oriented to information-dissemination, but such information as they derive from the former may be very temporary (Schram, 1961). It is also necessary in this context to bear in mind the fact that parents mediate in the process of socialization through the mass media because they exercise control over the quantity and quality of the programs which the children are allowed to watch. Steiner (1963; 95) has drawn attention to the complexity of the situation: "So all in all, so far as adult judgements are concerned, television helps to educate the child, but watching it interferes with his education. It helps keep him busy to do his chores. It keeps the kids in when you want them, which is good, except for some of the bad things they see. And it keeps them in when you want them out — which is bad even if they see good things." It has also been suggested that parents consider TV to be reducing the burdens of parental responsibilities, at least on occasions, while enabling the children to acquire some useful knowledge (Elkin, 1978: 168).

Children exposed to prosocial programs have been found to develop a significantly higher level of rule acceptance, tolerance and persistence than those exposed to aggressive programs. Children exposed to more balanced and neutral programs tend to show a behavioural pattern somewhere in between the two situations (Stein and Freiderich, 1973). In another study, using the popular information program for children, Sesame Street, it was found that maximum gain was made by children watching it with their mothers and subsequently talking about it (Lesser, 1974).

Another controversial area in this regard is the issue of violence in mass media. According to one study, children tend to be far more "stimulated to violence" than adults in a similar situation (Arnold, 1969 and Werthan, 1966). The thesis has also been maintained on the basis of empirical studies that the programs, including commercials and cartoons, carry a high level of violence in content, and, therefore, contribute to the generation and continuation of an atmosphere of high violence in American society. Children become inevitably influenced by this situation (Larsen, 1968, and Bronfenbrenner, 1970). An official document, the Surgeon General's Report on the problem (1972) came to the conclusion that there was no decisive evidence for establishing a causal connection between violence and structured behaviour. A recent survey of the relevant literature maintains: ". . . on the basis of evaluation of many lines of converging evidence, involving more than 50 studies which have included more than 10 000 normal children and adolescents from every conceivable background, the weight of evidence is clear: the demonstrated teaching and instigating effects of aggressive television upon youth are of significant importance to warrant remedial action" (Liebert, Neale and Davison, 1973). This has been countered by the argument that: "There is no reliable evidence that television exposures, whether general or violent, has any causal relationship. . . The essential variables such as sex are neglected. This failure confounds a relationship which becomes insignificant when appropriate controls are made" (Howitt and Cumberbatch, 1975: 106). This involves the claim that mass media do not intensify and magnify the existing levels of violence in society.

More recently, a new perspective and framework has emerged in the study of the impact of mass media. It has been argued that a more fruitful line of enquiry would be to focus on what people do *with* media rather than on what media do *to* people (Noble, 1975; Katz et al., 1974). The shift is away from a process of passive reception to a process of active participation. Children, for instance, may gain relief from the stresses and strains of everyday life by absorption in the TV program, and they may also be acquiring role models through TV characters. In this process of active interaction with mass media, violence constitutes only one among a variety of elements. The existing literature remains very uncertain, and it is at the moment not possible to state what sorts of behaviour lends itself to easy transmission (Maccoby, 1964).

An already confused situation is further complicated by other inconclusive and apparently contradictory evidence. On the one hand, it has been claimed that exposure to mass media involves stereotyped thinking (Bailyn). On the other hand, it has also been argued that there are cases in which children develop sympathy (Hyman, 1974). There is also empirical evidence to show that sixth graders "distrust" commercial messages, but this may well be attributed to the pattern of continuous disjunction in the programs created by the commercials (Comstock, 1975).

The overall effect of the existing evidence on the problem of the relationship between mass media and socialization is one of uncertainty and ambiguity. We are far from knowing beyond dispute the exact role of mass media in the socialization of children. There is, therefore, a serious gap in the existing literature. This can be filled up only by studies specifically structured to identify the concrete ways in which mass media and children are involved in a process of mutuality and interaction.

Church and Politics

Institutionalized religious activity is a major source of socialization into the values, roles and attitudinal expectations of the broader society. Religious teachings transmitted through churches, synagogues and mosques, are important in this context. While there has been a sharp decline in the role of religion in child socialization in North America, religion may yet be instrumental in enabling a child to draw a distinction between the sacred and the profane (Elkin, 1978: 182). While it is true that religious activities are no longer a structured part of the totality of the socialization process as is the case with traditional societies, it is also true that children who practice regular church-going with their parents tend to widen their network of social contact as a result of interaction with other church-goers. Children are known to be profoundly concerned to know and worry about such basic phenomena as illness, birth, injustice, aging and death (Crystal, 1977: 126). It is likely that religious teachings enable parents to offer reasonably satisfactory and acceptable explanations about such phenomena to their children.

Politics affects child socialization in terms of the influence exerted on children by political leaders, the police, judges and the personnel of the government. By the time a child reaches the end of his elementary school career, he would have had some awareness of authority outside his immediate context of the peer group, the neighbourhood and the family. It is possible that he may even become emotionally attached to political figures and identify with them as his role models. A recent study of Canadian children belonging to three public schools in Oshawa, Ontario, found that children in grades 4, 6 and 8, showed a relatively lower political identification in relation to the prime minister than that shown by comparable American children in relation to the president. While as many as 87 percent of the American children expressed the belief that the president would come to their aid when they needed it, only 27 percent of the Canadian children surveyed expressed a similar belief about the prime minister. However, the Canadian children demonstrated a high degree of respect and support for the more abstract and complex phenomenon of "government" (Goldlust, 1972). While the precise nature and extent of the role of these agencies in the process of child socialization remain far from clear, it has been suggested that "they all function to weaken the child's ties with the family, give the child new statuses, teach different perspectives, and broaden his or her range of experience" (Elkin, 1978: 183).

ORGANIZATION OF THE BOOK: SOME EMERGING THEMES

In the process of organizing the various Canadian studies on childhood and adolescence in this volume, three important themes have emerged. First, socialization as both process and outcome necessarily take place within a social context; second, while each of such important agents and models of socialization as the parents, the school, the religion, the peer groups, exerts its impact on the child and adolescent undergoing socialization, they also interact with them, and provide the child and the adolescent a 'total' socio-cultural environment, the major function of which is to socialize; third, an adequate understanding of the differential socialization processes and outcomes is contingent on our comprehension of the functional significance of such socio-cultural variables as the economy, the mass media, the educational and political systems. It is, therefore, the intention of this section to attempt a concise overview of these three major themes emerging from the papers in this volume.

Socialization in the Social Context

Unlike the modern social scientists who see a child undergoing the process of socialization in terms of learning the knowledge and skills to enable himself or herself to cope with a complex socio-cultural environment, Guemple's study of Inuit socialization indicates that Inuit perceive infants, children and adolescents as "social actors" endowed with a personality fully formed at birth. Inuit children are not taught to perform specific tasks, because they are seen as "diminutive adults" who can "socialize" themselves through observation and participation, and prepare themselves for the attainment of the adult statuses. With the interference of governmental programs such as housing and education, Guemple notes that the values, beliefs, and attitudes of Inuit are gradually eroded, and are in the process of converging to those prevalent in the larger society.

Using the modified version of the Spindler's Instrumental Activities Inventory, McElroy investigates the role preference of Inuit school children in two Eastern Canadian Arctic settlements, Frobisher Bay and Pangnirtung. The findings of the study indicate that males in both settlements preferred occupations bringing high and steady wage but without long-term training, whereas females preferred wage employment over traditional subsistence activities, though the role of seamstress was still popular. It was found by McElroy that both groups of children preferred "transitional roles" over modern or traditional ones but females less frequently than males. The possible explanation of the observed sex differences constructed by McElroy is that females chose modern or traditional roles without a threat to their autonomy or basic role definitions, while male role choices were dependent upon the contemporary issues of ethnic autonomy and community politics, thereby becoming less flexible in occupational choices and aspirations.

Traditionally, the Inuit did not see adolescence as a special period of maturation, and, therefore was able to avoid the abruptness and psychological stress inherent in the transition. Matthiasson's presentation reveals a prolonged period of adolescence among the Inuit resulting from a "double bind" situation: the Inuit is first socialized in the early years according to the traditional ways of life, and then placed in the modern education system which has little to do with the life-style of his parents and early life experiences. The imposition of formal education and modernization on the Canadian Inuit has produced a period of traumatic experience, and a "real time" for the adolescents, who might put off the inevitability of assuming the poorly understood adult roles as inculcated by the schools.

One significant observation in Preston's study is that the cultural uniformity of Eastern Cree Indians was maintained through "individual responsibility" and self-control taken on during short and long-term consequences. Mackie underscores the importance of gender socialization in terms of its consequences of sex-typing for adult man and woman by virtue of the fact that it operates as the axis of self-definition, permeating the smallest details of everyday lives and shaping life opportunities. Although the causal links between early gender socialization and sex-typed behaviour remain conjectural, successful internalization and identification of these stereotyped traits of masculinity and feminity, result in neither sex fully developing its human potential. Mackie notes that the costs are usually higher for women because of their constricted life chances and the ideology of male supremacy, and conclusively suggests that changing cultural values and familial behaviour would give healthier definitions of masculinity and feminity in the near future.

Theorizing along the line of differential socialization experiences and outcomes, Propper investigates the impact of mother's employment status on the adolescent roles, activities and parent-child relationships. Her data reveal a higher level of disagreement between working mothers and their children, that working mothers are more likely than their non-working counterparts to encourage their children to disagree. However, with respect to the feelings of closeness, parental interests, time spent with parents, or receiving help for school and personal problems, no difference was observed among children with working mothers and non-working mothers. Her findings also indicate that boys with working mothers are less likely to name their fathers as the most admired persons suggesting that perhaps the level of admiration for fathers may be differentially affected by the mother's employment.

Agents and Models of Socialization
Perhaps, the most logical and salient unit of analysis in childhood and adolescence socialization research is the parent-child interaction. Preston notes that "early indulgence" of socialization is an "antecedent" of self-control that permits and facilitates the development of a sense of individual Cree Pride. With the James Bay Project and the various institutions established in the area in recent years, the Cree process of socialization has undergone a shift of trajectory, from family and bush orientation to community and peer group orientation.
group orientation.

Data reported by Ishwaran and Chan in their study of the adolescents in a rural Dutch Community in Ontario point to the theoretical importance of conceptualizing the socialization process within its immediate socio-cultural context. While Calvinism strategically plays an all-pervading role in regulating the functioning of such institutions as the school and the family, the peer groups and the community — the high level of functional interdependence between these institutions and religion being the major operating force — provide the child and the adolescent a morally cohesive and integrative environment to grow up in. To borrow Benedict's phrase, the adolescent is "culturally conditioned by the religious ethos and moulded in such a way that he or she will become a functional participant in the community and a good Christian in the church."

In his analysis of the acquisition of adult responsibilities and insights by adolescents and discussion of the transition of role from adolescence to adulthood, Fasick, basing his judgement on census data and vital statistics of Canada, argues that expectations rather than statutory prescriptions, for instance, majority age, are more important in determining the adolescent's acquisition of the two essential roles, marriage and occupation.

One area that has attracted considerable empirical and theoretical attention of researchers in family studies is the differential in sex-role and gender socialization, and its immediate or, more specifically, the perceived impact of parental control and authority by children on their educational and occupational aspirations.

Focusing his research attention on the parents as strategic agents of socialization, Danziger, on the basis of his survey data on 222 fourteen-year-old boys and their mothers from immigrant and non-immigrant families, reports that the boys' occupational aspiration level is the highest when they perceive a lower degree of maternal control and manifest a lower level of rejection of that control. It was also found that while maternal involvement in decision-making was relatively higher and parental involvement relatively lower in non-immigrant than in immigrant groups, rejection of parental control was higher among non-immigrant adolescents. Though no consistent relationships was observed between occupational aspiration and parental control in the immigrant group, the general pattern of a negative association between rejection of maternal control and the level of occupational aspiration seem to have emerged for all groups.

Though the importance of the role of the school in child socialization has very seldom been overlooked by social scientists, the possibility that its saliency as an agent of socialization is differentially perceived by different groups of inhabitants in the social context still exists. Maykovich reports that while the Mennonites tend to see the school as an agent of religious and social organization to teach the child to follow a religious life and to respect rules of society, the Japanese parents consider the school as a preparatory ground for launching their children into the appropriate and desired occupations. Her data also reveal that though the white Protestant parents are concerned with the occupational function of the school, teachers and students are more concerned with individual development.

Another research attempt explicitly recognizing the significance of the school as an agent of child socialization is that of Maxwell and Maxwell who report data indicating that the private school serves to maintain the stratification system in Canada and to perpetuate and preserve the elitist norms and values through the socialization process. In further examination of the structure of private schools and their development, Maxwell and Maxwell note that the private schools facilitate the kinship and associational networks of various elites in Canada.

Based on the data obtained from 197 single, sexually experienced female teenagers, Herold and Goodwin examine the impact of reference groups on the adoption of oral contraceptives. It was found that peers were the source of information and support concerning the decision to use oral contraceptives and to come to the clinic. Boyfriends gave little information but provided legitimation, whereas parents were usually by-passed in the process. However, the general findings of the study also indicate that the reference group was not significant in determining whether or not the teenagers were early adopters of the oral contraceptives.

Synge explores the transition of role from school to work among working-class adolescents in the city of Hamilton, Ontario, in the early 20th century. She found that part-time employment was common among boys before leaving school to enter full-time employment, while girls usually stayed home and did household chores. Education was considered a luxury and they were expected to contribute to family income as soon as possible. The introduction to universal secondary education, increased income of parents, and the establishment of pension and welfare schemes, had given rise to a new ideology according to which the adolescents saw employment during education as a contribution to one's spending money. This, accordingly, resulted in important changes in the adolescent's conception of his own role in the economy and the family systems.

Social Structure and Socialization

One considerably comprehensive, theoretical attempt to place the phenomena of child and adolescent socialization in the socio-structural environment is made by Little and Ryan who, in locating the children in a social context, have adopted a social-ecological approach to human development. Within this framework, the authors conceptualize human development in terms of "a series of interdependent adaptations between children and their environments," and the environment as "social and material objects, events and resources which individually, and as interacting systems, influence human development." While the children and their environments are cast in a state of interdependence, the transactions and interactions between them are mediated by the child's sensory, cognitive, affective and behavioural processes. Accordingly, assessment of the adaptational competencies of the children is understood by Little and Ryan in terms of the extent to which children develop a sense of perceived control over their environments.

Perhaps one of the more important links between social structure and social process of the child and the adolescent is the mass media, its socio-cultural antecedents, and both long-term and short-term consequences. McCormack argues that the public subscribes to a common fallacy in treating television as a form of technology that has come into existence from nowhere and is accountable to no one, rather than as a social institution or a means of communication. She suggests that in order to understand the influence and impact of television on child socialization and its attendant consequences, we have to place television in the larger social context by examining how different classes of children use it and its meaning for them, and by drawing on our growing knowledge of the communication process. What is important is not television *per se*, but how the viewers perceive its meanings and uses.

In a meticulous attempt to look at the conceptual and empirical relationships between socialization and social structure, Peter's analysis of the childhood and adolescent socialization within the Hutterite community focuses on the socio-cultural factors which altogether make possible the development of socialization outcomes which are indistinguishable from the prevalent ideological and behavioural conformities of the contemporary society. While the religious world view propagated and maintained by the Hutterites serves various social and psychological functions, the structural and physical isolation of the Hutterite community also constitutes the major force that ensures degrees of self-determinate development for the religious community and facilitates the maintenance of distinctive cultural imperatives.

In his study of the working class male adolescents, West underscores the combined interaction effects of working-class background, adolescent status and employment problems, which are collectively responsible for the development of an occupational prospective of a "serious thief." His data support the hypothesis that a lack of conventional commitment leads to the eventual but temporary occupation of a serious thief. The short-term occupancy of the career of a serious thief stems from a general tendency to return to conventional commitments, e.g. marriage and occupation.

The importance of Landes' empirical work lies in his attempt to refocus his research attention on one largely overlooked aspect of socialization: political socialization. From his studies based on a purposive sample of approximately 600 children in grades 4 through 8 in one Canadian and one U.S. city, Landes reports data indicating apparent similarities in the patterns of political learning for the Canadian and American children on the one hand, but also important differences in specific areas (i.e., the child's affective response to government, the effects of the political structure on the institutionalization of political authority) in the development of political orientations between the Canadian and American students on the other. More importantly, the data of this study have confirmed earlier observations that the political affect expressed for government by children in these two cities is higher in Canada than in the United States. For the three indications of benevolence, dependability, and leadership, American children are found to have lower scores on the rating of governmental qualities in 1972 than in 1962.

In summing up, the three themes — socialization in social context, socialization means and models for adolescence, and social structure and socialization — indicate the three major angles from which the crucial problems of socialization may be fruitfully viewed and comprehensively organized for purposes of scientific understanding.

Bringing up children and adolescents in a modern complex society is no longer a purely informal process: it is an art as well as a science. Specialized institutions from outside the family constantly impinge on the processes of socialization that go on within the family. The interacting institutions and quasi groups which now envelope the adolescents tend to generate tremendous pressures not only on the parents but also on the adolescents themselves. To regulate the processes of socialization under these circumstances, to ensure that children are trained not only to function effectively as members of this or that national society but also as members of the human society, to ensure freedom of growth while curbing the traumatic trends inherent in growing up in modern societies — these increasingly require an understanding of the results of scientific studies on socialization. This volume represents good samples of such results in the specifically Canadian context.

The present volume is a clear indication that social scientists are beginning to display and unravel the complex issues concerning socialization in this country, instead of taking it for granted that all modern societies are the same, and if you know one — particularly the U.S.A. — you know all. Now that the results of painstaking research are available at one place, and the attempt has been made to systematize the results within a unified, interpretive framework, it is hoped that the available information will draw the attention of all those who, in one capacity or another, are connected with the problems, processes, and patterns of socialization in Canada.

Dr. K. Ishwaran

SOCIALIZATION IN SOCIAL CONTEXT

Inuit Socialization: A Study of Children as Social Actors in an Eskimo Community

LEE GUEMPLE
*The University of
Western Ontario*

This paper is about socialization among the Qiqiktamiut Inuit (Eskimo) of the Belcher Islands of Hudson Bay and, more generally, about techniques of socialization among Inuit of the Central Canadian Arctic. At this descriptive level it is a "just so" story of interest because of its relatively exotic content.

At another level, this paper is *not* about Inuit socialization at all for, in an important sense, Inuit do not socialize their children. Indeed, in a sense Inuit have no "children"! In describing *Qiqiktamiut* practices, I have chosen to stress the natives' own view of things: how they evaluate what is going on when the "teaching" of children is undertaken. This produces something of a paradox. In our society we see a child as an essentially empty vessel which, through the complementary acts of teaching and learning, is gradually filled with the knowledge and strategies which make it possible for it to cope with a complex social universe. Inuit, by way of contrast, see a child as already whole having a personality fully formed at birth in latent form. All of these he will manifest and use in good time with but little assistance. In that sense, this paper is not about socialization at all, but about the Inuit image of infants, children and adolescents as social actors, endowed as they are with already well formed social personalities.

The argument is divided into two parts. The first is a very compressed description of socialization using the terminology Inuit associate with age and sex statuses as an organizing structure. I describe each stage of development briefly stressing factors which Qiqiktamiut themselves focus on in rearing children. In the second section of the paper I deal with the ontological status of children as social actors. That is, an

inquiry is made into the Inuit formulation of the kind of beings children are; and this leads to a more general discussion of the status of all
social actors in Inuit society and of how the world works. The conclusions suggest how these facts might provide a useful commentary on
the status of children in contemporary Western society.

STAGES OF SOCIALIZATION

Inuit distinguish six stages or steps in the development of humans as
they pass through the life cycle. The stages, the appropriate age at
which each is assumed, and the criteria for attributing arrival at a given
stage are shown in Table 1. In the following description, it will be convenient to use the first four of these stages to discuss socialization in infancy, childhood and adolescence.

THE SOCIALIZATION OF INFANTS

Inuit have no special term to denote a fetus *in utero* and by custom do
not speak about it until after its birth. The fetus is never regarded as
"alive" until after it is born, so Inuit never think of it as a person. They
also believe that the fetus is vulnerable to attack by supernatural forces
and that to call attention to it by talking to it or about it might result in
a supernatural attack. Accordingly, an infant is never spoken of publicly before its birth and any reference made to the pregnancy is accomplished by circumlocution.

Even birth does not insure that the newborn is accorded the status
of a social person. Balikci (1970: 148) estimates that in some parts of the
Arctic as many as 50% of all those born alive were disposed of traditionally by infanticide. An infant which was to be disposed of was not
accorded the status of being a social person, though instead of being
exposed or smothered it might be given in adoption to another couple
who might then accord it such a status. A decision had to be made
within four days after parturition, for by this time an infant had to be
named. And, once named, the disposal of a child would be an act of
murder because a named infant was regarded as a social person and
exercised a powerful claim upon the living (Balikci, 1970: 148).

Infants are called *nutarak*. At this stage in the age hierarchy, Inuit
stress two tasks as essential to socialization: the complete integration of
the spirit of an infant into its body, and the creation of a happy, cheerful atmosphere of cooperation which will encourage the infant to develop attitudes and behaviours which Inuit value highly.

Inuit regard birth as the time at which the body of the infant is entered by an animating spirit. Presuming that it is to be allowed to live,
the child is named according to the spirit which is determined to have
entered its body. The spirit is presumed also to be volitional: it may
choose to remain in the body or it may withdraw. Outright withdrawal

TABLE 1
STATUS TERMINOLOGY ASSOCIATED WITH THE LIFE CAREERS OF MALES AND FEMALES AMONG QIQIKTAMIUT INUIT OF THE BELCHER ISLANDS, HUDSON BAY.

Approximate Age of Assumption	Terms for Males	Terms for Females	Criteria for Attribution
After 45-50 years.	*ituq* (old man) ↑	*ningiuq* (old woman) ↑	At 'retirement'; when they become dependent on their children for support.
Age 18 for males about 16 for females	*angutik* (man = husband) ↑	*angnak* (woman = wife) ↑	Individual is sufficiently well trained to be self-sustaining; when he or she marries.
Age 8 to 10	*angutiaru* (young man) ↑	*angnaru* (young woman) ↑	Indiv. can regularly produce some part of the traditional work pattern without supervision.
Age 3 to 3½	*tugusi* (boy) ↖	*niviaksi* (girl) ↗	Indiv. begins to act out sex-linked roles; when a child becomes betrothed.
Age 1 yr. to 18 months	*qitungak (kakalak)* (baby) ↑		When child can walk and make word-like sounds.
Birth	*nutarak* (infant)		Used only if child is allowed to live

Table 1. Status terminology associated with the life careers of males and females among Qiqiktamiut Inuit of the Belcher Islands, Hudson Bay.

can have serious consequences for the health of the child: the prolonged or permanent absence of the spirit can result in the death of the infant. Qiqiktamiut will sometimes say of a stillborn child that "it did not want to live." General or prolonged fussiness, a refusal to eat (see also Briggs, 1968: 151) or outright sickness — all these may be diagnosed as symptomatic of the spirit's withdrawal from the body. To secure its permanent integration with the body, the family and others make every effort to encourage it to remain. The measures necessary to insure this are thought to be the maintenance of a congenial atmosphere in which the infant spirit will be happy, expressions of concern and affection for the infant, and the creation of important ritual ties to members of the community outside the natal household. The infant is encouraged to respond actively to this atmosphere, and family members and others spend hours attempting to elicit smile responses from the newborn — the surest proof of its acceptance of the sentiments offered. Inuit stress cooperativeness and cheerfulness above all other values, and children express these values in their responses to others very early.

Inuit suppose that the most important bond between an infant and its family is the bond of "love." They work hard in the first months of its life to express love and to instill it in the child. Love is expressed by the use of terms of endearment addressed to the child, by acts of concern for its wellbeing, and by tokens of sentiment in the form of clothing, food, toys, and time spent attending to it. Expressions of sentiment by outsiders begin with visits paid to the infant immediately after it is named. They speak to the child as "lovable" and they bring it token gifts and accept token gifts from it in return.

The first months of an infant's life are viewed as crucial to the development of love. If the infant is estranged from its family they will develop anxiety concerning the love bond[1]; and in later life faults in the character of adults will sometimes be explained as owing to the failure of members of the community to engender love in the individual while still an infant.

In addition to this general atmosphere of help and affection the child becomes linked at birth to a number of community members outside the household in ritual relationships which symbolically express support and cooperation. The individual who cuts and ties the umbilicus and disposes of the placenta enters into a special relationship with the child. This person exchanges gifts with the newborn at birth and annually at the season of the infant's birth.

A second ritual connection is established in the person of a ritual sponsor who is selected by the parents of the child to prepare its first clothes, and is called immediately after the birth to dress the child for the first time. Thenceforth the sponsor and child become involved in a life-long reciprocal gift exchange which begins with the gift of clothes to the child.

Finally, an infant becomes ritually linked to one or more individuals with whom it shares a common name. Sociologically, the namesake relationship and the others stress the value of sharing and cooperation between the community at large and the newborn infant. The ritual relatives represent the community's interests to the child; they also represent the child's interests to the community — by insuring that a congenial, positive atmosphere is maintained and that community members behave decorously during the child's first months.

If there is evidence that an infant's spirit is separating from the body, or if the child becomes ill for what is judged to be other reasons, increased efforts are generally taken to see that relations with the child are positive and supportive. If these fail to alleviate the problem the difficulty may be judged to be an incompatibility between one or more relatives or ritual relations and the infant's name spirit, and efforts may be made to sever these harmful connections. Several remedies are available. The child may be put up for adoption or a series of rituals in which the child's hair is cut, his clothes burned and replaced, and his name changed may be performed.

Socialization in Babyhood

Once the infant's spirit is securely bound to its body and it is judged to have a commitment to being a member of the community, the family and relatives concentrate on securing the cooperation of the child in the social community. At first it will only nurse and eliminate, but it gradually becomes more animated and begins to make its first attempts at walking and speaking. At this stage it is regarded as a *qitungak* (*kakalak* is a less frequently heard synonym). Now parents generally exhort the child to be cooperative and reasonable, although they put no pressure on the child to conform.

Sharing is stressed by giving bits of food and toys to the baby and by eliciting gifts of these same items from it. This "drill" in reciprocity goes on continuously: at all times of the day; through work schedules and play periods; during visiting; when neighbors meet casually out on the land. The bonds of love which link the baby to the family and relatives are also reinforced. A child is told repeatedly that it is lovable and loved; and fits of temper, though they seldom occur, are explained as evidence that the baby has interpreted some act as thoughtless or unloving. The effort to maintain a cheerful, positive universe continues throughout this period and babies, by now taught to smile reflexively, will greet every visitor with a wide grin. Babies are given anything — even potentially dangerous objects such as razor blades — which they express an impulse to possess.[2]

Babies are drilled daily on their terms for relatives, either by name or by relational term. Mothers or older sisters take the babies visiting daily and during these visits some interlocutor will undertake the task of delivering the day's lesson. The relative addresses the child giving either the name or the appropriate relational term for someone present and asks the baby to identify the one designated. When very young the baby is expected to do no more than look directly into the face of the one designated and the baby's eyes are watched carefully to see if it can make the identification. Later the child will be expected first to point to the relative and finally to identify it either by name (given the relational term) or by relational term (given the name).

Socialization in Childhood

A boy becomes *tugusi* and a girl *niviaksi* when they develop a distinct consciousness of self. *Qiqiktamiut* say of them at this stage that they have become "shy" (*uningnatuq*)[3]. Children at this stage are quiet and easy to handle, and they are generally controlled by shaming — by laughing at their ineptitudes or by commenting sarcastically on any inappropriate conduct they may engage in. Children are expected to carry out small tasks when requested and gradually begin to be incorporated into whatever project is underway in any household they find themselves in. They are under no compulsion to accept work roles at this stage, however; and the only demand made on them is that they join with adults in lavishing attention and "love" on other infants and babies, forms of attention and gratification which at this stage they no longer enjoy themselves because they are now considered to be part of the established community.

Children are exhorted to give up suckling at this age. Inuit generally suckle their young up to age two or three. Because substitute diets are potentially dangerous to health even in the second year (Rasmussen, 1931: 212-213), weaning will generally be postponed until another child is born. As Briggs (1968: 158-159) has noted, weaning is sometimes traumatic, but is usually accomplished in a very short period of time.

At this time also there begins to be a separation between male and female play groups. Both boys and girls increasingly act out as play the tasks they will perform as adults. As manual dexterity increases and as children increasingly participate in the active work effort of the household and camp, they begin to display the skills they will use later in establishing and operating their own household as adults. These skills are developed both by direct participation and by knowledge derived from the discussions of those who practice these arts. By age five or six girls are performing routine tasks in the household including fetching water, hunting along the shore for clams, fetching fuel for fire, harnessing the dogs, cleaning up the tent or igloo, etc. Boys at a corresponding age accompany their fathers and brothers to hunt when the weather is good, at first merely to tend the dogs and stay with the sled, but later to help load the sled and eventually to actively engage in hunting. When not actually engaged in these tasks children learn from the conversations which center on these tasks. Hunting is a topic of seemingly inexhaustible interest to everyone in the camp, whether it be how a hunter stalked his prey, prevailing wind or ice conditions on the sealing grounds, or the probability that the geese, the eiders, or even the walrus will return on schedule during the coming season. Narrators describe and sometimes even act out the details of the hunt for their audience. Women too spend a good deal of time discussing sewing technique, the textures of thread or skin, the proper way to scrape hides, or how best to cut out a new pair of boots or trousers. Gradually, by easy steps, boys and girls gain competence in the tasks they must acquire to become fully participating adults.

It is at this time that Inuit anticipate that a child's latent character will begin to manifest itself. This will often be noticed by commenting on how typical of his particular name spirit some action is, or how characteristic of his particular social endowment the exercise of some skill is. Some name spirits, for example, are known to be particularly skilled kayak builders and it is anticipated that a boy who possesses one of those spirits will similarly manifest an extraordinary capability in this area of work. Even while young, his advice will be sought when boat frames are being repaired and parts replaced; and he will frequently be invited to help with the building or repairing or covering of the kayaks in his community. It is the same with a girl, although the impression is that variations in skills among females are not expected to be so marked. That is, every woman is expected to be able to sew well or tend a stone lamp; it is only among men that skills such as stalking walrus, building well balanced kayaks or carving walrus tusk are expected to be differentially distributed to any marked degree.

Sessions in which the personality or skill of a child is explained by attributing it to the child's name spirit are not infrequent in adult discussions. At these times one is struck by the similarity between these attributions of character and the ones commonly suffered by children from southern regions, when, at annual family gatherings such as Christmas, their relatives mentally dissect some youngster into constituent parts, attributing his blue eyes to his father, the color of her hair to her grandmother, etc. The exercise performed on the child by his Inuit relatives is remarkably similar in form, except that the principles on which the attributions are based are very different from those used by relatives in southern Canada. In our tradition, one inherits physical attributes and traits of character through the symbolic substance known as "blood." Inuit trace inheritance of many of these same attributes through the sharing of a common name spirit.

While there are no formally marked changes in the statuses of individuals as they move from childhood to young adulthood, the routine daily life of an Inuit community is periodically interrupted for the acclamation of minor victories. The acquisition of any new skill by a young person is always celebrated. Whenever a girl catches her first salmon trout or sews her first pair of socks, and whenever a young boy kills his first goose or traps his first fox, the community is given notice of the growing competence of the child. Here the ritual sponsor plays a crucial role. At birth the ritual sponsor dresses the infant and gives it gifts which symbolize the value placed on cooperation and sharing by the Inuit community. Later, when the child begins to participate in the productive life of the community it is the ritual sponsor who receives the benefits of the child's labour and brings its accomplishments to the attention of the community at large. Every milestone on the road to adulthood is similarly celebrated in this fashion.

SOCIALIZATION OF YOUNG MEN AND YOUNG WOMEN

When boys and girls have reached the point where they have passed all or most of the tests which serve as measures of adulthood they are gradually recognized in the community as being *angutiaru*, "young man" and *angnaru*, "young woman." These terms are formulated by using the base roots for "man" and "woman" with the addition of the suffix -*aru* which implies "approaching." They are thus viewed as close to full adulthood, a status which is attributable to individuals who possess the set of traditional skills associated with running a household; and it is at this point that a man or woman begins to think about marriage.

What is stressed at this young adult stage in the age/sex hierarchy is the ability to perform adult tasks routinely within the division of labor. Young men spend most of their daytime hours hunting and their evenings preparing for the next day's hunt. Any spare time they have is spent cultivating the families of marriageable women in the community. In the conduct of these affairs young men act with remarkable independence. They are in principle answerable to no one, although "maturity" is equated precisely with the ability to be cooperative and agreeable with everyone in the community, most especially with members of one's own family. So, in fact, young men are answerable to almost everyone older, for they must appear to be industrious, obliging, energetic, supportive, and competent. Gradually, their focus of concern will begin to narrow to a single household containing an unmarried young woman. Soon the youth will come alone to bring gifts of food or skins or tools to the family and to the household head and these are accepted as signs of his serious intent. If there are older unmarried brothers in the household the youth will begin to hunt regularly with them or with the male household head.

Young women are also encouraged to demonstrate their competence as skilled workers. They are generally the first members of the household to arise in the morning to make tea or help the younger children dress. They gradually take on responsibility for all the heavy work of the household — chopping wood, butchering and distributing meat, fetching water or hauling younger siblings around on their backs. Such household labour as cooking, tea-making, and the like are undertaken with an almost ritualized air of efficiency. Young women are hyperenergetic, excessively busy, dramatically competent at this point in their careers. In the presence of others they seldom say anything unless directly addressed, but they manifest a kind of work frenzy that will keep them going long after guests have left and other members of the household have retired. Almost their only relief from work during this period is on berry picking or fishing expeditions, usually in the company of other young women and often with a younger sibling carried in their roomy parka. These are also the occasions on which they have an opportunity to meet and talk to young men, although adults will sometimes contrive to leave young people alone at home for short periods as well. In these ways young women demonstrate their potentialities as wives.

Outright sexual relations at this time are generally discouraged, for the vast majority of Inuit now take Christian injunctions concerning chastity very seriously. Traditionally, men and young women were permitted to engage in overt sexual relations occasionally and this sometimes resulted in pregnancy. Young women who had children were never stigmatized in the traditional culture nor yet today, for a woman's ability to bear healthy children was highly prized and, if anything, enhanced her desirability as a prospective mate. Nor does the disposition of the child cause any real problem. The offspring becomes the child of its natal parents if they marry, or it becomes the offspring of the head of the household in which it comes to reside, most generally its own grandparents. Failing this it will be offered in adoption.

Full maturity is attained only at marriage, when a young couple establish their own household and begin to have children. Like the rest of the passage from infancy to adulthood the coupling occurs largely unheralded, the young husband simply moving his belongings into his wife's household where he will be a resident and do bride service until after the first child is born. After the period of bride service the couple will be free to set up an independent household wherever they please.

DEVELOPMENT OF HUMAN CHARACTER

In the foregoing description I avoided where possible the use of words like "teaching" and "learning" because Inuit do not view the movement toward adulthood precisely as a process in which children acquire knowledge at the hands of adults; and, as stated at the outset, the purpose was to portray the socialization process in terms of the Inuit's own conception of maturation. In their view, the individual becomes an adult through the interplay of inherent character and contact with relatives and community members whose aim is to set a good example, to draw out the individual's character by leading exemplary lives. Inuit think of character as having an immanent quality about it; it grows from the inside out. In this section the Inuit view of the development of human character will be described. This will be done, by describing their theory of how the world works, and how human character is a part of the orderly unfolding of that world.

Inuit regard the identity of an individual as embodied in his or her name, a label they confer no later than four days after birth and usually immediately after parturition. Actually, children are not thought of as being named. Naming is rather a process of discovering by divination what animating spirit has entered the child's body. This task is undertaken by parents or someone endowed with special skills at what might be called "interrogation." The task consists of mentioning all the name spirits likely to have entered the child and watching for signs of recognition. When the child appears to "recognize" its name, that name is generally considered to have entered the infant.

The process by which infants come to acquire their identities is no different in theory from that by means of which animals acquire their character. When a seal is killed its body is said to remain on earth to be consumed by the Inuit; but its soul, only provided that the correct propitiatory ritual is performed by the hunter and his family, proceeds to the underworld where a sea goddess named *nuliayuq* permits it to enter a new body and return to the upper world to be hunted by the Inuit again. The same is true of other animals, and also of human spirits. At death a human spirit remains around the body for a period of three to five days (cf. Rasmussen, 1929: 197-199), then proceeds to the underworld where it is kept until such time as it is permitted by the sea goddess to enter the body of an infant once more.

According to the theory, the name spirit animates the body in which it is housed and imparts personality and character to the individual. It animates the body in the sense that without it the infant would be still-born or the child or adult would sicken and eventually die. Even a temporary departure can have serious consequences. If the spirit departs, it may be replaced by a wandering spirit, either of an animal or of some malevolent being. Schizophrenia is commonly explained as the possession of the body by a wandering spirit of one sort or another. These altered states produce unstable personalities in theory; they are by definition "unnatural" and thus frightening. Consequently, Inuit are anxious to cement the name spirit to the body in order to stabilize the personality of the individual and, in the case of an infant, to insure that it remains alive.

As personality, the name spirit determines the temperament and traits of character an infant will manifest later in life and it also shapes the mechanical skills and aptitudes the individual will eventually develop. Some name spirits are associated with even temperedness, some others with tenacity, good humor, etc. Expertise at kayak building was associated with one name in the *Qiqiktamiut* repertoire; and another was said to embody the ability to hunt seal or even walrus at night.

These particular endowments are known to every member of the local community and serve as a basis for making judgments about the performance of any member, whether child or adult.

This is one of the chief differences between the animating name spirits of animals and those of humans. All animals of a particular species bear the name spirit of that species and for this reason all have the same character and skills. Inuit, of course, and dogs,[4] possess individuating name spirits which cause them to behave differently — to have different characters. But in the Inuit formulation, character is not individuated down to a one-to-one level as it is in our world. A given identity is commonly shared by as many as three or four people who participate in a particular name spirit, contributing to it by the way they live and drawing their identity from its historic "reputation." We can understand the matter better if we re-examine some of the facts of the name conferring process.

Inuit believe that naming is a process involving the discovery of what animating spirit has entered the child; but they also consider that naming involves a process whereby some living incumbent (or some close relative of a deceased name holder) gives permission for his or her name to be conferred on a child. Thus Qiqiktamiut assert that every individual has the opportunity to confer his or her name on at least three others and in practice it may happen that as many as five individuals may bear the same name in the Belcher Islands at any given time. The naming process thus involves what appears to be a paradox. What the Qiqiktamiut appear to mean is that any conferral of a name spirit must be consented to by some present incumbent, while the actual entry of the spirit into an infant is controlled by the supernatural world.

When the child is actually named it enters into community with the bearers of the name, its saunit or "bones," actually sharing the identity and collective personality and character associated with the name spirit with these people. The infant simply assumes the identity of an actor whose role in the human drama is already well established in the community the infant enters. For there are already a number of actors who have assumed that identity, some now living and others who have gone before. It is their collective history that forms the basis for attributions of character to the child; and his actions will eventually be compared to those which are embedded in that established identity.

A good deal more could be said about the Inuit formulation of how the world works. This would show the interconnections between such diverse topics as treatment of disease, traditional religious practitioners, formulae for sharing various kinds of food, and the social position of dogs and other pets. In the previous section an attempt has been made to indicate some of the beliefs which lend credence to the belief that children are not in fact children at all — at least not in our sense of that term — but diminutive adults. It remains for us to see whether a knowledge of their lifeways can enhance our insight into our own social universe.

Inuit children grow up in a society which is relatively simple, concrete, and directly related to experience. If the Inuit adult attitude toward children includes the view that they are nothing less than diminutive adults with all the potentialities of adults, this view can only be sustained because there is no great burden of knowledge to acquire that is not an ongoing part of the everyday life of everyone in the community. Children do not need to be "taught" how to perform tasks which they can experience through observation and participation. But life for the urban Canadian child is not so simply and directly accessible. Clearly, the lesson to be learned from examining the Inuit experience is not that we should close our schools and simply let our children grow into adulthood as best they can and in their own time.

There are, nonetheless, some important insights here. The first would appear to be related to the fact that the Inuit set but one task for the child: to become an adult. The process of growth into adulthood is a smooth, continuous one involving integration into an ongoing social tradition. It is relatively unambiguous in goal and simple in method. In Inuit society there is but one set of roles to play, those of men and women, and everybody is expected and encouraged to work for the attainment of those statuses as quickly and effectively as possible. In our society, by way of contrast, an individual must become two different sorts of persons before he is forced — or even encouraged — to take an adult view of the world. He or she must first be taught (which also means "must learn") to be a "child" and then an "adolescent." Much of what we encourage our children to learn is quite literally children's culture — virtually useless as adult knowledge. The singlemindedness with which Inuit approach living makes partners of adults and children; our conflicting and ambiguous treatment of development inspires the young to be our antagonists.

A second lesson to be derived from the Inuit example proceeds from the fact that they accept their young as having a social status equivalent to that of adults. There is a remarkable equanimity which pervades the relations of old and young in the Arctic. Children are allowed to explore the world using what skills they can muster; and there is remarkably little meddling by older people in this learning process. Parents do not presume to teach their children what they can as easily learn on their own; there is no patronizing attitude of "knowing it all" in the face of youthful innocence. The result is that children never perceive learning as a struggle for mastery, and they never feel the embarrassment which results from being forced to submit their accomplishments to the scrutiny of an approving assemblage of parents or relatives. They are permitted the luxury of conducting their lives with relative freedom and remarkable independence, turning to parents and others only when they truly need help with some skill that proves resistant to mastery. Adults are not teachers in such a learning context, they are resource persons. But more importantly, because they have a status equal to that of adults, children are consulted by their elders about decisions which involve them and the community as a whole. The effect is to produce a system in which equity takes precedence over authority.

Finally, there is an insight to be gained about the "politics" of family life in Southern Canada. In Inuit society children are not thought to be extensions of and therefore in some sense "owned" by their parents. Since their identity is not inherited in the form of some substance such as "blood" but is rather introduced into their bodies in the form of a name spirit, family members have nothing to gain or lose by the successes or failures of the child. The bond between parents and child is the bond of "love" and the only persons whose personal sense of self worth is affected by the actions of the child are his ritual relatives, most importantly his namesakes. In Canadian society parents feel a strong urge to exercise power over their children — running their lives, making their plans for them, insisting on this or that kind of career stream. The logic which requires this kind of control is the logic of blood relatedness which insists that children are substantive extensions of their families, and the definition of children as intellectually "empty." In our world, whatever a child does implicates the reputation of its family. Parents expect their children to accept their advice and authority in order that the reputation and dignity of the family as a whole can be maintained. The child's successes become explained in terms of family heritage — they serve to enhance the reputations of its parents. The child's failures, because they endanger the reputation of the family, invite disapproval by family members and, in serious cases, retribution. And so the child grows into adulthood striving to please his kin, struggling to preserve some of the merit parents bestow on themselves for his achievement, trying to hide or explain away his short comings so as to escape the cost of the family's disappointment. Inuit suffer no "generation gap" because they do not divide their social world into teachers and learners, knowers and empty vessels, parents and children.

EPILOGUE

In the preceding pages I have attempted to characterize the *traditional* — i.e. as practiced in the past — Inuit outlook toward children as social actors and to see the socialization of children as an outgrowth of, and therefore contingent upon, that outlook. But a caveat is in order concerning the status of these practices. The vast majority of Inuit now live in modern pre-fabricated houses, attend a Christian church of one denomination or another on Sunday, send their children off to public school, seek treatment for their ills at the local nursing station or hospital, and satisfy the greatest part of their material needs by trade at the local store. Even those who continue to hunt with some regularity go out to the sealing grounds on skidoos in the winter and in power driven canoes in the summer. Many hunt and fish only for sport or nostalgia; and some have even given it up as sport. The Inuit epitomized in literature have largely ceased to practice their ancient traditions; the classic Inuit now exist only in the fantasies of Southern Canadians and the rest of the Western World. To the extent that the outlook toward children and the universe sketched above captures Inuit traditional thinking (and it should be emphasized that there was always considerable variation in world view among various Inuit groups), that set of attitudes and beliefs has been steadily eroded by the values and beliefs of professional educators from the South in recent years. Modern Inuit increasingly think about and act toward their children just as we do.

Footnotes

1. In 1974 a Rankin Inlet Inuit couple sought and was awarded permanent custody of a child born to another couple because, it was explained in the custody hearing, the family had developed no love for the child. The child had become ill shortly after birth and been evacuated by airplane to a hospital in the south where it remained for a year. When it returned to the community it was returned to its natal household, but neither parents nor siblings took any interest in it. The child developed the habit of spending most of its time in a nearby household and eventually took up residence there. The adopted family developed love for it and finally asked for custody.
2. If a baby picks up a sharp object of some sort adults merely pick up whatever is readily at hand and give these items too to the baby. Distracted by these additional offerings the baby soon has its hands full of gifts and begins handing these back to the giver.
3. Briggs (1968: 111-112) notes that the Utkuhiqhalingmiut identify this stage as one at which children acquire 'thought' (ihuma).
4. Dogs are a special kind of animal which mediate in many ways between the animal world of nature and the human world of culture. Dogs bear individuating names just as humans do and in some instances function as surrogate human beings. In Inuit mythology the first humans were born to a woman who cohabited with a dog.

References

Balikci, Asen
  1970   *The Netsilik Eskimo.* Garden City, N.Y., The Natural History Press.

Briggs, Jean
   1968   *Never in Anger: Portrait of an Eskimo Family.* Cambridge, Mass., Harvard University Press.

Rasmussen, Knud
   1929   *Intellectual Culture of the Iglulik Eskimo.* Copenhagen, Reports of the Fifth Thule Expedition, Vol. VII.

The Assessment of Role Identity:

Use of The Instrumental Activities Inventory In Studying Inuit Children

ANN McELROY
Department of Anthropology
State University of New York at Buffalo

INTRODUCTION

This article discusses a study of the role model preferences of 153 Canadian Inuit (Eskimo) schoolchildren living in two Eastern Arctic towns. The testing method consisted of a set of drawings on cards of women and men at work in northern settlements. This research technique, called the Instrumental Activities Inventory, was first used by George and Louise Spindler (1965) in studying the Blood Indians of Alberta. The technique (to be referred to as the IAI), is particularly useful in studying a community undergoing acculturation to the larger Canadian society. Both traditional and modern roles can be depicted on the cards, and the role choices made by children taking the test reflect the culture change process.

This article will describe the reasons for choosing this particular test, the way the children were tested, and the results. Some of the advantages and disadvantages of using the IAI will also be discussed. In the last section the test results will be related to the community context.

The IAI was one of several research approaches used in an anthropological study of Inuit child socialization in Frobisher Bay and Pangnirtung, two settlements on southern Baffin Island. The research involved fourteen months of field study between 1967 and 1971.

A revised version of "The Assessment of Role Identity: Problems of Administering the Instrumental Activities Inventory to Inuit Children," presented at the 73rd Annual Meeting of the American Anthropological Association, Mexico City, 1974.

Frobisher Bay is a rapidly growing center of transportation, administration, medical services, and education (see Honigmann and Honigmann, 1965, for a history of the town). Approximately 1,200 Inuit and 1,000 Euro-Canadians of diverse ethnic backgrounds live in the community. Most of the Inuit depend on wage employment. In March of 1971, 87% of the Inuit men and 31% of the women aged 16-65 held jobs, and the average annual income per Inuit household was $6,590.

Pangnirtung is a smaller and more isolated community about 150 miles northeast of Frobisher Bay. Whereas Frobisher Bay's settlement began in the 1940s with construction of an Air Force base, it was only after 1966, when an epidemic reduced the sled dog population, that people from the Cumberland Sound region settled in Pangnirtung. About 650 Inuit and 100 southern Canadians live in the village. In 1969, 27% of all males in the community between 15 and 65 were employed full-time, and 40% of all households had one or more individuals (including women) employed either full-time or on a steady part-time basis. Thus fewer families had regular cash income than in Frobisher Bay, other than family allowance, pensions, and occasional social assistance. The average annual income per Inuit household in Pangnirtung in 1969 was $3,366.

Study of the socialization and role identity development of Inuit children and adolescents during initial field trips in 1967 and 1969 used standard cultural anthropology techniques. I lived with three Inuit families, accompanying two of them to hunting camps. In town, I interviewed teachers, community leaders, and parents of young children. Since I was still learning the language, Inuttitut, these interviews were actually focused conversations and relied heavily on informal questions about things I had observed in the family setting.

One of the most intriguing observations was that the training of young boys within the nuclear family and extended kin groups emphasized the traditional subsistence skills more than did the training of girls. Hunting skills were considered important for boys to learn, while girls were not urged to learn how to prepare animal skins for boots and clothing, for example. Similarly, observation of young adults pointed out considerable divergence in the attitudes of young men and women toward Euro-Canadian values and life-styles. Young women were clearly more interested in following Euro-Canadian role models. If young men were interested, they were also ambivalent, and many preferred a frontier-style of life.

These observations did indicate a general trend but also some variability, and a method had to be found to mesure actual role preferences in a larger sample and in several age groups. It seemed most productive to look for a projective technique like the TAT (Thematic Apperception Test), in which subjects express values and needs through the stories they make up about standardized pictures.

Projective techniques had rarely been used with Arctic groups. John Honigmann (1962) experienced some difficulty in giving Rorschach tests to Inuit in Great Whale River in Arctic Quebec, and the responses are rather constricted and don't tell much about personality. Preston (1964) gave a series of tests in studying the personality of northwest Alaskan Inuit and found the TAT especially difficult to administer because of language barriers. Berry (1966, 1969) gave Baffin Island Inuit a number of tests which show interesting relationships among cognitive style, ecology, and socialization. Parker's study (1964) of ethnic identity in two Alaskan villages used an original projective technique of pictures which elicited stories related to ethnicity. While Parker's study seemed valuable, my research problem required a projective technique which would tap attitudes toward socioeconomic roles. The Instrumental Activities Inventory, to be described in the following section, was a promising technique for this purpose.

METHOD

The Rorschach and TAT are deliberately ambiguous tests designed to elicit the inner feelings and perceptions of the subject. In contrast, the IAI was devised by the Spindlers to be unambiguous and useful in yielding data on perception of socio-environmental realities (Spindler and Spindler, 1965: 314). The inventory consisted of 24 line drawings, each depicting a male engaged in one type of instrumental activity or role — as a medicine man, priest, mechanic, farmer, bronc rider, and so on. Instrumental activities were defined as "those activities that an individual engages in for the achievement and maintenance of a life style and status in the social groups of which he is a member, or aspires to be a member" (ibid.: 312). The cards were shown to males and females ranging in age from 18 to 87. Respondents were asked by the Spindlers to choose at least three pictures which they valued most highly and an equal number which they disliked most. Female respondents were asked to choose "what they would like their sons or husbands (depending on age and family status) to do" (ibid.: 319).

In choosing the IAI as an appropriate technique for the study of role identity in Inuit children, I decided to depict female as well as male roles in the inventory and to include only those instrumental activities which were visible as models to the children in Frobisher Bay and Pangnirtung. Limits of time and finances required that only 24 pictures be prepared, so that each subject would be shown a set of 12 cards appropriate to his or her gender.

Pilot testing in Pangnirtung in the early winter of 1970 indicated that testing of adults would be difficult. Interpreter services were required and some individuals misunderstood the intent of my inquiries, believing that I was either offering them jobs or could influence local administrators to give them jobs. The people of Pangnirtung had never been exposed to projective tests (or for that matter, to anthropologists since the time of Boas in 1883) and it was difficult to elicit cooperation even from those adults I knew best. Therefore, I decided to test only schoolchildren, although the pictures showed adults at work.

The pictures represent three role categories: modern, transitional, and contact-traditional. The categories are defined as follows and are represented by the roles listed:

Modern
Occupations and activities currently monopolized by Euro-Canadians but open to bilingual Inuit with specialized training or advanced education.
Male roles: doctor, teacher, radio operator, office clerk
Female roles: nurse, teacher, radio announcer, secretary

Transitional
Occupations and activities currently characteristic of town Inuit of moderate or high levels of acculturation; learned by on-the-job training or adult education programs; also open to Euro-Canadians in the community but monopolized by Inuit.
Male roles: airplane mechanic, construction worker, store clerk, catechist (lay preacher)
Female roles: cook, post-office clerk, store clerk, housewife

Contact-Traditional
Activities characteristic of either town or camp Inuit which do not require formal education, bilingualism, and do not involve wage earning; roles exclusively occupied by Inuit.

The children were tested individually, coming to a testing room in pairs during regular school hours. The same instructions were given to each child, first in English and then in Inuttitut in the case of those younger children who appeared unsure of the procedure. The child was told that the pictures showed different kinds of work that a person could do in the North, and he was asked to sort the cards into two piles — one with those pictures showing work that he would like to do when he was older, and the other with pictures showing work that he would not like to do. No limit was put on the number of choices during the first task, and the subject was assured that he or she was not taking a test with right or wrong answers, choosing an actual job, or committed to the choices in the future.

The pictures were randomly ordered in respect to the three categories and were shown in the same sequence to each subject. After sorting the 12 cards appropriate to his or her gender, according to the initial "like-dislike" task (which I call the unlimited choice task), the child was then asked to choose the one card which showed the most preferred type of work (called the limited choice task).

Of the sample of 90 children originally chosen from class rolls in each settlement, it was necessary to delete the responses of 11 subjects from Pangnirtung and 15 from Frobisher Bay, leaving a final sample of 41 girls and 37 boys, ages 9 to 17, from Pangnirtung (63% of the total school enrollment). In Frobisher Bay 35 girls and 40 boys, ages 8 to 16, representing 27% of the enrollment, were tested. The total sample was 153: 76 girls and 77 boys.

Children who did not understand the testing procedure or who were uncooperative in taking the test were deleted from the sample. The results, therefore, represent the attitudes and orientations only of children amenable to being tested who could understand enough English (or Inuttitut as spoken by a foreigner) to comprehend the instructions.

RESULTS

Unlimited Choice Task

When the children could choose as many pictures as they liked, 74% of the boys chose between 2 and 4 cards. The three most popular male roles were store clerk (60% chose this), construction worker (53%), and airplane mechanic (52%). These jobs bring good wages and can be learned through on-the-job training, and there are many Inuit men in such positions.

Traditional subsistence tasks ranked in the middle. For example, 36% of the boys liked hunter with rifle, and 31% chose fisherman. Catechist and doctor are about the same (22 and 21%), while office clerk and teacher are not at all popular (10 and 9%). The less preferred roles, then, are those which require long-term education or involve competition with Euro-Canadians.

The girls tested tended to choose more cards than the boys had, although 2 to 4 cards is still the norm for 58% of the female sample. While only 3 roles were chosen by 50% or more of the boys, 5 roles were attractive to at least half of the girls: store clerk, seamstress, cook, secretary, and housewife. All of these cluster closely to the 50% mark except the very popular store clerk at 61%. The role of nurse was chosen by 47%. Office clerk, radio announcer, and teacher are in the middle. The pattern here is that work occupations which can be learned by on-the-job training are preferred over work requiring specialized training or advanced education. This is no different than the male responses, but what is striking about the female responses is the relative unpopularity of traditional roles: 20% chose skin worker (a woman scraping fat off a seal skin), 14% tentwife (a woman making bread in a tent while her family drinks tea), and 9% small game hunter (a woman with rifle walking in the hills to hunt hare or ptarmigan). Only seamstress is high among the traditional roles, ranking second in popularity (54%). There is some difference between settlements, though. Pangnirtung girls (66%) chose seamstress far more often than Frobisher Bay girls (40%), and skin worker was also more popular in the Pangnirtung sample (32% to 6%). The girls living in the smaller, less modern settlement have had more opportunities to learn traditional skills, especially those adolescents born in hunting camps.

Limited Choice Task
This part of the test asked the subjects to choose one card which they liked best as a job or activity. In this task, the boys most preferred airplane mechanic (27%) and store clerk (25%). Construction worker fell to the same rank as hunter with rifle (both 10%), and radio operator was chosen by 8%. No-one selected office-clerk or teacher, and only 3 chose doctor. While 21% (16 boys) liked the role of doctor in the first task, only 4%, all aged 11 and under, aspired most to this kind of role in the second task. As in the unlimited choice task, the modern roles are least popular.

In the limited choice task, the girls continue to prefer store clerk (30%) and seamstress (18%). Two of the modern roles rise in rank: secretary (14%) and nurse (12%), but teacher and radio announcer are not popular. Traditionally prestigious tasks, especially skin working, are not attractive under the pressure of a limited choice even to the 32% of the Pangnirtung sample who included skin worker in their unlimited choices. No-one chose skin worker or tentwife, and only one child selected small-game hunter.

Under the condition of limited choice, domestic roles are generally not preferred. While 50% of the subjects included the housewife card in their unlimited choices, only one out of 76 girls chose the housewife role in the limited choice task, putting that role on a rank with small-game hunter.

Differences between Male and Female Responses
The chi square method was used to test the significance of the differences between the two settlements and between males and females. The cards were grouped into three acculturative categories: traditional, transitional, and modern. The distribution of frequencies and percentages of responses by category is given in Table 1.

Combining male and female responses, there were no significant differences between the frequencies of the total samples from each settlement. This indicates that although Pangnirtung families have lived in town for a much shorter period of time than have Frobisher Bay Inuit families, the children have developed similar patterns of role identification in each settlement.

Because there are no significant differences between the settle-

TABLE 1

DISTRIBUTION OF UNLIMITED AND LIMITED CHOICES OF MODIFIED IAI CARDS BY ROLE CATEGORY BY MALE AND FEMALE INUIT SCHOOLCHILDREN, FROBISHER BAY AND PANGNIRTUNG, N.W.T., MARCH-APRIL 1970

| Frobisher Bay | Unlimited Choice | | | | | | Limited Choice | | | | | |
| | Modern* | | Transitional† | | Traditional‡ | | Modern | | Transitional | | Traditional | |
	N	%	N	%	N	%	N	%	N	%	N	%
Frobisher Bay												
Males	33	20	77	48	52	32	6	13	27	60	12	27
Females	60	41	63	43	23	16	13	36	15	42	8	22
Total	93	30.1	140	45.5	75	24.4	19	23	42	52	20	25
Pangnirtung												
Males	25	18	67	49	45	33	3	9	27	79	4	12
Females	59	29.6	89	44.7	51	25.6	13	32.5	20	50	7	17.5
Total	84	25	156	46	96	29	16	22	47	63	11	15
Combined Samples												
Males	58	19.4	144	48.2	97	32.4	9	12	54	68	16	20
Females	119	34.4	152	44.1	74	21.4	26	34	35	46	15	20
Total	177	27	296	46	171	27	35	23	89	57	31	20

*Male roles: radio operator, doctor, office clerk, teacher

†Male roles: store clerk, construction worker, airplane mechanic, catechist (lay preacher)

‡Male roles: hunter with rifle, spear hunter, carver, fisherman

*Female roles: radio announcer, nurse, secretary, teacher

†Female roles: store clerk, cook, post office clerk, housewife

‡Female roles: small game hunter, skin worker, seamstress, tent wife

ments, we are able to compare the total male sample with the total female sample. Differences between males and females in the unlimited choice situation are significant at greater than the .001 level of probability ($X^2 = 21.15$) and in the limited choice situation between the .01 and .001 level ($X^2 = 12.325$). While the highest percentages of responses for both sexes are in the transitional category, in both settlements a greater percentage of females than males chose those cards classified in the modern category.

Differences between the sexes in the Frobisher Bay sample for the unlimited choice situation are significant beyond the .001 level ($X^2 = 19.66$) and in the Pangnirtung sample, at the .05 level ($X^2 = 5.998$). This means that the divergence in role orientations of boys and girls is somewhat greater in the Frobisher Bay sample. In fact, in the limited choice task (with frequencies too small for reliable chi square treatment), there are more Pangnirtung females in the traditional category than there are males. It is in the more modern settlement, then, that females become significantly more oriented toward certain Euro-Canadian role models than males do.

Additional tests of statistical significance (see McElroy 1977 for details) showed that boys aged 8 to 11 chose modern roles more frequently than those aged 12 to 17. There was no significant difference in the choices of younger and older girls. Other variables tested, such as school attendance, absences to go to hunting camps, and age-grade retardation (age of the child in relation to the norm for that grade), showed no positive correlations.

ISSUES IN INTERPRETATION AND VALIDITY

In this section, I will discuss some of the problems which arose in interpreting the results. Some of these difficulties come from the research design, others from the testing procedures. This critique is presented to help students become aware of some of the disadvantages in testing children who are not fluent in English.

The most serious methodological problem is the classification of the roles into categories. The cards were classified according to three criteria based on observations in the settlements in 1969-1970: 1) the degree of education and bilingual ability required to carry out the instrumental activity; 2) the extent to which Inuit role models of the activity were present in the communities; and 3) the extent to which these jobs or roles were monopolized by Euro-Canadians.

The question which must be raised about classification of roles is the subjects' perception not only of the identity of the roles (the rights, privileges, rewards, and risk involved) but also of the opportunity to carry out the roles. It has been suggested, for example, that the classification of professional seamstress in a contact-traditional category leads to problems in interpreting the general trend of female responses. If the females are generally more oriented toward modern roles than are the males, then why the obvious popularity of the seamstress role?

In discussing the relatively popular male role of rifle hunter, the factor of prestige was introduced, and it is likely that the seamstress role is prestigious as well. However, skin working was traditionally prestigious and still is a valued role for Inuit women, and this role was not popular with the children. Sewing and skin working were formerly considered to be the most important attributes of a desirable wife, and Baffin Island women over the age of 30 have retained these skills. Why do girls dislike the role of skin worker but still aspire to being a seamstress? The critical difference here is in relative opportunity. Inuit girls do not disparage the skills of preparing skins. They like to watch their mothers at work and can judge whether a skin has been properly processed. But mothers are reluctant to allow their daughters to work with skins. Clumsy use of the *ulu*, the woman's knife, may tear the skin and lower its trading value. Sewing, knitting, and embroidery are profitable skills which most girls learn and which can provide earnings for adolescents and monolingual older women. The difference in the ranked order of these two traditional roles suggests that girls are responding in part to the factor of availability or opportunity and are not rejecting traditional roles entirely. But the test did not probe the issue of opportunity, a variable to be included in future studies.

In analyzing differences between age groups, the differences between younger boys and older boys could be interpreted in several ways. It is possible that older boys identified at an early age with the transitional male roles available to Inuit men in the settlements in the late 1950s and early 1960s, whereas younger boys have the opportunity to identify at the present time with Inuit men who hold positions as teachers and classroom assistants, office workers and radio operators. In the case of a role such as doctor, a popular choice for younger boys (13 chose this card in the unlimited choice situation, while only 3 of the older boys chose it), Inuit models have not been available. Older boys would be more likely to have been hospitalized in the south for treatment of tuberculosis than younger boys, who are now treated locally with chemotherapy. Perhaps the role of doctor is more negatively perceived by boys who have had unpleasant hospital experiences.

Another interpretation of the male age-group differences would be that boys aspire to Euro-Canadian roles less as they grow older, specifically because of their increased awareness of the difficulties of continuing in school and financing the training required. Professional training for an Inuk requires schooling in the south and separation from friends and family, a step which relatively few adolescents choose to take beyond six-month or one-year vocational training courses, even when tuition and support are provided by the government.

Another methodological problem involves sampling procedures. Selection of subjects from class attendance books initially allowed a balanced representation by criteria of attendance, age-grade retardation level, and absences connected with hunting. Loss of subjects due to lack of cooperation, as well as difficulties in finding satisfactory substitutes, effected an unbalanced representation of these categories for female subjects and for the Frobisher Bay sample as a whole. In the case of girls, there was a negative correlation between high attendance, advanced age-grade level, and cooperation in taking the test. In addition, many of those children scheduled for testing because they were representatives of the high-absenteeism category, based on the previous year's records, were never in school to be tested!

The problems in trying to get parents to respond to the inventory was one of the most difficult aspects of the study. Comparison of children's responses with parental perceptions and choices would be an invaluable addition to the study. However, the issue of whether it is feasible to use an assessment or projective technique with Inuit should be considered. Inuit adults are not used to taking tests and dislike questionnaires. They become characteristically withdrawn in situations structured as official queries, even when interpreters are present. Some of the schoolchildren responded well, but those most needed for a balanced sample (adolescents, students at an advanced age-grade level, and girls with high attendance) were among those subjects who gave minimal cooperation and brief responses.

SUGGESTIONS FOR FURTHER RESEARCH

I recommend that the present set of cards be expanded to 48 pictures, 24 for each sex group. All but three of the cards (catechist, tent wife, and housewife) presently depict occupations or subsistence activities, while the Spindlers' series represent a broader range of status-maintenance roles. Expansion of the number and range of stimuli should be done in consultation with Inuit assistants, who could provide classifications into categories based on their own perceptions of important types of traditional, transitional, and modern roles.

The problem of an Inuk's anxiety in being tested alone might be solved by training an Inuit classroom assistant to give the test in Inuttitut. The cards might be used more as a projective technique and less as a sorting technique by eliciting stories about the individuals in the pictures. Alternatively, one might ask the subjects to comment on the pictures in a generalized manner; e.g., by asking "which of these cards show work which Inuit boys would like to do when they finish school?" or "Is this a good job? Would Inuit boys like this kind of work?" A standardized set of questions following completion of choices would allow children to name the role as they perceived it and to give evaluative responses to the stimulus. Ranking of the cards by subjects would solve some of the statistical problems engendered by the variability in number of choices, and testing of all available children rather than drawing up samples would help compensate for loss of subjects. Allowing subjects to respond to *all* cards, both male and female roles, in terms of a generalized question such as "Is this a good job for an Inuk to do?" might yield interesting results. If the figures in the pictures had ambiguous ethnic affiliations rather than being clearly Inuit, one of the sorting tasks might be to ask the child which ethnic group usually (always, sometimes, rarely, never, etc.) did that kind of work. One of the ways that Inuit adults structure their choices, rationalize their decisions, and socialize their children is to classify behavior. Occupational roles, material goods, recreational styles, food, and many other components are grouped into one of two systems, *Inuttitut* or *Kadlunattitut* (white man's way). Focusing on ethnicity rather than role preference *per se* in using the modified IAI might yield interesting results, although the issue of ethnic relations in the community is a sensitive one at present.

A pertinent question raised by the editor of this volume, Professor Ishwaran, concerns the advisability of using a test like the Instrumental Activities Inventory in studying a non-western culture. Conventional anthropological methods include informal interviews with persons we call "informants," systematic observation of natural behavior and communication, and participation in the everyday life of the community. A census is usually taken, and a kinship chart is made. All of these methods add up to a research approach called ethnography.

One of the limitations of ethnography is that behavioral variability cannot easily be measured. Ethnographic data indicated differences in male and female responses to Euro-Canadian values and institutions, but there were no quantitative data to show how pervasive these differences were. Thus some type of measurement was needed. Check lists or questionnaires might be suggested by the sociology student, but such survey methods work best with literate adults, not shy children who do not read English well nor understand test-taking. The IAI had its own drawbacks, as the reader has seen, but it was a simple audio-visual test which was quickly administered and which did allow some quantitative assessment of the research problem.

No anthropologist would depend solely on an instrument like the IAI to study a non-western population. These communities have not been studied much by anthropologists with the exception of the early work of Franz Boas (1964), the fine ethnography by John and Irma Honigmann (1965), and a few recent projects. Therefore it would be inappropriate to use a single assessment technique and to fail to study family life, institutional processes, economic relations, and value systems. Even if one tested every person in the community, extensively interviewed subjects, and used sophisticated statistical analysis, the method would still waste an opportunity for a full community study. As it stood, the IAI involved less than a month of work out of 14 months of ethnography. It was an exploratory technique which raised as many new questions as it provided answers. Some of the questions raised can be approached through consideration of community dynamics, however, and in the next section we turn to ethnographic and historical material.

THE COMMUNITY CONTEXT

In the transition of the Baffin Island population from a hunting-gathering subsistence economy to a town-based, wage-earning economy in the 1950s and early 1960s, it was the male instrumental roles which came under greatest pressure for change. Frobisher Bay and Pangnirtung males were successful in obtaining employment, learning English, and participating in the development of local government and economic cooperatives. Women were not excluded from membership on community councils or from wage-earning opportunities, but the majority of women retained traditional roles in the domestic sphere. The economic components of the female role, particularly skin-working, manufacture of clothing and boots, and trade of skins and manufactured items, continued to be prestigious.

One would predict that this continuity in the female Inuit role would be reflected in general conservatism or traditionalism in the socialization and role orientations of female children and in the employment patterns of young women. The discontinuity of the male role would be predicted as contributing to a more modern socialization and role orientation of young boys and higher employment rates among young men.

Details of Inuit child socialization reported elsewhere (McElroy, 1975a), indicate an increasing emphasis among town-living Inuit parents on the learning of hunting skills by boys. There is little evidence of a parallel interest in transmitting traditional women's skills. Boys become skilled by the age of 12 in use and care of rifles, handling of outboard motorboats and snowmobiles, butchering animals, and ice-fishing. On the other hand, Inuit girls do not often work on skins, make boots, sew tents, or hunt small game, and only child care and sewing of trade items continue to be emphasized. While space restrictions do not allow elaboration of this point, it is clear that the continuity and conservatism of the roles of Inuit women over the age of 30 are not reflected in the current socialization of female children, while a number of traditional components of the male role are being transmitted to boys.

The question of female identification with traditional roles may be considered in relation to responses to the modified Instrumental Activities Inventory. To review the results of the unlimited choice task, 21.4% of all female subjects' choices were traditional, as opposed to 32.4% of all male subjects' choices. In only one category does our prediction that females would be more tradition-oriented than males hold, that of Pangnirtung females in the limited choice situation.

The prediction of higher employment rates for young men than for young women was tested by an employment survey carried out in Frobisher Bay by the author in 1971. The survey results shown in Table 2 indicate that 44% of the males and 53% of the females in the age group 18-23 were employed in July of 1971. The highest divergence in employ-

TABLE 2
NUMBER OF INUIT AGED 18-23 EMPLOYED IN FROBISHER BAY, N.W.T., IN JULY 1971

	18-19	20-21	22-23	Total
Females employed				
Category I (modern)				
clinic aide	1	4		5
clerk-typist	1		2	3
secretary			2	2
public health assistant	2			2
dental assistant		1		1
welfare assistant	1			1
vocational advisor			1	1
airline agent			1	1
radio announcer			1	1
telephone operator		1		1
				18
Category II (transitional)				
laundry worker	2			2
hospital kitchen worker		1	1	2
snack bar clerk	1		1	2
full-time babysitter	1		1	2
home management trainee			1	1
post-office clerk			1	1
store clerk		1		1
children's welfare home matron		1		1
				12
Total females employed	9	9	12	30
Percentage of resident females per age group	.56	.50	.54	.53

	18-19	20-21	22-23	Total
Males employed				
Category I (modern)				
clerk-typist			2	2
radio announcer			1	1
census-taker			1	1
R.C.M.P. assistant			1	1
				5
Category II (transitional)				
construction worker		3	3	6
cab driver	1	1	3	5
janitor	2			2
co-op clerk		2		2
store clerk			1	1
coffee shop kitchen worker			1	1
mechanic			1	1
plumbing apprentice			1	1
				19
Total males employed	3	6	15	24
Percentage of resident males per age group	.27	.40	.53	.44

ment is in the age group 18-19: 27% of the males versus 56% of the females.

The types of jobs held by young people may be classified in categories of "modern" and "transitional" analogous to the categories of the modified Instrument Activities Inventory cards, based on the amount of training, bilingualism, and identification with Euro-Canadian role models involved. We see a fairly even split in the female jobs shown in Table 2, 18 positions falling into the modern category and 12 in the transitional. In the case of jobs held by males, only 5 are classified as modern and 19 as transitional.

The modern jobs, in fact, overlap with what I have called "public liaison" occupations (McElroy 1975b). The occupations of clinic aide, welfare assistant, interpreter, vocational advisor, ticket agent, and Royal Canadian Mounted Police assistant all require bicultural flexibility, tact, patience, and ability to act as a liaison between Inuit clients and Euro-Canadian personnel. Most public liaison occupations are held by young women, who are usually under direct Euro-Canadian supervision. Supervisors' attitudes of sympathy and appreciation help young women adjust to the pressures of their jobs.

Males who take construction jobs, work as mechanics or other technical assistants are under greater pressure to develop technical skills. They are expected to respond appropriately to criticism, and to accept close supervision. Young Inuit men are sensitive to criticism and threats to their sense of autonomy. They also feel the pressures of supervision in public liaison jobs more strongly than do young women, who are less autonomous in the home and are allowed greater satisfaction of dependence needs than are males. Employers in Frobisher Bay consider young men to be a high risk and cite absenteeism and sensitivity to criticism as problems affecting work adjustment. It is likely that issues of male autonomy, as well as ethnic politics, come into play here and affect the job preferences of young men. Co-op clerk, janitor, cab driver, and construction worker are the most frequent forms of employment for males under the age of 22. Construction work is the only one of these four jobs which involves close supervision, and it is possible that the high wages and seasonal work routine compensate for the tensions of construction work.

In this section I have discussed the idea that the historical continuity in female Inuit role definitions would be correlated with conservatism in female acculturation. Data on patterns of child association, responses of schoolchildren to the IAI, and employment trends all fail to support this model. These findings suggest that continuity in roles does not inhibit individuals from behavioral flexibility. Are there alternative data which account for differences in male and female acculturation patterns? One approach is to look at the problem diachronically, that is over the course of contact history.

Using historical documents to trace the nature of the relationship between Europeans and Inuit from the beginning of contact in the 1840s to the present, I have shown elsewhere (McElroy 1976) that the customary autonomy and leadership prerogatives of Inuit males were systematically disparaged and threatened by British and American whalers, traders, employers, and other contact agents. There was considerable pressure on native men to change their roles during contact, and male leaders, particularly the shamans and work-group bosses (angiyuqaat), experienced what Hagen has called "withdrawal of status respect" in discussing the psychological impact of colonialism (1962, pp. 201-205). In contrast, there was little pressure on Inuit women to abandon their traditional roles. Moreover, the status of women may have been enhanced by their role as mediators in alliances and by their exclusive skills in providing skins and clothing for Europeans. While the subordination required of Inuit men by Europeans represented a departure from respected male behavior, the nurture, sexual services, and provision of material assistance which Europeans expected of Inuit women were essentially appropriate to the traditional role of women.

How does this historical reconstruction relate to the present divergence between young Inuit males and females? The explanation offered here is that the relative stability in female role identity over time may have provided a basis for female behavioral flexibility and emotional resilience in the town setting. The instability of male roles may have contributed to a symbolic linkage between gender identity and power in the transmission of male role models.

Young Inuit women gain power and status through education, employment in prestigious jobs, and general conformity to Canadian norms. A significant proportion of young men are choosing not to follow this pattern, gaining instead a sense of power and prestige within the peer group by standing in opposition to the choices made by women. At the same time they stand in opposition to the Euro-Canadian system. By affirming positive identity to the traditional male role, they give a political response to the intrusive system. They symbolically reject the continued subordination which participation in the Euro-Canadian system according to Euro-Canadian rules would entail. In emphasizing the traditional component of the male role in the socialization of young boys, parents are also affirming pride in their ethnic identity. By channeling their sons and daughters into somewhat different orientations, they may be engaging in a "silent negotiation" with Euro-Canadian socialization agents and thus minimizing the risks involved in total assimilation.

Playing into this negotiation is a whole set of Euro-Canadian expectations and attitudes about cultural assimilation (viewed positively) and ethnic resistance (viewed negatively). This set of expectations is translated into differential treatment of boys and girls in school, differential employment opportunities, acceptance of marriages between Inuit women and Euro-Canadian men but not the reverse, and more frequent arrests of young men for drinking offenses than of young women (McElroy 1975b).

If it is correct to assume that Inuit and Euro-Canadians have transactionally linked gender-identity and power in their 130-year history of contact, role continuity may be an intermediate variable in recent trends in patterns of male and female Inuit acculturation. The nature of contact transactions was conducive to female role stability, which in turn has promoted a certain flexibility in acculturation. Male roles have been far more unstable in the course of contact history, and at present they are not only unstable but also influenced by economic and political factors in these communities.

Footnote

1. *For further study of IAI technique see Spindler, G. and L. Spindler, Researching the Perception of Cultural Alternatives: The Instrumental Activities Inventory.*

References

Berry, J.W.
1966   Temne and Eskimo Perceptual Skills. *International Journal of Psychology 1* (3): 207-229.
1969   Ecology and Socialization as Factors in Figural Assimilation and the Resolution of Binocular Rivalry. *International Journal of Psychology 4* (4): 271-280.

Boas, F.
1964   *The Central Eskimo.* Lincoln: University of Nebraska Press.

Chance, N.A.
1966   *The Eskimo of North Alaska.* New York: Holt, Rinehart and Winston.

Hagen, E.E.
1962   *On the Theory of Social Change.* Homewood: The Dorsey Press.

Honigmann, J.J.
1962   Social Networks in Great Whale River. *National Museum of Canada Bulletin* #178. Appendix by F.N. Ferguson, Great Whale River Eskimo Personality as Revealed by Rorschach Protocols.

Honigmann, J.J. and I. Honigmann
1965   *Eskimo Townsmen.* Ottawa: Canadian Research Centre for Anthropology, University of St. Paul.
1970   *Arctic Townsmen.* Ottawa: Canadian Research Centre for Anthropology, University of St. Paul.

McElroy, A
1975   "Ethnic Identity and Modernization: the Biculturation of Baffin Island Inuit Children," in *Socialization and Values in Canadian Society*, Vol. II. Robert M. Pike and Elia Zureik, editors. Ottawa: Carleton Library. pp. 262-291.
1975   "Canadian Arctic Modernization and Change in Female Inuit Role Identification," *American Ethnologist 2* (4): 662-686.
1976   "The Negotiation of Sex-Role Identity in Eastern Arctic Culture Change," *Western Canadian Journal of Anthropology, 7* (3): 184-200.
1977   *Alternatives in Modernization: Styles and Strategies in the Acculturative Behavior of Baffin Island Inuit.* HRAFlex Books, ND 5-001, Ethnography Series, New Haven.

Parker, S
1964   Ethnic Identity and Acculturation in two Eskimo Villages. *American Anthropologist, 66* (2): 325-340.

Preston, C.E.
    1964 Psychological Testing with Northwest Coast Alaskan Eskimos. *Genetic Psychology Monographs 69*: 323-419.

Spindler, G. and L. Spindler
    1965 Researching the Perception of Cultural Alternatives: The Instrumental Activities Inventory. *In Context and Meaning in Cultural Anthropology.* M. Spiro, ed. N.Y.: The Free Press, pp. 312-338.

But Teacher, Why Can't I Be A Hunter: Inuit Adolescence as a Double-Bind Situation

JOHN S. MATTHIASSON
Associate Professor
Dept. of Anthropology
University of Manitoba

INTRODUCTION

Adolescence is a culture bound expression. As long ago as 1937, Margaret Mead, in her classic *Sex and Temperament in Three Primitive Societies*, demonstrated that the traumatic emotional period between childhood and adulthood which North American middle-class young people experience is neither regarded as a separate period of life nor experienced as one in other societies (Mead, 1937). Physical changes brought about by the advent of puberty are real for the youth of any culture, but their behavioural correlates vary considerably from culture to culture.

The traditional culture of the Inuit did not recognize adolescence as a special period of maturation. So far as I have been able to determine, there is no word for it in the Inuit language. A boy becomes a man and a girl a woman, but the transition from one to the other is more one of flow than of abruptness and psychological turmoil. In North American middle-class society, adolescence is an extended liminal time during which the young is betwixt and between, or, in Turner's words, "neither-nor" (Turner, 1969). Neither a child nor an adult. Traditional Inuit society was devoid of anything resembling an initiation ceremony for either sex, other than social recognition of a boy's first kill, or of any other special way of marking the transition. A boy became a man, and a girl a woman. Little note was taken of the transition, other than by the subtle shaping by elders of the boy into a hunter and the girl into a prospective wife.

The intrusion of southern Euro-Canadian agencies into the lives and world of the Inuit has changed all this. Young Inuit are exposed to many of the same influences as middle-class southerners, such as prolonged attendance in day schools or, until recently, residential schools, long after they have reached sexual maturity. Children whose parents at the same age were already hunters or wives now continue to carry their books to school daily, awaiting the time when they can step into the "real" world of adulthood. Unfortunately, we know little about their responses to this imposition of a period of adolescence onto their lives. However, there is undoubtedly some trauma as part of it. Chance has indicated that a decade ago Eskimo adolescents of Alaska, who were given a large dose of formal education before it became a common experience of Canadian Inuit of the present generation, were caught in a particularly difficult bind (Chance, 1966: 28). It was the double bind situation of having been socialized during the early years to a traditional way of life and then taken away from the aspirations which would realize that training, and placed in schools to be "educated" for a place in a modernized society which had little to do with the lifestyles of their parents and the aims of their early socialization. The adult role for which they were being prepared was unclear to them. The rationale behind their formal educational experiences were not easily understood. Adult life possibly became something not to be eagerly awaited, but rather, dreaded. A consequence may have been a readily identifiable period of prolonged adolescence. A period of adolescence which was traumatic, but held on to because it put off the inevitability of stepping into the unknown waters of newly introduced and poorly understood adult roles.

This double bind experience is making a time of adolescence a real time in the life cycle for contemporary Inuit of both Alaska and Canada. But before discussing it at length perhaps I should review what this time of life meant before the imposition of formal education and of modernization on the Canadian Inuit.

GROWING TO ADULTHOOD IN TRADITIONAL INUIT SOCIETY

The literature on traditional Inuit Society is substantial and valuable (Rassmussen, 1927; Boas, 1888; Weyer, 1932). While rich in descriptions of material culture, economic activities and kinship patterns, it is almost devoid of information on the processes by which Inuit youth became Inuit adults. In order to reconstruct this phase of the traditional Inuit life cycle, we have to read between the lines of the classic ethnographies, and "tease out" information. One way to do this is to examine descriptions of sex-based roles. If nothing else, adolescence in any society is a time of socially imposed sex-role behaviour based upon earlier socialization experiences and aimed at adult acquisition of one role or the other.

Inuit children were highly regarded in traditional Inuit society.

The practice of female infanticide suggests a preference for male children, but the practice was not as widespread as has been commonly believed, and was a difficult act for both fathers and mothers to carry out. The recent literature on the place which women held in traditional Inuit society supports the thesis that girls were both desired and valued as family members (Matthiasson, 1977). Little distinction was made between male and female offspring until they began to reach puberty. Girls were given more tasks to perform, such as taking care of younger siblings, but both sexes were in general treated equally. By the time they reached nine or ten years of age, though, differential treatment began to be applied. Girls were expected to have acquired at least the rudiments of the skills required of a wife, such as sewing, handling meat brought home by a hunter, and the elaborate techniques of interpersonal relationships which are necessary in a band society, where face-to-face contacts with others are limited by existence in a small-scale society. By that age, young girls were expected to be ready to become women, and wives, and the transition from the one to the next was not considered to be one of hardship (Minnie Freeman: personal communication).

Boys began to be trained by fathers and uncles and grandparents as hunters. The transition from one status to another for them was more difficult than for their female siblings. Life in the day-to-day existence of the band was more easily accommodated to adult female life because day-to-day female activities were there to be observed and absorbed by the young girl, whereas the boy saw little of what his father did while on the hunt. He could watch adult males repairing sleds, making new dog harnesses or, in more recent times, carving soapstone, but he couldn't be in at the kill, and that was when the male sphere was openly revealed. That was when men would take the animal from its place of death and discuss the luck, the skill and the mistakes which were involved in the kill.

Boys at the age of ten began to be taken along on hunts, not to hunt themselves, but to participate by handling the dogs while the adult male crept slowly up on a seal, if it were spring hunting, or stood stoically by the breathing hole in winter, waiting for the sound of an animal. In time, the boy would be given more responsibility, and slowly, as he learned from older males, and acquired the necessary skills, he would emerge from boyhood to manhood. Along the way, men would tease him and challenge him, but he would know that he was not in a liminal period, but moving along a road which progressed, and in time would allow him full adulthood. Possibly the sons of craftsmen in medieval Europe experienced something similar, as they slowly acquired skills which would enable them to produce a finished product, just as young Inuit males worked to the point where they would finally be allowed to make the kill.

There was, then, no formality associated with the transition from child to adult in traditional Inuit society. Hardships were surely encountered by individuals going through the process, but most made the transition without experiencing the problems faced by probably most North American youths as they pass through a liminal period in which they can no longer behave as children and yet are not permitted to be adults. Our own society's uncertainty and ambiguity about this period is reflected in a continuing public debate about drinking laws in Manitoba. Is a youth able to handle alcohol when he is eighteen, or nineteen, or not until he is twenty years of age? By the time Inuit youths were eighteen in traditional society they were fully participating adults, and often married as well. Today, however, they also live with a period of adolescence, largely a product of the implementation during the 1960s and 1970s of formal educational programs in most settlements in the Northwest Territories.

SCHOOLS AS A HARBINGER OF CHANGE

Formal education was never a part of traditional Inuit society. During the contact-traditional period, when settlements were established which became the residences of traders, missionaries and police, and a few Inuit hired as guides, store clerks and so on, Inuit continued in the main to live on the land, and children to be socialized by parents and other older relatives. Their parents learned to write in syllabics from missionaries, and they in turn taught the system to their children. In some settlements missionaries opened mission schools, but attendance was largely hit and miss. Students might attend classes while their parents were visiting in the settlement, but then they would return with them to the land.

In the late 1950s and early 1960s, however, a massive school building program was initiated by the federal Department of Northern Affairs and National Resources (DNANR). Elementary schools were built in all of the larger settlements and many of the smaller ones, along with hostels to house students, and teachers brought in from the south to staff them.

At first, Inuit parents were ambivalent about these new schools, and their potential value for their children. They continued to live on the land in most cases, and were reluctant to accept the idea of their younger children living in hostels. On the other hand, most saw value in the acquisition by the children of a knowledge of the English language. One technique employed by at least some civil servants to ensure attendance at school was use of the threat of withholding family allowance payments, which for most land dwelling families was the only guaranteed source of income. In time, however, virtually all Inuit children were enrolled in schools and began to move through the progressive grades.

The transition was not easy for these children. I recall one young boy of ten years of age who, in 1963, was deriving immense satisfaction from the fact that he was now allowed to accompany his father on the hunt, when this was suddenly disrupted and he was placed in the settlement school. His case was not unique.

One of the more serious aspects of this discontinuity from land life to hostel living has been identified by the Honigmanns as a discontinuity in the use of discipline as a socializing technique (Honigmann and Honigmann, 1965). As mentioned earlier, in the traditional Inuit family young children were given a degree of personal freedom which would probably shock even the most permissive southern parent. In the case of boys, it may well have been intentional on the part of the parents, for they were aware that they were socializing children who would become hunters in one of the most demanding and often dangerous environments on the face of the earth. Young girls were also given almost unlimited freedom. The school and hostel contexts were markedly different. In the schools teachers applied the same techniques which they had learned in education faculties and used in their own teaching in the south. Students were expected to be in the classroom promptly at nine o'clock each morning. They were to perform the tasks given to them, often within a set period of time, and almost always in a standardized fashion. For hours at a time they were expected to sit in rows of chairs, speaking only when called upon and even having to request permission to leave the room when they felt a need to urinate or defecate. At lunch time, and after school, they were expected to return to the hostel, where food would be served at pre-ordained times each day, and early in the evening they had to have washed their faces, brushed their teeth and been ready for bed. In the camps of their parents they had eaten when they felt hungry, and during the summers when the midnight sun circled the skies constantly, slept only when they felt the need, which might be at any time of the day or night.

Unfortunately, we know little about the psychological consequences of this sharp discontinuity in the expectations of adults which were experienced by the first children to attend federal day schools. There is some suggestion, however, that to a considerable extent it continues today. McElroy has claimed that:

> Adults who grew up in small bands of semi-nomadic hunters and trappers are now attempting to prepare their children for participation in a bicultural social system (McElroy, 1975: 662).

She may in fact be correct for larger communities such as Frobisher Bay, but it is doubtful whether this is true of most Inuit parents, even in the late 1970s. While many parents may be striving to prepare their children for life in a bicultural social system, the task becomes difficult, if not impossible, when the parents themselves have been, through their own socialization experiences and most of their adult lives, firmly embedded in a traditional socio-cultural system. Few Inuit continue to live on the land today, for during the centralization period of the 1970s virtually all have taken up residence in settlements, where husbands and fathers have usually found employment. The transition has been a hard one for the older generation as they have struggled to come to grips with the alien society of which they are now a part. In many instances, they have held on to the familiar ways practiced while they still lived on the land, and this is often true of socialization practices. Mothers make efforts to ensure that their children will be at school on time, but it is not uncommon for a mother in an isolated settlement to send her child to school and then go to bed herself, having been up all night visiting with friends and relatives. She is often loathe to make sure that her child goes to bed early, because she does not want to impose her will on his or her own decisions. The school age Inuit child of today, consequently, continues to live under two differing sets of expectations about his or her behaviour.

The school environment to which the Inuit adolescent was exposed in the 1950s and 1960s was foreign in other respects as well. Some efforts were made by curricula planners to create a curriculum which was meaningful to the experiential world of Inuit children, but they rarely succeeded. A cultural system is a complicated phenomenon, and when the first schools were built in the Northwest Territories educators knew little about possible resolutions of the problems inherent in transcultural education. Teachers were frustrated at what they perceived as a lack of responsiveness on the part of their students. The curriculum content was usually irrelevant to the children, and teachers, with only the most cursory knowledge of Inuit culture, and that often stereotyped, were dismayed at the difficulty they faced in trying to make it relevant. These difficulties were compounded by the fact that both teachers and pupils were, in the early years at least, monolingual, but in different languages. A consequence was that many teachers concentrated on the teaching of English language skills exclusively, which satisfied the wishes of parents, or simply came to regard their role as one of care-taker, and sought ways to keep their wards busy during school hours drawing pictures and doing other non-educational activities.[1] Response on the part of the pupils was to do what was required of them on a minimal level, but to see little point in the exercise.

In time, and this corresponded with the advent of adolescence for those children who were enrolled in the first schools at an early age, some students did progress through the grade system until they were ready for high school. Many arctic communities now have their own high schools but that is a fairly recent development. Residential schools in Churchill, Manitoba and Frobisher Bay, Northwest Territories, were where the first generation of formally educated Inuit were sent for the higher grades. Attendance at high school meant being separated from parents, friends and familiar surroundings. Parents worried about the experiences their children would have in these large communities which had gained an unsavory reputation as a result of stories told by and about adults who had spent time in them, often in transit from hospitalization in tuberculosis sanitaria in the south. By this point, however, their children were firmly entrenched in an alien educational system about which they, as parents, understood little, and over which they felt they had no control. I have talked with several mothers who told me that they grieved at having their children taken away from them for ten months at a time, but accepted the prospect because they felt that since the children had not learned the traditional skills of an Inuit adult, it was imperative that instead they continue to acquire the skills needed to participate in "the white man's world." Fathers were more reluctant to accept the idea, but they found themselves in a powerless situation; one to which they applied a traditional posture of stoicism. They, also, were aware that their sons would not be hunters, or their daughters the wives of hunters.

The experience of attending high school in Frobisher Bay or Churchill was traumatic for many Inuit adolescents. Family ties were strong, and in traditional Inuit society one's identity was in large part predicated on who one's parents were. Inuit society was highly egalitarian, but at the same time more social stratification existed than many observers have noted, and kinship was one base for position within the system (Matthiasson, 1977).

One of the features of the residential high schools which disturbed many Inuit students was what seems to have been a conscious effort by administrators to mix together children from various parts of the territories. A young girl from the eastern arctic might be placed in the same room with a girl from the central region and a third from the western. Reasons for this practice can only be speculated on, but it demonstrated an absence of understanding by administrators of traditional Inuit social arrangements, or, possibly, an intended abuse of them. Beyond a certain geographical limit, usually defined by the broadest use of the -miut concept of shared social identity, Inuit traditionally did not identify with other Inuit. I remember flying south with two young Inuit girls in the early 1960s who were going "out" for a YWCA summer camp experience. When we had an unplanned stop-over in Fort Chimo, I watched them laugh at what they considered to be the ungainly dress of the local, and in their estimation, less-than-true-Inuit people. Mixing of students from different areas in the dormitories of the high schools surely exacerbated the adjustments these youths had to make in a new-found period of extended adolescence. A sharing of a dormitory room by two girls two decades ago, one black and the other white, and both from the southern United States, may have led to some mutual understanding of the insigificance of racial differences, but for these youths from the arctic, cut off from all personal ties for the better part of each year, the sharing only intensified what was already a strong case of culture shock.

Many young Inuit with whom I have discussed their residential school experience have told me that it seemed to them that there was a deliberate attempt by teachers and other supervisors to cut them off from their cultural background. Their experiences seem to have paralleled those of Indian children in residential schools in the early part of this century, who often discovered that any demonstration of Indian identity, such as use of their native language, was disapproved and often led to punishment. When the Inuit children returned home each summer they discovered that the techniques of their caretakers had worked, and they found themselves to be marginal to Inuit culture while not fully part of that of Euro-Canadians. The betwixt and between phenomenon had taken on a new meaning in their own period of adolescence. Not only were they neither children nor adults, but also neither Inuit nor white.

DIFFERENTIAL RESPONSES OF MALES AND FEMALES

The settlements to which these youths returned had gone through a radical transformation. During their years of formal education the camp life, or, "life on the land," into which they had been born, had disappeared, and their parents had taken up a sedentary residence in a settlement. No longer were the only Euro-Canadians available as role models traders, missionaries or policemen. Now there were nurses, teachers, mechanics and administrators. In their early years these adolescents had been socialized toward a role in a hunting economy; one in which only two roles were accessible, hunter or wife of hunter. Now, career possibilities were broadened. During their high school years they had been told that they could aspire to whatever status and role they desired. How to achieve them was another matter, though, because the double bind situation still entrapped them.

Anecdotally, I think back to a year in the early 1960s, when I was leaving the Arctic after a year's field trip, and on the ship on which I travelled met a young girl who had been "sent out" for higher education and was acting as interpretor on the ship until it reached her home settlement. She told me that she was terrified of returning home, for she had been betrothed as an infant to a man several years older than her, who was a hunter. She was dressed in modish clothes, and could discuss Shakespeare, and she dreaded her impending marriage to a man whom she did not know and whose life style was foreign to her, even though both were Inuit. Her adolescence had not prepared her for the life her own culture had destined for her.

Euro-Canadian women in the settlements lived in a world to which young Inuit girls aspired, but found difficult to enter. It was easier for young males. Euro-Canadian women were nurses or teachers, or wives of administrators. Their homes contained furniture and decorative objects which were never found in Inuit homes. These women had professional training far beyond that provided by the high schools in Frobisher Bay or Churchill, or, if they had no professional training, they had the skills needed to find a husband who would give them the material benefits of modern life. How were these young Inuit girls to achieve the same? It takes too long to train as a nurse or teacher. Far easier to marry a Euro-Canadian, and until recently many Inuit girls aspired to just that.

Young males, on the other hand, had other options open to them. The range of occupations held by Euro-Canadian males in settlements was wider, and many of them were accessible to Inuit youths. Learning to drive a tractor meant only a brief training period in the south. Inuit boys had been brought up to work with their hands, and the transfer of training to visible jobs held by Euro-Canadians was not hard to make.

Male adolescents, then, on returning to their home settlements from residential schools, found it easier to adjust to the new bicultural setting than did girls. They had been socialized in their early years to be hunters, or, achievers. Working a piece of heavy equipment while helping build a road in a settlement gave them something of the same satisfaction they might have gained from hunting. For girls, the abilities to sew a sealskin slipper or to make bannock were not as easily transferable to a new context. Many of them wanted to break any thread of cultural continuity, and to step into roles held by Euro-Canadian women. Males could still gain status among their peers by taking on the better jobs available to them. Females found less possibility, and so often jumped into the new world to which they had been exposed with both feet forward.

Ann McElroy, one of the few anthropologists to study Inuit youth, while beginning with an hypothesis that Inuit girls in an acculturative situation would be more conservative than their male counterparts, was surprised to find the opposite. Working in Pangnirtung and Frobisher Bay, she discovered when she administered the Spindlers' Instrumental Activities Inventory[2] to youth of both sexes that males showed a preference for new occupational roles which offered high wages and high prestige (McElroy, 1975). But females showed an even higher set of aspirations toward "modern" occupations than the males. She also found that Inuit youths in the two communities are putting off marriage until they are in their twenties, another indice of the extended period of adolescence with which they now must cope. They wait hesitantly before making decisions which their own parents made at a much earlier age.

Adolescence has become part of the "growing up" process of virtually all modern Inuit youth. They live between two worlds, one swiftly replacing the other and placing new expectations on them. At the same time, they are seeking ways to objectify and keep alive remnants of the culture from which they have sprung. There are problems inherent in such a transition. Anti-social behaviour on the part of some is one response to these difficulties. At the same time, most Inuit youth of today are using their time of adolescence to think about what they want for themselves. I remember sitting in an office in a settlement in the high arctic a few years ago, and watching young people walk along the only street in town, holding hands and talking together intently. I worried about the problems they must have been struggling to resolve for themselves, but then I remembered that they are Inuit, and they will adapt, and in the final analysis, on their own terms. That is a central feature of their cultural heritage which will help them to live with adolescence, and in time, make their own valid choices.

Footnotes

1. *I do not mean to denegrate the sincere efforts of many dedicated teachers in the early years of formal education in the Canadian arctic. Many demonstrated an intuitive and sympathetic understanding of the adjustment problems faced by their students. Others, on the other hand, regarded their northern sojourn as a personal adventure of short tenure, and gave up the fight too easily.*
2. *The Instrumental Activities Inventory, designed by George and Louise Spindler, is a series of 24 cards depicting occupations. Respondents are asked to rate them.*

References

Boas, Franz
  1888   *The Central Eskimo*, Bureau of American Ethnology Annual Report, Washington, D.C.

Chance, Norman
  1966   *The Eskimo of North Alaska*, Holt, Rinehart and Winston, New York.

Honigmann, John J. and Irma Honigmann
  1965   *Eskimo Townsmen*, Canadian Research Centre for Anthropology, Ottawa.

Matthiasson, John S.
  1977   "The Continuation and Transformation of Traditional Inuit Power Bases Into the Modern Context," (in) Williams, Gerry, (ed.), *Essays in Anthropology in Honor of Morris Edward Opler*, University of Oklahoma Press, pp. 33-42.

McElroy, Ann
1975 "Canadian Arctic Modernization and Change in Female Inuit Role Identification," *American Ethnologist*, Vol. 2, no. 4, pp. 662-686.

Mead, Margaret
1937 *Sex and Temperament in Three Primitive Societies*, William Morrow, New York.

Rassmussen, Knud
1927 *Across Arctic America*, Putnam, New York.

Turner, Victor
1969 *The Ritual Process*, Aldine, Chicago.

Weyer, E.M.
1932 *The Eskimos*, Yale University Press, New Haven.

The Development of Self-Control in the Eastern Cree Life Cycle[1]

RICHARD J. PRESTON
McMaster University

It is a universal condition of mankind that societies can function pre-dictably and with stability only when there are cultural patterns that effectively regulate the desires, will, and behaviours of the individuals who, viewed collectively, are the society. For us this means several institutions that seem ever-ready to influence our lives, from schools, teams, clubs, churches, and other peer groups, to the expectations of our neighbours, our local political administration, and the police. But what of a culture that lacks virtually all of these influences for stand-ardizing of belief and behaviour?

The ideas and perspectives offered here describe one such culture, and stem from my field work beginning in the early 1960s, in several Cree Indian communities on the east coast of James Bay, Quebec. The traditional, relatively stable cultural patterns will be described first, and will then serve as a point of departure for examining the processes of rapid change and de-stabilization of the 1960s and 1970s.

EASTERN CREE TRADITIONAL CULTURE

The traditional culture was that of widely dispersed Boreal Forest hunters, organized on the basis of kinship, convenience, and congenial-ity into small groups that only occasionally coordinated their activities with other small groups. In spite of their sparse population and very ar-duous life, and an apparent lack of integrating cultural stuctures[2], East-ern Algonquian-speaking peoples like the Cree are noted for cultural uniformity over a very large geographical space, and probably over a substantial period of time (Morgan, 1871: 206-208, Hallowell, 1946: 198, Voegelin and Voegelin, 1946: 191-192).

Their cultural uniformity and stability was in part a consequence of ecological limitations and historical factors but was also importantly dependent upon their effective, yet largely *implicit*, means for social control. In the absence of specialized roles or associations that might act as agents or agencies of social control, the regulation of belief and behaviour was more essentially a matter of personal psychology — of predictably uniform individual participation in shared understandings and values. For the neighboring Ojibwa, Hallowell has shown the importance of anxiety regarding punishment in the form of sickness or sorcery as a reason for maintaining "proper" behaviour (Hallowell, 1955: 266ff). While fear of sorcery or other calamity is also a part of the Cree cultural tradition, the relative importance of these threats was, and is, I believe, less than that described for the Ojibwa.

Social Control by means of self-control

For the Eastern Cree, I believe that social control was, and still is maintained largely through self-control, where norms are imbedded in each individual's personality. Part of this process of imbedding is the anticipation or actual occurrences of teasing or threats by other persons, and so compares with the anxiety Hallowell described for the Ojibwa. In this context, it is worth noting that physical punishment is rarely inflicted on children or adults, and threats of physical harm are normally given a sense of social-psychological distance by being attributed to sources of danger which are outside of the immediate group. Related to this sense of the social distance of threats is the potentially dangerous quality of the non-human, but personalized environment: the sub-arctic bush with its animal and spiritual persons. These factors constitute the major restrictive influences on human behaviour.

Facilitating influences on social control have been relatively less studied by social scientists, and it is this area that I wish to treat here in more detail. I propose that facilitating influences, like the restrictive influences mentioned above, operate more usually and significantly in the process of socialization than in direct, event-specific actions of social control. Through socialization, the norms are internalized by each individual, and social control then takes the form of *self*-control. My basic premise is that a strongly developed sense of self-esteem is the basis against which the restrictive or "negative" qualities of teasing, threats, concern not to fail in a task once it is undertaken, caution towards the non-human environment, and so on, may become effective. Self-control is therefore closely related to a well developed sense of self-esteem, for competently controlled action is the means of maintaining one's self-esteem. The background for my presentation is that of traditional child-rearing practices.

Traditional patterns of child rearing

Traditionally, then, the child's socialization group was a small commensal group (*bekodEno*), that would sometimes join others to form a larger hunting group of up to fifty persons. The nursing infant was swaddled and carried on its mother's back while the mother went about her daily routine of cutting firewood, tending snares and fish hooks, scraping hides, pulling the toboggan when shifting camp, drying meat, making clothes, and cooking meals.

Infancy was characterized by strong emphasis on indulgence of the child's wants, by such manifestations of parental affection and admiration as kissing, nose rubbing and intimate talking. The mother was scarcely able to carry and to look after more than one child while going about her outdoor work. After weaning, usually at about age 2, and until they were able to look after themselves and to keep up with their parents (beginning at about age seven or eight), either the mother or an older person would remain at the camp to look after them. When no adult was remaining at the tent, usually due to work demands, the children were swaddled and left in the tent. Swaddling past infancy served two manifest functions: (1) to keep the child warm, and (2) to control the child's mobility.[3] The parent's realistic fear that the child might come to harm if left unbound is explained in narratives of children left alone in the tent who, in playing near or tending to the fire, have been burned. Often these narratives end with the return of the adults to a smouldering ruin of children and property. To prevent this and other dangers, when all adults were needed away from the camp, the children who could not follow were bound in warm skins and left just enough freedom to get the bite of lunch left next to them into their mouths. The child was advised not to eat the food right away, or he would be hungry before the adults returned.

Safeguarding of the children by an older member of the group, or by means of swaddling restriction, continued until the child was deemed able to accompany the father (if a boy) or the mother (if a girl) on their respective daily rounds. One informant recalled his last swaddling at (he estimated) age ten, when he felt indignant at this treatment. The task of getting a living in the Eastern Sub-Arctic was often very demanding on the strength and stamina of adults, and thus on the child who followed the adult. The memory of wearily snowshoeing along the trail his father had broken, with his father almost out of sight up ahead, remains vivid into the old age of some Cree men. Yet boys would try to accompany their fathers, and by age five would be able to follow for substantial distances.

Traditional apprenticeship to adult standards

At this point in the child's life history, emphasis was placed on an informal but understood adult role apprenticeship, in which the child was directed towards goals of adult behaviour, rather than encouraged to express his particular level of childhood. The child learned the techniques of economic endeavour by example. No teacher explained the techniques in schematic terms, or took the child's hand and helped with the appropriate motions. Instead, the child was advised to watch the adult as the task was done, and then to try it for himself without help. Although the level of technological elaboration of the Eastern Cree culture is rated as very low, the knowledge and skills of hunting and trapping were subtle and very difficult to master, and required many years of apprenticeship. During these years, the child was constantly learning through comparing his or her skills and knowledge directly with that of a considerably more able adult. Instead of competing within a peer group, where competition offers the opportunity to scale oneself against others with some success, the Cree child was relegated to a more modest status in which competitive comparison was rarely gratifying, yet the goal of adult competence remained essential and of primary importance.

The character of parent-child relationships was one in which adult behaviour was repeatedly and subtly held up as an example for the child to emulate. Expressions of anger or aggressive intent were (ideally) not allowable in the adult world, and so were not often found in the behaviour of the adults towards children. The adult ideally embodied the teaching example for the child, and very rarely resorted to physical punishment. Strong remonstration was occasionally used, but the vehemence ideally expressed the fault of the child, more than the anger or impatience of the adult. If two small children were competing for the same object or for attention, adults would expect the older child to give way to the younger, carrying on the pattern of permissiveness even where the permissive "elder" is scarcely older than the child indulged. This apparently indulgent atmosphere was tempered with a subtly elaborated pattern of teasing, threats, and withdrawal of emotional response. For example, one small child, who did not wish to go where she was told, responded with protests and finally with a jumping and screaming tantrum. The protests were teased; then, the tantrum that followed was ignored and the child was left behind, alone, until fear made her run, still crying, to catch up.

Less extreme behaviour was teased, or a bogey-man threat might be used, as when the threat that a nearby cannibalistic monster would hear their noise quickly silenced a group of obstreperous three- and four-year-olds. But the children mature, and the threats seem less scary, and gradually the child learns to respond with the emotional reserve and self-control that the adult had shown. For example, when one boy of about ten (mentioned earlier) decided to assert his status as competent to follow his father rather than be left at the tent, he worked himself loose from the swaddling clothes and then kept a fire going and had the tea water hot when his parents returned. He then explained with dignity that he was too big to be bound up and left behind. His father responded by laughing, by which he accepted his son's ability but teased his assertive manner.

Self-control as personal competence

Throughout his socialization, then, the individual was taught the value of self-control, a closely defined sense of social skills and a quiet but persistent competence in coping with difficult or stressful situations. Tendencies to express focussed emotions or to assert one's individuality within the intimate, personal group milieu were offset primarily by the unwillingness of an individual to suffer the loss of self-esteem that would accompany such a manifestation of personal incompetence, and secondarily by the blunting effects of teasing, verbal threats, and emotional reticence. This way of viewing personal competence appears eminently rational and appropriate in a milieu that presents each person with the great difficulty of mastering necessary hunting and trapping techniques and kinds of wisdom needed to deal with a highly personalized "bush" world where the contingencies were often unpredictable, and sometimes severely trying.

Focusing now on the boy, his apprentice-like relationship to his father was learned early and well in an intense and intimate milieu. This relationship is well suited in its particular kind of psychological strength, as a framework for coping with the contingent world that he will face as an adult. Here are some examples of how I think the father-son relationship serves as a model for subsequent relationships between an individual and his environment.

a) The father provides food to the son-apprentice, and the (personalized) world provides food-animals to the competent adult. The father-son affective bond is maintained where the adult looks to a world in which animals are believed to love the man who hunts them (Preston, 1975). The child must develop the skill, mental competence, and physical energy that allows him to adequately participate, first, in the small milieu of his family, and then in the larger world of human and other-than human persons.

b) The personalized world in some sense symbolizes a somewhat more vast and diffuse image of teacher and provider, where learning still takes place on a case-by-case basis, requiring the learner to watch and then to coordinate his actions in the way that careful observation has shown him to be appropriate.

c) The corpus of Cree oral tradition represents a similarly scaled-up and diffused form of the more immediate and personally directed communications of father to son. Both contain at least implicit moral rationale and a concern to perceive some aspect of existence within its precise context.

Because the maturation of the child's father-milieu into a personalized world of adult action is a culturally patterned phenomenon, it is not created anew by each individual. Rather it is imbedded in the child at the time that he is learning the content of the father-son relationship and the competencies of the father. The resulting understandings that define the personal world, are consequently highly congruent with the understandings of the other Cree individuals. Each father's competence is closely related by action and perception to the common Boreal Forest physical environment, and by this means incorporates environmental uniformity into a uniformity of personality content and structure.

In passing, I might observe that the Mistabeo (the attending spirit of conjurors) is partially similar to the father, in that the spirit knows what is in the conjuror's mind, (as an intimate father-son relationship enables a father to know his son's thoughts and feelings), and explicitly thinks of himself as helper, provider, and ethical guide. Also, fear of sorcery may, in part, grow out of childhood threats that are similarly occasional, event-specific, and usually a consequence of some behavioural incompetence on the part of the child.

To summarize the characteristics of traditional Cree socialization, I have described a balance between indulgence in early childhood, and apprenticeship in the maturing of personal competence, as the individual grows to adulthood. Indulgence in child rearing may heighten the contrasting impact of a less-than-indulgent environment, and of later deprivation. But it might also prepare a man to persevere in hope of success, and to feast with deep pleasure when he is able to feast. Also, indulgence of small children can hardly be seen as simply a projection, into the family milieu, of the spectre of a threatening environmental world view, and I doubt that this quality is often a part of the Cree world view.

Self-control in a contingent world

The world is more likely viewed, not as an abstract, threatening whole, but rather as a relational complex of event-specific contingencies, some harsh or threatening, and others that support men and are gratifying (Preston, 1975). Hunger is a very real, though occasional problem, but life in the bush is best maintained through effective self-control, that one's associates will know they can depend on. The similarity between dangers in early childhood (from fires, cannibal attacks, kidnapping, etc.) and the contingencies and hardships (dangers) of later adult life may explain why a child who "doesn't care what he does" and requires constant watching for his boldness and appearance of fearlessness (even thoughtlessness?), is both amusing and highly regarded. These qualities may be recognized, implicitly or explicitly, as evidence of a psychological makeup that will be better able to cope with adversity and danger when the child is an adult. When his behaviour warrants interference by an adult (who will almost always be close kin) it typically comes in the form of a lecture that details the fault of the child rather than the anger or shame of the close kin or the larger group. The criticism is preferably public, but the fault is typically not seen as having implications beyond the individual transgressor. This contrasts with the use of negative sanctions in some of the more complexly integrated cultures, where cooperative activities and kin-structured values result in the inverse: censure coming privately, after others are out of earshot, and conceived in terms of shame to kin and to ideals.

Self-esteem, private fault, and public censure

The Cree pattern of private fault and public censure facilitates the maturation of a self-image that emphasizes individual autonomy of one's self and respect for that autonomy in other individuals. This aspect, plus the early childhood setting of parental warmth, clearly defined limits, and respectful treatment, allows the maturation of a kind of self-esteem that is unlikely to suffer from an accumulation of internal recriminations or guilt, but rather develops internal confidence in one's knowledge and actions, within the limits of each individual's talents, acquired competence, and self-control.

Cree pride, then, is not an obvious or focussed emotion, but is more controlled and seemingly diffuse in its manifestations. While pride is not *purely* internal or self-directed, the external manifestations are careful and controlled, expressed more in the range of tasks a person will undertake, and in the satisfaction found in the successful performance of the tasks. In some cases, the satisfaction has a social context (e.g., the bear feast when a man kills a bear; the narration of events that he was a part of, or a conjuring ceremony) and in others the context is private and individual (e.g. the effects of power for a man who has an attending spirit but does not conjure publically; the efforts and hardships that are never told to others, but coped with to the satisfaction of the individual; or in the competent management of difficult emotionally charged or ambiguous social relationships).

Summary of Traditional Patterns

To recapitulate, social control via self-control involves the restrictive influences of teasing, threats, sorcery, and ecological deprivation. But often more important and basic are facilitating influences derived, as a part of socialization, from the internalization of norms. A basis of self-esteem allows for social control without external intervention, in the form of self-control. Socialization begins in indulgence, affection and admiration, but with external control in the form of physical restraint of swaddling or close watching by an adult (including tethering), to prevent harm.

As the child matures, the role of apprenticeship develops. The goal of technical, social and mental competence (Preston, 1976) is taught by example, where the adult is the ideal, and criticism expresses the fault of the child, more than the anger of the adult. Emotions mature from strong and focussed form, into more controlled and perhaps diffuse form as an integral part of quiet and persistent competence. Variance from this norm involves a loss of self-esteem (at perceiving one's own incompetence) and the diffuse mockery of others in the form of teasing. In this fashion, adult teachings are replaced by self-control.

Early indulgence is an *antecedent* of self-control, while the synthesis of "heart" and competence are consequences of self-control. Self-control, in turn, permits the development of a sense of individual pride that is felt internally more than it is expressed to others. Pride that is expressed in a social context normally is controlled and diffuse, since focussed pride is quite inconsistent with the ideals that I have described, would invite teasing or even mockery. Cree pride, then, is largely an inner-directed feeling, and its expression in social contexts is typically diffuse and controlled; self-control is basic to the complex of actions, thoughts, and emotions that the pride is derived from.

CONTEMPORARY REINTERPRETATIONS OF TRADITIONAL PATTERNS AND PROCESSES

Now that we have established a feel for the traditional cultural patterns that influence social stability and self-control, we are in a position to understand how these traditions are reinterpreted or modified by rapid cultural change. Government services like education, health and welfare, and housing and transportation have had far-reaching effects, strongly felt in the 1960s. In the 1970s the massive James Bay Hydroelectric Project has greatly accelerated the rate of change, with the influx of people, wage-labour and construction subcontracting, the formation of a Cree political and administrative Grand Council that has negotiated an agreement with provincial and federal government, and other significant new conditions.

Culture change is usually treated as a part of the history of a culture or community as a societal or collective whole. But here we will treat the processes of change in terms of individual or personal history; that is, as changes in the trajectory of the individual's socialization process. While there is no necessity demanded by the nature of the data for giving up the collective view in favour of such an individual orientation, the cultures of the Eastern Sub-Arctic Algonquian speaking Indians, such as the Eastern Cree, do focus more strongly on individual autonomy and responsibility, than on collective responsibilities and actions. Traditional Cree culture did not develop elaborate political, economic, social or ritual institutions. Much of the cultural elaboration in this area was (and still is) personal and psychological, covert more than overt.

Variations on traditional patterns
Today's picture is complicated by wide variations in the manner and degree to which specific families participate in the winter bush life. But differences in family situations are not independent of cultural pat-

terns. I will first outline the pattern in modal terms, and then turn to a discussion of variations seen in different families.

The style of socialization through the first five or six years is not greatly altered from the traditional pattern. Today the child is swaddled only during infancy; and leaving the older children swaddled, alone in the tipi, no longer occurs. When families leave the settlement for bush camps, the availability of staple foods such as flour, baking powder, and sugar relieves the mother of most hunting and gathering duties, and the use of a snowmobile to pull the toboggan allows other foods and goods to be enjoyed as well. But the general pattern of life in the "bush" is still family-oriented and the premium on competent behaviour is only somewhat diminished by the security of staple foods. Life in the bush is still a hard way to get a living, but it is cherished by many Cree people.

From the trap-line to the peer group

At about six or seven years, the child in traditional Cree culture had his autonomy submerged in the demands of following the adult. Today, however, the Cree child is more often a part of a peer group and operates less within the family or *bekodEno* environs, except during fishing trips and, for some children, during winters in the bush. Replacing these traditional activities, there is play, and school, with the peer group. Many parents would like to see their children learn the bush life (including values and the style of social behaviour), but they also recognize the pressure of the school administrators and some of the rationale behind that pressure. Most parents feel school is the means to a better living than bush life for their children. Their attitude towards participation of the children in peer group activities is not so easily discovered, and probably is actually less well defined in the parent's mind. The reason is that in the eyes of the parents the peer group is not a clear cut departure from "normal" behaviour. It appears to be nothing more radical than ordinary child's play in a context of residence in a larger social setting than the bush-life group. But the child's internalization of social controls has changed radically in the shift from family groups to peer groups, even though it may not be apparent to Cree adults. The quality of social control imposed by the peer group (and by their school setting) is not focussed on family-responsibility and bush-competence. The peer group milieu accommodates individual expressiveness and competitive assertion with increasing ease and recognizes leadership in these terms. These qualities are reinforced by the values and standards of social relations introduced in school. Today's peer group freedom involves expressions of focussed emotions and self-assertions that would have been repressed by traditional adult sanctions, if such expressions were a part of the bush-life situations. But the adult sanctions are not a part of the peer group milieu, and the child learns to enjoy and desire these new freedoms. For example, the older child, who traditionally was expected to give way to the younger child, in keeping with a pattern of permissiveness, now may assert himself over the younger and weaker members of his peer group when competition exists between them. In Cree terms the children do not learn to be "shy." Instead, they care less for the social controls of the adult group. When confronted by adult controls, children may flaunt their freedom to test the limits of the controls. If they are thwarted in this, the response is usually stubborn persistence coupled with the more or less controlled expression of resentful anger. This is the response that traditionally would have been made to unwarranted *external* interference, such as attempts at discipline by some adult outside the family. If their persistence is thwarted, the child may give up his struggle against interference, and regress to tears and impotence. Crying is less allowed by children as they mature, yet it will occasionally occur among boys through their teens.

The loosening of self-control
A relatively tight, traditional structure of social control by self-esteem and avoiding of threats, and the traditional, family-oriented dependence upon parents' emotional response is replaced in the peer group setting by a loose structure of controls, based on partially internalized traditional patterns of control, plus new patterns, including public reward for achievement and public shame for failure. The traditional goal of competence undergoes a radical re-interpretation. Traditional competence involved a progression from the child's difficult emulation of his father, to the adult's participation in his harsh environment. Contemporary competence involves a progression from the child's competition within his peer group, to the adult's alternatives of participation in the Indian community or within a large-scale Euro-Canadian peer group.

Some individual's variance from the traditional norms
With respect to the father's position of authority over the son, I find a range of variation from the father who enjoys bush-life independence to the father who is community-life dependent. A large part of the father's authority derives from his somewhat distant position as the teaching example of competence. The son is largely dependent upon his father's teaching, and mature informants have explained to me the gaps in their knowledge as due to the early death of their father. With a decrease in bush life, there is a decrease in this dependency and in the demands for emulation of the father's competence. The relation between mother and daughter is similar but characterized by less social distance.

Two sons of bush-oriented parents
I have selected "Edward" and his wife as an example of bush-oriented

parents, and their two eldest sons as examples of bush-orientation and community-orientation. Edward is a successful trapper and is recognized by other trappers as very competent in the bush-life milieu, although he is not a leader in affairs within the town. Edward's authority over his oldest son was considerable, and some years ago he required this son to marry a girl that he did not wish to marry. He gave way to his father's competence, and is respected by other adults for his abilities and for his quiet and self-controlled personality. Like his father, his use of non-Cree languages is minimal, and his interest in the Euro-Canadian world is slight. In fact, his participation in community life is also rather slight, and most of his activity and interest is family oriented, and bush-life oriented.

Edward's second son has a markedly different situation. He was sent to residential school as a young boy and returned to school each winter, completing his grade twelve without spending any time in the bush except for brief summer trips. He is a capable, intense young man, and while his relationship with his older brother is close during his visits home, his values and attitudes are markedly different. A large part of the difference, I believe, may be attributed to the distinctive residential school experience. In the residential school, the peer group was paramount and the family group totally absent. In spite of usually fairly high standards in the quality of personnel and in the concern of the school for the welfare of the children, the residential school student experiences a profound loneliness. He gradually adapts to this through increasing participation in, and dependence upon, the peer group.

The school aspect of the peer group milieu adds a complex and often disjunctive quality to the socialization process, since it appears on the scene of one major break in the socialization continuity (the shift from the family group to the peer group) and adds its own, additional break. In the school setting, children dissociate learning from the life which their families have to offer them. With the new modes of learning, they acquire Euro-Canadian values and habits of social behaviour. Rather than say that the children abandon the security of familiar family life, it is more accurate to say that family life abandons the children, and they find their security where they can, in the peer group and in an approximation of Euro-Canadian values and behaviour.

The younger son's competence, then, is a new competence as a member of an adult, Euro-Canadian peer group. While he is welcome at home, he no longer feels a part of the community and finds few satisfactions there. In the years following school he sought success in assuming a southern urban job and in finding satisfactions in his new milieu.

Two sons of transitional bush-to-town parents
As an example of an intermediate father, "Charles" also has two grown sons whose adaptation to the process of culture change is different. In

the past years, Charles did little trapping himself, until, about fifteen years ago, he gave it up altogether. His two sons went to the bush for a few months by themselves, with moderate success. The older son followed his father's example more closely than his younger brother, although both had participated in peer group and school experience. The younger brother has been most influenced by this experience and left the Indian community to find a job, rather than stay to trap. His father observed, "I guess no one can blame me if he gets into trouble." As far as Charles is concerned, what the younger son does is his own affair.

Two sons of town-oriented parents
For the final example, a community-oriented father, "Michael" is quite dependent upon the community for his livelihood. He is now in his 50s, has been regularly employed by the government in a service-type job for many years, and has not trapped during this time. His sons did not learn bush life, and Michael had very little effective authority over them, a fact which was sometimes brought up as public knowledge in the Indian community. Michael's two sons are about the same age as the other sons described previously. The oldest is married and has several children. His social relationships, during the first years of his marital relationship, were unstable and sometimes rather apathetic. Normally young men withdraw abruptly from their peer group at marriage and return to a family orientation (but not necessarily to a bush orientation). He withdrew only slowly from the group of single boys to assume the status of manhood, and the process took a few years to complete. His younger brother was for several years unable to arrange a marriage, due to the girl's parents' refusal to consider him as suitable. The lack of competence and self-control shown by both brothers, and especially the younger, left them with a tenuous status in the community, and their peer group status was also only partially satisfactory. The younger brother has still not matured and found composure and stable relations in the Indian community or in an adult Euro-Canadian peer group.

CONCLUSIONS AND PROSPECTS

Since the 1950s, and particularly in the 1970s, with the impact of the James Bay Hydroelectric Project, the Cree process of socialization has undergone a shift of trajectory, from family and bush orientation to community and peer group orientation. The degree to which traditional values and psychosocial skills of self-control are being replaced by community and urban values and social habits is variable but obviously of radical significance. Social control, and thereby Cree cultural uniformity and stability, has been transformed and elaborated with political, economic, educational, and religious institutions. The nearly exclusive focus on individual autonomy has given way to band councils, a grand council, a school board, a pentecostal movement; and self-control is yielding in a parallel fashion.

The three examples of particular families given here are, of course, merely illustrative. Nonetheless, it is interesting to note that the oldest son of each family remained, or returned to, a relatively traditionalist position in the community, while the younger son (each of these families had several, still-younger children) did not. Speculatively, one could see the weakening of traditional socialization affecting younger children, as if parental authority was strong enough for only the first child. But this kind of interpretation requires further research on the development of families over a period of years.

The prospects for the Cree culture are for greater variety and complexity, with a guaranteed annual wage for trappers drawing families to the bush, and their children to a traditional orientation to the land. On the other hand, planned economic development will offer an increasingly urban milieu and its more cosmopolitan socialization processes.

Footnotes

1. *Field work was supported in 1965, '66, '67, '68 and '69 by contracts from the National Museum of Man. An earlier version of this paper was read at the 10th Annual Meetings of the Northeastern Anthropological Association, Carleton University, Ottawa, May 7-9, 1970.*
2. *Exogamy was apparently not a very significant factor for social integration. Eggan describes ". . .a relatively new type of social structure for North America: a bilateral band held together by cross-cousin marriage" (1955: 521). Also, the integrative consequences of a common language are not well understood.*
3. *An interesting latent function of swaddling has been described, that of isometric muscular development (Hudson 1966: 470-474).*

References

Eggan, F
   1955   "Social Anthropology: methods and results." *Social Anthropology of North American Tribes*, ed. F. Eggan, pp. 485-551. Chicago. Aldine Publishing Co.

Hallowell, A.I.
   1946   "Some psychological characteristics of the Northeastern Indians." *Man in Northeastern North America*, ed. F. Johnson, pp. 195-225, Andover, Mass. Papers of the R.F. Peabody Foundation.

Hallowell, A.I.
   1955   *Culture and Experience*. Philadelphia, University of Pennsylvania Papers. Reissued 1967, Schocken Books.

Hudson, C.M.
1966 "Isometric Advantages of the Cradle Board: A Hypothesis." *American Anthropologist* 68: 470-474.

Morgan, L.H.
1871 Systems of consanguinity and affinity of the human family. *Smithsonian Contributions to Knowledge.* Washington, D.C.

Preston, R.J.
1975 Cree Narrative: Expressing the Personal Meanings of Events. *National Museum of Man,* Mercury Series No. 30.

Preston, R.J.
1976 Reticence and self-expression: a study of style in social relationships. In, W. Cowan (ed.) *Papers of the Seventh Algonquian Conference,* 1975. Carleton University, pp. 450-494.

Rogers, E.S. and J.H.
1963 The individual in Mistassini Society from birth to death. *National Museum of Canada Bulletin* 190: 14-36.

Voegelin, C.F. and E.W. 1946
1946 "Linguistic considerations of Northeastern North America." *Man in Northeastern North America,* ed. F. Johnson, pp. 178-194. Andover, Mass. Papers of the R.F. Peabody Foundation.

The Socialization of Rural Adolescents

K. ISHWARAN
York University

KWOK CHAN
Concordia University

THE LITERATURE AND THE PROBLEM

It has now almost become a sociological truism to suggest that the social scientists have made considerable contribution to the construction of and rationalization with the social reality. However, adolescence as a separate phase of the socialization of a person and as a distinct social phenomenon was given neither pragmatic nor theoretical recognition until the fifteenth century, during which a sharp, almost mutually exclusive distinction between childhood, stressing subordination of the wishes and needs of the child to his elders, and adulthood, granting the adult rights and responsibilities to the growing person, prevailed (Muuss, 1968). Hollingshead (1946) pioneered in his research on and theorizing with the adolescent in terms of "the period in the life of a person when the society in which he functions ceases to regard him (male or female) as a child and does not accord to him full adult status, roles and functions." Koller and Richie (1978: 274) succinctly summarized the popular modern conceptions by sociologists and psychologists of the adolescent in terms of "neither a child nor an adult, lost in 'between' being a child and an adult." Accordingly, the status of the adolescent is conceptually characterized as marginality that stems from the absence of a careful articulation of the standards and procedures of the transitional period.

Another tangent of theory and research in adolescence, in parallel with the historical interest in the origins and the definitions of the adolescent, is affiliated with the professional controversy in regard to whether an adolescent subculture does exist. Sebald (1968: 198), in an attempt to dissect the anatomy of this professional controversy, indicates that such writers as Coleman (1963), Cohen (1955), Davis (1944), Parsons (1942), Williams (1960) and Green (1968), take an affirmative stand about the existence of the adolescent subculture on the assumption that the typical adolescent is recognizable by manifestations of various problematic, behavioral symptoms which can be described as socially-caused "storm and stress." According to Sebald (1968: 198), "the youth culture is a social reaction to the young individual's uncertain status in the adult world."

In an attempt to carry the affirmative stand about the "storm and stress" of an adolescent culture further, Winch (1971) views the adolescent as one craving for social acceptance by the peer groups whose values and behavior are exactly those forbidden and opposed by the parents. To the extent that the adolescent's commitment to his peer group is high, the parents become an "out group," sometimes almost an opposing group. While the literature has led us to believe in the popular conception of the adolescents as persons occupying an uncertain and marginal status, and constituting a subculture characterized by "storm and stress" and infiltrated by values and attitudes that run diametrically against those of the adults, it has also generated considerable research interest in the emergence and maintenance of parent-youth conflict. Davis (1940) looks upon parent-youth conflict as a historical inevitability, and attributes its etiology to such factors as the rapid social change in modern civilizations which establishes a hiatus between the generations, the problems and difficulties in enforcing parental authority as a result of conflicting norms operating within different generations, education and other institutions competing with the parents for authority, and lack of explicit institutionalization of steps in parental authority.

An altogether different view of the adolescent that distinguishes itself from those presented in the mainstream of conventional literature on adolescent socialization is presented by Elkin and Westley (1955, 1957). Their intensive study of twenty adolescents and their families in a suburban town in Montreal has marshalled data indicating a clear continuity in socialization, a continuity evidenced in the congruence of attitudes of adolescents and parents, not discrepancy, towards heterosexual relationships, career aspirations and economic matters. They conclude that it is the patterns of continuity rather than discontinuity in socialization that is warranted by the data.

The research data reported by Elkin and Westley have thus cast serious doubt on the universal inevitability of adolescence as a period of "storm and stress" resulting from patterns of socialization discontinuity. Anthropological research by Mead (1930, 1950) has also carefully documented the close association between social organization and the form and content of the adolescence phase of socialization. Mead (1950) marshalled impressive anthropological data indicating how the Samoan society has avoided the "discontinuity of cultural conditioning" as it is happening in the North American society by rendering the Samoan boys and girls responsible for a diverse range of adult responsibilities early in the socialization process. Initiation into the adult world, including training in expression of sexuality, has thus become a spontaneous and continuous facet of cultural conditioning and training. Benedict (1954: 142-148) distinguishes two kinds of societies. The first is one in which the primary task is to prepare him to achieve adulthood continuously and gradually. The second is that in which to be an adolescent one must undergo a discontinuous and disruptive process of relinquishing acquired behavioral and attitudinal sets.

Theorizing in the context of the historical controversy among social scientists regarding the conceptions of the adolescent, Winch (1971) proposes four sets of variable structural conditions under which adolescence is most unlikely to be under stress: first, the society designates clearly which adult position the adolescent will fill and permits no alternative; second, that position and its constituent roles are seen as attainable and highly rewarding; third, the course of preparation for that position is not believed as either too long or too costly relative to the prospective rewards; fourth, the culture provides a means for the individual to be aware of the time when he passes into adulthood.

Accordingly, the specific aims of this paper are to report and interpret data on the adolescents in the Holland Marsh community, and to assess to what extent they bear on the controversy among the social scientists regarding the issues of continuity versus discontinuity of the adolescence as a phase in the entire socialization process on the one hand, and the degree of the inevitability of the "storm and stress" of the adolescence, and the universality of the "adolescent culture" on the other. The general aims of the paper are to make contributions to our cumulative theoretical understanding of the impact of social organization on the form, content, and consequences of the socialization process as far as the development of the personality and behavioral systems is concerned.

THE METHOD

The data to be reported in this paper came from a larger pool of information gathered between October, 1977, and March, 1978, by the authors on the family life of the rural Dutch in the Holland Marsh. Since one of us had done some intensive field work in the community between 1965 and 1971, with the gathered data resulting in a community study monograph (Ishwaran: 1977), prior working relationships with key informants of the community and heads of households, which were essentially pleasant and satisfactory, had greatly facilitated attempts in soliciting agreement of the respondents to participate in this study, and in making arrangements for conducting interviews.

All interviews with the parents were conducted in the evening by us in their homes, and lasted between two and three hours. While these interviews were intended to be intensive, in-depth and semi-structured, the two-man research team enabled one of us to concentrate on making detailed and comprehensive notes of the dialogues, and the other to pose questions to the respondents, to establish rapport, to maintain the continuity of the interview, and, most importantly of all, to effect the eventual completion of the interview process. Since we did not adhere visibly to a set of preconceived questions, the resultant flexibility and ease of the interview situations were conducive to pursuing issues and concerns which were deemed interesting or important on particular occasions. In general, we usually started an interview with basic questions eliciting demographic and socio-economic data, then with questions on marital stability and commitment, and on attitudes, values and patterns of behaviour of the adolescents in the community, and ended with a discussion of the conceptions of time and space of rural Dutch Canadians.

The statistical data to be reported in this study were elicited by administration of a seven-page questionnaire consisting of both open- and close-ended questions to 72 adolescents, 32 males and 40 females, after their catechism classes in the church building. The counsellors of catechism classes and the ministers were very helpful and cooperative in getting our questionnaires filled out by the adolescents. While the adolescents themselves provided us with one source of data about themselves by responding to the questionnaire, the other source of information supplied by the parents of the adolescents, the ministers, the school-teachers and several key informants of the community, enabled us to compare qualitative with quantitative data, and to check the general validity and reliability of the data as a whole.

Some Demographic Characteristics
A total of 72 adolescents, 32 males and 40 females, in the age category of 16 to 20, living in two farming communities of Ansnorveldt and Springdale, constituted the sample of this study. The two communities, located in the geographical region of the Holland Marsh area, are about 40 miles north of Toronto. Ansnorveldt was born in 1934, and Springdale, largely an outgrowth of the first community, was conceived in 1948.

Roughly 60% of the inhabitants in the Marsh are Dutch and live closely among each other, spatially and socially. The Dutch inhabitants who profess Calvinism would like to describe the Marsh as an integrated, multi-ethnic community, though our field data indicate that they are highly segregated from other ethnic groups primarily composed of the Polish, Hungarian, Ukranian, German, Chinese and Japanese. Socio-culturally, the Dutch express a strong sense of ingroup solidarity and manifest considerable loyalty to the institutions of the community, especially the church, the school and the family. The social organization of the Dutch people is very much centered around these institutions, which serve as strong barriers for others to make entrance into the community. Socially and structurally speaking, the community of the Marsh bears striking resemblance to other better known religious communities such as those of the Hutterites and the Mennonites.

In terms of age composition of our sample, 41% (30) of the respondents were in the 14-16 age category, 42.5% (31) in the 16-18 age category, while the rest were in the 18-20 age category. There were more females (55.6%) than males (44.4%) in our sample. Community-wise, there were more females (65.9%) than males (34.1%) in Springdale. In Ansnorveldt, there were more males (86.2%) than females (13.8%). While the two communities reveal a common pattern of social organization, a common life-style, a common design of living, and similar attitudes toward religion, education and the family, we decided to refer to them as one community in this paper.

Self-Images and Self-Conceptions

While there seems to be a general inclination of the literature on the urban adolescents in the North American society to stress their feelings of ambiguity and ambivalence regarding issues such as personal and occupational responsibilities, psycho-social maturity and growth, and independence, the adolescents in the Holland Marsh, in striking contrast, seem to manifest a definite and unfailing sense of striving for maturity, independence and responsibility. Though the conventional sociological conception of the adolescent in terms of a marginal person maintaining ambiguous connections to the worlds of the child and the adult is by and large correct in many urban, industrial settings, the Dutch adolescent in the agrarian community views his induction into the adult roles as inevitable, gradual and, essentially, unproblematic.

The Marsh adolescent sees himself or herself firmly rooted in a stable agrarian community with its well-guarded rules and regulations. It is a time of life which is partly care-free and partly responsible. They have their freedom defined for them by the culture of the community, but are also fully aware of their obligations. While their freedom gives them occasions to express themselves, their rights and obligations keep them aware of their parents and the community — the chief sources of independence.

There were remarks by the adolescents illuminating their sense of maturity and responsibility:

> "An adolescent is different from a child. He or she has his or her opinions and is more mature."
> "It is an adventurous time of life. He is a mature person and has more responsibilities."

"It is different because we are given more responsibilities and treated as being more mature."

"He is quite different from a child. A child follows the adults' footsteps while we have to start making our own but within guidelines given to us by our parents, teachers and elders."

"I am trying to find an identity that will suit me for the rest of my life. My youngest brother, still a child, does not worry about that whereas I want to belong."

Regarding self-conceptions as an adolescent distinguishable from those as a child or as an adult when asked to describe what a teenager is like, the typical remarks were as follows:

"A teenager is in between a child who is innocent and a mature adult who is experienced and usually more wise. He is ready to take his place in the community. However, he needs independence at times. He has his own ideas."

"A teenager is a growing person, between a child and a fully mature male or female. It is not very easy when you are expected to do things that you were not used to. It is not, of course, easy growing out and into a teenager."

"A teenager is like a young person, growing up discovering what is right or wrong, being happy, not having many worries and exploring the future."

"I find myself at a stage capable of doing many things and competing with adults. Yet I find myself often put down by adults in the family and community as being incapable of any responsibility."

"To me, being a teenager is a good part of life, even though there are problems that cannot be dealt with. I am very happy and enjoy being a teenager. Life always isn't a bed of roses, there are a lot of thorns, but the rewards are also there."

"A teenager is like a bud about to flower. It is undecided as to whether to show the world what it is like. We don't know how people will react to our real selves. We copy parents and elders but go partly our own way."

It is misleading to infer from the above remarks that the adolescents fail to see the sequential and qualitative distinctions between the child, the adolescent, and the adult. On the contrary, they not only clearly perceive the conceptual distinctions, but are also able to see the appropriate roles and duties attendent to each phase of the life process. While the typical adolescent in the Marsh tends to see himself as "a growing person with own ideas", "ready to take his place in the community", and "capable of doing many things and competing with adults", he is also be looked upon by the adults and the outside observers as a gradually maturing person gravitating toward adulthood and assumption of responsibility. More importantly, adolescence is looked upon by our respondents as a necessary and useful transitional period during which he or she is socially and psychologically prepared for the assumption of adult duties and rights, responsibilities and liabilities. Accordingly, our data on adolescent self-images and self-conceptions seem to indicate a dominant and clear pattern of continuity of socialization during which the growing person feels confident and productive, ready and prepared.

OCCUPATIONAL AND RELIGIOUS SOCIALIZATION

It has already been indicated in the literature overview that one of the many important determinants of the emergence of a youth culture in some urban areas, and its behavioral consequences such as parent-child conflict and generation gap, is the increasingly high degree of social, and, correspondingly, occupational segregation of the youth from the values and roles of the adult, a phenomenon partly attributable to the lengthy confinement of the youth within a secluded and well-protected environment of the school system. In many urban areas, gone were the days when the child was considerably exposed to and familiarized with the social and occupational aspects of his father's life. With the abrupt disappearance of a child's occupational apprenticeship with the father since the Industrial Revolution, the child is seldom occupationally or socially socialized to jobs and careers he is most likely to pursue, especially that of his father. The absence of the father at home and the confinement of the child in the school during most parts of the day thus operate to undermine the nature and frequency of parent-child interaction.

However, our data indicate that not all of the situations and problems confronting the urban child in the modern, industrial society are immediately applicable to the rural adolescents in the Holland Marsh community. While residing in an essentially farming community, the father, who is more often a farmer by occupation, inducts his children, male or female, into various agricultural activities very early in their socialization process out of the need to maximize children's contributions to the production of the household unit. Right from the beginning of his early years, the adolescent participates in various phases of agricultural production, and is gradually trained in terms of acquiring knowledge of the skills, the technology, and ideology of the farming career. The toys, or playing objects, of the adolescent in the Holland Marsh thus consist of machinery and garden tools, rather than the various sophisticated artifacts the urban adolescents have found themselves indulged in. We were told by the farmers that they started their children on routine chores on the field when they were as young as six years old; eleven-year-old kids can handle the tractor competently and efficiently while the thirteen-to-fourteen-year-olds have already learnt how to repair and maintain old machinery.

In our first survey conducted between 1965-70, we noted that 86.5% of the heads of family had elementary education, whereas only 5.2% had some high school education, and none had gone to university. Incentives for higher education are not forthcoming from parents, though we found about half-a-dozen graduate students in both communities between 1965 and 1978. Parents do not seem to provide enough motivation for university education in these gardening communities, whereas the church emphasizes primarily morals and religion. In consequence, the aspirations of teenagers are limited by the environmental conditions, and are sought within the framework of the existing opportunities in the Marsh. Teachers complain of the increase in the student's drop-out rate, and indicate that most of the junior high school students at Springdale have not attained high school standard before they go out to seek higher education in the nearby King City.

With regard to our question concerning future occupational plans after education, 30 respondents did not answer the question. "Farming" seems to be the majority answer for those who have specific plans, and was mentioned 10 times by the respondents, who generally said, "I would like to go into farming, but it is hard to get land now" or "I would like to form a partnership with my dad on our farm." The other favourable occupations for boys are carpentry, plumbing, factory work, trucking, police, wild-life management, and for girls, legal secretary, nursing, stewardess, hairdressing, or bank-teller. The following illustrative responses are indicative of the pattern of occupational career for the Marsh teenagers:

"I plan on giving farming a try. If I am not successful, I still would enjoy working for a farming organization."
"Getting my licence for carpentry, and planning to travel throughout Canada and Europe."
"I intend to be a police officer or a carpenter."
"A teller in a bank, a receptionist at a motel, somewhere working with people."
"Would like to be a nurse in a psychiatric ward."
"Get my licence and get a job."

Nevertheless, it is very important to note that most of the occupations aspired to by the adolescents demand skills which have already been learnt and practiced in early years of socialization during which they were to aid the family in farm work. While the occupational and educational aspirations of the typical adolescent may not be as high as we expect, the final occupations he or she will enter as an adult continue with his or her early apprenticeship experiences.

While occupational segregation of the adolescent is effectively coped with and avoided via early apprenticeship with and induction into the occupation as a result of joint family participation, social segregation is also appropriately dealt with via considerable family involvement in religious activities. In the Holland Marsh community, the child partakes in various phases and modes of religious activities both in the church and at home almost right from birth. Not only does the church organize occasions on a routine and scheduled basis for religious worship and celebrations, it is also the most important social institution. Most social gathering involving persons of all ages revolves around the church. The Marsh community has developed religion-oriented and voluntary organizations based on age and sex differentiations. There are the Calvinist Cadet Corps for boys and the Calvinette Club for girls in the age group of 8-16. Then there is the Young People's Society, one each for boys and girls between 16-20. These organizations hold regular monthly meetings in the evenings from October to March. In an earlier analysis of the religious socialization of the child in the Marsh, Ishwaran (1977: 91-92) observes that "formal socialization among the peer groups begins when a Young Calvinist is first initiated into his Cadet Corps (while) the official motto of this organization is living for Jesus." Throughout the entire process of early socialization, religious occasions almost invariably provide opportunities for intensive family interaction between spouses, and between parents and children. Among others, the religion of the community serves to establish operating norms, rules and regulations for family interaction, to provide ideological and behavioral scripts for child-rearing practices, and to provide ultimate and absolute standards of morality according to which the behavior of the family member is measured and assessed.

An overwhelming majority of the respondents (82.2%) said that their parents did and would object to their irregular church attendance on Sunday. As many as 90.2% of the respondents in Springdale indicated they attended Sunday School regularly. In regard to their feelings about parents' objection to their irregular church-attendance, most seemed to have given only positive and approving remarks as "It is fair", "I don't mind", "I have no objection to regular church attendance", "It is the way it should be", and "I feel it is a great necessity to go to church".

To recapitulate, the dominant argument, as based on our qualitative data from intensive interviews with adults and on impressionistic observations of the form and functions of the community, is that the Dutch adolescent, compared to his urban counterparts, is less subjected to social and occupational segregation or transitional discontinuity of growth, throughout the psychosocial development of his personality. This empirical observation has also led us to find few behavioral consequences of youth segregation such as parent-youth conflict, generation gap, and deviancy or delinquency.

PARENT-ADOLESCENT INTERACTION: OBLIGATIONS OF THE ADOLESCENT

While our data were not specifically collected to probe the dynamics and processes of parent-child relationships, however, some glimpses can be caught by assessing the pragmatic and practical applicability of the concept of reciprocity to family life in the Marsh in terms of mutual obligations to render favors and services. In his conceptualization of the family as "a unity of interacting personalities," Burgess (1926) implicitly assumes a nexus of interpersonal relationships based on mutual reciprocity and exchange of benefits and services between all involved family members. The essense of the family life is thus cast in a different theoretical light with an immediate recognition of the elements of mutuality, relative causality, and reciprocity as norms for familial operations, development, and maintenance.

The practical applicability of the concepts of mutuality and reciprocity is to be understood and assessed in this paper in terms of what kinds of obligations and how much of it one family member owes to the others with what kinds of rewards or benefits. In a closely knit family unit, it is important to underscore that no one single family member is completely immune from participating in the operating dynamics of reciprocity and mutuality. However, the atypical distribution of power, authority, and resources between different family members might, under some circumstances, provide some family members (for example, the parents) with more control over the familial operations than other family members (in this case, the children).

In our foregoing discussion on the "occupational socialization" of the adolescent in the Holland Marsh, we have reported data including how the adolescent's apprenticeship in the farming career over the years of growing up and becoming an adult is operated at the expense of himself rendering service to the process of production by contributing labour and time. Data have also been reported in regard to the adolescent contributing labour to domestic chores. What is important is the gradual development of a sense of personal and occupational responsibility in the growing person during the process of practicing the trade.

While the adolescent feels responsible to the farm, he or she is also responsible to his or her younger siblings, and to the broader concept of the parental family. When asked the question "Do you think that an elder brother or an elder sister has a responsibility toward taking care of the younger ones?", 91.8% (67) of the respondents gave positive responses, with only 5.5% (4) indicating negative responses.

Sex-roles are blurred to some extent at the stage of life of the adolescent. Both boys and girls help Mom in domestic work and Dad in farm work, though adults' roles are by and large clear-cut with mother's work mainly limited to domestic work and father's work committed to farm work. However, this is a transitional period in the lives of boys and girls, leading gradually toward differential roles. In farm families with small acreages which are in no position to hire labour, boys and girls invariably work together with the parents. However, upper-class families do not regularly utilize daughters' labour on farm work. All the families, however, do seek teenagers' help on the farm, particularly during harvest.

With regard to help being given to father in Springdale, there were 11 respondents in Springdale whose fathers do not now own a farm. In both communities, 65.8% gave father help on his farm work, and 16.4% did not help because it was not needed. The kinds of help given by these adolescents to their father in the field are revealed by the following remarks:

> "Help him with the machinery on the farm, and the regular maintenance of the farm land during planting and harvesting"
> "Anything I can, work in the chicken barn, cut grass, pull potatoes"
> "Work with the field like picking beans, corn, beets, pees, spinach and go to market"
> "Driving tractors"

Regardless of the non-helping and non-applicables categories stemming from having no farm or working outside the community, 63% (46) of the respondents said that they did get paid from their fathers for working in the field, whereas only 24.8% (18) did not get paid. It seems that a higher percentage of respondents from Ansnorveldt (75%) than from Springdale (53.7%) were paid for their jobs. This data may be misleading due to the higher proportion of respondents' fathers from Springdale who either work outside the community or do not own farms.

Over half of the respondents (54.8%) who earned money from helping the father were allowed to keep money and there is no difference between respondents from the two communities. The money was mainly spent on clothing, education, entertainment and buying presents for parents' birthdays.

In response to the question "Do you help your mother in domestic work?", an overwhelming majority of the respondents (84.9%) gave positive answers while only 13.7% gave negative answers. Kinds of help given to mother in her domestic work include doing laundry, sewing, making supper, cleaning own rooms or anything around the house. The corresponding percentage of the adolescents not giving help to the mother is only 29.2%.

Instead of seeing teenage as an irresponsible and carefree time of life, the *weltenschaung* of the community is that teenage is a gradual and natural process of integrating the life of a growing and maturing person into the provider role of the adult. The process of growing up in this rural community, perhaps like any other agricultural community, is continuous, and, thereby, provides a systematic link between different generations.

To most adolescents in the Holland Marsh, the socialization process is one of acquiring and practicing the necessary and appropriate trade skills, of developing and maintaining a certain level of devotion and loyalty to God by attending regularly both religious and non-religious activities organized by the church in conjunction with the family, and of developing a sense of responsibility to the family by assisting in family production on the one hand, and by fulfilling obligations to the younger siblings on the other. Ways of demonstrating personal responsibility by the adolescent to the family include assisting the parents in rearing younger children, setting to them good and respectable examples, and demonstrating to the young how specific role-expectations can be fulfilled.

"We have obligations. We are our 'brother's keeper.' "

"He or she has a *responsibility* to help the younger ones. Sometimes he/she can understand a problem of the younger ones better than parents."

"*Help* them with their problems. Let them know that life involves hard work and that they have to start working right at home."

"An adolescent is very much involved in his parental family and expected to do more around the house. Expected to act in a mature way since you are the eldest."

"He or she should set a good example to the younger ones. Should help with homework, and be sure to talk to."

"Help the young ones with school work, teach him how to handle money, teach him with work at home and on the farm."

"A teenager should help his parents guide the children. Since he is the oldest, he should set an example for the young ones to follow."

"The elder brother's or sister's responsibility would be to bring them up in the way of the Lord."

"A teenager is a person who is beginning to feel *responsible* for what he does. He does not like getting pushed around by his parents but has little chance to escape their restrictions — which are generally in his interest."

The involvement of the adolescents in the Marsh in sharing household responsibilities, specifically in terms of aiding in rearing younger siblings, has several immediate consequences. First, the adolescents provide appropriate role-models for the younger siblings, and their own behaviour necessarily exerts considerable impact on the content and process of socialization of the latter. Second, the adolescents mediate between adults and the younger siblings, interpret and act upon messages from the adults, and personally exemplify and demonstrate the hows of undergoing the transitional period of the adolescence with comfort and ease. One of the important roles of the adolescents is, therefore, that of providing their younger siblings with patterns and modes of anticipatory socialization. Third, the fact that the adolescents are held responsible for their younger siblings by adults provides them with the opportunities to confirm their sense of worth and competence, and to reinforce their ideologies and values in regard to what is normal, desirable, and good, and what is not. Fourth, there are also good reasons to believe that the intimacy of interaction between the adolescents who act as interpreters and transmitters of adult values and the siblings contributes considerably to familial solidarity and cohesiveness.

PARENT-ADOLESCENT INTERACTION: PARENTAL OBLIGATIONS

In explicit recognition of the contributions of the adolescents to family productivity and domestic chores, the parents in Holland Marsh, like most parents in other communities, reciprocate their favours by fulfilling the basic, necessary duties and obligations of the parenting role. Data have already been reported to indicate that the contributed labour of the adolescents in the work field are more often than not financially rewarded. Over half of the respondents (54.8%) who have earned money from helping in the field are allowed to keep it. Although 58.9% (43) of the respondents received no pocket allowance from their parents, as many as 39.7% (29) did receive some allowance.

At a time when the adolescent is craving personal recognition and acknowledgement of his or her ability to be responsible, mature, involved and productive, the fact that the parents in the Marsh are beginning to conceive the adolescent as a grown-up person socially and occupationally involved in the adult world on a full scale is most psychically gratifying in the eyes of the adolescents. Nearly 70% (51) of the adolescents revealed that they were not looked upon as children by their parents, when they were asked the question, "Do you feel that your parents still look upon you as a child?" In response to a parallel question, "Do you feel that your parents treat you like a grown-up person?" 63% (46) of the adolescents said that they were treated by their parents as a grown-up person while 31.5% (23) said no, with 5.5% (4) not having given a response to the question.

It has long been stressed by researchers on the adolescents (e.g., Coleman 1963) that ownership of an automobile is one of the first essential indications of the rising status and social worth of the adolescent in the community. In the Holland Marsh, more than half (58.9%) of the adolescents indicated that they were allowed to drive their family car.

While the adolescent would, under most circumstances, like to see themselves productive, worthy and responsible, the fact that they are indeed treated as such by their own parents has largely confirmed his or her sense of competency and potency, which, in turn, aids greatly in building a strong sense of self-esteem. The implications of high self-esteem and competence as far as our theoretical understanding of the social psychology and behaviour of the adolescents have yet to be further explored in future studies on child socialization. Recognition and mutuality, within a context of differential distribution of power and authority, can very seldom be operated on all the absolute premises of democracy, neither can they completely do away with personal discipline on the part of some members, nor the exercise of control by some members over the others. In the atypical power structure of the Protestant family in the Holland Marsh, the prevailing Christian ideology dictates that the father be the authority figure, the disciplinarian, the controller, the ultimate decision-maker in regard to the distribution of costs and rewards. Over half of the respondents (57.5%) indicated that the final decision with regard to a major purchase of a car or a house was made jointly by "father and mother." However, in terms of "father only" compared with "mother only," considerable difference was noted: 38.4% of the respondents reported that the decision was made by "father only" while only 2.7% indicated "mother only" made the decision. The pertinent question is two-fold. First, how much control does the father have over his children in what areas of behavioural enactment, and second, how much resistance from the adolescents is met with by the parents while exercising disciplinarian control?

We have collected some interesting data on several specific disciplinary areas where potent parental control is most readily and explicitly exercised.

Parents' obligations to their teenage sons and daughters are in conformity with those standards of the community and the larger society. The adolescents are expected by both the community and their parents to attend Sunday school, catechism classes and Sunday services, to attend school and to come home at regular hours, to make the right friends, to date the right person, etc.

With regard to the attendance of Sunday school, 90.2% said that they did attend Sunday school, and only 9.8% said that they did not attend. Catechism classes were frequently attended mainly due to sponsored independence acquired by teenagers in the process of growing up. As one respondent put it, "I come here with some reluctance but to please and oblige my parents. When once I am here I am happy, I have my friends around here. Now that I have grown, I find it natural to come without any parental pressure." That sums up the attitudes of the teenagers who are reluctant to attend Sunday school and catechism classes.

It has already been briefly alluded to in the above that Holland Marsh parents take strong objections to irregular attendance by their children at Sunday church services, and that 90% of the adolescents indicated that they do attend church regularly. When asked what their feelings were about parents' objections to irregular church-going, only 17 expressed negative feelings. The reasons given are more or less similar, such as, "I wish that I would make my own decision whether I want to go or not." However, the majority of the respondents seem to have basically positive feelings about their parents' objection to irregular church attendance. Their typical responses were as follows:

"I don't really mind going. I go partly to please my parents and partly to learn something so that I could apply religion to my own life behaviour."

"I was brought up in a God-fearing home. Therefore, I enjoy attending church. If I have a good reason to stay home, like homework or sickness, it is left to me to decide whether or not I should stay home."

"Since my parents have brought me up to go to church, twice a week, I would feel guilty for not going regularly."

"I think it is good to listen to parents. It strengthens my obedience toward my parents and teaches you to be a true Christian. We should serve God as much as we can."

"I don't mind compulsion of my parents to attend church. I agree with the idea of regular church attendance anyway. I think that every one, if that is at all possible, should attend church twice on Sunday and whenever there is another service on Thanksgiving Day, Christmas and pray, etc., etc."

"Well, I think it is up to me if I want to go or not. But it is still their duty to tell us while we are young that we should go."

Parents in the Marsh, as everywhere, are very much concerned with the patterns of dating behaviour of their teenage sons and daughters to ensure that their children are dating the right person, socially and culturally speaking. Thirty-eight of our respondents gave no answer to the parents' reactions to their dating. Among those who did express or perceive to know their parents' reactions, only 3 respondents said that there were 'objections,' while the rest either said, "It is okay," or simply "No objection." The typical responses were as follows:

"I would never date and marry someone who isn't a Christian. My parents know that I have good judgment, and would terminate a relationship with a non-Christian if it got too serious. Religion is one of the first topics I talk about with my dating partner and let that person know my views and hope that he will respect them."

"My parents usually like my dates, because they are mostly from our church, so they can't really disapprove."

"My parents don't mind so long as they know who it is and where we are going."

About time limits for coming home, many respondents (32) did not express their feelings. Among those respondents who gave answers to the question, only one respondent did not agree with the time-limit set by his parents. The others either said that the limit is reasonable and fair, or that it is great. The response pattern is as follows:

"My parents let me stay out on special occasions. I think they have a right to set a time-limit for coming home in the evening. They worry about us. If we come late they think something happened to us."

"Before the age of 18, you need guidelines to follow and need to have respect for your parents' decisions."

"I think it's fair, because we shouldn't be out all hours of the night."

"I feel great about it. I have no objections at all. I think of it as a necessity to all teenagers between 14-16."

"I respect what my parents say and try to abide by it. If I don't, I have a good reason."

"I think it is right for parents to be concerned because they want their child to grow up in the fear of God."

The unerring impression gathered from our analysis and interpretations in terms of the obligations of the parents and of the adolescents, and also of parental control and discipline, points very convincingly to the emergence and maintenance of a well-integrated family unit in the Marsh in which all family members interact as an interlocking unit based on a considerable level of mutuality and reciprocity. The exercise of parental control and discipline in such areas as church attendance, joint family labour production, dating patterns, and time limits for coming home, etc., is more often than not met with acquiescence and cooperation, rather than hostility and antagonism. In a typical Dutch-Canadian family in the Marsh, the authority structure, with most of the rights, duties and privileges all vested on the father-husband, is operated with the least tension and resistance.

VALUE CONVERGENCE ACROSS GENERATIONS

The relative lack of resistance and hostility, in both ideological and behavioural terms, manifested by the adolescents as a group on the whole to parental control and discipline, as demonstrated by our empirical data, necessitates some words of explanation. We have stressed in our earlier writings on the Holland Marsh (Ishwaran: 1977) the saliency and centrality of the ideology and practice of Calvinism in giving form and content to the social organization of the community, such institutions as the school, the polity, the economy, and the organization of leisure included. What has not been emphatically stressed before is the impact of Calvinism on the socialization of the child, which is immediately measurable in terms of the child's value and behaviour systems. While the infiltration and dominance of Calvinism in the family can be understood in terms of the extent to which it provides norms and scripts in operating various modes of intra-familial relationships, it also provides an absolute external standard of morality according to which the competence and worth of all family participants are to be measured and judged. In other words, in providing a more visible external code of behavioural ethics, Calvinism in the Holland Marsh functions to generate and maintain a substantial amount of "value convergence" shared by family members of all generations. With the historical practice of Calvinism over the years, family members have gradually learnt to formulate concrete and unambiguous sets of role expectations. Occasional role tensions and role strains can be subjected to routinized and ritualized ways of arbitration, which invariably mean consultation with the Bible and the church on the part of the family members.

To recapitulate, the logic of the argument is that a Calvinistic socialization process, which, in the Holland Marsh, has occupational, economic, cultural and educational connotations, historically functions to develop and stabilize a considerable level of value convergence and neutrality, which, in turn, becomes a "normative bind" for all family members in all families. The functional application of value convergence to persons of all generations, noting its continuity and consistency, is by and large demonstrated by the tendency of the youth to adhere to the values and standards of morality and behaviour prescribed by the church, the community, and the parents in the family.

The family, in functional conjunction with the church, the school and the community, becomes the primary agent in instilling in the growing child conceptions of the normal versus the abnormal, the good versus the bad, the law-abiding versus the deviant, and the desirable versus the undesirable. We have gathered data indicating a maximal degree of "convergence" between the conceptions of the adolescent and those of the adults about the "desirable" qualities of a teenager.

Family, church and community consistently and systematically uphold qualities that are desirable in boys and girls, and these are held before children in the process of growing up. Basically, the Marsh is a well-integrated community with trust and cooperation at the base of the ethical structure.

When asked to describe the five most desirable qualities in a friend, the following were more frequently mentioned by the respondents than others: loyal, friendly, honest, trustful, and responsible; loving, caring and understanding; considerate and helpful when needed; sharing things (money, goods, cigarettes, ideas, interests); fun to be associated with, and having a sense of humour. Among the more frequently mentioned desirable qualities, "trustful" has been mentioned 52 times; "loyal," 48 times; "helpful," 31 times; and "honest," 31 times.

When asked to describe the five most undesirable qualities in a friend, the following were most frequently mentioned: lying, distrust and conceited, gossip behind, hypocritical and deceiving, inconsiderate and mean. "Distrust and conceited," the one most frequently mentioned response, was cited 17 times by the respondents, followed by "gossip" which was mentioned 10 times.

When asked the question, "Do you have a friend(s) with all these desirable qualities," 79.5% (58) of the respondents said yes and 19.2% (14) said no.

Altogether, "drinking, smoking and drug use," "not going to church," and "having no faith in religion" are frequently cited as "deviant things." However, some respondents replied that they did not find more than one individual in the two communities who was a habitual deviant or who "messed up with the laws because of drugs, stealing and alcohol." Other responses indicating known deviancy in the Marsh were as follows:

> "P. is a deviant. He doesn't go to church and works on Sunday."
> "I myself am a deviant. Don't take advice of parents, want to quit school, drink a bit, drive fast, play rock music loud."
> "This deviant in our community broke into the church and continues drinking and stealing. He has now problems with his parents and police."
> "Even in a Christian community like ours there are drinking problems and swearing."

The Holland Marsh community is culture-bound, and its people know what is right and wrong, moral and immoral, what is expected and not expected of them. Here family values such as subordination of the individual to the interests and wishes of the family, and being Dutch and maintaining Dutchness through endogamous marriages, which in turn operate in close accordance to the prescriptions and proscriptions, the precepts and dogmas of the church, are all guarded and indoctrinated into children in various phases of the socialization process.

Here the adolescent does not form his own sub-culture, for two reasons: first, adolescence is only a limited passing phase of life, inhibiting distinct formation of a set of values and objectives different or in opposition to that of the adults; second, adolescence in this rural community constitutes part of the continuous process moving gradually from childhood and adolescence into adulthood. Here, living space and work space are in one area, the age-graded clubs are centered around church, and the close linkage between intimate interaction of the three generations do not pose any threat to continuities in cultural conditioning, thereby providing role-merging at different stages of the life-cycle.

Borrowing a concept from Gottlieb and Ramsey (1964: 105-117), Holland Marsh's first adolescent generation may be described as "the cool generation," whose values do not conflict with values and norms of the community and do not fit with the values and norms of a rebellious youth. Here 90% of adolescents attend Sunday services, catechism classes, church-centered clubs and leisure activities like camping, hockey games and picnics. They find their security in being conformistic and are not easily led away to take risks in seeking pleasures typical of a rebellious adolescent. The Marsh community does provide appropriate outlets for emotions and frustrations, but within its bounds. The adolescents fully realize that their rewards in this stage of life rest upon their participation in activities centered around the church, the community, the home, and the farm.

The Holland Marsh adolescents are not "escapists," either. Their roles are well set for them by their families and institutions of the community. This awareness came through to us in seeking answers to the question, "What would you do with the money if you were given a gift of ten thousand dollars?" The responses given range from, "giving to my church" to "saving in the bank for interest." "Save in the bank for interest of future education," the most frequently chosen way of spending the ten thousand dollars, was mentioned altogether 68 times. "Give it to parents for debt or for mortgage" was mentioned 28 times, "give some to the church and to the charity organization," 24 times, "buying a car or truck," 16 times. Each of the other responses, "clothing," "buying a house," "buying land for farming," and "helping a boy friend" was mentioned less than 10 times. Some of the illustrative remarks are as follows:

"I'd give 20% to the church, deposit 70% in the bank, and the remaining 10% I would spend for myself."
"Send $2000 to church funds for poor countries and put most of it in the bank and spend the rest between my parents and myself."
"Give as much as my parents need and give some to the church and foreign missions and put the rest in my bank."
"I would give some of it to my church and half of it to my parents."
"I would put it in the bank and give some to my mom and dad."
"I would divide it between my family and take my share and put it in the bank for my future plans."
"Invest one-tenth of it in the high school, sports equipment and give some to my church and the rest in bonds for use in later life when I may need it."
"Give $500 to my dad, $2000 to church, and put the rest in the bank or buy a car."

One clear fact emerging from the above remarks by the adolescents is the high level of adolescent commitment to the parental family on the one hand, and to the institutions of the community on the other. While the adolescent sees himself as an individual with own preferences and wishes, he also, simultaneously, places high premium on his integral connections to the community as an entity.

DISCUSSION

If it is acceptable to suggest that one of the major objectives of socialization is to develop in an individual a certain level of social and occupational competence which will enable him or her to acquire a sense of social responsibility and independence, the important theoretical question then becomes: What kind of independence is to be cultivated and developed via what mechanisms or processes with what costs and consequences? Farber (1964: 369) distinguishes two types of independence, sponsored and unsponsored. In the instance of sponsored independence, the parents strive to develop in their children a sense of autonomy, independence and competence within the larger framework of parental authority and control. The parents act as supervisors and guardians, and attempt to strike an appropriate balance between granting independence and exerting control. In the instance of unsponsored independence, the parents act as sheer passive observers while the children strive for independence in the absence of parental guidance, supervision and control.

Our portrayal of the adolescents in the Marsh seems to fit quite well into the "sponsored independence" type. In our discussion of the occupational and religious socialization process in the Marsh, we have reported data indicating how the child begins to strive for independence in his very early years, with the parents acting as the primary socializing agents, both within and without the family.

What is happening in the Marsh as far as child socialization is concerned is that the historical development of independence and autonomy is completed not at the expense of storm and stress, or rebellion and antagonism against the parental or institutional authority. On the contrary, the entire process of independence development is operated within the framework of conformity, respect, tolerance, and cooperation. Our data have already indicated the high frequency of parent-adolescent interactions, the high congruence of values and beliefs between parents and children, the containment of parent-youth conflict, the unproblematic enactment of parental authority and control, and the low level of adolescent delinquency. The dynamic operation of norms of reciprocity and mutuality within the family, which in time generates a considerable level of intergenerational value convergence and congruence, makes it altogether unnecessary for the adolescents to establish a sub-culture on their own to undermine the values held by the parents and the community. While we are prepared to be recognizant of the existence and functions of the peer groups which might have their own versions of most aspects of community life, it is equally important to note that the sense of responsibility and commitment of the adolescents to the parents and the family is also high.

In regard to the long-standing controversy about the universality and inevitability of the "storm and stress" of the adolescent subculture, we might want to conclude that the most important variable to be examined is the nature of the social organization of the special community under study, which seems to have enormous impact on the modes of child-rearing practices, the nature of parent-child relationships, the form and content of the socialization process, and lastly, the kinds of adolescents living in the community. The Holland Marsh community, as we have portrayed it in this paper and in our earlier writings is an interesting illustration of a stable, well-integrated and considerably self-contained community in which Calvinism has found in-roads into all other social institutions, the family, the economy, the polity and the education system included. It provides an ideological foundation for the social organization of the community and also, more importantly, provides an explanation for the high level of value congruence across generations.

References

Benedict, Ruth
    1954   "Continuities and Discontinuities in Cultural Conditioning" in W. Martin and C. Stendler (eds.), *Readings in Child Development*, New York: Harcourt, Brace, pp. 142-148.

Burgess, Ernest
    1926   "The Family as a Unity of Interacting Personalities," in *Family*, pp. 3-9.

Cohen, Albert K.
    1955   *Delinquent Boys: The Culture of the Gang*, Glencoe, Ill., The Free Press.

Coleman, James S.
    1963   *The Adolescent Society*, New York: The Free Press.

Davis, Kingsley
    1940   "The Sociology of Parent-Youth Conflict," *American Sociological Review*, (4), pp. 523-35.

Davis, Kingsley
    "Adolescence and the Social Structure," *The Annals of the American Academy of Political and Social Sciences*, Vol. 236 (Nov. 1944) pp. 8-16.

Elkin, F., and W.A. Westley
    "The Myth of Adolescent Culture," *American Sociological Review*, 20 (Dec. 1955), pp. 680-684.

Farber, Bernard
    1964   *Family: Organization and Interaction*, San Francisco: Chandler.

Gottlieb, David and Charles Ramsey
    1964   *The American Adolescent*, Homewood Illinois: The Dorsey Press.

Green, Arnold W.
    1968   *Sociology*, New York: McGraw-Hill Book Co.

Hollingshead, A.B.
1949   *Elmtown's Youth: The Impact of Social Classes on Adolescents*, New York: Wiley.

Ishwaran, K.
1977   *Family, Kinship and Community: A Study of Dutch Canadians, A Developmental Approach*, Toronto: McGraw-Hill Ryerson.

Koller, Marvin R., and Oscar W. Ritchie
1978   *Sociology of Childhood* (2nd edition), Englewood Cliffs, New Jersey: Prentice Hall.

Mead, Margaret
1950   *Coming of Age in Samoa*, New York: New American Library, 1950; "Adolescence in Primitive and Modern Society," in V.F. Calverton & S.D. Schmalhausen (eds), *The New Generation*, New York: Macauley, 1930.

Muuss, Rolf E.
1968   *Theories of Adolescence*, (2nd edition), New York: Random House.

Parsons, Talcott
        "Age and Sex in the Social Structure of the United States," *American Sociological Review*, Vol. 7 (Oct. 1942), pp. 604-16.

Sebald, Hans
1968   *Adolescence: A Sociological Analysis*, New York: Appleton-Century-Crofts.

Westley, William A., and Frederick Elkin
1957   "The Protective Environment and Adolescent Socialization," *Social Forces*, Vol. 35, No. 3, March.

Williams, Robin M., Jr.
1960   *American Society: A Sociological Interpretation*, New York: Alfred Knopf.

Winch, Robert F.
1971   *The Modern Family*, (3rd edition), Holt, Rinehart and Winston, Inc.

Acquisition of Adult Responsibilities and Rights in Adolescence

FRANK A. FASICK
University of Waterloo

Adolescence is usually defined as a transitional period between childhood and adulthood. As a rule the end of adolescence is signaled by young persons taking on adult obligations and acquiring adult rights. An understanding of the factors that affect this process provides valuable perspectives on the ways this transition occurs. In this paper the purpose is to explore two factors which are frequently overlooked in the analyses of the transition from adolescence to adulthood — biological development and minimum age legislation.

ADULT RESPONSIBILITIES AND RIGHTS IN THE LIFE CYCLE

There is no doubt about physical and mental capabilities being related to the life cycle. In the early years of life children obviously lack such capabilities. At the end of the life cycle capabilities also often become problematic, especially if one lives to an advanced age.

In Canadian society, and indeed most industrial societies, the denial of adult rights and obligations toward the end of the life cycle is handled very differently from the way in which they are granted in youth. With the exception of retirement, older adults are not denied responsibilities and privileges categorically because they have reached a specific age. Denial, if it occurs at all, is on a case by case basis involving a direct test of competence or is a consequence of institutionalization. Retirement differs in that most older adults must give up their principal occupation at a specified age. Mandatory retirement, however, is not universal. The self-employed have no such restriction and some occupational groups, particularly high status ones, often circumvent compulsory retirement. For the young the situation is quite the reverse. The age at which they acquire obligations and rights is often prescribed by law.

The legislation of minimum age limitations raises a number of questions. Are minimum legal age requirements actually related to the capabilities of the young? If so, what is the nature of the capabilities implied in the law? Are the age limitations consistent with one another? If not, what factors help to explain the inconsistencies? No definitive answers to these questions are possible, but these issues can be explored. The following discussion is an effort in this direction.

Perhaps the most important stumbling block in attempts to explore these questions lies in the ambiguity of the term, *capability*, in relation to social behavior. By defining capability in adolescence as a matter of physical and mental maturity, the problem of ambiguity is reduced. Development of physical and mental capabilities in relation to age can be determined with reasonable precision despite considerable variation from individual to individual. Furthermore, the importance of physical and mental maturity in the assumption of adult responsibilities seems abundantly clear. By comparing what adolescents *can* do in terms of physical and mental development with what they *may* do in terms of age limitations on the legitimate assumption of adult behaviors one can begin to explore systematically the questions raised above.

PHYSIOLOGICAL AND INTELLECTUAL DEVELOPMENT IN ADOLESCENCE

Humans attain full intellectual capability and near physiological maturity during adolescence. The three main dimensions of development taking place during adolescence are: (1) physical growth associated with the height spurt, (2) sexual development, and (3) intellectual development.

Physical Development

Although there is a general decline in the rate of physical growth from birth onward, this decline is reversed for a period of a year or more during adolescence when a surge in growth occurs. The most obvious indication of this spurt is a rapid growth in height. Other important changes, however, also occur at this time. Muscles widen and become stronger, the heart enlarges, and there is a loss of fat.

As shown in Table 1, the height spurt typically begins at about twelve for girls but may not begin until as late as fourteen and a half. Boys typically begin the height spurt about two years later at around fourteen. It may not end among boys until as late as seventeen and a half and still be within normal limits.

Associated with the growth spurt is sex differentiation. During this period boys become heavier and taller than girls. They develop larger

TABLE 1
AVERAGE AGE AND UPPER LIMIT OF THE NORMAL AGE RANGE
FOR COMPLETION OF THE HEIGHT SPURT,
SEXUAL DEVELOPMENT AND INTELLECTUAL MATURATION
IN ADOLESCENT GIRLS AND BOYS

	Average Age at Completion	Upper Limit of Normal Age Range for Completion
The height spurt		
Girls	12	14.5
Boys	14	17.5
Sexual development: girls		
Menarche	13	16.5
Completed breast development	15	18
Sexual development: boys		
Completed penis development	14.5	16.5
Completed testis development	15	17
Intellectual maturity		
Stage of formal operations	14-15	not established

Sources: Tanner, J.M., "Sequence, Tempo, and Individual Variation In the Growth and Development of Boys and Girls Aged Twelve to Sixteen," in Grinder, R.E., Studies in Adolescence: A Book of Readings in Adolescent Development 3rd Ed., New York: Macmillan Publishing Co., Inc., 1975, p. 508.
Muuss, Rolf E., Theories of Adolescence 3rd Ed., New York: Random House, 1975, p. 190.

muscles, more force per gram of muscle, and such related characteristics as the ability to carry larger amounts of oxygen in the blood.

Sexual Development
The most dramatic physiological change that occurs during adolescence is sexual development. As noted in Table 1, menarche ordinarily occurs at about age thirteen but may not begin until sixteen and a half. Often, however, girls are not fecund until about a year to eighteen months after menarche. Breast development is usually complete by about 15 years of age, although complete development as late as eight-

een years is normal. In males, the penis ordinarily is not fully developed until about age fourteen with complete development occasionally occurring as late as sixteen and a half. The first ejaculation ordinarily occurs in males about a year after the beginning of accelerated penis development.

The Secular Trend

Both the height spurt and sexual development have been occurring typically at progressively earlier ages for a considerable number of years.

In North America the median age at menarche has declined from a little over fourteen years in 1900 to a little under thirteen years at the present time. The age at which boys reached full adult height in 1880 was twenty-three or later; today the average age is eighteen. Girls reached full adult height at eighteen or nineteen in 1900; the average age is now sixteen. Adults of both sexes have become, on the average, taller and heavier in each generation. Young persons today are biologically closer to adulthood at a younger age than were earlier generations.

The declining age of biological development contrasts sharply with prolonged adolescence defined in sociological terms. The countervailing pressures of the secular trend and changing educational standards that tend to lengthen the period of economic dependency among young persons clearly contribute to the ambiguities of adolescence (cf Sebald, 1977: 1).

Intellectual Development

The best known work in the field of intellectual development has been done by Piaget and his co-workers. Piaget has constructed a comprehensive theory of cognitive development from infancy through adolescence. In his theory the final stage of intellectual development is the stage of formal logical operations. It is divided into two substages. The early substage covers the years eleven or twelve to thirteen or fourteen and the latter substage continues indefinitely from thirteen or fourteen onward. What distinguishes the stage of formal logical operations from earlier stages in cognitive development is the ability to reason abstractly. This development signals full intellectual capability. The principal logical components in the stage of formal operations are the Combinatorial System and the INCR Group. Development of the Combinatorial System means that one can take into account systematically all the possible combinations of the values of the variables under consideration. The INCR Group consist of four logical operations: Identity, Negation, Reciprocity and Correlativity. These operations allow one to manipulate the matrices formed through the Combinatorial System. Together these two logical capabilities form the foundations of abstract reasoning.

In most persons the logical capabilities that characterize formal operations develop gradually during the period of early and mid-adolescence (11-12 to 15-16). Other researchers, e.g. Dulit (1975), question the extent to which all persons fully achieve these capabilities.

When one uses the height spurt, sexual development, and Piaget's scheme of intellectual development as criteria, the vast majority of young persons achieve maturity, or near maturity, by the age of sixteen.

Since social adolescence as defined in Canadian society lasts at least until the age of eighteen (cf Muuss, 1975b: 1; Sebald, 1977: 7), it extends well beyond the point at which most young persons attain full sexual and intellectual powers, as well as the bulk of their overall physical growth.

There is, of course, a great deal of individual variation among adolescents in growth and development. This variability may cause some adolescents to become confused and concerned when they compare themselves with their age mates, considering themselves excessively over or under developed.

Variability in maturation during this period may appear extensive to the participants, but in the context of the whole life cycle, the processes of adolescent growth and development occur within a very brief time span. One consequence of this situation is that young persons in the later years of adolescence differ substantially from younger adolescents in terms of biological and intellectual development. Although from some perspectives it may be possible to speak of adolescence as a single stage in the life cycle covering most of the second decade of life, biologically one must distinguish between early and late adolescence.

THE ACQUISITION OF ADULT RESPONSIBILITIES AND RIGHTS

If one is willing to accept the view that most adolescents are physically and biologically capable of assuming adult responsibilities and rights at sixteen, it is possible to compare this age at which one infers that most adolescents *can* assume these responsibilities and rights with the age at which they *may* legally assume them. From this comparison one can commence exploring the questions raised at the beginning of this discussion.

Table 2 gives for each of the ten provinces the minimum age at which young persons may legally assume four important responsibilities and at which they acquire four rights or privileges. The four responsibilities are: employment, military service, marriage, and legal independence (i.e. age of majority). The rights or privileges are: the right to vote, to drive a passenger car, to be served alcohol in a public establishment, and to attend adults only movies.

TABLE 2
MINIMUM AGES AT WHICH YOUNG PERSONS CAN ASSUME SELECTED RESPONSIBILITIES AND OBTAIN SELECTED RIGHTS IN CANADIAN PROVINCES

Selected Responsibilities	Minimum age at which responsibility or right can be assumed									
	B.C.	Alta.	Sask.	Man.	Ont.	Que.	N.B.	N.S.	P.E.I.	N.F.
Employment[a]	15	15	16	16	16	16	16	14	15	16
Marriage:										
with parental consent	16	16	15	16	16	(14) (12) (boys) (girls)	*	16	16	*
without consent	19	18	18	18	18	18	18	19	18	19
Military service[b]										
with parental consent	17	17	17	17	17	17	17	17	17	17
without consent	18	18	18	18	18	18	18	18	18	18
Age of majority	19	19	18	18	18	18	19	19	18	19

Selected Rights	Minimum age at which responsibility or right can be assumed									
	B.C.	Alta.	Sask.	Man.	Ont.	Que.	N.B.	N.S.	P.E.I.	N.F.
License to drive passenger car	16	16	16	16	15	16	16	16	16	17
Right to vote: 1969										
in Provincial elections	19	19	18	18	21	18	21	21	18	19
in Federal elections[b]	21	21	21	21	21	21	21	21	21	21

Right to vote: 1977									
in Provincial elections	19	18	18	18	18	18	18	18	18
in Federal elections[b]	18	18	18	18	18	18	18	18	18
Use of Alcohol									
in 1969	21	19	21	21	21	21	21	21	21
in 1977	19	18	18	18	18**	18	19	18	18
Admission to									
adult only films	18	18	18	18	18	18	18	18	18

[a] Permitted at an earlier age with the approval of appropriate authorities.
[b] Established by federal statute.
* No minimum age established by statute. English common law minimums of 12 for girls and 14 for boys would apply.
** Became 19 years of age in September 1978.

Sources:
W.H. Jennings, Canadian Law. Toronto: McGraw-Hill Ryerson, 1972, p. 120
Canadian Almanac & Directory. Toronto: Copp, Clark, 1977, pp. 48-49.
Qualter, Terence H., The Election Process in Canada. Toronto: McGraw-Hill, 1970, p. 8.
Anstett, Andrew and Terence Qualter, "Election Systems," in Bellamy, David J., John H. Pammett and Donald C. Rowat, The Provincial Political Systems: Comparative Essays, Toronto: Methuen Publications, 1976, p. 150.
Personal communications from: Censor Board of Ontario, Toronto; Armed Forces Recruiting Centre, Kitchener, Ontario.
Statutes of the various provinces.
The Canada Year Book, Ottawa: Statistics Canada, 1975, p. 604.

ASSUMPTION OF ADULT RESPONSIBILITIES

Employment

All provinces permit adolescents to obtain employment at the age of sixteen or earlier; the minimum ages being sixteen in Saskatchewan, Manitoba, Ontario, Quebec, New Brunswick, and Newfoundland; fifteen in British Columbia, Alberta, and Prince Edward Island; and fourteen in Nova Scotia. Employment below the minimum age is allowed with provincial approval. Conditions of employment are set so that requirements for school attendance are met.

Traditionally young persons have begun productive labour early in life. It is not surprising, therefore, that present day restrictions on employment by age are set at the mid-teens. If anything, age limitations are relatively high in terms of basic physical capabilities for most types of employment open to young persons.

There are no restrictions on the sixteen-year-old's decision to seek employment. This situation contrasts with the requirement of parental approval in order to marry prior to eighteen or nineteen (a matter which is discussed below). A number of factors seem to play a role in the autonomy granted young persons regarding employment. In the first place employment is the principal means, often the only means, by which youths may achieve independence — partial or complete — from a family situation they find unsatisfactory. In such circumstances requiring parental approval might run counter to adolescents' efforts at meeting the need for economic independence. Furthermore, the relationship to an employer is contractual, with obligations by both parties specific and closely regulated. They are nothing like the open-ended and all pervasive responsibilities assumed at marriage. Finally, employment is a private contractual arrangement that may be terminated at will by either party. (The need for parental approval to enter the armed forces prior to eighteen may reflect the fact that it involves a commitment to a highly regulated life in a potentially hazardous occupation for a minimum of three years.[4] See the discussion below.) On the other hand, marriage is an important social institution in which one ideally makes a life long commitment to one's partner in a publicly sanctioned ceremony and in which the legal protections of the spouses are limited.

Military Service

Military service is of special interest in terms of minimum age requirements, since it is a potentially very hazardous occupation that places great emphasis on physical strength and endurance. In addition, military service is a tax supported occupation and so subject to public scrutiny and political pressure. Under these circumstances, it is especially noteworthy that adolescents may enter this occupation with parental consent at the age of seventeen. The widespread public acceptance of military service at seventeen can be interpreted to imply a general — if tacit — public recognition of fundamental biological and emotional maturity at this age.

Marriage

The situation regarding marriage is very similar to that of employment. With parental consent adolescents may marry at sixteen or earlier in all provinces: the minimum age being sixteen in British Columbia, Alberta, Manitoba, Nova Scotia, Prince Edward Island and Ontario; fifteen in Saskatchewan; and fourteen for boys, twelve for girls in Quebec. Since there is no statutory minimum age in New Brunswick or Newfoundland, the English common law minimums of twelve for girls and fourteen for boys would apply. Ordinarily there is provision for marriages below the minimum age, usually limited to instances of pregnancy.

The minimum age for marriage with parental consent is obviously much more firmly based in biological maturity than the minimum age for employment. In Canadian society marriage presumes sexual maturity, and a minimum age for marriage of fifteen or sixteen is close to the typical age of full sexual capability. As noted above, the typical age for menarche among girls is approximately thirteen, but they ordinarily are not fecund until around fourteen or fourteen and a half. The full development of related sexual characteristics, such as breast development, ordinarily does not occur until around fifteen. The average age of full penis development in boys is about fourteen and a half, but the ability to impregnate may not occur until later.

Since Canadians, as most other peoples, place great emphasis on legitimacy and on the tie between children and their natural parents, the minimum age at marriage cannot be expected to depart much from the age at which adolescents can have children. In fact, the minimum ages in Saskatchewan and Quebec approach the lower limit of the age range for the normal development of reproductive capacity among young persons.

Although marriage imposes heavy mutual obligations on the partners and legitimizes parenthood, the qualifications needed to enter marriage are usually only a marriage license and freedom from venereal disease. This latter requirement is typically waived in cases of pregnancy. Under these conditions the requirement of parental consent at the minimum age for marriage acts as a screening device in establishing the appropriateness of the marriage in each instance. Presumably, the judgment of experienced adults, familiar with the circumstances of the young couple and committed to their welfare, is brought to bear in the decision to marry. Parental consent can be interpreted as a qualification on the right to marry that reflects a concern by Canadians about the social maturity of adolescents below the age of eighteen or nineteen.

In line with the reasoning regarding parental consent outlined above, the minimum legal age of marriage without parental consent could be interpreted to indicate a legal definition of social maturity. In this regard the provinces are remarkably consistent. British Columbia, Nova Scotia, and Newfoundland set the age at nineteen; all the others at eighteen. The notion that social maturity appears to be defined in law at about the age of eighteen or nineteen is a point that comes up again in the discussion to follow.

Age of majority

None of the provinces set the age of majority in close relation to biological and intellectual maturity as it is being defined here. The age is eighteen in Alberta, Manitoba, Ontario, Quebec, and Prince Edward Island. In British Columbia, Saskatchewan, Nova Scotia, New Brunswick and Newfoundland it is nineteen. It appears that the age of majority, like the age of marriage without consent, is established in terms of some conception of social maturity. As one would expect, the age of majority and the age of marriage without parental consent are identical in all but two provinces, Alberta and New Brunswick.

It is possible to rank the selected adult responsibilities discussed above on the degree to which the age they are granted occurs after sixteen, the presumed age of fundamental biological and intellectual maturity. Employment is the one most unequivocally granted by the sixteenth year. No province has a higher minimum age for employment and no constraints other than compulsory school attendance requirements are imposed. Marriage ranks next to employment. No province denies marriage at the age of sixteen, but none grants the right to marry below the age of eighteen without parental consent. Military service would seem to rank third, although the situation is complicated by the fact that age requirements for military service are established federally and so do not vary from province to province. Limitation of military service to young persons aged seventeen with parental consent and eighteen without, however, is clearly more restrictive than the age limitations on employment and marriage. The age of majority ranks last. In no province is it granted below the age of eighteen.

ACQUISITION OF SELECTED RIGHTS

With the exception of the right to drive a passenger car, all of the rights listed in Table 2 are granted by the provinces at age eighteen or nineteen. Since the minimum age for obtaining a driver's license differs from the other rights, it will be discussed first.

License to drive a passenger car

The age at which one may obtain a license to drive a passenger car is eighteen in Alberta and New Brunswick, seventeen in Newfoundland,

and sixteen in the remaining seven provinces. Most provinces grant the right to drive at the age being used in this discussion to indicate biological and intellectual maturity.

Safe driving involves a combination of skills and judgment. Sixteen-year-olds obviously have the motor development needed to drive skillfully, but serious questions can be raised about the adequacy of the judgment exercised by many young drivers. The evidence from accident records suggests that an adult level of judgment isn't widely developed among young persons until the early twenties, especially in males. It would seem that the granting of driving privileges in most provinces reflects an uneasy compromise between adequate motor skills and the need for emotional maturity in which basic biological maturity (i.e. sixteen) is the most frequently chosen option.

Rights conferred at age eighteen or nineteen
Three of the rights listed in Table 2: the right to vote, to be served alcoholic beverages in public establishments, and to attend adults only movies are granted by the provinces at eighteen or nineteen. This uniformly high age contrasts with the variability in the ages at which the responsibilities listed in Table 2 are granted. Social factors apparently related to the age level for granting these rights are discussed below.

Until recently, such rights as voting or drinking in public establishments were granted at twenty-one. As noted in Table 2, this was the case as late as 1969 in many provinces. It is not clear what accounts for the widespread lowering of the minimum age regarding these rights. As Anstett and Qualter (1976: 150) note regarding sufferage, the lowering of the age requirement is a worldwide phenomenon which has occurred in the absence of any strenuous effort on the part of young persons to obtain it.

SOCIAL DIMENSIONS IN MINIMUM AGE REQUIREMENTS

Social considerations related to minimum age requirements for particular adult behaviors have already been discussed. In this section the focus is on three social dimensions related to the *patterning* of age limitations among the various rights and responsibilities. These dimensions are: (1) social maturity, (2) personal relevance, and (3) social ambiguities.

Social Maturity
One consequence of the lowering of the drinking and voting age to eighteen or nineteen is a greater consistency among the provinces in the age at which young persons can act independently. This consistency extends to responsibilities, such as the decision to marry or enter the armed forces without the consent of one's parents as well as the age of majority.

Currently there are only a few years between the lower age limit at which adolescents can take on adult roles and the age of eighteen or nineteen when almost all restrictions are removed. The lower age limit for taking on adult responsibilities and rights seems to be based in part on considerations of biological maturity. Do a few more years represent the acquisition of additional social experience sufficient to warrant the granting of unfettered legal adult status?

The answer is ambiguous at best. On the one hand, most adolescents continue to live at home and attend secondary school between their sixteenth and eighteenth year. The social setting within which they live remains much the same. On the other hand, all of adolescence is a rush to new experiences. By the time they are eighteen or nineteen most adolescents have had some kind of employment, have completed their formal education, and carry on a relatively independent social life with their peers. A sizeable minority have obtained full-time employment and a small percentage have married. Some have children of their own. Although late adolescence is very brief viewed in the context of the life cycle, it clearly represents a time of rapid social maturation for most young persons. The secular trend in physiological development and the marked increase in the proportions of eighteen and nineteen-year-olds with secondary education or more are also factors that can be expected to contribute to the perception of young persons as socially responsible at these ages.

Personal Relevance

The matters for which the minimum legal age is under eighteen in most provinces (employment, marriage, military service, and a licence to drive) are of importance to the persons concerned. The right to drive a passenger car ordinarily does not impinge as heavily on one's life as the other concerns, but it is often of great relevance. In contrast, the matters in which the minimum age is eighteen or nineteen (the age of majority, voting and drinking ages, and admission to adults only movies) are issues whose bearing on one's life is usually perceived as less fundamental. This distinction cuts across responsibilities and rights, although only one responsibility (age of majority) and one right is involved (driver's licence).

A partial explanation for the lower age limitations on such matters as employment and marriage may lie in the persistence of traditional social norms. There is a widely supported norm (although it has come under attack in recent years) that it is better for adolescents to marry than to live in "sin." The importance of adolescents marrying in the case of pregnancy is subscribed to even more widely. These norms are especially strong among ethnic groups with a high proportion adhering to the Catholic faith; e.g., French-Canadians, southern Europeans, eastern Europeans, etc. Similarly, there is much support for the notion that young persons who are nearly grown should be permitted to seek employment rather than continue formal education (cf Mitchell, 1975). In fact the right to marry in mid-adolescence implies the right to seek employment in the absence of some other socially established way for the couple to obtain support.

Military service is a special case of employment which can be particularly appealing to some adolescents. It provides young persons who are in good health an opportunity to leave their old environment and enter a new one, to get started in the world of work, and to obtain economic security. There are many instances when the availability of such an option may be considered very desirable by adolescents and by adults concerned for them.

Traditional social norms are less persuasive as an explanation for the minimum age of sixteen to obtain a driver's licence in most provinces. The age limit on driving privileges, however, does seem to satisfy the general principle that lower minimum age limits are attached to those matters of most immediate concern.

In contrast to matters such as employment and marriage, there is no established basis in traditional social norms to support the right of adolescents to drink in public establishments, to vote, to be exposed to "adult" presentations in the mass media, or to obtain legal independence. The failure of such norms to develop may very well lie in the fact that these latter concerns are seldom perceived by adolescents and their families as being of crucial importance. In the absence of deeply felt self-interest, age limitations can be — and are — more restrictive.

Social Ambiguities

The division of minimum age limitations so that those attached to occupational and family roles are lower than those for the acquisition of social rights tends to create ambiguities.

Today adolescents in all provinces may marry or join the military service but may not see films with exceptionally erotic or violent scenes. They may assume the responsibilities of a job and family, but they may not participate in forming a government or drink in a public establishment.

It is not clear why such ambiguities are tolerated. The most likely possibility seems that tolerance derives from a combination of apathy and circumvention. On the basis of voting participation rates by young adults who are eighteen or over, it appears that the vast majority of adolescents are apolitical. Similarly, drinking in public establishments or attending adults only movies is unlikely to be high on late adolescents' list of priorities. In those situations when there is a desire to participate in such activities as drinking or attending adults only movies, it appears that the age limits are readily violated. Under these conditions it is not difficult to understand the lack of concern by adolescents over the ambiguities reflected in the various minimum age limitations.

MARRIAGE AND PARTICIPATION IN THE LABOUR FORCE BY ADOLESCENTS

This discussion has dealt with a comparison between what adolescents presumably can do in terms of biological development and what they may do legally. It is only appropriate to end by noting the extent to which adolescents act on the legal entitlements they obtain prior to the general dropping of restrictions at eighteen or nineteen.

The focus will be on employment and marriage because these are the most important roles adolescents may assume under the age of eighteen. The figures on employment and marital status among adolescents are based on the fifteen to nineteen year age group, since this is the classification used in the census and relates closely to the age group under discussion.

About half of all adolescents take advantage of the opportunity to seek employment. In 1976, based on the annual average, 52.7% of males and 47.0% of females between the ages of fifteen and nineteen were in the labour force (Statistics Canada, 1977b, Table 47). Although many of these young persons were students who sought employment on a temporary basis, a sizeable proportion were adolescents who had opted for employment rather than continuing their secondary education. The figures for adolescents of secondary school age who have moved into full time employment are not readily available, but the move is reflected in school enrolment figures. Nearly 90% of sixteen-year-old males and females were enrolled in school during 1975-76 (Statistics Canada, 1977a; Table 27). The figure for seventeen-year-olds of both sexes drops sharply to approximately 60%. Most of these young persons can be assumed to have entered the labour market.

On the other hand, a very small percentage of adolescents take advantage of the opportunity to marry. In 1971, 01.7% of males and 07.5% of females between the ages of fifteen and nineteen had married (Statistics Canada, 1973a; Table 1). Of the females, 49.7% had at least one child (Statistics Canada, 1973b; Table 24). This last figure indicates the importance of pregnancy as grounds for marriage in adolescence. When one recalls that in 1975 the median age at first marriage among females was 21.5 years and among males 23.6 years, it is readily apparent that marriage is concentrated in the immediate post-adolescent years (Statistics Canada, 1977c; Table 3).

CONCLUSIONS

What are the answers to the questions raised at the beginning of this dicussion? Does the evidence indicate that minimum age requirements are related to the capabilities of the young? The answer would seem to be a tentative yes, but this reply must be qualified by the nature of the capabilities implied in the law. The minimum age limitations on the acquisition of social roles that make an important difference in the life of the adolescent, such as employment and marriage, seem to be set in terms of biological and intellectual development. In particular, the minimum ages for marriage of twelve to sixteen for girls and fourteen to sixteen for boys appear to reflect the likelihood that pregnancy can occur. On the other hand, minimum age limitations on acquiring social roles of less immediate relevance to most adolescents are consistently set at a later age. These more conservative age limits would seem to reflect a definition of capability based on social maturity. In general the important social roles with lower age limits involve social responsibilities and the less relevant social activities with higher limits rights or privileges, although the relationship is not entirely consistent.

The explanation for the relatively low age limits on marrying or seeking employment seems to lie in traditional social norms that support both early marriage and adolescent employment when there is a socially recognized need, such as pregnancy or economic hardship. Simply a strong desire on the part of adolescents to marry or to enter the job market is also widely supported as sufficient grounds for allowing them to do so. The persistence of these norms is no doubt due, at least in part, to the fact that adolescents, their families, and authorities who deal with adolescents each perceive them as relating to their individual self-interest in some circumstances.

The higher minimum age limits placed on less relevant activities, such as voting, drinking in public establishments, or attending adults only movies seem to reflect the fact that there are no traditional social norms supporting adolescent participation in these types of activities. The absence of normative support for lower age limitations when associated with a low level of self-interest on the part of adolescents has provided the social context for the limitations currently imposed.

Regarding the question of consistency in the various minimum age limitations, the answer is that they are inconsistent. This inconsistency is reflected not so much in age limitations relating to the more relevant and less relevant obligations and rights taken separately, but in the age differences between them. Adolescents are permitted to take on important social obligations years before they obtain ordinary adult rights and privileges. The apparent widespread acceptance of this situation seems to reflect a general apathy on the part of adolescents regarding issues such as voting rights, as well as their ability to circumvent age limitations in matters such as drinking in public establishments and attending adults only movies.

About half of adolescents take advantage of the opportunity to seek employment, but only a small percentage seize the opportunity to marry. In many cases teenage marriages are the result of pregnancy. The fact that adolescents tend not to assume these two important social roles, even though they are legally entitled to do so, highlights the extent to which social expectations rather than laws serve to define the ages at which young persons take on these responsibilities.

Footnotes

1. *Many thanks to Daniel Kubat and K. Ishwaran for comments on an earlier version of this paper and to Beverly Bell-Rowbotham for assistance in obtaining statistical data.*
2. *The discussion of physical development, sexual development, and the secular trend is based on Tanner (1975).*
3. *The discussion of intellectual development is based on Muuss (1975a) and Dulit (1975).*
4. *Young persons may request a discharge prior to the end of their three year enlistment, but must ordinarily serve nine months as a minimum.*

References

Anstett, Andrne and Terence Qualter
1976 "Election systems," in Bellamy, David, J., John H. Pammett and Donald C. Rowat (eds.) *The Provincial Political Systems: Comparative Essays.* Toronto: Methuen Publications.
1977 Canadian Almanac & Directory. Toronto: Copp-Clark.

Dulit, Everett
1975 "Adolescent thinking à la Piaget." Pp. 536-556 in R.E. Grinder (ed.), *Studies in Adolescence: A Book of Readings in Adolescent Development.* New York: Macmillan.

Jennings, W.H.
1972 *Canadian Law.* Toronto: McGraw-Hill Ryerson.

Mitchell, John J.
1975 *The Adolescent Predicament.* Toronto: Holt, Rinehart and Winston of Canada.

Muuss, Rolf E.
1975a *Theories of Adolescence.* 3rd ed. New York: Random House.

Muuss, Rolf E.
1975b "Adolescent development and the secular trend." Pp. 56-68 in R.E. Muuss (ed.), *Adolescent Behavior and Society: A Book of Readings.* 2nd ed. New York: Random House.

Qualter, Terence H.
1970 *The Election Process in Canada.* Toronto: McGraw-Hill.

Statistics Canada
1973a 1971 Census of Canada. Population: Marital Status by Age Groups. Catalogue 92-730 Vol. I Part: 4 (Bulletin 1:4-2). Ottawa. April.

1973b 1971 Census of Canada. Population: Women Ever Married by Number of Children Born. Catalogue 92-718 Vol. I Part: 2 (Bulletin 1:2-6). Ottawa. October.

1977a Education in Canada: A Statistical Review for 1974-75 and 1975-76. Catalogue 81-229. Ottawa. July.

1977b The Labour Force — December, 1976. Catalogue 71-001. Ottawa. January.

1977c Vital Statistics Vol. II: Marriages and Divorces — 1975. Catalogue 84-205. Ottawa. July.

Tanner, J.M.

1975 "Sequence, Tempo, and Individual Variation in the Growth and Development of Boys and Girls Aged Twelve to Sixteen." Pp. 502-522 in R.E. Grinder (ed.), *Studies in Adolescence: A Book of Readings in Adolescent Development.* New York: Macmillan.

Gender Socialization in Childhood and Adolescence

MARLENE MACKIE
Department of Sociology
University of Calgary

METHODOLOGICAL CONSIDERATIONS

Before proceeding, several general observations must be made about the literature in this area. The first concerns the somewhat confusing vocabulary. "Sex" refers to the physiological differences between males and females. "Gender," on the other hand, is a "socio-cultural-sociological-psychological fact." (Lipman-Blumen & Tickamyer, 1975: 302). It involves the psychological and cultural definitions of masculinity and femininity which have been erected upon the anatomical distinctions. According to Green (1974), gender has three dimensions: the conviction of being male or female, the culturally learned behavior that is appropriate to the gender, and the preference for male or female sexual partners. Although considerable controversy surrounds the precise linkages between sex and gender, most authorities (Ambert, 1976: 69; Chafetz, 1974: 4) consider the latter to be learned rather than innate.[2] Finally, "sex roles" is generally used to refer to the societal scripts or standards for appropriate masculine and feminine attitudes, temperament, and behavior. Despite the currency of the term, Lopata's (1976: 172) objection seems well-founded:

> I am very uncomfortable with the concept of sex roles; what seem to exist in [our] society are not social *roles* of men or women but a pervasive sexual identity which affects all, or almost all, social roles. (Emphasis in original.)

The purpose of this paper is to explore the processes of gender socialization in childhood and adolescence and to consider the consequences of sex-typing for adult men and women. Although the topic has been approached from a variety of disciplines[1], the emphasis here will be social psychological. Special attention will be given to the available Canadian literature.

It should also be remembered that sex role prescriptions for behavior are not necessarily how people actually behave (Keller, 1975: 2). That is, the societal expectation that women should be warm and sympathetic does not necessarily describe how women do indeed relate to others.

A second problem is the literature's tendency to exaggerate differences between the sexes and to overlook important human similarities (Tresemer, 1975). This distortion stems partly from journals' reluctance to publish studies which failed to find differences, and partly from researchers' attempts to rectify social sciences' historical neglect of women. Although feminists have alerted us to the arbitrariness of much of the content of sex roles and the resulting victimization of women, we must be aware of this bias.

The difficulties resulting from polarization of male-female distinctions have been compounded by constricted samples. When there is insufficient knowledge of the variability of definitions by culture and sub-culture, region, social class, ethnicity, and religion, the gender differences found in the American middle-class are apt to be unduly emphasized. This hopefully temporary situation is especially acute for Canadian scholars. Williams (1975) warns us against assuming that American and Canadian child-rearing patterns are identical. Tomeh (1975: 79) suggests that Canadian youth socialization practices are more traditional than their American counterparts. A great deal of work remains to be done before Canadian-American differences are documented and before we understand the demographic correlates of gender socialization within our own country.

SEX ROLE DIFFERENCES

Gender role socialization involves the processes through which individuals learn to become masculine and feminine, according to the expectations current in their particular society. Because they are abstract guides to behavior, the exact specification of Canadian sex role norms does not present the sociologist with an easy task. However, the organization of the pivotal family and work institutions indicates that men are expected to work outside the home, marry, and support their families, while women are expected to marry, carry the major responsibility for childrearing, and rely on men for financial support and social status. For women, attracting a suitable mate takes priority over serious occupational commitment. These future adult activities require cultivation of appropriate skills, attitudes, and comportment in children. Indeed, in a cross-cultural survey of sex differences in socialization, Barry et al. (1957) reported that most societies emphasize nurturance and responsibility in the socialization of girls and independence and achievement in the socialization of boys. Greenglass (1973: 110) suggests that attributes such as independence, aggressiveness, and competitiveness are encouraged in boys because they are essential for their future occupational success. Girls, on the other hand, are expected to derive their self-esteem from heterosexual relationships. Consequently, attributes such as dependency, passivity, and compliance are rewarded. Considerable attention has been given to Horner's (1969) much-popularized conclusion that women fear success because it threatens their femininity. However, follow-up studies have found that males also fear success. (See Kimball, 1977; *Journal of Sex Roles*, entire September, 1976 issue.)

Although the empirical content of Canadian sex roles could ideally be established by systematic study of how men and women behave, and the reactions elicited by nonconformity, the best available indicators are stereotype studies which describe the traits which people *believe* typify males and females. The actual truth-value of the imagery is, of course, another matter.

Sex Stereotypes

The author's study (Mackie, 1971) of 300 Edmonton, Alberta adults found that only 2% of the sample were unable to comply with the instructions to supply adjectives describing "women in general." As Table 1 shows, women are seen to be socio-emotional specialists and their identity is perceived to revolve about their relationship with men. They are either guardians of an established family or heeding the dictates of the fashion world in order to attract men. Although these results are similar to Broverman et al.'s (1972) findings that Americans assign an expressive cluster of traits to females and a competence-independence cluster to males, the Canadian sample also ascribed some of the latter characteristics to women.

TABLE 1
OPEN ENDED DESCRIPTION OF "WOMEN IN GENERAL," N = 300

Traits	% N
Concerned with family responsibilities	37.7
Warm, nurturant	29.0
Extroverted/talkative	27.9
Emotional	25.6
Fashion conscious	24.2
Ambitious	17.2
Attractive, sexy	16.2
Dominating	13.5
Cold, manipulative	13.1
Competent workers	11.8
Submissive	9.8

Mackie, 1971

Lambert's (1969) questionnaire study of the sex role imagery of 7,500 Canadian children, 10 to 16 years old, established that children are aware of differential societal expectations for masculinity and femininity. He measured perception of sex role differentiation in terms of appropriate traits, behavior, tasks, and peer and authority relations. Boys were considerably more traditional in their thinking about the sexes than were girls. Among Lambert's many interesting observations, perhaps the most important is his proposition that children perceive greater differences between males and females generally when the sex distinction is pivotal to the organization of their own family.

Children's sex stereotyping of occupations is a key dimension of their knowledge of the societal script for masculinity and femininity because internalization of these beliefs may unduly restrict their future occupational choices. Schlossberg and Goodman (1972) discovered that five-year-old kindergarten children had already learned the traditional sex norms for occupational achievement. When these children were asked to set occupational goals, 83% of the girls and 97% of the boys chose occupations consistent with the traditional sex norms. Barty (1971) (described in Kimball, 1977) found that when 10 to 13-year-old Vancouver students were asked to choose between being a doctor and being a nurse, 70% of the girls chose to be a nurse, while 80% of the boys chose to be a doctor. However, sex-typing did not occur when they were asked whether a boy or a girl would win a hypothetical university scholarship.

In summary, a number of studies such as Lambert (1969) and Williams et al. (1975) indicate that children are aware of sex role norms. Although we can assume that these norms have some impact upon their own behavior, recognition and expression of stereotypes in a research setting is not the equivalent of "real life" behavior.

Differential Evaluation of the Sexes

Children learn not only that society has different expectations for males and females, but that the sexes are ranked. Males have more prestige, power, and freedom than females (Chafetz, 1974). According to Vaughter (1976: 128), "the theme that the masculinity of men is more highly valued than the femininity of women is one of the most consistent themes to be found in current research data."

Much of the research on this question concerns evaluation of the performances of men and women. For example, Labovitz (1974) asked 335 University of Calgary students to evaluate a brief description of a sociological study. This same article was attributed to four different fictitious authors in order to determine the extent to which sex and ethnicity influence student reactions. The alleged authors were: Edward Blake (English-Canadian male), Edith Blake (English-Canadian female), Joseph Walking Bear (Canadian Indian), and Marcel Fournier (French-

Canadian). The same work was judged to be of lower quality when it was attributed to a woman than when it was attributed to a man. (However, the non-Anglo Saxon names elicited more critical evaluations than the female name.) American studies (Goldberg, 1968) also show that the performance of females is rated as lower than the performance of males, unless the performance is in a female-stereotyped area (Mischel, 1974), or other special circumstances prevail (Pheterson et al., 1971). Further, success of males is attributed to ability, success of females to luck or effort (Deaux & Emswiller, 1974; Feldman-Summers & Kiesler, 1974).

Both parents and children seem cognizant of the cultural devaluation of females. Many studies (e.g. Markle, 1974) report that couples prefer boys as first- and-only children. If they plan to have more than two children, they want the majority to be boys rather than girls. Markle concluded that the ideology of male superiority was an important determinant of this preference for male offspring. Brown (1957) found that although a significant number of girls wish they were boys, few boys wanted to be girls. Fashion is a symbolic recognition of the sex hierarchy: female fashions often copy male fashions, but the reverse is rare (Chafetz, 1974: 75).

As Keller (1975) points out, the fact that the sexes are culturally ranked as well as differentiated greatly complicates our attempts to understand gender socialization:

> . . .it is not possible, without explicit controls, to determine which findings reflect the differential training and experience of the sexes, and which the fact of super- and subordination. Without separating these two dimensions we cannot . . . make inferences about the influence of gender alone (p. 3).

The above discussion has outlined the *content* of the lessons involved in North American gender socialization. In the section to follow, the emphasis will be placed on the *processes* of gender socialization.

THE MECHANISMS OF GENDER SOCIALIZATION

At the present time, the complex literature on the processes of gender socialization is highly speculative. As yet, there is a shortage of studies in natural (as opposed to laboratory) settings, and careful cross-cultural studies are scanty. Although concerted efforts are being made to sort out the roles played by male-female differences in temperament, hormonal levels, and inherent psychological distinctions (Bardwick, 1971), the research so far remains inconclusive.[3] Nevertheless, consensus exists that gender identity is, for the most part, learned not innate, that training begins early[4], and that the family is the primary agent of socialization. Since sex norms are linked with age, standards for appropriate gender behavior vary over the life cycle. Later on, the family's influence is augmented by those of peers, school, mass media, and so on.

Early Childhood Socialization

From the beginning, male and female infants are perceived differently. Indeed, Rubin et al. (1974) suggest that sex-typing begins at birth. These researchers interviewed 30 pairs of parents at a suburban Boston hospital within 24 hours of the birth of their first child. Fifteen of the couples had daughters and fifteen had sons. Infant girls were seen as "softer," "finer," "littler" and boys as "stronger," "firmer," and "more alert," despite hospital records which showed that the male and female infants did not differ on any physical or health measure. Names are the key to selfhood (Denzin, 1972: 306) and personal names classify infants by sex. A feminist's parable of a "Secret Scientific Xperiment" to undermine sex stereotyping tells the tale of a child named "X":

> Once upon a time, a baby named X was born. This baby was named X so that nobody could tell whether it was a boy or a girl. Its parents could tell, of course, but they couldn't tell anybody else (Gould, 1972: 74).

According to Lewis (1972), young infants are handled differently. Girls are cuddled and talked to more; while boys are jostled and played with more roughly. Up to six months of age, boys are handled more than girls, but after that, the amount of handling of male infants diminishes. Goldberg and Lewis (1969) found that the play behavior in year old infants showed sex differences. Girls were more dependent, less exploratory, and quieter in play style. Fox (1977) concludes that early childhood studies of sex role learning show that,

> even as infants, girls are expected to be, taught to be, and rewarded for being quieter, more passive, more controlled — in short, "nicer" babies — than are boys (p. 809).

Parents' choice of toys reinforces their gender expectations. Ambert (1976: 71) says that boy toys "encourage rougher play, activity, creativity, mastery, and curiosity; girl toys, on the other hand, encourage passivity, observation, simple behaviour, and solitary play." Rheingold and Cook (1975) inventoried the contents of the rooms of children from one month to six years of age. Boys' rooms contained toys of more classes than girls' rooms (machines, sports, animal toys, vehicles, educational art, etc.). The toys provided the older boys encouraged activities away from home, while girls' toys encouraged domesticity. Cultural norms, to a certain extent, determine which toys are appropriate for each sex. Toy manufacturers comply with these norms (Chafetz, 1974), and parents supply their children with sex-typed playthings.

Theories of Gender Socialization

Several general explanations of the specific processes involved in gender socialization have been put forth. The social learning position (Mussen, 1969: 713-714) argues that gender behavior is learned through rewards and punishments from the environment. Parents reinforce children for behavior consistent with their notions of societal sex roles (e.g. initiative in boys, passivity in girls) and punish them for inappropriate behavior (e.g. male crying and female aggression). Since many of the lessons of gender are subtle, the position of Kagan (1964) that children identify with adult models, especially parents, and learn through imitation (as well as direct instruction) seems sensible. Sex norms are learned through identification with the parent of the same sex and complementation with the parent of the opposite sex. Mussen and Parker (1965) present evidence for the hypothesis that parents who are warm and nurturant facilitate their children's imitation of them, even without specific instruction or reward for such imitation.

A third perspective upon gender socialization is provided by Kohlberg's (1966) cognitive developmental theory. The emphasis here is the child's need to make sense of his/her cognitive environment. The label "girl" or "boy," applied to self and others, becomes a major organizing cognitive schema and determines attitudes, values, and activities. Conviction of gender identity lends stability to the self-image and structures the social world. Although sex role learning is conceptualized here as a part of the child's cognitive growth, the child is motivated to imitate same-sex models. Clearly, the three general positions outlined above should be viewed as complementary, rather than competing models.

A number of studies show that until puberty, the male role is more inflexible than the female role. That is, more pressure is placed on boys to act like boys, than for girls to act like girls; tomboys are sanctioned less than sissies (Brown, 1957; Fling & Manosevitz, 1972). A recent Canadian study (Berger & Gold, 1976) of problem-solving performance in young children reported that boys have a greater need to differentiate themselves from opposite-sex activities than do girls.

One likely reason for this is the cultural devaluation of femininity and the prestige and privileges accorded males. However, if Lynn's (1969) hypotheses are correct, greater male anxiety over gender points to important differences in male-female gender socialization. Lynn postulates that because of the greater availability of the mother and the relative absence of the father during early childhood, females easily develop their gender identity through imitation and positive reinforcement. However, males must shift from their initial identification with the mother to masculine role identification. Since male models are scarce, they have greater difficulty than females in achieving gender identity. According to Lynn, males must learn through abstractly piecing together the intellectual problem of definitions of masculinity. Some of this learning comes from peers and media presentations of sex stereotypes. Some results from punishment for displays of female behavior. Consequently, males remain anxious over gender. As adults, they are considerably more hostile towards both the opposite sex and homosexuals than are females.

Selected Familial Variables

All of the theories of gender socialization emphasize the role of the parents as either providing same-sex and complementary models to their children or meting out rewards and punishments for appropriate gender behavior. However, the discussion thus far over-simplifies the dynamics of family interaction. Though the available literature is still very limited in scope, a more detailed understanding of gender socialization is provided by studies on the effects of maternal employment, father absence, and siblings.

A number of researchers have compared the gender conceptions of children of housewives with those of children whose mothers are employed, and concluded that the latter children perceive smaller differences between masculine and feminine roles (Etaugh, 1974; Vogel et al., 1970). However, Canadian researchers have reported a social class difference. Gold's (1976) study of 10-year-old children found that while children of employed mothers generally had more equalitarian sex role concepts than those of non-working mothers, sex role distinctions were especially salient for the sons of employed mothers in working-class families. This evidence that the processes of gender socialization may differ in middle-class and working-class homes receives further support from Propper's (1972) survey of Toronto high school students. She reports that fewer sons of working-class employed women choose their father as an adult ideal than sons of non-working mothers from the same social class. Studies of American college (Almquist & Angrist, 1971) and high school students (Rey, 1974) found that females with working mothers have higher work aspirations than do females with nonemployed mothers. However, a recent Canadian study (Brinkerhoff, 1977: 294) reported that "mother's work does not appear to have a great deal of effect on daughters' role innovativeness." The girls still aspired to traditionally female occupations.

Although more research is required to sort out both Canadian-American and social class differences, the general conclusion that children of working mothers hold more flexible sex stereotypes supports the identification theory's position that children pattern their ideas of appropriate gender roles upon the parental behavior they observe. Such observational learning explains Lambert's (1969) finding that children who perceived the sexes as quite different came from homes organized along traditional sex divisions. The fact that in 1973, 35% of

Canadian mothers were in the labor force (Boyd et al., 1976) suggests that a substantial number of children are being exposed to experiences which may lead to some blurring of gender distinctions. Nevertheless, radical changes cannot be predicted. Children are privy to parental behavior in the home, not in the workplace, and women still bear most of the burden of household tasks (Meissner et al., 1975).

The interest in mothers' work has been paralleled by concern with the impact of fathers' absence on male gender development. Research so far indicates that the absence of the father (through death, divorce etc.) has little influence on the sex-typed behavior or masculine identification of sons after age five (Barclay & Cusumano, 1961; Hetherington, 1966). Biller (1971) presents many interesting ideas on this subject which warrant the attention of future researchers. He points out the importance of variables such as mothers' attitudes toward the absent fathers, peer group interaction, and the length and timing of fathers' absence.

Finally, evidence is accumulating that gender socialization involves sibling-sibling as well as parent-child influences. Rosenberg and Sutton-Smith (1968) report that girls with sisters scored significantly higher on the Gough Scale of Psychological Femininity than girls with brothers. Similarly, Brim (1958) found that five and six-year old boys with older brothers were more masculine than boys with older sisters. However, Vroegh (1971) found little evidence that the presence of older like-sex siblings reinforces appropriate gender identity. Finally, Kammeyer (1967) discovered a relationship between birth order and traditional gender behavior. First-born girls tended to be more traditional than later-born girls. (However, Rosenberg and Sutton-Smith (1968) reported that birth order did not affect femininity scores.)

Mass Media
Though the family is the primary agent of gender socialization, its influence is augmented by those of mass media, school, church, peers, etc. Because the sex stereotypes portrayed in the media (though not the actual influence processes) are easily accessible to measurement, many studies exist on this topic. The one exception is television, where the author was unable to locate any Canadian studies and only one American one (Sternglanz & Serbin, 1974). These authors' analysis of children's programs found twice as many male as female characters. The males were portrayed as aggressive, the females as deferent. The research on children's books shows characters engaged in "highly stereotyped sex role behavior, a preponderance of male images, and an emphasis on variety and creativity in male portrayals not found in female characterizations" (Lipman-Blumen & Tickamyer, 1975: 304). Pyke's (1975) survey of 150 children's books reported that females are

not shown to work outside the home: the "perennial apron is their trademark and is worn even by female squirrels" (p. 68). Weitzman et al. (1972) also found rigid sex role definitions, with males in the instrumental roles, and females in the expressive roles. Wilson (1978) analyzed *Chatelaine* and *Maclean's* magazines over a 40 year period. Very few fictional heroines were pictured as employed and almost never if they had children. Brabant (1976) reports sex stereotyping in the Sunday newspaper comics. Studies such as the above have been widely publicized and some attempts are being made to reduce sex stereotyping in media content. Dargauel (1976) examined 131 Anglophone Canadian libraries and discovered that although children's librarians consider the issue of sexism in children's literature to be an important one, 96% of these libraries had no formal policy on the acquisition of books which avoid sex role stereotyping.

School

The classroom experiences of children are a further source of gender socialization which reinforce sex distinctions (Baumrind, 1972; Saario et al., 1970). The *Report of the Royal Commission on the Status of Women in Canada* (1970) analyzed the sex role imagery in a representative selection of anglophone and francophone elementary school textbooks. The Commission reported that "a woman's creative and intellectual potential is either underplayed or ignored in the education of children from the earliest years" (p. 175). The versatile characters who have adventures are seldom women. The sex-typing even appeared in arithmetic books, with children being presented with problems such as this: "A girl spent one-quarter of an hour sewing and one-quarter of an hour reading. What number of hours did she spend sewing and reading?" (p. 175). Although the curriculum is the same, with the exception of home economics and shop classes, the textbook models provide children with clearly differentiated sex imagery.

Several studies suggest that teachers behave differently towards young male and female students. Serbin and O'Leary (1975) observed nursery school children, and reported that teachers encouraged aggression and assertiveness in boys and passivity in girls. In the early years, children mostly confront female teachers who model feminine patterns for them. Fagot and Patterson (1969) report that female teachers reinforce feminine behavior for nursery school children of both sexes. However, for boys, the reinforcement from family and peers counters teachers' reinforcement and maintains masculine behavior. A longitudinal study of middle-class anglophone Montreal children from kindergarten through grade five (Lester, Dudek & Muir, 1972) also found elementary school to be a congenial atmosphere for girls. The authors suggest that girls' higher academic achievement was related to male-female personality differences measured by the Cattell Personality Questionnaire. Girls were more obedient, dependent, sober-minded, quiet, practical, and realistic; boys were more assertive, independent, excitable, happy-go-lucky, and free-thinking. (Though these feminine traits give girls the advantage in their early schooling, their functionality is short-lived.) Finally, the counselling of students appears to be sex biased (Pietrofesa & Schlossberg, 1972). Lambert (1969: 63) says that the educational and vocational counselling girls receive results in their consignment "either to the role of housewife or to one of a very few occupations."

Play

Though some references to the topic have been made in the foregoing, little systematic information is available on the undoubtedly important role children's peers play in their gender socialization. However, the segregation of children into same-sex groups and the sex-typed nature of their play activities has provoked some discussion. Keller (1975) suggests that,

> by keeping the sexes apart and away from certain life experiences, each is reinforced in its partial view of the world and its limited identity (p. 22).

Such sex segregation permits contrived fictions about the opposite sex to survive untested. Moreover, the actual play activities differentially socialize children. Although empirical support is required, Ambert's (1976) observations are worth quoting:

> Girls tend to congregate in small groups in which a considerable amount of time is devoted to verbalizing and socializing. The games they engage in do not require the codification of complex rules nor much team coordination. Little "bonding" is encouraged in little girls' games while much more of it is forced on the boys because of the very nature of their activities. Male games act as anticipatory socialization elements towards their future occupational, economic, and political roles: they require mastery, social coordination, striving, and competition based on achievement. . . . Girls activities sharpen their sociability, interpersonal and affective skills to the detriment of their mastery, intellectual, and decision-making skills (p. 79).

One might also speculate that boys' greater participation in organized team sports accustoms them to accepting criticism of their performance. As adults, they may be in a better position than women to benefit from criticism without too many hurt feelings.

The above section has considered only some of the major mechanisms of gender socialization. Probably the only area where empirical data are not urgently required is the measurement of media sex stereotypes. We need much more detailed knowledge of adult-child and child-child interaction, particularly opposite sex influences. Moreover, the cultural expectations (and evaluations) of gender roles are also conveyed by the masculine-oriented organization of politics (McCormack, 1975), religion, the economy, etc. We can do little more, at this point, than speculate about its subtle effects on children. Finally, symbolic interactionists tell us that language is a crucial determinant of the self-concept. Canadian children are immersed in languages which differentiate the sexes. In the case of the English language, linguistic disparities reflect the social inequality of men and women (Lakoff, 1975).

GENDER SOCIALIZATION IN ADOLESCENCE

The volatile period of adolescence is marked by pressure to solve the problems of "Who am I?" and "What shall I become?" As adolescents mature into creatures with sexual urges, masculinity/femininity becomes an increasingly more fundamental component of their identity. Moreover, the decisions they make at this time carry life-long consequences and these decisions are made within the context of societal sex role expectations.

As children reach the teenage years, they are exposed to more complex and more precisely defined norms of sex-appropriate behavior (Kohlberg, 1966). Whereas the pressures for sex-appropriate behavior in early childhood were relatively stronger for boys than for girls, such pressures become stronger for girls at puberty. Tomboyish behavior is no longer tolerated. Longitudinal research (Brun-Gulbrandsen, 1971) shows that teenagers are more rigid in their notions of masculinity and femininity than are elementary school children. Peer groups are vital to adolescents and appropriate gender behavior is one of the most important criteria of acceptance (Ambert, 1976: 78).

Male and female adolescent interests become increasingly differentiated as their future aspirations crystallize. Although both sexes must prepare themselves for some occupation, males view work as a life commitment. For females, on the other hand, work is often viewed as a temporary matter and attracting a suitable mate takes priority over protracted occupational training. Douvan and Adelson's (1966) national U.S. survey showed that while male-female attitudes in early adolescence were similar, within a few years, boys were focusing on occupational success and girls on social success.

Although the situation may be changing under the influence of the feminist movement, two recent Canadian studies (Brinkerhoff, 1977; Kimball, 1977) suggest that adolescent females are still charting their destiny according to traditional sex role patterns. Even much of the trouble adolescents have with the law seems to revolve around problems in establishing gender identity. Most teenage delinquents are male and a good part of this activity is involved with "establishing their 'masculine' prowess and independence" (Chafetz, 1974: 63). According to Clark and Haurek (1966), male offences involving risk and aggressiveness increase to mid-adolescence, perhaps because these acts are seen as a testimonial to masculinity, and then decrease as the anxiety surrounding masculine identity decreases in later adolescence. Though larceny is the most frequent offence for both sexes, boys appear in court for burglary, auto theft, and vandalism, while girls are charged with sexual immorality, truancy, or "unmanageable" behavior (Landau, 1975).

Although gender socialization does not, of course, stop with adolescence, male-female differences appear to be most salient during this stage. Less sex stereotyped behavior is permitted later on, particularly after the reproductive years. However, the fate of most adults was decided by their adolescent experiences.

DEMOGRAPHIC VARIATIONS IN GENDER ROLE SOCIALIZATION

Canadian society is a heterogeneous one, with ethnic, social class, and regional differences in family processes which might well influence gender socialization. Though much more work needs to be done, we do have some indication of the general relationship between gender socialization and social class (along with education), rural versus urban residence, and French-Canadian versus English-Canadian family environments.

Social Class[5]
Lambert's (1969) study of sex role imagery in Canadian children found parents' education and socioeconomic status to be strongly related to their (the parents') perception of sex roles. The less the education and the lower the social class, the more traditional were the views. Lambert's finding regarding social class is in accord with Mussen (1969: 711) who states that lower class children were aware of sex role patterns earlier, and they conform to these preferences more clearly than do middle class children. Gaskell (1975) reports that working-class high school girls have more traditional sex role ideologies concerning division of labor in the home and the desirability of change in sex roles. The reason for this well-established relationship seems to be the more patriarchal patterns in working-class homes (Hall & Keith, 1964).

Rural-Urban Residence
When Lambert (1969) analyzed sex role imagery in terms of rural-urban residence, he found no relationship whatsoever. He concludes that,

the mass media and centralized schooling have presumably urbanized even the nominally rural, so that there is no sign that people outside the cities cling to traditional conceptions of the sexes (p. 26).

French-Canadian versus English-Canadian Patterns
Sociologists are well aware of the distinctions between the English-

Canadian and the French-Canadian family (Tomeh, 1975: 75), and possible differences in their sex role ideologies have been explored. Though the French-Canadian family is developing equalitarianism in husband-wife and parent-child relations (Tremblay, 1966), French-Canadian attitudes differ from English-Canadian ones, often in unexpected ways.

Lambert (1969) reported that while French-Canadian children had less differentiated views of appropriate gender behavior than did English-Canadian children, the latters' parents were less traditional than French-Canadian parents. Lambert suggests that the parental difference may stem from the lower educational level of this sample of French-Canadian adults. The English-Canadian/French-Canadian parental difference was reversed in Lambert et al.'s (1971) analysis of working class parents' reactions to a taped version of a child's demands for attention, help, and comfort and displays of anger and insolence etc. Here, although both French-Canadian and English-Canadian parents demanded more of boys than of girls, the French-Canadians perceived fewer sex role differences than did the English-Canadians. However, there is some evidence to support the proposition that French-Canadians remain quite traditional about gender relations where the family is concerned. In his study of college students, Hobart (1973) discovered that French-Canadian students continue to expect a clear differentiation of mother and father parental roles. Boyd's (1975) analysis of Gallup Poll results found that French-Canadians entertain two attitudinal complexes with respect to women. They support equality between the sexes, but only when the mother and husband images are not evoked by the Gallup questions. When these roles become salient, French-Canadians become more traditional in their attitudes towards women. Obviously, it is impossible at this point to draw any firm conclusions about how gender socialization processes differ in French-Canadian and English-Canadian homes.[6]

CONSEQUENCES OF GENDER SOCIALIZATION

Although some of the causal links between early gender socialization and sex-typed adult behavior remain conjectural, successful internalization of stereotyped masculine and feminine identities results in neither sex fully developing its human potential. The costs are especially high for women, whose life chances are constructed by both their own internalized barriers and the ideology of male supremacy. More specifically, women's adult roles and experiences are more limited than men's because of their metamorphosis into dependent, noncompetitive specialists in social relationships, as well as the external barriers of discriminatory policies, sex-typing of jobs, and lack of role models (Lipman-Blumen & Tickamyer, 1975: 305).

The range of women's adult roles is much narrower than men's, and their lack of competence in society's instrumental roles places them at a disadvantage (Baumrind, 1972). Lack of training and lack of self-confidence leaves them "ill-equipped to cope with an increasingly complicated world" (Keller, 1975: 17). Despite their earlier success in school, substantially fewer Canadian women than men, aged 16 to 24 years, attend school or university (Robb & Spencer, 1976: 65). Regardless of their abilities, the majority of women are channeled into the housewife role, either on a full time or part time basis. Most of the women who also work outside the home are concentrated in a small number of low-skilled, poorly paid jobs (Armstrong & Armstrong, 1975). Their occupations are congruent with traditional sex role learning and primarily nurturant and person-centered (Klemmack & Edwards, 1975: 511).

The problem goes beyond the fact that most women are denied access to the challenging work and experiences available to many men. Adherence to the traditional feminine role appears to produce frustration, unhappiness and personal maladjustment for some women (Bem, 1975). Although more research is needed to establish just how widespread this situation is, the following studies suggest that a very real problem does exist. Cumming et al. (1975) compared the suicide rates of British Columbia women who work with those of women who do not, and found that work outside the home offers protection from suicide. For women (but not men), adoption of highly "appropriate" sex role identification is associated with low self-esteem (Stericker & Johnson, 1977). Connell and Johnson (1970) concluded that the male role may have reward value in itself, whether adopted by a male or a female.

Despite suggestions that the masculine role is healthy for both sexes (Broverman et al., 1970; Connell & Johnson, 1970), a number of scholars (Balswick & Peek, 1971; Pleck & Sawyer, 1974) are calculating the costs of sex typing for males. The gender boundaries are more inflexible and the pressure to conform stronger for young boys than young girls. However, realization is growing that masculinity, as defined by our society, also restricts adults. Insistence that males achieve, be aggressive, and competitive and prescriptions against emotional expression create considerable stress. Jourard (1974) talks of the "lethal aspects of the male role" and suggests that the "male self-structure will not allow man to acknowledge or to express the entire breadth and depth of his inner experience, to himself or to others" (p. 22). The higher male adult suicide rates and earlier death rates may be, in part, consequences of gender socialization.

Women's (and men's) liberation groups, academicians and Canadian young people (Kallen & Kelner, 1976) all appreciate the fact that traditional sex stereotypes are arbitrary and damaging. Although the difficulties inherent in altering cultural values and familial behavior cannot be under-estimated, thought is being given to healthier definitions of masculinity and femininity (Bem, 1975), and to the possibility that adult gender identities are not immutable (Tresemer, 1975). Nevertheless, the ambiguity surrounding proper masculine and feminine behavior is bound to produce confusion in gender socialization patterns well into the foreseeable future.

Footnotes

1. *For a summary of the sex differences literature from biology, anthropology, and sexology see Lipman-Blumen and Tickamyer (1975).*
2. *This emphasis upon environmental, as opposed to biological influences accords with feminist movement proclivities to change the social world.*
3. *Maccoby and Jacklin (1974) systematically reviewed over 1,400 sex difference studies in the area of psychology. They identified only four areas of consistent differences — boys' greater aggressiveness and mathematical and visual-spatial abilities, girls' greater verbal ability. They dismissed many myths and failed to draw firm conclusions in many areas.*
4. *Mussen (1969: 710) uses evidence of people born with genital anomalies to emphasize the importance of the early years for gender socialization. He says that "attempts to reassign sex in accordance with predominant physical attributes are usually unsuccessful and may result in severe psychological stress, unless the change is made before the child is two years old" (emphasis in original).*
5. *Social class variations were also discussed under the section "Selected Familial Variables."*
6. *Almost no research seems to have been published which directly addresses the problem of gender socialization in Canada's many other ethnic groups. However, Danziger's (1976) observations on the acculturation of Italian immigrant children may have wider applicability. He reports that, "whether it is a question of role specialization or of individual autonomy, traditional patterns affect the girl more than they do her brothers." He attributes this to the "special importance that the immigrant group attaches to the maintenance of strong and reliable family ties" (p. 211).*

References

Almquist, Elizabeth M., and Shirley S. Angrist
  1971 "Role model influences on college women's career aspirations." Pp. 301-323 in Athena Theodore (ed.), *The Professional Woman.* Cambridge, Mass.: Schenkman.

Ambert, Anne-Marie
  1976 *Sex Structure,* 2nd Ed. Don Mills: Longman Canada.

Armstrong, Hugh, and Pat Armstrong
  1975 "The segregated participation of women in the Canadian labour force, 1941-71." *The Canadian Review of Sociology and Anthropology* 12 (November, Pt. 1): 370-384.

Balswick, Jack, and Charles Peek
1971   "The inexpressive male: a tragedy of American society."
        Family Coordinator 20: 363-368.

Barclay, A., and D.R. Cusumano
1961   "Father absence, cross-sex identity and field-dependent
        behavior in male adolescents." *Child Development* 38: 243-
        250.

Bardwick, Judith
1971   *Psychology of Women: A Study of Bio-Cultural Conflicts.*
        New York: Harper & Row.

Barry, Herbert, Margaret K. Bacon and Irwin L. Child
1957   "A cross-cultural survey of some sex differences in socializa-
        tion." *Journal of Abnormal and Social Psychology* 55: 327-
        338.

Barty, M.
1971   "Fear of success." Unpublished manuscript.

Baumrind, Diana
1972   "From each according to her ability." *School Review* 80: 161-
        197.

Bem, Sandra L.
1975   "Sex-role adaptability: one consequence of psychological
        androgyny." *Journal of Personality and Social Psychology*
        31: 634-643.

Berger, Charlene, and Dolores Gold
1976   "The relation between sex-role identification and problem-
        solving performance in young boys and girls." Paper pre-
        sented at Research for Women: Current Projects and Future
        Directions, An Interdisciplinary Conference, Mount Saint
        Vincent University, Halifax, Nova Scotia.

Biller, Henry B.
1971   *Father, Child and Sex Role.* Lexington, Mass.: D.C. Heath.

Boyd, Monica
1975   "English-Canadian and French-Canadian attitudes toward
        women: results of the Canadian Gallup polls." *Journal of
        Comparative Family Studies* 6: 153-169.

Boyd, Monica, Margrit Eichler, and John R. Hofley
1976   "Family: functions, formation, and fertility." Pp. 13-52 in Gail
        C.A. Cook (ed.), *Opportunity for Choice: A Goal for Women
        in Canada.* Ottawa: Information Canada.

Brabant, Sarah
1976 "Sex role stereotyping in the Sunday comics." *Sex Roles 2*: 331-337.

Brim, Orville
1958 "Family structure and sex role learning by children: a further analysis of Helen Koch's data." *Sociometry* 21: 1-16.

Brinkerhoff, Merlin B.
1977 "Women who want to work in a man's world: a study of the influence of structural factors on role innovativeness." *Canadian Journal of Sociology* 2: 283-303.

Broverman, I.K., D.M. Broverman, F.E. Clarkson, P.S. Rosenkrantz, and S.R. Vogel
1970 "Sex-role stereotypes and clinical judgments of mental health." *Journal of Consulting Psychology* 34: 1-7.

Broverman, I.K., S.R. Vogel, D.M. Broverman, F.E. Clarkson, and P.S. Rosenkrantz
1972 "Sex role stereotypes: a current appraisal." *Journal of Social Issues* 28: 59-78.

Brown, D.G.
1957 "Masculinity-femininity development in children." *Journal of Consulting Psychology* 21: 197-202.

Brun-Gulbrandsen, Sverre
1971 "Sex roles and the socialization process." Pp. 59-78 in Edmund Dahlstrom (ed.), *The Changing Roles of Men and Women*. Boston: Beacon Press.

Canada.
1970 *Report of the Royal Commission on the Status of Women in Canada.* Ottawa: Information Canada.

Chafetz, Janet Saltzman
1974 *Masculine/Feminine or Human?* Itasca, Illinois: Peacock.

Clark, John P., and Edward W. Haurek
1966 "Age and sex roles of adolescents and their involvement in misconduct: a reappraisal." *Sociology and Social Research* 50: 495-508.

Connell, David M., and James E. Johnson
1970 "Relationship between sex role identification and self-esteem in early adolescents." *Developmental Psychology* 3: 268.

Cumming, Elaine, Charles Lazer, and Lynne Chisholm
1975 "Suicide as an index of role strain among employed and not employed women in British Columbia." *The Canadian*

Review of Sociology and Anthropology 12 (November, Pt. 1): 462-470.

Danziger, Kurt
1976   "The acculturation of Italian immigrant girls." Pp. 200-212 in K. Ishwaran (ed.), *The Canadian Family*, Rev. Ed. Toronto: Holt, Rinehart & Winston.

Dargauel, G.J.
1976   "Sex-role stereotyping and children's librarians." *Emergency Librarian* 4: 20-23.

Deaux, K., and T. Emswiller
1974   "Explanations of performance on sex-linked tasks: what's skill for the male is luck for the female." *Journal of Personality and Social Psychology* 29: 80-85.

Denzin, Norman K.
1972   "The genesis of self in early childhood." *The Sociological Quarterly* 13: 291-314.

Douvan, Elizabeth, and Joseph Adelson
1966   *The Adolescent Experience.* New York: Wiley & Sons.

Etaugh, Claire
1974   "Effects of maternal employment on children, a review of recent research." *Merrill-Palmer Quarterly* 20: 71-98.

Fagot, Beverly I., and Gerald R. Patterson
1969   "An *in vivo* analysis of reinforcing contingencies for sex-role behaviors in the preschool child." *Developmental Psychology* 1: 563-568.

Feldman-Summers, S., and S.B. Kiesle
1974   "Those who are number two try harder: the effects of sex on attributions of causality." *Journal of Personality and Social Psychology* 30: 846-855.

Fling, Sheila and Martin Manosevitz
1972   "Sex typing in nursery school children's play interests." *Developmental Psychology* 7: 146-152.

Fox, Greer Litton
1977   " 'Nice girl:' social control of women through a value construct." *Signs* 2: 805-817.

Gaskell, Jane S.
1975   "Sex-role ideology of working class girls." *The Canadian Review of Sociology and Anthropology* 12 (November, Part 1): 453-461.

Gold, Dolores
1976 "Full-time employment of mothers in relation to their 10-year-old children." Paper presented at Research for Women: Current Projects and Future Directions, An Interdisciplinary Conference, Mount Saint Vincent University, Halifax, Nova Scotia.

Goldberg, Philip A.
1968 "Are men prejudiced against women?" *Transaction* 5: 28-30.

Goldberg, Susan, and Michael Lewis
1969 "Play behavior in the year-old infant: early sex differences." *Child Development* 40: 21-31.

Gould, Lois
1972 "X: a fabulous child's story." *Ms.* 1 (December): 74-76, 105-106.

Green, Richard
1974 *Sexual Identity Conflicts in Children and Adults.* New York: Basic Books.

Greenglass, Esther
1973 "The psychology of women; or, the high cost of achievement." Pp. 108-118 in Marylee Stephenson (ed.), *Women in Canada.* Toronto: New Press.

Hall, Marjorie, and Robert A. Keith
1964 "Sex-role preference among children of upper and lower social class." *Journal of Social Psychology* 62: 101-110.

Hetherington, Mavis E.
1966 "Effects of paternal absence on sex-typed behaviors in Negro and white preadolescent males." *Journal of Personality and Social Psychology* 4: 87-91.

Hobart, C.W.
1973 "Attitudes toward parenthood among Canadian young people." *Journal of Marriage and the Family* 35: 93-101.

Horner, Matina
1969 "Fail: bright women." *Psychology Today* 3: 36, 38, 62.

Jourard, Sidney M.
1974 "Some lethal aspects of the male role." Pp. 21-29 in Joseph H. Pleck and Jack Sawyer (eds.), *Men and Masculinity.* Englewood Cliffs, N.J.: Prentice-Hall.

Kagan, J.
1964 "The acquisition and significance of sex-typing." In M.

Hoffman (ed.), *Review of Child Development Research*, Vol. 1. New York: Russell Sage Foundation.

Kallen, Evelyn, and Merrijoy Kelner
1976 "Parents and peers: who influences student values?" Pp. 213-226 in K. Ishwaran (ed.), *The Canadian Family*, Rev. Ed. Toronto: Holt, Rinehart & Winston.

Kammeyer, K.
1967 "Sibling position and the feminine role." *Journal of Marriage and the Family* 29: 494-499.

Keller, Suzanne
1975 *Male and Female: A Sociological View.* Morristown, N.J.: General Learning Press.

Kimball, Meredith M.
1977 "Women and success: a basic conflict?" Pp. 73-89 in Marylee Stephenson (ed.), *Women in Canada*, Rev. Ed. Don Mills: General Publishing Co.

Klemmack, David L., and John N. Edwards
1975 "Women's acquisition of stereotyped occupational aspirations." *Sociology and Social Research* 57: 510-525.

Kohlberg, L.A.
1966 "A cognitive-developmental analysis of children's sex-role concepts and attitudes." Pp. 82-172 in Eleanor Maccoby (ed.), *The Development of Sex Differences.* Stanford, California: Stanford University Press.

Kuhn, Manford H.
1960 "Self-attitudes by age, sex, and professional training." *Sociological Quarterly* 9: 39-55.

Labovitz, Sanford
1974 "Some evidence of Canadian ethnic, racial, and sexual antagonism." *The Canadian Review of Sociology and Anthropology* 11: 247-254.

Lakoff, Robin
1975 *Language and Woman's Place.* New York: Harper & Row.

Lambert, Ronald D.
1969 *Sex Role Imagery in Children: Social Origins of Mind.* Studies of the Royal Commission on the Status of Women in Canada. Ottawa: Information Canada.

Lambert, W.E., A. Yackley and R.N. Hein
1971 "Child training values of English Canadian and French

Canadian parents." *Canadian Journal of Behavioural Science* 3: 217-236.

Landau, Barbara
  1975   "The adolescent female offender: our dilemma." *Canadian Journal of Criminology and Corrections* 17: 146-153.

Lester, Eva P., Stephanie Dudek, and Roy C. Muir
  1972   "Sex differences in the performance of school children." *Canadian Psychiatric Association Journal* 17: 273-278.

Lewis, Michael
  1972   "Culture and gender roles: there's no unisex in the nursery." *Psychology Today* (May): 54-57.

Lipman-Blumen, Jean, and Ann R. Tickamyer
  1975   "Sex roles in transition: a ten-year perspective." *Annual Review of Sociology* 1: 297-337.

Lopata, Helena Znaniecki
  1976   "Sociology: review essay." *Signs* 2: 165-176.

Lynn, David B.
  1969   *Parental and Sex Role Identification: A Theoretical Formulation.* Berkeley: McCutchan Publishing Corp.

Maccoby, Eleanor Emmons, and Carol Nagy Jacklin
  1974   *The Psychology of Sex Differences.* Stanford, California: Stanford University Press.

Mackie, Marlene
  1971   "The accuracy of folk knowledge concerning Alberta Indians, Hutterites, and Ukrainians." Unpublished Ph.D. dissertation, University of Alberta.

Markle, Gerald E.
  1974   "Sex ratio at birth: values, variance, and some determinants." *Demography* 11: 131-142.

McCormack, Thelma
  1975   "Toward a nonsexist perspective on social and political change." Pp. 1-33 in Marcia Millman and Rosabeth Moss Kanter (eds.), *Another Voice.* Garden City, N.Y.: Doubleday Anchor Books.

Meissner, Martin, Elizabeth W. Humphreys, Scott M. Meis and William J. Scheu
  1975   "No exit for wives: sexual division of labour and the cumulation of household demands." *The Canadian Review of Sociology and Anthropology* 12 (Nov. Pt. 1): 424-439.

Mischel, H.N.
1974 "Sex bias in the evaluation of professional achievements." *Journal of Educational Psychology* 66: 157-166.

Mussen, Paul H.
1969 "Early sex-role development." Pp. 707-731 in David A. Goslin (ed.), *Handbook of Socialization Theory and Research.* Chicago: Rand McNally.

Mussen, Paul H., and Ann L. Parker
1965 "Mother nurturance and girls' incidental imitative learning." *Journal of Personality and Social Psychology* 2: 94-97.

Pheterson, G.T., S.B. Kiesler, and P.A. Goldberg
1971 "Evaluation of the performance of women as a function of their sex, achievement, and personal history." *Journal of Personality and Social Psychology* 19: 114-118.

Pietrofesa, J.K., and N.K. Schlossberg
1972 "Counselor bias and the female occupational role." Pp. 219-221 in N. Glazer-Malbin and H.Y. Waehrer (eds.), *Counselor Bias and the Female Occupational Role.* Chicago: Rand McNally.

Pleck, Joseph H., and Jack Sawyer (eds.).
1974 *Men and Masculinity.* Englewood Cliffs, N.J.: Prentice-Hall.

Propper, Alice Marcella
1972 "The relationship of maternal employment to adolescent roles, activities, and parental relationships." *Journal of Marriage and the Family* 34: 417-421.

Pyke, S.W.
1975 "Children's literature: conceptions of sex roles." Pp. 51-73 in Robert M. Pike and Elia Zureik (eds.), *Socialization and Values in Canadian Society,* Vol. 11. Toronto: McClelland and Stewart.

Rey, Lucy
1974 "Predicting women's educational aspirations." *Sociological Focus* 7: 99-110.

Rheingold, H.L., and K.V. Cook
1975 "The contents of boys' and girls' rooms as an index of parents' behavior." *Child Development* 46: 459-463.

Robb, A. Leslie, and Byron G. Spencer
1976 "Education: enrolment and attainment." Pp. 53-92 in Gail C.A. Cook (ed.), *Opportunity for Choice: A Goal for Women in Canada.* Ottawa: Information Canada.

Rosenberg, B.G., and B. Sutton-Smith
1968   "Family interaction effects on masculinity-femininity." *Journal of Personality and Social Psychology* 8: 117-120.

Rubin, J.Z., F.J. Provenzano, and Z. Luria
1974   "The eye of the beholder: parents' views on sex of newborns." *American Journal of Orthopsychiatry* 44: 512-519.

Saario T. et al.
1973   "Sex-role stereotyping in public schools." *Harvard Educational Review* 43: 386-416.

Schlossberg, N.K., and J.A. Goodman
1972   "Woman's place: children's sex stereotyping of occupations." *Vocational Guidance Quarterly* 20: 266-270.

Serbin, L.A., and K.D. O'Leary
1975   "How nursery schools teach girls to shut up." *Psychology Today* 9: 56-57, 102-103.

Stericker, Anne B., and James E. Johnson
1977   "Sex-role identification and self-esteem in college students: do men and women differ?" *Sex Roles* 3: 19-26.

Sternglanz, Sarah H., and Lisa A. Serbin
1974   "Sex role stereotyping in children's television programs." *Developmental Psychology* 10: 710-715.

Tomeh, Aida K.
1975   *The Family and Sex Roles.* Toronto: Holt, Rinehart and Winston.

Tremblay, M.A.
1966   "Modèles d'autorité dans la famille Canadiénne-Francaise." *Recherches Sociographiques* 7: 215-230.

Tresemer, David
1975   "Assumptions made about gender roles." Pp. 308-339 in Marcia Millman and Rosabeth Moss Kanter (eds.), *Another Voice.* Garden City, N.Y.: Doubleday Anchor Books.

Vaughter, Reesa M.
        "Psychology: review essay." *Signs* 2: 120-146.

Vogel, Susan R. et al.
1970   "Maternal employment and perception of sex role among college students." *Developmental Psychology* 3: 384-391.

Vroegh, Karen
1971   "The relationship of birth order and sex of siblings to gender role identity." *Developmental Psychology* 4: 407-411.

Weitzman, Lenore J., Deborah Eifles, Elizabeth Hokada, and Catherine Ross
1972 "Sex role socialization in picture books for pre-school children." *American Journal of Sociology* 72: 1125-1150.

Williams, John E., Susan Bennett, and Deborah L. Best
1975 "Awareness and expression of sex stereotypes in young children." *Developmental Psychology* 11: 635-642.

Williams, Tannis M.
1975 "Canadian childrearing patterns and the response of Canadian universities to women as childbearers and childrearers." *Canada's Mental Health* 23 (Special International Women's Year Supplement): 6-9.

Wilson, Susannah J.
1978 "Sex-role socialization and the mass media in Canada: a study of employment characteristics of magazine heroines." Pp. 79-86 in J. Ross Eshleman and Juanne N. Clarke (eds.), *Intimacy, Commitments, and Marriage: Development of Relationships.* Boston: Allyn and Bacon.

The Relationship of Maternal Employment and Sex to Adolescent's Parental Relationships and Participation in Household Tasks and Leisure Activities

ALICE PROPPER
Department of Sociology
York University

This research has two major purposes. One is to examine the effects of maternal employment on some typical activities and parental relationships of youth.[1] Another is to examine the extent of male and female differences on these dimensions. Specifically the analyses deal with youth's participation in household tasks and extracurricular activities, and with youth's parental relationships.

The theoretical underpinning of the study views the nuclear family as a social system with the four interdependent roles of husband-father, wife-mother, son-brother, and daughter-sister. The system of role relationships differs depending on the mother's employment status. A mother who works outside the home has less time for domestic tasks. Thus, her adolescent children might be expected to take increased household responsibilities. If they do, they may have less time available for social and leisure activities, or for taking part-time or summer jobs.

In terms of parental relationships the mother's employment can result in more or less parent-youth conflict. More disagreements are likely if parents encourage more independence, including the freedom

Revision and update of "The Relationship of Maternal Employment to Adolescent Roles, Activities, and Parental Relationships," Journal of Marriage and the Family, 1972, 34, 417-421, by permission of the publisher. The author wishes to thank D. Ayres, E. Douvan, D. Drever, F. Elkin, F. Fasick, K. Lilienstein, K. Ishwaran, V. Marshall, W. Merrick and the Canada Council for their help and encouragement in various phases of the project.

to disagree with parents, when the mother works. Increased conflict can also result if youths feel that doing more household chores entitles them to increased responsibility and freedom in other spheres of life, including the freedom to disagree. On the other hand, if youths are freer to do as they wish, fewer parent-youth conflicts could result.

Perhaps the most central issue is the quality of the parent-youth relationship. Youths may resent being pressured to help with household chores or they may feel closer to their mothers because of their increased contribution to the family welfare. The mother's employment might deprive her adolescent children of supervision, love, and companionship and youths might perceive her absence as rejection. The working mother could also be a better companion to her children, however, because she gains confidence, positive self-regard, and interesting experiences to relate from her job. As a result, she might have more positive interaction time with her children than the full-time homemaker. Yarrow found that college-educated working mothers compensated for their absence in the home by planning more activities with their children[2], and Jones that mothers employed as professionals spent more time reading with their 6th grade children than did nonworking mothers.[3] The positive quality of the working mother's deliberate efforts to spend time with her children could be more beneficial to the mother-youth relationship than the time spent by nonworking mothers with their children.

Effects of maternal employment on the father-youth relationship might also be positive or negative. If a father became more active in caring for his children's emotional needs when the mother is working, a more gratifying relationship might result. A father and his children could gain increased understanding of each other as they share household tasks. Considerable positive interaction may take place among people preparing dinner or doing the dishes together. On the other hand, negative effects are possible if the father loses respect and status because he is perceived as an inadequate provider.

In the analyses to follow we will explore, in adolescent males and females separately, the extent to which maternal employment is associated with their (a) assuming responsibility for household tasks, (b) spending time on leisure activities and nonacademic interests, (c) having disagreements with their parents, and (d) being close to their mothers and fathers.

METHOD

The data used in exploring these relationships came from self-administered questionnaires given to 268 male and 415 female students in regularly scheduled health classes in a Toronto high school in December, 1969. This is the total population of females and about two-thirds of the school's male population. Some classes of males were not given the opportunity to answer the questionnaire because it would have been inconvenient. The school was in a working-class area, and the respondents were in grades 9 to 12 and ranged in age from 14 to 19 years. They were told that the purpose of the study was to learn about adolescent activities and problems.

The analyses to follow are based on a sub-sample consisting of 72 females and 44 males whose mothers had at least seven years full-time employment since their birth, along with 65 females and 48 males whose mothers had never been employed full-time since their birth. The employment history of the mothers is not typical, but it represents the extreme ends of a continuum of employment history; thus we enhance the likelihood of uncovering any real differences between groups.[4]

Inferential tests of significance are used as a guide to decide if we can reasonably infer that a relationship found in this sample of youths is great enough that we can say it is "real" or "significant," and not the result of chance. I assume these students are fairly typical of working-class Toronto youths although the sample was selected because it was convenient and not by the strict processes of random selection assumed by the tests. Any significant or real relationship reported in this paper is at the conventional .05 level of significance, designated as $p <$ .05 in the tables. A rough interpretation is that when the odds are that a difference could occur by chance in fewer than five times out of a hundred, we infer that it is likely to indicate a real difference.

All respondents come from intact families with employed fathers. In addition, respondents with working mothers are similar to those with nonworking mothers in terms of religion and socioeconomic status. About 20% of each group are Protestant and 60% are Catholic. Roughly 60% of parents have less than grade 11 education. The mean rating for fathers on Blishen's socioeconomic index for occupations in Canada is similar for youths with employed mothers and unemployed mothers.[5] Together, the socioeconomic indicator, both parents' education, and the school's geographical location indicate most respondents are from working-class families.[6]

The big difference between families with working and nonworking mothers is size. The mean number of siblings reported by youths with working mothers (mean = 1.7) is roughly half that of nonworking mothers (mean = 3.0). Table 1 shows this relationship is similar for male and female respondents.

RESULTS

Approximately two-thirds of the sons and daughters with working mothers report that their mothers work outside the home primarily for

TABLE 1
MEAN NUMBER OF SIBLINGS, BY SEX AND MOTHER'S
EMPLOYMENT STATUS

Types of siblings	Mean Siblings for females		Mean Siblings for males	
	Employed full time	Non-employed	Employed full time	Non-employed
Older brothers	.31	.85	.48	.94
Older sisters	.39	.52	.23	.52
Younger siblings	.99	1.68	.93	1.75
Siblings of all ages	1.69	3.05[a]	1.64	3.21[a]
Number of respondents	72	65	44	48

[a] $p < .05$ using a one-tailed test between employed and nonemployed groups.

economic reasons — either to supplement the father's income or to buy necessities. While youth's reports may sometimes differ from their mother's perceptions of why she is working, it would appear that many mothers entered the work force because of a real or perceived need to supplement the family income. Although economic motives dominate, most youths (roughly 70%) report that their mothers like their jobs. The majority of youths (55%) approve of their mother working outside the home, and two-thirds report that their fathers approve.

Household Responsibilities
A review of evidence by Vanek shows that, in the 1960s, employed women spent only about 26 hours per week on housework.[7] This is about half as much time as the full-time housewives devoted to household tasks. Although there is some evidence that husbands of employed women help with household tasks and child care, working women spend more time on these tasks than do their husbands.[8] Vanek says that the husbands' willingness to help does not explain the fewer hours spent by working wives on household duties. Thus the question remains of why nonemployed women spend so much more time doing household chores than employed women.

One possibility is that the employed mother's adolescent children take on some additional household duties. This hypothesis was examined by asking our respondents how frequently they performed a list of 23 common tasks. The list included caring for children, preparing meals, making beds, washing and drying dishes, taking out garbage, cutting and raking grass, shovelling snow, washing and ironing clothes, running errands, shopping and cleaning. Respondents indicated the frequency of performing each chore by checking one of three columns — (1) once every day or two, (2) once or twice a week, or (3) once every two weeks. If the chore was performed less frequently than once every two weeks, no column was checked.

A chore score index was computed by summing the scores assigned for each chore performed every day or two (score of three), once or twice a week (score of two), once every two weeks (score of one), and less frequently than once every two weeks (score of zero). The mean chore score of 20.1 for sons of working mothers is significantly higher than the 16.5 score for sons of nonworking mothers, but the difference is very small. Although the mean chore score of 34.5 for daughters of working mothers is slightly higher than the 31.5 for daughters of full-time homeworkers, the difference is not statistically significant.

Sex differences on the chore score index are much larger than differences related to maternal employment. Females' scores (mean = 33.3) are almost double those of males' (mean = 18.2), regardless of the mother's employment status. That is, boys whose mothers are employed do far less housework than girls whose mothers are or are not employed.

Leisure Activities
Since the data on household chores indicate very small differences in the amounts of housework done by youths with working and nonworking mothers, we may expect few differences between the two groups in the extent of leisure activities. This expectation is based on the assumption that commitment to leisure activities is inversely related to the household responsibilities assumed by adolescents. The same reasoning would lead us to expect greater participation in leisure pursuits by males than females.

To compare the leisure and nonacademic activities of youths with working and nonworking mothers, respondents were given a check list of 43 activities and a space to indicate others. The list included 10 hobbies, 17 sports and 16 other activities including dancing, parties, picnics, games, discussions, church services and watching television. Youths were asked to check the activities in which they participated "fairly regularly," and to indicate whether the activities were done with parents, with friends, or alone. They were asked also what clubs, organizations, and teams they belonged to; how many books they read for pleasure the previous month that were not school assignments; whether they took lessons in dancing, dramatics, speech, art, music, or language outside of regular school classes; whether they held a part-time or summer job; whether they had dated yet or gone steady; and how many times they went on a date the previous month.

Their responses are summarized in Table 2. The data indicate no strong and consistent relationship between the mother's employment status and most leisure activities.

TABLE 2
SOCIAL ACTIVITIES AND WORK FOR PAY, BY SEX AND MOTHER'S EMPLOYMENT STATUS

Leisure activities and paid employment	Females		Males	
	Employed full time	Non-employed	Employed full time	Non-employed
Mean number of activities checked on list of 43 items				
Hobbies[b]	5.3	5.2	3.4	3.1
Sports[b]	6.8	6.0	8.2	8.2
Activities with parents[b]	8.7	7.7	5.5	5.3
Activities with friends	16.2	15.4	13.5	15.0
Other activities				
Mean number of clubs and organizations	.8	1.4[a]	1.0	1.3
Percent reading for pleasure[b]	83%	89%	77%	73%
Percent taking lessons in dancing, dramatics, speech, art, or music	52%	43%	50%	23%[a]
	(62)	(54)	(32)	(31)
Percent with paying job previous summer	43%	51%	55%	62%
	(69)	(64)	(42)	(47)
Percent with part-time job	29%	26%	21%	29%
	(65)	(58)	(39)	(42)
Percent dating	52%	52%	45%	43%
	(71)		(42)	(44)
Percent going steady	11%	19%	18%	3%
	(46)	(43)	(28)	(29)
Mean number of dates last month[b]	1.7	1.8	.7	1.0
Maximum possible number of respondents (N)[c]	N = 72	N = 65	N = 44	N = 48

[a] $p < .05$ using a two-tailed test of differences between employed and nonemployed groups.
[b] $p < .05$ using a two-tailed test of difference between male and female groups
[c] Where N is not maximum, the actual number of respondents is indicated in parentheses. The difference between the value in parentheses and the maximum N is the number in the "no answer" category.

Youths report sharing twice as many leisure activities with friends (mean = 15.5) as with parents (mean = 7.0), indicating the importance of peers in their lives. The only real differences between youths with employed and nonemployed mothers are that daughters of working mothers belong to slightly fewer clubs, organizations and teams (mean = 0.8) than daughters of non-working mothers (mean = 1.4). Also, a higher proportion of sons of working mothers (50%) report taking lessons in dancing, dramatics, speech, art, or music than do sons of non-working mothers (23%). Some respondents report that the mother's earnings made the extra lessons financially possible.

There are large sex differences in activity patterns. Boys report playing more sports (mean = 8.2) than girls (mean = 6.5). However, girls are more active than boys in other activities. A high proportion of both sexes read, but more girls (86%) than boys (75%) report reading at least one book that was not a school assignment in the month preceding the questionnaire administration. Girls report sharing more activities with parents (mean = 8.2) than boys (mean = 5.4), having more hobbies (mean = 5.2) than boys (mean = 3.2), and having more dates (mean = 1.7) than boys (mean = 0.8) in the previous month. Girls may report more frequent dating than boys because boys define fewer shared coed activities as dates, or because girls date older boys outside their high school. Except for sports these results are not in the predicted direction. Although we cannot tell from our data it may be that the sports activities of boys represent a greater overall time commitment to leisure pursuits than the array of activities in which girls predominate. For the moment this matter must remain unclear.

Frequency and Topics of Parent-Youth Disagreements

Another area where we might expect differences by sex and mother's employment status is parent-youth disagreements. Males may have more parental disagreements because they have been socialized to greater independence, or fewer disagreements because they are given more freedom. Disagreements might also increase or decrease when the mother works for similar reasons. Fewer conflicts might result when the mother is employed if youths are given more freedom to do as they wish. Disagreements could also increase, however, if the mother's employment caused parents to encourage independence and to tolerate more disagreement. Increased disagreement would not necessarily reflect a negative parent-youth relationship.[9] The quality of the parent-youth relationship needs to be examined independently from the degree of parental disagreement. This is done later in this report.

The degree of parent-youth disagreement was measured by asking if respondents had a quarrel or serious disagreement with their parents "yesterday." They were also asked if they had parental disagreements about dating, curfews, or frequency of going out; style of clothing or

TABLE 3
DISAGREEMENTS WITH PARENTS, BY SEX AND MOTHER'S EMPLOYMENT STATUS

Indicators of parent-youth disagreement	Females		Males	
	Employed full time	Non-employed	Employed full time	Non-employed
Had a quarrel or serious disagreement "yesterday"	20%	13%	32%	4%[a]
	(70)	(63)	(38)	(46)
Topics of disagreement				
When to date or come home, or how often to go out[b]	73%	43%[a]	81%	79%
				(43)
Style of clothing or wearing make-up	48%	36%	72%	46%[a]
				(43)
Choice of friends	51%	43%	63%	52%
				(43)
Politics	42%	35%	42%	25%[a]
				(43)
Religion	57%	17%[a]	49%	26%[a]
				(43)
Future education or occupation	52%	41%	58%	50%
				(43)
Maximum possible number of respondents (N)[c]	N = 72	N = 65	N = 44	N = 48

[a] *p < .05 using a two-tailed test of differences between employed and nonemployed groups.*
[b] *p < .05 using a two-tailed test of difference between male and female groups*
[c] *Where N is not the maximum, the actual number of respondents is indicated in parentheses. The difference between the value in parentheses and the maximum N is the number in the "no answer" category.*

make-up; choice of friends; politics; religion; and future education or occupation.

Their responses are summarized on Table 3. The proportion of males and females disagreeing on various questions are similar, except that more males (80%) than females (59%) report disagreements on dating and/or curfew and/or frequency of going out.

Youths with working mothers consistently report more disagreements than youths with nonworking mothers. Real differences between daughters of working and nonworking mothers were on the topics of religion, and when to date or come home or how often to go out. Significant differences between sons of working and nonworking mothers were on having a quarrel or serious disagreement "yesterday," style of clothing, politics, and religion.

The higher level of parent-youth disagreement that is associated with maternal employment does not necessarily mean that the quality of parent-adolescent relationships is damaged by her employment.

Quality of Mother-Youth Relationship

To determine if the quality of the mother-youth relationship was affected by the mother's employment, youths were asked six questions about their relationship with their mothers. Two questions were direct indicators of the mother-youth relationship. These were, "How do you feel toward your mother?", and "How often is your mother interested in what you are doing?" On the first question responses of "close" or "very close", and on the second question responses of "always" or "usually" were regarded as indicators of a positive mother-youth relationship. The high percentage of positive youth responses on these two questions is shown in the first two rows of Table 4. There is no significant or consistent pattern of differences between adolescents with working and nonworking mothers. The same is true for differences by sex, except that a slightly higher proportion of males (91%) than females (83%) report being "close" or "very close" to mother.

Respondents were also asked four indirect questions about their relationship with their mother. These questions did not specifically ask youths to evaluate the quality of the relationship. "Mother" was only one of several possible responses to the questions: "With whom do you spend most of your spare time? Whom do you ask for help with a school assignment? Whom do you go to for help with personal problems? What woman that you know do you admire most?" A "mother" response to these questions was interpreted as indicating a positive relationship.

Youth responses in Table 4 show that a slightly higher proportion of female (48%) than male (35%) youths ask for help with personal problems. There are no significant associations between the quality of mother-youth relationship and maternal employment. Thus, our findings clearly do not support the notion that the quality of mother-youth relationship is affected by the mother working outside the home.

Let us now examine the effects of maternal employment on the father-youth relationship.

Quality of Father-Youth Relationship

One of the arguments feminists use in support of maternal employment is that fathers become more nurturant figures to children because they are more likely to share child-care roles with their working wife. On

TABLE 4
RELATIONSHIP TO MOTHER, BY SEX AND MOTHER'S EMPLOYMENT STATUS

Relationship to mother	Females Employed full time	Females Non-employed	Males Employed full time	Males Non-employed
Feels close or very close to mother[b]	81%	84%	93%	89%
		(70)	(43)	(47)
Mother always or usually interested in activities	83%	91%	91%	81%
			(43)	
Spends most spare time with mother	6%	10%	2%	2%
		(63)		
Asks mother for help with school assignments	6%	2%	2%	2%
	(71)		(39)	(43)
Asks mother for help with personal problems	49%	45%	39%	31%
	(70)		(33)	
Mother is most admired female adult	16%	26%	21%	20%
	(66)	(58)	(29)	(41)
Maximum possible number of respondents (N)[c]	N = 72	N = 65	N = 44	N = 48

[a] $p < .05$ using a two-tailed test of differences between employed and nonemployed groups. There are no real differences in this table.
[b] $p < .05$ using a two-tailed test of differences between male and female groups.
[c] Where N is not the maximum, the actual number of respondents is indicated in parentheses. The difference between the value in parentheses and the maximum N is the number in the "no answer" category.

the negative side is evidence from McCord's study of lower-class boys from intact families. This study found that sons of employed mothers were more likely than sons of full-time housewives to indicate disapproval of their fathers.[10] Douvan found that lower-class, but not middle-class, sons of working mothers were less likely than sons of full-time homemakers to choose their father as the person they most admired.[11]

To determine the perceived quality of father-youth relationships youths were asked two direct and four indirect questions. The ques-

TABLE 5
RELATIONSHIP TO FATHER, BY SEX AND MOTHER'S
EMPLOYMENT STATUS

	Females		Males	
Relationship to father	Employed full time	Non-employed	Employed full time	Non-employed
Feels close or very close to father	63%	74%	70%	75%
	(71)		(43)	
Father always or usually interested in activities	65%	75%	74%	71%
	(71)		(43)	
Spends most spare time with father	0%	0%	0%	0%
	(69)	(63)		(43)
Asks father for help with school assignments	11%	9%	13%	5%
	(71)		(39)	(43)
Asks father for help with personal problems[b]	3%	3%	8%	19%
	(70)		(39)	
Father is most admired male adult	20%	25%	18%	38%[a]
	(61)	(57)	(28)	(40)
Maximum possible number of respondents (N)[c]	N = 72	N = 65	N = 44	N = 48

[a] $p < .05$ using a two-tailed test of differences between employed and nonemployed groups.
[b] $p < .05$ using a two-tailed test of differences between male and female groups.
[c] Where N is not the maximum, the actual number of respondents is indicated in parentheses. The difference between the value in parentheses and the maximum N is the number in the "no answer" category.

tions were identical to those on the mother-youth relationship, except that the word "father" was substituted for "mother."

Youths' responses on all the questions are summarized in Table 5. Comparisons of the responses on father relationships (Table 5) with those on mother relationships (Table 4) show more positive mother-youth relationships on four of the six items. Higher proportions of youths report close relationships with mothers, and also more often claim that their mothers are likely to be interested in their activities. Few youths spend most of their spare time with mothers, but none report spending most of their spare time with fathers. In addition, more youths ask mothers for help with personal problems.

In contrast, similar proportions of youths choose their mothers and fathers as their most admired adults, and a slightly higher proportion of youths ask fathers for help with school assignments.

There are no real differences between males and females on the quality of relationship with fathers, with the one exception that males (14%) are slightly more likely than females (3%) to ask their father for help with personal problems.

The differences between youths with working and nonworking mothers on the father relationship items are inconsistent and, with one exception, not statistically significant. The exception is that a higher proportion of nonworking mothers' sons name their father as the adult they most admire. These data are consistent with McCord's and Douvan's findings of greater admiration expressed for fathers by sons of nonworking mothers within the lower class.

Douvan has suggested that lower-class sons perceive their father's lack of economic success as the cause of the mother being forced into working outside the home. The boys devalue their father for not adequately fulfilling his societal role. This explanation appears plausible in light of Douvan's finding that sons of working and nonworking mothers in middle-class families were equally likely to choose their fathers as models. It may only be in working-class families, where the mother's employment is an economic necessity, that youths are less likely to admire their fathers. If this is the case, both the father's occupation and the mother's employment status influence the son's choice of most admired adult.

I am somewhat sceptical of Douvan's explanation. If it were true, daughters of working mothers would also be less likely to choose their father as the adult male they most admire. Presumably, females are as likely as males to perceive their fathers as economic failures and therefore admire them less. Douvan presents no data on female's choice of admired male. In our study, however, differences on this item between daughters of working and nonworking women were not statistically significant. The effect of maternal employment on the prestige of the father in working-class families requires more attention than it has so far been given.

CONCLUSIONS

There is clearly still much that we can and should do to learn more about the effects of maternal employment. In general, the findings here show little difference between youths with working and nonworking mothers. This accords with the overall conclusions reached by reviewers of British and American studies.[12] The few observed differences between youths with working and nonworking mothers were generally smaller than differences between males and females. Girls did far more household chores than boys, regardless of their mothers' employment status. Sons, and daughters, of working women reported slightly more household responsibility than their counterparts with nonemployed mothers but the differences were only significant for sons. This may be because sons are asked to do more household chores when their mothers work because their usual household responsibilities are so small that the extra tasks are unlikely to become too burdensome. Employed mothers may deliberately avoid giving their daughters increased household responsibilities to prevent overburdening them. The commitment to leisure pursuits and related activities by youths with working mothers was similar to that by youths with nonworking mothers, but there were sex differences in the kinds of activities reported.

Although youths with working mothers reported more disagreements with parents, they were similar to those with nonworking mothers in feelings of closeness, parental interest, time spent with parents, and receiving help with school and personal problems. These two sets of findings appear incompatible, unless they indicate that parents in families where the mother works encourage independence and autonomy. They may, therefore, be more tolerant of youths expressing opinions with which they disagree. Clearly, the validity of this explanation should be more fully examined in future studies. The interpretation fits well with the finding that more males than females report disagreements on dating, curfew or frequency of going out. It seems likely that males are allowed more independence than females on these dimensions.

There is no consistent evidence that the mother's absence from the home while she is working results in loss to her adolescent children of love, concern, support, or supervision. This may be because working mothers are usually away from home when their children are in school, or because mothers take effective remedial measures to counterbalance any negative effects of their employment. Mothers who work may also have personal characteristics which negate any problems caused by their employment. Compared to the woman in similar economic circumstances who does not work, the working mother may have more training, work experience, competence and intellectual ability. Her physical and mental health may be better and in this sample at least, she has fewer children. Full-time maternal employment in low income families may also be more common when the children are well-adjusted. The mother with a problem child is probably more reluctant to take a full-time job than the mother who is confident her children will cope successfully.

Footnotes

1. The effects of a mother's employment on herself and other family members becomes a matter of considerable controversy as increasingly high proportions of wives and mothers are employed outside the home. In 1975, 44.2% of the female population aged 15 years and over, was in the Canadian labour force. This compares with 37% in 1971, 31% in 1965, and 16% in 1911 (Labour Canada. Women in the Labour Force, 1975: Facts and Figures). The labour force includes both people who are working and people looking for work. In 1971, 37.9% of wives in husband-wife families with no children participated in the labour force. For families with at least one child under six years of age, the wife's participation rate was 26.2%. The participation rate is 39.9% for families with children between the ages of 6 and 14 years only, and 40.0% for those families with children between the ages of 15 and 24 years of age only (Labour Canada. Women in the Labour Force, 1971: Facts and Figures).

    The two wars are often considered a turning point for increased labour force participation among both married and single women. In contrast to the Great Depression of the thirties when there were some restrictions placed on the employment of women who were self-supporting, the two wars opened more jobs to women.

2. Yarrow, M.R., Scott, P., DeLeeuw, L., and Heinig, C. "Child-rearing in families of working and nonworking mothers." Sociometry, 1962, 25, 122-140.

3. Jones, J.B., Lundsteen, S.W., and Michael, W.B. "The relationship of the professional employment status of mothers to reading achievement of sixth-grade children." California Journal of Educational Research, 1967, 43, 102-108.

4. The average duration of employment reported by daughters of working mothers was 10 years. For sons, the average was 11 years. All the girls' mothers were fully employed at the time of the study. The employment status of the boys' mothers at the time of the study was 75% fully employed, 16% employed part-time, and 9% not employed. To be considered fully employed the mother must have worked 30 or more hours per week for at least 10 months of the year.

    Previous researchers have usually asked only whether mothers were fully employed, employed part-time or not employed at the time of the questionnaire administration. They do not take account of such important variants as the number of hours she works, or the regularity, or duration of her employment. One is thus left wondering whether some of the nonemployed mothers were only temporarily out of the labour market and if the employed mothers had been working long enough for their employment to have had an effect upon their children's attitudes and behaviors. See, for example, Douvan, E. "Employment and the adolescent." Pp. 142-64 in I. Nye and L. Hoffman (eds.) The Employed Mother in America. Chicago: Rand McNally, 1963; Essig, M., and Morgan, D.H. "Adjustment of adolescent daughters of employed women to family life." Journal of Educational Psychology, 1946, 38, 219-233; Mathews, S.M. "The effects of mothers out of home employment on children's ideas and attitudes." Journal of Applied Psychology, 1934, 14, 116-136; Nye, I. "Adolescent-parent adjustment: age, sex, sibling number, broken homes, and employed mothers as variables." Marriage and Family Living, 1952, 14, 327-332; Nye, I. "Maternal employment and the adjustment of adolescent children." Marriage and Family Living, 1959,

21, 240-244; Roy, P. "Adolescent roles: rural-urban differentials," Marriage and Family Living, 1961, 23, 340-349.

5. For a description of the scale construction see Blishen, B.R. "A socioeconomic index for occupations in Canada." The Canadian Review of Sociology and Anthropology, 1967, 4:1, 41-53. The mean of 32.5 for youths with employed mothers was not significantly different (t = .55 p > .05) than the mean of 33.6 for youths with nonemployed mothers.

6. This is desirable in a study of working mothers since most North American women with children work more for economic reasons than for self-enrichment. Some time ago, a Canadian study found nearly 80% of married women respondents stressed economic motives as their primary reason for working (Women's Bureau, Department of Labour. Occupational Histories of Married Women Working for Pay. Ottawa: Queen's Printer, 1958). An analysis of 1961 census data and the 1974 Statistics Canada labour force survey shows a strong relationship between the wife's tendency to work outside the home and her husband's income among families with children (Sylvia Ostry. The Female Worker in Canada. Ottawa: Dominion Bureau of Statistics, 1968; Labour Canada. Women in the Labour Force, 1966: Facts and Figures).

7. Vanek, J. "Time spent in housework." Scientific American, 1974, November, 116-120. Vanek finds the full-time housewife spent 55 hours per week on household tasks in the middle 1960's. This was slightly more than 52 hours per week by similar housewives in 1924. Vanek suggests that increased levels of consumption require the modern housewife to spend more time on laundry, despite the availability of automatic washers and dryers, probably because their families own more clothes and change them more frequently. Increased time spent on child care reflects societal modifications in standards of care. In addition to the older concern with health, discipline, and cleanliness, today's mother is responsible for the child's social and mental development.

8. Blood, R.O. and Hamblin, R.L. "The effect of the wife's employment on the family power structure." Social Forces, 1958, 36, 347-352; Hall, F.T., and Schroeder, M.P. "Time spent in household tasks." Journal of Home Economics, 1970, 62 23-29; Weil, M.W. "An analysis of the factors influencing married women's actual or planned work participation." American Sociological Review, 1961, 26, 91-96.

    Some 1971-72 data from Halifax suggest the time husbands spend on housework may depend on the ages of the children as well as the mother's employment status. When the youngest child was under 12 years old, men whose wives worked spent from 2 to 12 hours more than men whose wives did not work. By contrast, husbands of employed wives spent 12 hours less when there were two or more children and the youngest was 13 to 17 years (See Table 2.15 in Perspective Canada 11: A Compendium of Social Statistics, 1977, Ottawa. Statistics Canada).

    In the Soviet Union where mothers have been encouraged to work outside their homes since the 1917 revolution, there are numerous facilities provided to help with the care of children. Yet, mothers are still apparently carrying a disproportionate share of domestic responsibility (Mace, D.R. "The employed mother in the USSR." Marriage and Family Living, 1961, 23, 330-332).

    In a British survey, 50% of husbands of working wives did not help with the housework (Yudkin, S., and Holme, A. Working Mothers and Their Children. London: Sphere Books, 1973).

9. I am indebted to Lois Hoffman for suggesting this interpretation in "The

effects of maternal employment on the child — a review of research." Developmental Psychology, 1974, 10, 204-228. Hoffman reviews some evidence suggesting that working mothers encourage independence and autonomy in adolescent children.

10. McCord, J., McCord, W., and Thurber, E. "Effects of maternal employment on lower-class boys." Journal of Abnormal and Social Psychology, 1963, 67, 177-182.
11. Douvan, E. "Employment and the adolescent." Pp. 142-64 in I. Nye and L. Hoffman (eds.) The Employed Mother in America. Chicago: Rand McNally, 1963.
12. See Etaugh, C. "Effects of maternal employment on the child — a review of research." Developmental Psychology, 1974, 10, 204-228; Yudkin, S., and Holme, A. Working Mothers and Their Children, London: Michael Joseph, 1963, 100-111, 138.

SOCIALIZATION MEANS AND MODELS FOR ADOLESCENTS

Attitudes to Parental Control and Adolescents' Aspirations: A Comparison of Immigrants and Non-Immigrants

KURT DANZIGER
Department of Psychology
York University

The search for possible antecedents of the level of adolescents' aspirations may be conducted on two levels. In the first place, one may establish empirical associations between aspirations and social class or value systems. One may establish that lower aspirations are correlated with working class or ethnic status and then attempt to explain this relationship in terms of differences in values and/or realistic estimates of life changes. For example, one may choose to regard high educational aspirations as part of a "delayed gratification" pattern, characteristic of the middle class, or as a product of a sub-cultural value system that defines individual worth in terms of career goals rather than some other set of values, like family loyalty, physical prowess, etc. But in that case no questions are raised about the *process* by which such values are internalized so that they become a force within the individual. This is precisely what the social psychological level of analysis attempts to do. The first step in such an undertaking is to identify the interpersonal situations that are crucial for the transmission of different value orientations. Values are not disembodied entities; they express themselves in the concrete interaction of individuals with one another. Only in this way can they be transmitted.

This question immediately resolves itself into a two-fold search, namely, the identification of the agents of value transmission and the identification of the relevant modalities of social interaction. Among the agents, parents, teachers, peers and mass media represent obvious possibilities. Parents have generally seemed to play a special role in this context. Not only are parents in a position to influence the child in the most impressionable and pliable stage of its development, but their influence normally has a duration and continuity which is denied to other socialization agents.

The simplest and most obvious way in which parents may influence the aspirations of adolescents is by direct pressure, emphasizing such things as school performance and occupational plans. It seems that there is a strong association between the educational plans that mothers have for their children and the children's own plans, quite independently of certain specific socialization techniques (Sandis, 1970). The next question concerns the possible effect of the degree of pressure with which parental plans are presented to the children: Perhaps too much pressure has a negative effect? However, it is misleading to conceptualize parental pressure simply in quantitative terms. The important distinction is a qualitative one, between pressure that takes the form of encouragement and support, and pressure that operates in a punitive context. There is some evidence to suggest that high achievement levels in children are more likely to be associated with the former than with the latter type of parental pressure, and achievement levels in turn affect educational aspirations. It therefore appears appropriate to assess not only the goals which parents have for their children, but also to address the question of whether these goals operate in a supportive or a punitive context. In view of existing evidence that at lower socio-economic levels maternal influence on adolescents' aspirations may be far more important than paternal influence (Bennett and Gist, 1964), it seems advisable to obtain direct evidence of mothers' educational goals in particular.

While parental goals may have their role, it would clearly be naive to suggest that parents have only to announce their goals for them to be transmitted to their children. The question of whether children truly make these goals their own or whether they react against them, ignore them, merely pay lip service to them, etc. depends on subtle aspects of the parent-child relationship. Besides, it is not entirely unknown for children to develop high aspirations in the absence of any obvious and direct form of parental influence. It is therefore necessary to pay some attention to possible indirect influences.

It may be helpful to think of the distinction between direct and indirect parental influence in terms of the common sense distinction between what parents *say* and what they *do*. The two may not coincide and in the long run children probably take more notice of deeds than of words. A parent may well announce high goals, but his behaviour towards the child may be such as to evoke personal reactions that are incompatible with high levels of motivation for achievement.

There is one aspect of parental behaviour which appears to have exceptional importance in this context, namely, the degree and kind of control which the parent exercises over the child's activities. A parent who severely limits the child's initiative in the major divisions of life and who arbitrarily and rigorously enforces his own authority may not be providing the best soil for the growth of effective levels of aspiration. For example, excessive father dominance has been held responsible for low levels of achievement motivation among boys in such countries as Brazil (Rosen, 1962) and Turkey (Bradburn, 1963). On the other hand, high levels of maternal dominance tend to be associated with low educational achievement in some groups (Bowerman and Elder, 1964; Gill and Spilka, 1962). In general, a negative relationship between parental dominance and level of schooling reached by the children has been demonstrated for a number of countries, including Italy and Germany (Elder, 1965).

Unfortunately, some of the studies in this area are methodologically unsatisfactory in that they rely on retrospective data and very general questions about parental dominance. But replies to questions about experiences that occurred many years before are subject to such profound distortions that they really cannot be used as evidence for what really happened. And very general questions about parental dominance are unlikely to yield anything but stereotyped responses; to study the actual pattern of authority in any given family it is necessary to ask concrete questions about specific areas of decision making.

By far the most elaborate study of family authority among Italian immigrants in relation to needs and values relevant for worldly achievement has been undertaken by Strodtbeck (1958). His basic hypothesis has been sufficiently influential to be quoted verbatim: "The power distribution in the family will condition the way a boy expects power to be distributed in the outside world, and his adjustment to family power will generalize to external systems." According to Strodtbeck, many Italians grow up with a belief in *Destino*, a belief which implies that an individual's fate is decided by powers outside himself and is not affected by the individual's own efforts; an orientation which is unlikely to encourage strong social or intellectual ambition. In his sample of American Italian and Jewish adolescents, Strodtbeck does find that a significantly (5% level) higher percentage of the latter disagree with the following statements: (1) "Planning only makes a person unhappy since your plans hardly ever work out anyhow." (2) "When a man is born, the success he's going to have is already in the cards, so he might as well accept it and not fight against it." However, it should be noted that a clear majority of the Italian adolescents do disagree with these statements, and it is not clear to what extent the group difference simply reflects a peculiarly high level of disagreement among the Jewish group. That this may be a more appropriate interpretation is suggested by the fact that when social class is held constant, more Jewish than Italian American adolescents expect to go to college, but the latter do not differ from the general population in this respect.

Be that as it may, Strodtbeck attempts to show that there is a relationship between such general beliefs about the world and the distribution of power in the family. To assess the latter he makes use of his "revealed differences" technique in which family members (father, mother and son in this case) are confronted by differences of opinion among them and are asked to reach agreement, if possible. When this is done for a number of issues it is possible to assign a "power score" to each member in terms of the number of instances in which the final agreed opinion of the family corresponds to his original opinion. While the Italian fathers in Strodtbeck's sample do not have a significantly higher power score than the Jewish fathers, the gap between the power scores of fathers and mothers is far greater among the Italian parents. On this measure there is therefore greater equality among Jewish than among Italian parents.

Unfortunately, there are serious doubts about the meaning of this finding in view of the unanimity with which anthropological accounts emphasize south Italian cultural prescription that makes it mandatory for wives to defer to their husbands in public, even when they dominate them in private (Cronin, 1970). The technique of "revealed differences" gives evidence of the degree of ritual public deference of wives which may be of little or no significance for the socialization of the children.

The results of Strodtbeck's study hardly confirm the stereotype of the authoritarian Italian father. In fact, in their verbal reports Jewish and Italian boys did not differ in the power which they assigned to their fathers. On the contrary, an examination of the interaction which precedes the reaching of family consensus in the "revealed difference" situation shows that Italian fathers actually displayed more supportiveness towards their sons than Jewish fathers.

While Strodtbeck's study does nothing to confirm the popular stereotype of the authoritarian Italian father, an interesting footnote is added by a more recent anthropological study on a small sample of Sicilian immigrants in Australia (Cronin, 1970). In that instance it is reported that paternal authoritarianism was strongly associated with upward social mobility among migrants; on the other hand, relatively non-mobile migrants seemed to become more egalitarian in the family relationship as a result of migration. It is difficult to reconcile such reports with the belief that authoritarianism and personal ambition are in some way antithetical.

While the attempt made in Strodtbeck's study to link certain verbalized value differences among Jewish and Italian American adolescents to differences specifically in paternal authority must be regarded as unsuccessful, it is still likely that the general level of parental (rather than exclusively paternal) control is relevant to youthful plans and aspirations. Indeed, in reply to a question about the supervision of homework a greater proportion of Italian than of Jewish adolescents in Strodtbeck's sample reported such supervision. The proposition that adolescent aspirations will be affected by parental control of adolescent activities remains a plausible hypothesis.

But the definition of what is meant by different levels of parental control raises problems. A purely objective definition of levels of control will clearly be irrelevant to the effects which any given level of control can be expected to exert in a particular case. Such an "objective" definition of levels of control simply substitutes the interpretation of an uninvolved observer for the definitions that operate for those actually affected by the situation. It is these definitions, and not those of the uninvolved observer, that are crucial for the determination of the effects of different levels of control. What may appear to be high levels of control to the observer, may not be so experienced by the participants. Moreover, there are at least two participants, parent and child, and it is entirely possible that they will disagree as to whether a given level of parental control remains within reasonable limits or not. Such disagreements are crucial for the effects which any given level of parental control can be expected to produce. Moreover, parent and child may not even agree about who makes the decisions in the first place. Human interaction, especially in the family, is sufficiently complex and ambiguous to allow for different interpretations by each of the participants. Before we can make a meaningful analysis of the effects of different levels of parental control, it is necessary to assess, firstly, whether there is agreement among the participants as to who actually makes the decisions, and secondly, as to whether the perceived pattern of decision is considered to be legitimate or not. In other words, we must be careful to make at least two types of distinctions; we must distinguish situations in which there is an agreed distribution of authority from those in which the distribution of authority is ambiguous, and we must distinguish the exercise of authority that is regarded as legitimate from the exercise of authority regarded as illigitimate.

What this amounts to is a deliberate attempt to get away from the model of the socialization process in which the child is essentially a passive reactor to various externally imposed conditions. On the contrary, his responses to any given interaction with socialization agents will depend on his own interpretation of that interaction. It is not someone else's interpretation of the situation that is crucial for his reaction to it, but his own; and his own interpretation may differ completely from that given by either an uninvolved observer or the other participants. The child, especially at the adolescent stage, reacts very actively to parental claims at control, and their effect on him will depend very largely on the nature of this reaction. A parental attempt at control which is accepted as legitimate is likely to have very different psychological consequences than one which is rejected as unjustified. It therefore seems quite unsatisfactory to assess the effect of different levels of parental control on social aspirations without taking into account the reaction of the child to such parental influence attempts.

For the purpose of assessing the child's reaction to actual parental control, his own report of the level of such control is inadequate. His own reaction to such control is bound to distort his perception of the situation. Whether his attitude to parental control is distinctly positive or distinctly negative he is likely to exaggerate the actual level of parental control, although for different reasons. In the one case this exaggeration enhances his feeling of security, in the other case he justifies his rebellion by magnifying its target. One way of correcting for these distortions is to compare his report with that of one or both of his parents and accepting only those instances where these independent reports corroborate each other. Even this measure is not foolproof but it provides a more solid base against which to compare the child's reaction. It is therefore necessary to obtain parental reports as well as reports from the children.

There is a further issue which has not been faced in previous studies in this area. Even if some kind of relationship between parental control and the son's aspirations exists it does not follow that such a relationship follows a regular linear trend. It is quite possible that it only manifests itself at relatively extreme levels of either variable. In particular, parental control may only function so as to facilitate or inhibit very high or very low aspiration levels and may be irrelevant at intermediate levels. There is at present a real lack of information on these possibilities.

METHOD

Subjects
All grade eight boys in seventeen Toronto schools who stated that Italian was used in their homes were selected and their mothers were interviewed in Italian (the median age of the boys was fourteen years). The total immigrant sample consisted of 153 boys and their mothers. In addition, a group of 67 non-immigrant English speaking boys were selected so as to give roughly the same occupational distribution as the immigrant group; (it was impossible to match the groups exactly due to the preponderance of Italians at lower socio-economic levels). The fathers of 89.7% of the immigrant group and 80.6% of the non-immigrant group were manual workers. The mothers of the non-immigrant group were also interviewed.

Because the members of the immigrant group differ considerably among themselves in regard to their level of acculturation to Canadian society, it is appropriate to split them into sub-groups defined by this variable. An index of English language usage was used for this purpose which has been described elsewhere (Danziger, 1975). Although this index correlates with length of residence in Canada, it is clearly a more meaningful measure of acculturation than mere physical residence on Canadian territory. For present purposes the sample of immigrant mothers was split into those falling above and those falling below the median on the index of English usage. The former are referred to as the High Acculturation and the latter as the Low Acculturation group.

Instruments

(a) The sons were asked: "What kind of work would you most like to do when you grow up?" Their replies were classified on a three-point scale of occupational aspiration as follows:

Highest level — professional, managerial and entrepreneurial

Middle level — semi-professional and white collar

Lowest level — manual occupations.

An occupational rather than an educational aspiration scale is used because in the present sample it yields a greater spread of responses among the subjects.

(b) Both mothers and sons were given a set of 12 items referring to decisions involving the son's social life, his appearance and his welfare and were asked to indicate who usually made these decisions and who ought to make them. The following decision items were used: when to go to bed, when to go out for entertainment, when to come home, what friends to have, what kind of shoes to buy, when to have a party, when to have a haircut, whether to be punished, whether to get a job, what to have for breakfast, when to visit friends, when to have friends in the house. Only a negligible number of replies involved decision agents other than the son, the mother, and the father and only these three decision agents are considered in the analysis of the results.

Measures of three distinct aspects of the control relationship between parent and child can be derived from this instrument:

(i) A measure of the relative control exercised by each parent as perceived by the son. This is obtained by calculating the mean number of decisions (possible total 12) which the son attributes to each of the parents irrespective of whether he feels that they ought to exercise this control or not. Note that there may be discrepancies between the reports of parents and sons but only the perception of the sons is of interest in the present context.

(ii) A measure of the number of items where there is agreement among mother and son about which of the parents makes the decisions and *ought* to make them. This constitutes an estimate of the extent to which actual parental decision making is accepted as legitimate by both parties. The mother's report is used as a check on the son's perception of the situation.

(iii)   A measure of the number of items where there is agreement among mother and son about which of the parents makes the decisions but where the son states that the parent ought *not* to make them. This constitutes an estimate of the extent to which the son rejects the legitimacy of decisions actually made by each of the parents.

DATA

Each of the three measured aspects of the parent-child control pattern shows a different relationship to the level of the adolescent son's occupational aspiration. It is therefore convenient to present each of these relationships separately in the following three tables. In each case the three levels of aspiration are related to the control pattern for mother and for father in the non-immigrant and the immigrant groups. Among the latter, the abbreviation "H.A." in the tables identifies the High Acculturation group, and "L.A." the Low Acculturation group.

Reading across the rows of this table a consistent trend for higher levels of perceived maternal control to be associated with lower aspiration levels emerges only in the non-immigrant and the Low Acculturation immigrant groups. For paternal control such a trend exists only in the latter group.

One-way analyses of variance were applied to each of these trends, but in no instance did the F values reach the 5% level of significance. For each group, levels of perceived maternal and paternal control at each aspiration level were then compared with the overall mean level of perceived control at the other aspiration levels. It emerged that at the highest aspiration level the mean level of perceived maternal control was significantly lower (5% level) than the mean level of perceived maternal control for the other aspiration levels, at least for the

TABLE 1
SON'S PERCEPTION OF MEAN PARENTAL INVOLVEMENT IN DECISIONS FOR VARIOUS LEVELS OF OCCUPATIONAL ASPIRATION AMONG DIFFERENT GROUPS

| | Occupational Aspiration Level | | | | | |
| | Low | | Middle | | High | |
Group	Mother	Father	Mother	Father	Mother	Father
Non-immigrant	5.90	3.80	5.75	4.19	4.50	3.75
Immigrant H.A.	4.68	4.18	4.66	4.22	4.87	4.67
Immigrant L.A.	4.56	4.38	5.40	4.27	3.90	4.19

non-immigrant group (F = 4.12) and for the Low Acculturation immigrant group (F = 4.05).

The data therefore provide somewhat tenuous evidence that relatively low levels of perceived maternal involvement in decisions affecting the son may be associated with high levels of occupational aspiration in some groups. The absence of this relationship in one of the groups indicates that any effect of perceived levels of maternal control on aspirations is subject to modification by other factors and cannot be generalized across different groups.

Turning now from the son's perception of levels of parental control to his judgment of the legitimacy of actual control we have to restrict ourselves to those instances where the son's report is supported by the mother. As previously indicated, we now use a measure of parental control based on those items for which mother and son agree that the parent makes the decisions and the son also feels that the parent ought to make them.

Separate one-way analyses of variance for each group and each parent showed no significant relationship between accepted levels of parental decision making and occupational aspiration. Contrast effects between different aspiration levels for each group yielded only one significant difference: For the Low Acculturation immigrant group the mean level of accepted paternal decision making is higher among subjects with the lowest aspiration level than the overall mean among subjects with higher aspiration levels (F = 5.12). It is therefore possible that relatively high levels of *accepted* (not perceived) levels of paternal control may be associated with a depression of occupational aspiration under some circumstances. It may be noted that those numbers of the Low Acculturation group with the lowest aspiration level have the highest level of accepted paternal control of any of the sub-groups. However, there is clearly no general relationship between levels of accepted parental control and occupational aspiration.

TABLE 2
MEAN NUMBER OF PARENTAL DECISIONS CONFIRMED BY
MOTHER AND ACCEPTED BY SON FOR VARIOUS LEVELS OF
OCCUPATIONAL ASPIRATION

| | Occupational Aspiration Level | | | | | |
| | Low | | Middle | | High | |
Group	Mother	Father	Mother	Father	Mother	Father
Non-immigrant	1.80	0.90	2.88	1.31	2.75	0.75
Immigrant H.A.	2.23	1.05	1.78	1.89	2.13	2.00
Immigrant L.A.	1.81	2.25	2.20	1.13	1.33	1.38

TABLE 3
MEAN NUMBER OF PARENTAL DECISIONS REPORTED BY SON, CONFIRMED BY MOTHER AND REJECTED BY SON, COMPARED FOR VARIOUS LEVELS OF OCCUPATIONAL ASPIRATION

| | Occupational Aspiration Level | | | | | |
| | Low | | Middle | | High | |
Group	Mother	Father	Mother	Father	Mother	Father
Non-immigrant	3.50	1.90	2.63	0.94	1.00	1.25
Immigrant H.A.	1.36	1.23	1.22	0.22	0.40	0.93
Immigrant L.A.	1.31	0.81	1.33	0.73	0.86	1.05

Finally, we may examine the effect of different levels of *rejection* rather than acceptance of parental control. For this purpose we restrict ourselves to those items on which the mother confirms the son's report of actual parental control while the son states that the parent should not make these decisions.

Reading across the rows of Table 3 it is apparent that there is a consistent trend for rejection of maternal control and level of occupational aspiration to be negatively associated. No such trend is discernible in the case of rejection of paternal control. While separate one-way analyses of variance do not yield significant F values for any of the three groups the mean level of rejection of maternal control is significantly lower for subjects with the highest aspiration level than for the rest of the subjects, at least for the non-immigrant group ($F = 5.93$; $p <$ .02) and for the High Acculturation immigrant group ($F = 4.14$; p. $<$ .05).

There is therefore some evidence that the son's reaction to maternal control has some association with occupational aspiration in the sense that the highest aspiration level is unlikely to be found in sons with high levels of rejection of maternal control. Comparing the groups at the highest aspiration level with those at lower aspiration levels, it emerges that the relative degree of rejection of maternal and paternal control changes. Those sons which have the highest aspiration level seem to show a (relatively) stronger tendency to reject paternal, rather than maternal, control, while those at lower levels of aspiration reject maternal control more frequently than paternal control.

DISCUSSION

The general factor in the parent-child control situation which seems to relate to high levels of aspiration in all groups is the son's reaction to parental control rather than the level of parental control as such. Moreover, this effect works in opposite directions for paternal and maternal control. Among those with the highest occupational aspirations there is likely to be relatively greater rejection of paternal control, while among those with more modest aspirations there is likely to be relatively greater rejection of maternal control. This can probably be best understood in terms of social class. The great majority (over 80%) of the fathers of these boys were manual workers, while those boys who were located at the highest aspiration level had ambitions for professional status. In other words, the boys at this level were those with considerable aspirations for upward social mobility. Under these circumstances the authority exercised by their working-class fathers may well be resented. The effect is, however, only a relative one, because the overall level of rejection of parental control (i.e., the sum of maternal and paternal measures) tends to be lower among those at the highest aspiration level than among those at lower aspiration levels. The upward aspiring boys could be described as relatively "oversocialized," but where rejection of parental control occurs at all, it is more likely to be directed at paternal than at maternal control.

The key to the interpretation of the differences among immigrants and non-immigrants lies in the differential involvement of mother and father in decisions affecting the adolescent son. While, for the twelve decisions sampled, maternal involvement is usually somewhat higher than paternal involvement, this higher level of maternal involvement is consistently more marked in the non-immigrant than in the immigrant group. This is true at all levels of aspiration and holds both for *perceived* level of involvement (Table 1) and essentially also for *accepted* level of involvement (Table 2). (In half the immigrant subsamples the level of accepted paternal involvement is actually higher than the level of accepted maternal involvement.) This clearly indicates that, in general, the degree of paternal involvement is *relatively* higher in the immigrant groups, while the degree of maternal involvement is relatively higher in the non-immigrant group. Of course, this simply confirms the impressions of observers, and we might have had reason to question the validity of our data if they had turned out differently.

Given the relatively much greater perceived involvement in control situations among mothers of non-immigrant boys (the group differences are significant at the 1% level), it is perhaps not surprising that the level of rejection of this involvement is also much higher in this group (group differences significant at the .001 level). The factor of maternal control is presumably more salient for non-immigrant than for immigrant boys. Hence it is in this group that attitudes to maternal control are fairly consistently related to the son's social aspiration level. The boys in this group who are at the highest aspiration level indicate a significantly lower degree of perceived maternal control and of rejection of that control than those boys who are at lower aspiration levels.

Among the boys in this group who are at the lowest level of aspiration there is also a much lower degree of accepted maternal control than among the others (Table 2), though this difference just fails to reach statistical significance. All aspects of the son's reaction to maternal control show a consistent relationship to aspiration level in the non-immigrant group, but among the immigrants no consistent pattern emerges.

On the basis of these observations it is possible to advance the hypothesis that where overall levels of maternal involvement in decision making are high it will be those members of the group who perceive relatively little maternal control and show relatively little resentment of that control who are most likely to have the highest occupational aspirations. It is in such groups that the relationship between reactions to maternal control and sons' aspirations is likely to emerge in a relatively consistent pattern.

Apart from the overall level of maternal involvement in decisions affecting the son the level of the mother's own aspiration for the son constitutes a second factor which appears to modify the relationship between maternal control and the son's level of occupational aspiration. If the mother actually has high aspirations for the son and encourages such aspirations in him the level of control she is perceived as exercising may become irrelevant to the level of his aspiration (Sandis, 1970). In another part of the present series of studies it was found that mothers in the High Acculturation group had significantly higher aspirations for their sons than mothers in the Low Acculturation Italian group (Danziger, 1975). The lack of any consistent relationship between perceived level of maternal control and sons' aspirations (see Table 1) may be attributed to this factor. As long as the overall level of maternal control is relatively low the effect of her own high expectations washes out the effect of differences in perceived level of control. This occurs in the High Acculturation Italian group but not in the Low Acculturation group where mothers tend to have much lower expectations.

The effect of rejection of maternal control, however, remains important, even when her expectations are high. This clearly indicates that the effects of maternal control cannot be assessed without taking into account the son's reaction to such control. His rejection of her control will also negate the influence of her expectations, and if that rejection is pronounced some inhibition of the highest aspiration levels is to be expected.

We must therefore see the relationship between maternal control on sons' aspirations in terms of the interaction of three factors, namely, the level of perceived maternal control, the son's rejection of that control and the level of maternal aspirations for the son. The last factor becomes important under conditions of relatively low maternal control and high maternal aspirations, while the son's rejection of maternal control exerts its greatest influence when maternal control is generally high or when it is lower but not counterbalanced by high maternal expectations.

In view of the fact that all our groups were overwhelmingly working class in composition these findings have some relevance for the determination of antecedents of strong motivation in the direction of upward social mobility. It appears that such motivation is likely to be strengthened in adolescent working-class males by a combination of relatively low maternal involvement in decisions affecting the son, little resentment by the son of such involvement and a high level of maternal aspiration for the son. It would seem that among the groups studied in the present investigation it is the High Acculturation Italian group that most closely conforms to this pattern. It would therefore not be surprising to find considerable upward mobility in this group in the course of time.

The data on the relationship of paternal control to occupational aspiration are more tenuous than the data on maternal control. This is partly due to methodological limitations. It was not practicable to obtain direct reports from fathers, and the estimate of their level of involvement in decisions affecting the son is based on agreement among mothers and sons. Had direct reports from fathers been available, a different picture might well have emerged. It is also possible that the choice of items on which paternal involvement was assessed favoured maternal rather than paternal involvement. Finally, it is conceivable that the father's influence becomes more pronounced at a somewhat later age than that of the subjects covered by this study.

The only group in which paternal control (independently of its relation to maternal control) seems to have some relation to occupational aspirations is the Low Acculturation immigrant group. In this group we get a pattern of low occupational aspiration associated with a relatively high level of acceptance of paternal authority. We must remember that this group is defined by a low level of English usage, an indication of its relatively greater closeness to the patterns of its traditional south Italian culture. It is not surprising that in this context the role of the father emerges as more salient.

The factor of salience does not necessarily refer to the range of decisions in which the parent participates, but rather to the significance of his or her culturally sanctioned authority for the child. An examination of Tables 1 and 2 indicates that neither the father's perceived nor his accepted involvement in decisions is greater in the Low Acculturation than in the High Acculturation immigrant group; if anything, the reverse relationship may be true. It is, however, safe to assume that members of these two groups differ in their degree of commitment to the south Italian culture stereotype of paternal authority. Thus, contrary to Strodtbeck's hypothesis, it appears that it is cultural patterns which determine the role played by parental (i.e., paternal) authority, and not patterns of familial authority which determine cultural attitudes. The implication of this conclusion is that it is not necessary to wait for a change in familial authority patterns in order to be able to observe a change in social ambitions. The High Acculturation Italian group illustrates this.

Finally, it is of some interest to note the consistently greater rejection of both paternal and maternal involvement in decision making among the non-immigrant group, as compared to both immigrant groups (Table 3). This finding clearly contradicts the stereotype of the immigrant family as inordinately subject to conflicts about paternal authority. There are good grounds for treating this stereotype with considerable scepticism. Much of the literature in this area owes more to the ideology of the melting pot than to objective evidence (Kunz, 1968). The exaggeration of the speed of acculturation of migrants, which is supposed by this ideology, leads to a dramatization of intergenerational conflicts among immigrants and to a convenient ignoring of the intense and widespread nature of intergenerational conflicts among non-immigrants. Once an appropriate comparison group of non-immigrants is used, as in the present study, it is possible to gain a better perspective on the incidence of the rejection of parental authority among immigrants. Melting pot ideology also overlooks those very real factors which increase parent-child solidarity and reinforce traditional authority patterns in immigrant families. These range from the ideology of "familism," not irrelevant in the case of south Italian immigrants (Danziger, 1975), to the sense of a shared challenge in coming to terms with an unsupportive environment. It may not be uncommon for the children of immigrants to feel a stronger sense of obligation towards their parents than the children of non-immigrants.

In conclusion we may note that while the factor of parental control is not quite unrelated to the social aspirations of adolescent boys, that relationship is certainly not a simple one. In the first place, it is clearly the child's attitudes to such control which are important rather than any "objective" level of control which automatically leaves its imprint on a passive child. It is the degree of control perceived by the child, and its acceptance or rejection of any such control, with which we must concern ourselves. Any relationship between these attitudes and social aspirations will, however, be decisively modified by a number of factors. Among these, the factor of social class must not be forgotten. The child's social aspiration must be seen in relation to the parents' social level — professional aspirations cannot have the same psychological significance in the children of professional parents and in the children of working-class parents. Secondly, variations in sub-culture patterns will play their role, especially insofar as they influence feelings of solidarity and obligation in respect to parents, and not least, insofar as they are associated with variations in the differential involvement of the two parents in the control relationship and the differential salience of this involvement for the son. The role played by acts of control on the part of the mother is not likely to be the same as the role of similar acts by the father. But there are no absolutes here — precisely what significance each of these controlling agents has for the child will depend on the prevailing distribution and salience of control as exercised by each parent. But such patterns of control can be expected to vary from group to group and from one historical period to another.

Footnote

This study was supported by a Canada Council Research Grant.

References

Bennett, Jr., Wm. S., & Gist, N.P.
  1964   Class and family influences on student aspirations. *Social Forces, 43*, 167-173.

Bowerman, C.E., & Elder, G.H.
  1964   *Variations in adolescent perception of family power structure. American Sociological Review, 29*, 551-567.

Bradburn, N.M.
  1963   n Achievement and father dominance in Turkey, *Journal of Abnormal and Social Psychology, 67*, 464-468.

Cronin, C.
  1970   *The sting of change: Sicilians in Sicily and Australia.* Chicago: University of Chicago Press.

Danziger, K.
  1975   Differences in acculturation and patterns of socialization among Italian immigrant families. In E. Zureik and R.M. Pike (Eds.). *Socialization and values in Canada.* Toronto: McClelland and Stewart.

Elder, G.H.
  1965   Family structure and educational attainment: A crossnational analysis. *American Sociological Review, 30*, 81-96.

Gill, L.J., & Spilka, B.
  1962   Some non-intellectual correlates of academic achievement among Mexican-American secondary school students. *Journal of Educational Psychology, 53*, 144-149.

Kunz, P.R.
  1968   Immigrants and socialization: A new look. *Sociological Review, 16*, 363-375.

Rosen, B.C.
1962 Socialization and achievement motivation in Brazil. *American Sociological Review, 27,* 612-624.

Sandis, E.E.
1970 The transmission of mothers' educational ambitions as related to specific socialization techniques. *Journal of Marriage and the Family, 32,* 204-211.

Strodtbeck, T.L.
1958 Family interaction, values and achievement. In D.C. McClelland et al. *Talent and society.* Princeton: van Nostrand.

Japanese and Mennonite Childhood Socialization

MINAKO K. MAYKOVICH
California State University

BACKGROUND

Dominant versus Minority Values of Canadian Society

A society as complex and diversified as the one in Canada is nonetheless characterized by certain values shared by the majority of the people. Such a value system consists of instrumental activism, representing a commitment to an active mastery of the world (Maykovich, 1975; Lipset, 1964; Naegel, 1964; Porter, 1967; Truman, 1971; Wrong, 1955). Although the objective of such a commitment is activity itself, it is usually accompanied by a positive evaluation of material success. This activity orientation entails individualism, that is, utmost realization of individual potentiality through active pursuit of goals.

Typical family and school socialization processes have been conducted according to these values. Parents and teachers are likely to expect that the school should teach children to develop individuality and to learn how to prepare themselves for a productive life.

In contrast, both the Japanese and Mennonites have traditionally subscribed to a collectivity orientation which subordinates the interests of the individual to the welfare of the social group. In both cases the collectivity orientation has been derived from religious doctrines. Thus Japanese and Mennonite parents are likely to expect from the school an education for religious and social responsibilities.

Another contrasting feature of Japanese and Mennonite socialization against the dominant pattern in Canada is the former's emphasis on self-control. While individualism encourages spontaneous expression of self, a collectivity orientation inhibits it. Further similarity between the Japanese and Mennonites is that, unlike other lowerstatus minorities, they maintain relatively high socioeconomic status and are proud of their cultural heritage.

Mennonites in Ontario

The Mennonites are descendants of the Anabaptists of sixteenth century Europe. They withdrew from the state church and formed voluntary fellowships in imitation of the early primitive Christian church. As dissenters, they suffered persecution but survived by migrating to many regions (Hostetler, 1963).

The geographic origin of the Mennonites migrating to Ontario stem from a wide variety of areas. The earliest Mennonites came from Pennsylvania in the late eighteenth and early nineteenth centuries, whose forefathers had fled from Switzerland to Germany, and to Pennsylvania. Later, other Mennonites came from Russia, France, Mexico and other areas (Hostetler, 1963).

The Mennonite population in Ontario is approximately 40,000, which is about twenty percent of all Mennonites in Canada. Eighty-five percent of them are concentrated in seven counties including Waterloo. Among Ontario Mennonites there are seventeen separate groups. They range from the most conservative in belief and nonconformist in behavior to being completely assimilated to the society around them (Fretz, 1967).

Five religious themes among Mennonites have significant implications for socialization: (1) separation from the world; (2) voluntary acceptance of high social obligations symbolized by adult baptism; (3) the maintenance of the disciplined church community; (4) practice of shunning of trespassing members; and (5) a life in harmony with the soil and nature.

The emphasis on separation from the world has given rise to a view of themselves as a "chosen people" or "peculiar people." A key biblical passage epitomizing the message is "Be ye not unequally yoked together with unbelievers, for what fellowship hath righteousness with unrighteousness? And what communion hath light with darkness?" (II Corinthians 6:14). These teachings forbid the Mennonites from entering into social or economic relations with non-Mennonites.

Isolationism enables them to provide for their members a sanctuary from competing value systems. Material success is devalued. They believe that a Christian life is maintained only on the farm. Hard work, thrift, and mutual aid are virtues upheld in the Bible. The city, by contrast, is viewed as the centre of leisure, non-productive spending, and often wickedness.

Traditionally Mennonites have viewed education as "the cultivation of humility, simple living, and resignation to the will of God." They have centered their instruction in reading, writing, arithmetic, and the moral teaching of the Bible. Education beyond that has been looked upon with suspicion. Traditional Mennonites send their children to parochial school up to the eighth grade but are against higher education. They are afraid that higher education at public schools will corrupt their children into leading a non-religious way of living.

Among traditional Mennonites family and church, rather than school, are the main socialization agents for children. Parents are responsible for training their children and morally accountable to God for teaching them right from wrong. Strict obedience to parents is a religious duty for Mennonite children. School is viewed as an instrument for teaching children skills needed to live in an environment where values taught at home are continuous (Hostetler, 1971).

Mental health of children who live in a stable, well integrated, and highly structured social system has been studied by many (Gutkind, 1952; Maykovich, 1970; Kurokawa, 1969b). For instance, Hutterites, who are relatively free from overt manifestations of psychopathology, tend to internalize their difficulties (Eaton and Weill, 1955). Neurotic Hutterites are reported to react to most stresses with signs of depression rather than with anxiety symptoms. Eaton and Weill noticed children with habit disturbances such as nail-biting, enuresis, and thumb-sucking. Gutkind (1952) observed that publicly well-behaved, obedient, quiet, and joyful Amish children showed aggressiveness and viciousness when they were left alone. Mennonite children are at the crossroad of social change. Despite their conscious resistance against outside influences, Mennonites have adopted some of the values, attitudes, and behaviours of the larger society. In fact, the liberated Mennonites live in an urban area, engage in urban occupations, and endorse material success values. Children who are exposed to socializing agents with contradictory values are likely to suffer from emotional disturbances as reported by many (Maykovich, 1970).

Japanese Canadians

According to the 1971 census there were 37,260 persons of Japanese descent in Canada, which amounts to 2.1% of the total Canadian population. Approximately forty percent of them reside in Ontario (Inaba, 1968).

The Japanese in Ontario are traced to two major sources of migration. The first group moved from the West Coast to Ontario after World War II and they are the descendants of early immigrants who left Japan between 1890 and 1920. Now the Japanese Canadians of this group have reached the stages of middle-aged second generation and have third generation children. The second group of Japanese immigrants came directly from Japan after World War II. The second group who left an industrialized Japan of the twentieth century is quite different from the first group. In this paper attention is focused on the earlier immigrants who constitute the majority of the Japanese in Canada.

Despite the long time since their departure from Japan, the Japanese descendants in Canada still retain traditional family values (Hosokawa, 1969; Maykovich, 1971). The possible reasons for this are two-fold. On the one hand, the culture which their forefathers brought from Japan is a traditional one derived from the feudal period of the seventeenth through the early nineteenth century. On the other hand, as victims of a prejudiced and segregated minority group the Japanese developed closely-knit communities of their own where the retention of cultural heritage was easy (Laviolette, 1948; Young, 1938).

According to their traditional values the Japanese placed a premium on collectivity rather than individuality. The entire nation was considered one large family. Each family was held accountable that its members not disgrace the honour of the nation. The family was the major socializing agent for children. Parents taught their children values related to the family as well as to society as a whole. Among them were respect for elders and authority, control of self-expression, primacy of social obligations against individual needs, and diligence for the sake of the family and the nation. Hard work and success were encouraged not for the actualization of individual potentiality but rather for the reputation of the family (Kurokawa, 1970).

In Canada these values were translated to suit their needs for survival. As a racial minority the Japanese knew that the key to success was education. Parents pressured their children to do well in school so that they could secure good occupations, which would enhance the honour of their family and of the Japanese Canadians as a whole.

A typical socialization method used by parents is that of comparison. Parents compare the performance of their child against that of other children and let the former know if he has brought shame to his family by his poor performance or his bad conduct.

Unlike orthodox Mennonites, the Japanese in Canada send their children to public school. Thus the child is under conflicting demands of various socializing agents: parents, teachers, and peers. Parents are likely to emphasize a collectivity orientation including respect for authority, and control of self-expression, while teachers and white peers tend to endorse individualism and spontaneity.

According to previous research (Kurokawa, 1969a) Japanese children are likely to suppress frustration and aggression resulting from value conflicts as well as from authoritarian treatments.

RESEARCH FINDINGS

In order to compare socialization practices and consequences among Japanese and Mennonites, the following study was conducted in Toronto and Waterloo counties in Ontario in 1975. Each sample consisted of 100 boys and their fathers from Mennonite, Japanese and white Protestant groups respectively, and 30 teachers each from parochial and public schools.

The study deals with (1) the degree of verbal agreement among teachers, parents, and students on the roles of schools categorized as religious, social, individual, and occupational; and (2) the association of such an agreement with the mental health of the children.

Methodology

Four areas of socialization at school were examined: religious, social, individual, and occupational. Teachers, parents, and students were asked if they agreed with the following statements strongly (4); moderately (3); slightly (2); or not at all (1).

The religious category included such items as "At school a child must (1) learn to follow a religious life; (2) learn to avoid worldly temptations; and (3) learn to have faith in God." The social issues referred to are: "At school a child must (1) gain an understanding and respect for the rules of society; (2) become more accommodating to the needs of other people; and (3) learn to consider the welfare of the group before personal desires." On the individual level, there were statements such as: "At school a child must (1) learn to be self-reliant; (2) learn to develop his potentialities; and (3) learn how to make decisions." Finally, occupational issues were stated as: "At school a child must (1) learn how to prepare for careers in which he/she is interested; (2) become aware of the need to update skills and maintain a flexible career plan; and (3) become aware of the need to understand money matters and to provide for himself/herself."

The 20-item scale of psychosomatic symptoms was developed, modifying Gurin's (1960) scale to suit the samples of this study. Internal consistency of the scale was attested to by the average intercorrelation of items, which amounted to .56. The score at one standard deviation above the mean was used as a cutting point to distinguish between those with "many" and 'few" psychomatic symptoms, or between the "maladjusted" and the "normal."

From the Mennonites, 100 boys in the eighth grade were chosen from three parochial schools in Waterloo County. Their fathers (100) and teachers (30) were also interviewed.

The Japanese sample was selected from the directory prepared by the Japanese Canadian newspapers in Toronto. One hundred boys in the eighth grade in public schools and their fathers were interviewed. As a control, 100 white, Protestant, non-Mennonite boys in the eighth grade in three public schools in Toronto and their fathers were selected. Thirty teachers from these public schools were also interviewed.

Hypotheses were developed as follows:

    1:   Mennonites are likely to emphasize religious and social functions of the school as a socializing agent.

    2:   Japanese are likely to stress social and occupational roles.

    3:   Whites are likely to stress individualistic and occupational roles.

4:    The child whose views are exceedingly different from those held by teachers, parents, or peers is likely to show signs of maladjustment in the form of psychosomatic symptoms.

FINDINGS

The degrees of verbal agreement among Mennonites, Japanese, and Whites

The first hypothesis is supported that Mennonites tend to consider school as an agent of religious socialization — to teach the child to follow a religious life; to have faith in God; and to avoid worldly temptations. Note that parents in this study, without exception, consider these functions very important. As hypothesized, Mennonites are also concerned that the social functions of the school should teach children to respect rules of society; to accommodate to the needs of others; and to

TABLE 1
FUNCTIONS OF SCHOOL REPORTED BY CHILDREN, PARENTS, AND TEACHERS (MEAN SCORES)

Function of School		Mennonites		
	N:	Children 100	Parents 100	Teachers 30
Religious		10.25	12.00	10.80
Social		9.78	11.04	10.44
Individual		8.03	6.32	7.13
Occupational		6.23	4.22	5.34
		Japanese		
	N:	Children 100	Parents 100	Teachers* 30
Religious		4.50	6.80	7.30
Social		8.32	12.00	6.40
Individual		10.55	7.47	11.43
Occupational		8.01	12.00	8.33
		Whites		
	N:	Children 100	Parents 100	Teachers* 30
Religious		5.03	8.40	7.30
Social		6.38	9.30	6.40
Individual		11.31	8.50	11.43
Occupational		7.32	11.83	8.33

Notes:
1. Score range: 3-12
2. *White teachers in public schools

place the welfare of a group above the needs of the individual. Individualistic and occupational socialization is disregarded by Mennonites as unimportant for a school to perform. In fact, training for individuation and nonagrarian skills is perceived as a threat to the religious life. Among Mennonite parents, teachers, and children, parents are most anxious to protect the religious functions of parochial schools against secular influences from outside.

The second hypothesis is supported that the Japanese parents without exception in this study consider the social and occupational functions of the school as very important. They send their children to public school so that the latter will learn to conform to the social order and to prepare themselves for the future careers. However, this second hypothesis is acceptable only among parents. Japanese children do not subscribe to their parental values and tend to consider the function of the school as developing potentialities of the individual. Their perceptions of school are closer to those held by the public school teachers than those of their parents.

It is interesting to note that, in spite of their traditional value orientations based on Buddhism and Confucianism, the Japanese separate religious functions from the domain of socialization at public school. In the minds of the Japanese Canadians religion seems to imply Christianity which is associated with church rather than with school.

The third hypothesis is partially supported that white teachers and students, though not parents, tend to emphasize individuating aspects of socialization, while white parents are more concerned with the occupational function of the public school. White students and teachers tend to de-emphasize the vocational aspect of the school. White respondents tend to separate religion from public school.

Perceptive discrepancy and mental health

The child who is at the crossroads of conflicting socialization agencies is likely to suffer from psychological stress which may result in psychosomatic symptoms. In order to test this fourth hypothesis, the individual child's score is compared with the average scores calculated for parents, teachers, and peers. Table 2 presents the number of children whose scores are higher or lower than the mean scores of parents, teachers, and peers by one point.

No Mennonite child is more religiously inclined toward school than Mennonite parents or Mennonite teachers. Among those children whose scores are lower than those of parents, 44% report "many" psychosomatic symptoms. Among children whose perception of school as a religious agency is lower than the parental perception, 30% show many psychosomatic symptoms. Among those whose religious score is lower than their peers', 15% show maladjustment symptoms. In other words, deviation from parental views is most likely to accompany

TABLE 2

DEVIATION FROM THE SCORES GIVEN BY PARENTS, TEACHERS, AND PEERS, AND PSYCHOSOMATIC SYMPTOMS

Deviation	Mennonites		Japanese		Whites	
	# of children	% showing "many" psychosomatic symptoms	# of children	% showing "many" psychosomatic symptoms	# of children	% showing "many" psychosomatic symptoms
Religious						
Deviation from parents						
Above ($\bar{X}+1$)	0	—	10	—	0	—
Below ($\bar{X}-1$)	64	44	63	21	70	23
Deviation from teachers						
Above ($\bar{X}+1$)	0	—	5	*	13	*
Below ($\bar{X}-1$)	48	30	73	22	62	19
Deviation from peers						
Above ($\bar{X}+1$)	20	30	48	17	35	23
Below ($\bar{X}-1$)	30	23	33	19	38	24
Social						
Deviation from parents						
Above ($\bar{X}+1$)	0	—	0	—	0	—
Below ($\bar{X}-1$)	54	32	89	28	68	21
Deviation from teachers						
Above ($\bar{X}+1$)	7	*	58	24	36	22
Below ($\bar{X}-1$)	46	26	18	24	37	24
Deviation from peers						
Above ($\bar{X}+1$)	28	18	20	40	35	23
Below ($\bar{X}-1$)	31	16	35	38	36	22
Individual						
Deviation from parents						
Above ($\bar{X}+1$)	55	33	70	24	63	8
Below ($\bar{X}-1$)	0	—	15	*	25	35

Deviation from teachers						
Above $(\bar{X}+1)$	47	29	0	—	0	—
Below $(\bar{X}-1)$	22	27	51	26	38	36
Deviation from peers						
Above $(\bar{X}+1)$	32	56	30	38	0	—
Below $(\bar{X}-1)$	41	24	38	42	39	38
Occupational						
Deviation from parents						
Above $(\bar{X}+1)$	67	35	0	—	0	—
Below $(\bar{X}-1)$	0	—	98	26	93	19
Deviation from teachers						
Above $(\bar{X}+1)$	47	38	37	27	13	*
Below $(\bar{X}-1)$	28	36	42	28	50	18
Deviation from peers						
Above $(\bar{X}+1)$	21	48	40	10	35	23
Below $(\bar{X}-1)$	44	23	40	45	34	20

Notes:
1. *Percentage is not shown due to the small number of cases.

many psychosomatic symptoms, followed by deviation from teachers', and then from peers' perspectives.

In relation to peers, a Mennonite child is likely to suffer from maladjustment symptoms when he deviates from the peer norms by either a greater amount (30%) or a lesser (23%) in religious inclination.

In the areas of social, individual, and occupational socialization by the school, similar trends are seen as in the religious socialization discussed above. Children are less likely than parents or teachers to consider the function of the school as teaching social conformity but rather as guiding students toward self actualization. Deviation from parents is most likely to induce stress upon the children, followed by deviation from teachers, than from peers.

Among the four areas of socialization religious deviation is most likely to be accompanied by symptoms of maladjustment in children. In short, among the Mennonites parental role in socialization is more important than teachers' or peers' roles, and religious socialization overrides other areas.

In contrast, religious deviation from parents or teachers does not seem to affect a Japanese child as much as a Mennonite child. Approximately one-fifth of those whose views are different from parents, teachers, or peers show many psychosomatic symptoms.

Japanese parents and public school teachers are more likely than Japanese children to emphasize social conformity or anti-individuation as the goal of education. A quarter of the Japanese children who hold more individualistic views than teachers or parents indicate many psychosomatic symptoms. On the other hand, approximately 40% of the children who deviate from peers either in the direction of social conformity or individuation show signs of maladjustment. Forty-five percent of those who deviate from their peers' perception of education in the area of vocational training suffer from many psychosomatic symptoms.

In short, among Japanese Canadian children, deviation from peer group norms is more closely associated with psychosomatic symptoms than deviation from norms held by parents or teachers. This is in agreement with the previous findings (Lyman, 1971) that "generation" as an age group serves as an important determinant of behaviour for Japanese Canadians.

In the areas of religious, social, or occupational socialization by the school whether or not a white child deviates from the perspectives held by parents, teachers, or peers does not make much difference upon his mental health. Approximately 22% of deviant children show many psychosomatic symptoms.

On the other hand, whether or not a white child holds a deviant view concerning the individuating function of the school is closely associated with the symptoms of maladjustment. More than a third of the white children who are more individualistically inclined than parents, teachers, or peers manifest many psychosomatic symptoms.

Thus, when white children are compared to Mennonite or Japanese children, there appears to be no singular socialization agent which exerts exclusive power.

CONCLUSION

As minority groups in Canada both Mennonites and Japanese children are at crossroads because of various socializing agents. Mennonites with religious doctrines of isolationism are able to insulate their children from outside influences. Parents play the most important role in the religious socialization of their children. Deviation from parental views seems to induce anxiety in a Mennonite child more than deviation from teachers' or peers' opinions.

Japanese Canadian children are exposed to the central values of Canadian society through the public school. Placed between the opposing forces of parents representing traditional Japanese culture and teachers with Canadian values, a Japanese Canadian child seems to value the opinion of his peers. His frame of reference is provided by other Japanese Canadian children who similarly suffer from marginality. Hence deviation from peers tends to produce stress in the mind of a Japanese Canadian child.

Finally, the above research findings should be viewed with caution in the light of the small and nonrepresentative sample size as well as the narrow focus on socialization issues. The data serve to illuminate some of the mechanisms of socialization rather than to give conclusive generalizations. Also, it should be noted that the usefulness of sweeping generalizations concerning any ethnic group or a society is highly controversial.

References

Eaton, J.W. and R.J. Weil
  1955 *Culture and Mental Disorders*, Glencoe: Free Press.

Fretz, J. Winfield
  1967 *The Mennonites in Ontario*, Kitchener: The Mennonite Historical Society of Ontario.

Gurin, Gerald, et al.
  1960 *Americans View Their Mental Health*, New York: Basic Books.

Gutkind, P.C.W.
  1952 "Secularization versus the Christian Community: The Problems of an Old Order House Amish Family," Unpublished M.A. Thesis, University of Chicago.

Hosokawa, William
  1969 *Nisei: The Quiet Americans*, New York: Morrow.

Hostetler, John A.
  1963 *Amish Society*, Baltimore: Johns Hopkins.
  1971 *Children in Amish Society*, New York: Holt, Rinehart & Winston.

Inaba, M.
  1968 "Japanese Community in Metropolitan Toronto," A report submitted to the Ontario Human Rights Commission, Toronto.

Kurokawa, Minako
  1969a "Cultural Conflict and Mental Disorder," *Journal of Social Issues*, Vol. 25, pp. 195-214.

Kurokawa, Minako
1969b "Psycho-Social Roles of Mennonite Children in a Changing Society," *Canadian Review of Sociology and Anthropology* Vol. 6, pp. 15-35.
1970 "Linear Orientation in Child-Rearing Practices among Japanese," *Journal of Marriage and Family*, Vol. 30, pp. 129-136.

Laviolette, F.E.
1948 *Canadian Japanese and World War II*. Toronto: University of Toronto Press.

Lipset, Seymour M.
1964 "Value Differences, Absolute or Relative: The English-speaking Democracies," in B.R. Blishen, *et al.* (eds.), *Canadian Society*, Toronto: Macmillan, pp. 325-340.

Lyman, Stanford M.
1971 *The Asian in the West*. University of Nevada System.

Maykovich, Minako K.
1970 "Beyond Integration and Stability: Mental Health of Mennonite Children," *British Journal of Social Psychiatry*, Vol. 3, pp. 215-226.
1975 "Ethnic Variation in Success Value," in Robert M. Pike and Elia Zureik (eds.), *Socialization and Values in Canadian Society*, Toronto: McClelland & Stewart, pp. 150-179.

Maykovich, Minako K.
1971 "The Japanese Family in Tradition and Change," in K. Ishwaran (ed.), *Canadian Family*, Toronto: Holt, Rinehart & Winston, pp. 33-46.

Naegle, K.D.
1964 "Canadian Society: Some Further Reflections," in B.R. Blishen, *et al.*, (eds.), *Canadian Society*, Toronto: Macmillan, pp. 497-522.

Porter, John
1967 "Canadian Character in the Twentieth Century," *The Annals of the American Academy of Political and Social Science*, Vol. 370, pp. 48-56.

Truman, T.
1971 "A Critique of Seymour M. Lipset's Article "Value Differences: Absolute or Relative: The English-speaking Democracies," *Canadian Journal of Political Science*, Vol. 4, pp. 497-525.

Wrong, D.H.
1955 *American and Canadian Viewpoints*, Washington, D.C.: American Council on Education.

Young, C.H. et al.

1938   *The Japanese Canadians*, Toronto: University of Toronto Press.

Private Schools: The Culture, Structure and Processes of Elite Socialization in English Canada

MARY PERCIVAL MAXWELL
JAMES D. MAXWELL
Queen's University at Kingston

In non-literate societies the socialization process is a part of everyday life, and the major part of it is usually carried out by parents or kin. In our society, until relatively recently, the patterns were similar. Prior to the nineteenth century, some families retained tutors and others founded or supported private schools. While the church and the wealthy occasionally operated schools as charities, for most children and adolescents, the major part of the socialization process now carried out in the school was carried out in the home and family. The advent of state-funded education in the nineteenth century made the system of tutors, governesses and private schools unnecessary insofar as the availability of instruction was concerned. However rare private instructors may now be, the private school remains an integral part of the Canadian social structure. Support for this type of school comes from those who for reasons of religion beliefs, ideas about educational quality, or outright snobbery are willing to pay privately for the privilege of schooling their children outside the state system, in addition to paying the taxes for education in that system itself.

In this study, we first look at the structure of private education in Canada. In particular, we focus on the development of private schools and the relationship of private education to the power structure. Subsequently we want to look at the structure of the socialization process in the private school system and the way in which it is related to the structure of the larger society. This study is an attempt to provide a synthesis and review of the research on private school socialization in Canada.

PREVIOUS WORK ON PRIVATE SCHOOLS IN CANADA

Social histories of Canadian private schools and biographies of former principals including recent work by Gossage (1977), Simmonds (1972), Lamont (1972), Penton (1972), Sowby (1971) and Steele (1971) are more numerous than sociological studies of private schools in Canada (Maxwell, 1970; Maxwell and Maxwell, 1971, 1975; Weinsweig, 1970, 1977 and Podmore, 1976). With the exception of Podmore, both types of work tend to focus on individual schools and their role in Canadian society. Despite the fact that Porter (1965), Clement (1975) and Newman (1975) discuss the role of private schools as class institutions in the perpetuation of elites, little if any systematic attention has been paid to comparative organizational structures, socialization processes and personality formation, and the formal ties these schools have to national elites and inter-generational access to power and privilege. Work done in the United States and Britain is more comprehensive (Ollerenshaw, 1967; Wilkinson, 1964; Weinberg, 1967; McArthur, 1954; Wakeford, 1969).

Undoubtedly, the neglect of private schools by sociologists in Canada reflects the limited amount of work done in this country in the sociology of education (Card, 1976; Clark, 1973) as well as the more specific problem of research access to the more elite institutions (Weinberg, 1968; Weinsweig, 1970). In addition, the relatively low enrollments of students in private secondary schools in Canada's nine anglophone provinces (3.41% in 1975), in comparison with 8.09% in Great Britain, 7.74% in the United States and 24.19% in Australia may have led to them being overlooked because of their small numbers.[1] We shall argue later on that this makes them more crucial in relation to elite socialization.

THE DEVELOPMENT OF PRIVATE SCHOOLS IN CANADA

The first schools in what is now Canada were private schools established first by the Roman Catholic Church and later by the growing involvement of the Protestant denominations. The first formal secondary school for boys was founded in 1635-36 by the Jesuits who opened a college (Petite Ecole) at Quebec which served as a model for the later *collèges classiques* developed under British rule. In 1642, the first school for girls in Quebec was founded by the Ursulines. What were to become the *collèges classiques* followed the traditional French curriculum of Greek, Latin, philosophy and theology which constituted the appropriate educational background for careers for men in the professions, church and academie. All of these colleges were private feepaying institutions as were the privately sponsored schools and academies of the English speaking population. Outside Quebec, the oldest private school still in existence is King's College School, (Windsor, Nova Scotia) founded by Bishop Inglis in 1788. The oldest existing girls' school in Anglophone Canada is Bishop Strachan School, Toronto, founded the year of Confederation.

While some private schools continue to exist in Quebec, in 1962 the Quebec government undertook to pay fees in all the classical colleges. In 1967, legislation based on the Parent Commission established the CEGEP's (Collèges d'enseignement géneral et professionnel) which replaced the collèges classiques. While many of Quebec's formerly private schools continue their traditions, government subsidization has ceased to make them anything more but nominally private in terms of the fees paid.

In the nineteenth century, there was increasing debate over the need for mass schooling. Although the Common Schools Act was established in 1816 in Upper Canada, private schools continued to be founded. Generally, Roman Catholics fought to retain their own distinctive schools while most Protestant denominations accepted the principle of interdenominational schools. Some, mainly Anglican groups were an exception and continued to found private schools which have come to form the core of the elite private schools in English Canada today.

The position of power wielded by Anglicans in Upper Canada was enhanced by their access to the Clergy Reserves. Led by Strachan, Bishop of Toronto, the Anglicans strove to maintain power against the Methodists led by Ryerson, the champion of state schools. Despite the growth of the public school system, private schools continued to be established and enrollments continued to grow in absolute numbers if not as a percentage of children attending school. It was not until 1865 that grants for girls were established in grammar schools (high schools) and that was calculated at half that given for a boy. Finally in 1871, grammar schools were declared co-educational. Podmore maintains that the sociological role of private schools changed with the introduction of state systems: "Perhaps they (private schools before the rise of public schools) were class institutions but they were certainly not elitist institutions. It was the passage of the fee-less state school legislation which converted the private sector into a more elitist direction." (1976: 193).

A common distinction between private schools in Canada is between the "schools of privilege" (the elite schools) and the "schools of protest" (ethnic, linguistic, free schools and those which serve the smaller Protestant denominations). In total there are 552 private schools in English Canada (Statistics Canada, 1975-76). The formal association of the schools of privilege was established in the 1930s with the founding of the Canadian Headmistresses' Association in 1931 (later changed to the Canadian Association of Principals of Indpendent

Schools for Girls — CAPISG) and the Canadian Headmasters' Association (CHA) four years later. To become members in either association, the schools must offer courses designed to prepare students for university entrance and for CHA membership they must be Protestant. Some of the smallest private boys' schools are not members of the Association (e.g. Rousseau Lake School, Ontario and Qualicum College, B.C.). Recently CAPISG opened its membership to schools of all religions, but only three English Catholic schools have joined. At present, these two associations have a combined membership of 51 schools. The size of the schools ranges from Sedbergh School, Montebello, Quebec with 73 boys to 900 at Upper Canada College, Toronto. For girls, the range is from 150 at Queen's Margaret's School, Duncan, B.C. to 675 at both Havergal College and Bishop Strachan School, Toronto. These schools have a combined enrollment of 17,000 students over half of whom are female. This enrollment represents only about two percent of the primary and secondary school population in Canada.

It is these 51 schools which constitute the schools of privilege in English Canada and it is upon these schools that the study focuses. Although many of these schools operate primary schools as well, our concern here is with the secondary level. While we have discussed the structural features of boarding schools elsewhere (Maxwell and Maxwell, 1971) we focus here on the secondary level as it functions as an integrated unit of day and boarding students. While a comparison of English and French private school traditions in Canada is desirable, the difficulties of getting comparable statistical data, and the problems of comparability due to government funding of private schools in Quebec make it necessary to confine this study to the other nine provinces, and the anglophone schools in Quebec.

PRIVATE SCHOOLS AND THE NATIONAL CHARACTERISTICS OF EDUCATION

The constitutional division of powers which has resulted in variation by province in the system of public education in Canada has also created provincial variations in the private school sector. While the adage "He who pays the piper calls the tune" does not hold as strongly for private schools, provincial educational standards, with some exceptions, have been adopted by private schools. The economic structure of the society and its historical development have also affected the distribution and pre-eminence of private schools in Canada. While the first schools were founded in the Maritimes, and private schools were also founded in Western Canada, the largest number and the most prestigious schools are to be found in Toronto and Montreal and the areas surrounding them. Private schools are found in the most highly urbanized areas and in the centers of economic power. Ontario has 20 private schools of privilege, Quebec, 12; British Columbia, 10; and Nova Scotia, 4. Manitoba and New Brunswick each have two schools and Alberta has one school.

The most distinctive characteristics of the Canadian system of private education is that it is almost entirely confined to the pre-university level. By contrast, the United States, in addition to its "prep schools" has had a tradition of private college and university education where the level of tuition and fees works to exclude all but the well-off. Although there may be financial barriers to post-secondary education in Canada, the fee structure among universities is relatively similar and there are no universities where fees are five or six times the national average. Consequently, although studies of Canadian universities show them to be disproportionately the preserve of the middle and upper classes (Pike, 1970; Porter, Porter and Blishen, 1973) they are all equally restrictive or equally open. There is no set of universities beyond the total group where fees exclude those with high academic achievement. While some universities are able to attract students with above average records, and these may well be the children of the privileged (who may themselves aspire to sending their children to these particular institutions) the concentration of the children of the elite is not as great as in a system with a sub-set of private universities. Consequently, the role of the private school becomes more significant as a differentiating agent in the social system. In particular, secondary school attendance becomes a significant factor. While attendance at an elite primary school may be interesting, without attendance at a private secondary school, it is not likely to have much impact. It is the importance of peer group relations at the stage of the socialization cycle which is reached in the high school years which contributes to the significance of the role of the private secondary school. The congruence between private school attendance and this process results in the establishment of friendships and networks which continue and endure throughout the life cycle. The proposition that the greater the interaction the greater the liking, advanced by Homans (1950) appears to hold in the majority of cases. Although some may rebel in later life against their position and former friends from their private school days, for the majority their favourable orientation continues. For a significant segment of this majority, the interaction itself does not cease but continues in different structures throughout their lives.

While there is obviously some element of parental determination in sending children to private schools, for the adolescents themselves, the result is an experience which is more carefully selected and arranged than in most Canadian high schools. In addition to the process of self (or parental) selection, the schools themselves are very conscious of the requirements of offering a superior education as defined by their clientele. The result is a socialization process with a structure and culture which is carefully controlled and administered and which, if successful in the individual case, results in a certain form of integration of the individual in Canadian society which endures throughout the life cycle.

PRIVATE SCHOOLS AND THE LARGER SOCIETY

In *The Vertical Mosaic* (1965) Porter demonstrated that persons who had attended private schools exerted considerably greater social power than their mere numbers would suggest. Clement (1975) has demonstrated that the pervasiveness of private school background is on the increase among the economic elite. While 34.2% of the 611 Canadian born members of the economic elite had attended private schools in Porter's 1965 study, this had increased to 39.8% by the time Clement examined the same group. The actual years to which the data pertain are 1951 and 1972, and while the percentage increase is not overwhelming in itself, it becomes more dramatic if one had assumed that the Canadian power structure was becoming more open during that period. Caution, however, is in order in interpreting this as a continuing elitist trend. Entry into the elite comes relatively late in life and the 1972 data reflect little of the educational change following World War II.

Despite questions of trends, both Porter and Clement attribute a critical and strategic role to the private schools in Canada. Clement summarizes that role as follows:

> Although they may be examined as educational institutions, private schools are most appropriately understood as class institutions designed to create upper class associations and maintain class values both by exclusion and socialization; that is, exclusion of the lower classes and socialization of the potential elite. Private school education is a life long asset for the select few who experience it. (1975: 244)

Clement goes on to argue that private school experience coupled with university attendance, residence in exclusive areas of Canada's metropolitan centres, and membership in the most exclusive clubs such as the York Club in Toronto and the St. James Club in Montreal are facilitated by and contribute to one's elite social status. Whereas university education and post-graduate and professional degrees are becoming more important as prerequisites for membership in the economic elite, among those who hold multiple directorships, (what Oswald Hall (1949) in another context has called the 'inner fraternity') the percentage of those who had attended private school increased from 52.9% in the 1951 data to 72.2% in the 1972 data (Clement, 1975: 458). The role of the private school is underscored when we recall that the percentage of students attending private elementary or secondary schools was two percent in 1971 (*Canada Year Book*, 1972: 400). Such high representation calls for further examination of the relationship between the schools and society.

Formally, and to a great extent in reality, the relationships of the schools with the larger society are presided over by a Board of Governors. At what Parsons (1960) has called the institutional level, they mobilize financial resources and secure political support. With the Board of Governors, length of service tends to be one of the most striking characteristics. The Board is usually a self-perpetuating body with new members being appointed by the old. This procedure provides for great continuity in the recruitment of "like-minded individuals." The fact that in the past many members served for over twenty years reinforces continuity and tradition within the school and many of the more conservative values. In the case of Havergal College in Toronto (founded 1894) there was a total of only seven board chairmen in seven decades and one man held the office for twenty-five consecutive years. In addition, virtually all members of the boards of these schools attended private schools themselves and the majority also have other elitist connections (Maxwell, 1970).

Since the board is responsible for financial matters, including salaries and fees, and contractual matters such as the appointment and terms of office of the principal and other personnel, it is often rationalized that the girls' schools as well as the boys' schools require male trustees. Until recently the relative lack of female lawyers, architects, chartered accountants and corporate benefactors resulted in stronger male concern than one might expect with the socialization process in private schools (particularly girls' schools). Membership on the board, of course, offered yet another opportunity for the contact with other members of the elite in the overlapping directorships which form a part of the confraternity of power. In this context the private schools were like private clubs for the very small number of men who ran them for their children (and of course the children of others). While there was to some extent a vested interest (hardly a strong one) it is not only tradition but also the ability to mobilize resources and to manage them that keeps men on the boards of these schools. The structural and cultural repercussions of male dominance on the boards has led one "old girl" to comment:

> . . .it is still a female community designed by men, overseen by mostly a male board, and plunked into a culture with male values. It (the girl's school) preached feminine achievement but also feminine submission. (Swan, 1977: 116)

We shall explore this further when we look at the socialization process and its consequences.

In the case of private schools, alumni also act at the institutional level to mobilize support in the larger society. Whereas in most other organizations those who leave seldom sustain or wish to sustain a commitment, schools have potentially strong support from those who pass through their doors. In recent years universities and private schools have moved to involve their former students in a more active way, particularly with regard to financial support. Money is seldom forthcoming unless the alumni can identify with the school. Private schools have an advantage because in addition to the enriched experiences they supply in both the curriculum and the extra-curriculum they are likely to retain the academic staff which supplied them. Low rates of turnover, which we will subsequently discuss, allow the school to retain a core of committed teachers with whom, board members, former students (and sometimes their children) can clearly identify. The goals and purposes of the school, although they may change somewhat, have a continuous physical embodiment beyond the bricks and mortar which in the case of the ordinary high school are often the only symbols remaining.

"Old boys" and "old girls" form the alumni of the private schools and play a strategic role in the maintenance of elitist norms and values, and in supporting the school financially and sponsoring it in the larger society among friends and in relation to the power structure. The functions of the "old school tie" and the "old boy network" are well-known. When one becomes a "new boy" or a "new girl" one becomes a member of this network. More than ordinary school attendance, going to a private school means one is a member for life. This involves sponsorship of the school, and of the careers of its members. Class reunions, membership on the board of governors, attendance of relatives' children, and the children of associates at the school keep the alumni closer to the school than they might be to their former high school. An alumni magazine keeps those who may be more peripheral in formal contact with the school. For those who are more central, particularly the males, the reciprocal interaction between school and work may continue throughout their lives; they are socialized into a world from which they continue to support their school. From a structural point of view the two are highly complementary; not only has the school contributed to the sense of belonging and community in the world which Porter and Clement have described but support and contributions to the school give personal immediate satisfaction and ensure strong possibilities of a similar sense of community among the upper classes of the next generation.

SOCIALIZATION — STRUCTURE AND PROCESS

To understand the socialization process in these private schools, the major cultural features of the schools and their inter-relationships must be examined. These include the ideology, the goals and values, and recruitment and selection processes. In the following section some of the unique organizational features of the school are explored in conjunction with the cultural variables. We want to demonstrate how processes of selection, socialization and social control contribute to a class based experience for the private school student during the adolescent years.

Weinsweig has used the concept of "compliance" (Etzioni, 1961: 3) in his study of Upper Canada College. Primary processes of selection and identification and secondary processes of boundary maintenance and legitimate authority complement each other in the socialization process. Because of their stringent selection processes the schools can exercise more control over their members' values. Because they attempt to select those students whose values are already congruent with the school identification (which facilitates compliance), compliance is initially strong. Through the complex effects of role models, structural features and rewards for identification and conformity this identification is typically strengthened over the course of the years at the school. Boundary maintenance also facilitates compliance by blocking or obscuring countervailing influences external to the school and reinforcing the saliency and effectiveness of processes and influences internal to the school. While this is more possible in boarding schools, day schools have important mechanisms of boundary maintenance as well. Uniforms which symbolically separate the students from those attending public high schools, and compulsory after-school sports which reduce contact with non-private school students as well as the organization of exchanges with other private schools on social occasions and for sports events, make for a "separate world."

In two independent analyses of private schools, one a boys' school (Weinsweig, 1970) and the other a girls' school, (Maxwell, 1970), the same set of cultural themes and values, structural features and mechanisms of socialization and social control emerged. It is the dynamics and effectiveness of these that we shall examine in the following sections.

THE PRINCIPAL AND THE TEACHING STAFF

Prior to the turn of the century the majority of the principals and the academic and service staff were recruited from Britain and had been raised in the ethos of the English public school system. It was this group which established the tradition of private schools in Canada which meshed with the culture of the upper classes in Anglo-Canada. Today the vast majority of staff at all levels are Canadian born, and the academic staff are very likely to be graduates of Canadian private schools; the principals are not infrequently graduates of the schools they head. The tradition of private school attendance may also be a family tradition of private school teaching and administration. For instance the father of the present headmaster of Lakefield College School (founded in 1879) was headmaster of Ridley College (founded 1889) and his grandfather was the first headmaster of Upper Canada Prep School and founding headmaster of Appleby College, Oakville (founded 1911). Other patterns of intergenerational continuity exist and the traditions they support are reinforced by the long periods of tenure of many of the principals. For instance St. Andrew's College, Aurora, Ontario (founded 1899) has had only five principals in the school's history. The similarity of educational background, social class, as well as the long periods in office provide a unique source of continuity and stability over the generations of the ideals, ethos and practices traditional to the private schools and the clientele they serve.

While this continuity and ethos is not as strong in the case of the teachers, it is highly detectable. Since the role of private school teachers is typically more diffuse than that of the teachers in the public system, the recruitment of teaching staff is relatively more important. Parents paying fees are likely to be more concerned about the quality of the socializing agents and their concern is not only in terms of competence in formal subjects but also with the teachers' credibility as role models (although not particularly in relation to occupation). Since the teachers are expected to exemplify the ethos of the school and to participate in the myriad of activities the school provides for its students, the importance of the role demands is more likely to be recognized by teachers who are themselves private school graduates. The professional role model with which they identify may have been strongly influenced by their high school experience and recruitment to the private school system becomes in part a process of self selection. Staffing summer camps, conducting tours of Europe, running weekend programs for boarders, sports programs, clubs and cultural and charitable events often make the school a total institution for teachers as well as students in boarding. Homogeneity of origins of the teaching staff is often coupled with long tenure as in the case of principals. Weinsweig (1970: 62) found that 34% of the teachers at Upper Canada College had been to private schools and that the span of service for all teachers at the school was 15 years. Maxwell (1970) reported similar findings in the case of a girls' school. Teachers are expected to have wide ranging interests to contribute to the enrichment of the lives of students at the school. Individuals with such capabilities and desire to exercise them are more likely to be the products of the private school system and more likely to gravitate back to it to find an outlet for their talents. The consequence is a core of teachers devoted to the school and its ethos and who remain there for a long period of time. These people are dedicated to providing continuity in the socialization process and they are symbols of beliefs and traditions that alumni and board members trust and respect. As in the case of alumni support, the private schools rely on their own graduates to continue the traditions in teaching.

STUDENTS — SELECTION AND RECRUITMENT

In organizations, recruitment and selection processes influence subsequent socialization processes and modes of social control. As opposed to prisons which must accept those who are assigned to them, and have non-voluntary inmates, most private schools, despite their increasing fees, now have larger pools of applicants from which to select than they did in the past. These application ratios (sometimes 10: 1) make it possible for the school to select, from those who wish to come, those most likely to be compatibile with the school. Problem children or children who are applicants because of parental insistence may be excluded during the selection process. The schools of privilege can then accept those who already identify strongly with the private school ethos, values and modes of socialization and control and are likely to be high on academic achievement as measured by the entrance examination. In relation to the social structure in the larger society, this process tends to "cull out" those children of the elite and upper classes who do not have the relatively high potential. Resources are thus allocated to the most promising, and there is a certain conservation of resources because the most promising are also highly committed to the socialization process in which they are participating.

Lying behind this commitment are a number of structural variables which have led to the high level of anticipatory socialization referred to above. Both Weinsweig and Maxwell found that 50% of the students' same sex parent had attended private school, and of these, almost a half had attended the same school as their children were now attending. Moreover, a majority of the students at both the schools studied had a relative who had attended the school. Not only does this allow selective recruitment to reduce the effort required for socialization and social control (Etzioni, 1961: 70) but it reinforces the generational continuity within the school and the making and conserving of traditions and family alliances among the elite. Weinsweig found two brothers attending Upper Canada College who could trace connections with the school back 136 years through six generations. The long history of a school and family connection exemplifies the reciprocal relationship between the school and the social structure and how structural relationships facilitate cultural transmission and reinforcement in the socialization process.

Other structural factors complement those we have already discussed. Our reference to an elite and upper class origins are borne out by empirical findings which indicate that virtually all of the occupations of the fathers of students at two Toronto schools fall into Class I or II of the Blishen Scale. (Maxwell, Weinsweig, 1970). An examination of *Who's Who in Canada* and the *Canadian Who's Who* indicates that a significant percentage of parents are in one or both of the two Canadian social registers. This simply confirms the evidence of the attendance at private school of elites and their children and the consequent linkages pointed out by Porter (1965) and Clement (1975). The religious affiliations of the elite are also reflected in private school attendance, and although there are certain denominational affiliations, Anglicans are overrepresented in the private school system just as they are among the elite (Clement, 1975). Weinsweig has pointed out that the belief that the schools have religious preferences inhibits applications and that religious "outsiders" help create the social conditions they perceive (1970: 43). Religion, social class and intergenerational continuity influence and mesh with the patterns of recruitment and selection, and these features work in such a way as to facilitate the socialization process insofar as motivational and ideological aspects are concerned. A presently high selectivity ratio in most private schools also reduces the problems of transmitting the content of the curriculum itself, since the students admitted to the school have been well-prepared academically.

THE GRADE-STRATIFIED PRIVILEGE SYSTEM

The grade-stratified privilege system and its ideology is a universally and systematically employed socializing technique and method of social control. The system is such that each grade theoretically enjoys all the privileges of the preceding grades and some, but not all, of those of the succeeding grades. It is a system of *privileges* and not rights since they can theoretically be withdrawn by staff. This implicit threat provides a potent means of gaining behavioural compliance from the group and through peer group pressure, from the individual. Privileges are earned through increasing identification and compliance and increasing responsibility in relation to the ideology and structure of the school which is *assumed* to increase with each succeeding grade. Privileges cover a wide range of practices (e.g. unsupervised study, eligibility for grade linked offices) and they are more extensively used in the boarding schools than in the day schools. These privileges all offer a carefully measured additional amount of autonomy and require less staff supervision and control. Privileges are either age graded maturational rewards or performance rewards not specifically contingent on one's status or the age-graded hierarchy, e.g. earning the privilege of unsupervised study by consistently good study habits for a period of time in supervised study.

DELEGATED AUTHORITY AND THE PRIVILEGE SYSTEM

The homogeneity of social class and value systems coupled with the voluntarism of recruitment permits these schools to utilize organizational features and processes of social control by which students themselves are co-opted as agents of socialization and control. The schools are able to assume an identity on the students' part while at the same time attempting to strengthen that identity through the privilege system and its corollary, increasing amounts of authority in the status hierarchy of the school. Weinberg (1967) and Wilkinson (1969) have described the way in which British public schools use the prefect system (which is part of the system of delegated authority) to co-opt senior students into roles where they assist in the administration and discipline of the rest of the student body. Wilkinson states: ". . .the communitty conferred high status only as a *quid pro quo* offering prefectorial privileges, special living comforts, freedom from certain rules, and so on — in return for duty" (1964: 31). The prefect system not only co-opts the most senior students but relieves the principal and staff of much of the detailed, time consuming aspects of social control. At the same time that it acts as a reward for conformity it also, in the word of Weinberg, "co-opts the senior, most mature and articulate boys into the authority hierarchy at a stage when they could cause infinite trouble if excluded" (1967: 123-4). Regardless of whether prefects are elected or appointed, the myriad of activities and the carefully planned system of rewards which accompany them appear to be highly effective in producing the behavioural and ideological conformity among the prefects who, by their visibility and responsibility, serve as role models for the school. The result is that there are highly visible "career lines" in the school and at the time that the prefects are put in office, their contribution to the school is thoroughly discussed. Having such a "career" at the school involves identification with the formal authority structure and the reward system. Since this structure pervades all the school sponsored activities few students can avoid being rewarded and being co-opted by the system. In addition to the psychic rewards, elaborate installation rituals and insignia of office (badges, pins, belts, ties, crests, blazers) put conformity and rewards clearly in the public domain of the school. Students have difficulty in playing down their commitment to the system.

While there is a system of punishments — negative marks which count against the "house" collectivities and against the individual, the schools rely heavily on positive rewards in a pluralistic opportunity structure as a means of promoting identification, co-operation and group morale.[2] Co-optation into the authority structure and the privilege system results in most students seeing the system of formal authority as it is exercised by staff as beneficial to themselves and the school and as training them in exercising responsibility. The structure as it exists is congruent with the ideology and values articulated at the cultural level in the organization. It is this complementariness which perhaps accounts for the absence of "youth culture" (a set of values antithetical to those of adults). This absence has been observed by researchers in Canada's private schools (Maxwell, Weinsweig, 1970). The student culture demonstrates a dramatically high conformity to the official norms of the school and the beliefs of parents.

IDEOLOGY, VALUES AND PROCESSES

The ideology of the private schools cannot be considered in isolation from those of their clientele, particularly their parental clientele. Socialization in the home and socialization in the school may not be completely congruent in values and techniques but they appear to complement each other extremely well. The schools serve a segment of the most highly privileged families in Canada. According to Gossage, the independent school claims that its function is "to train those already privileged by virtue of talent or birth to social responsibility" (1977: 6). The idea that *with privilege goes responsibility* is an overarching ideological tenent of most private schools which finds expression not only in the culture of the schools but in their social structure as well. Students are sent to the school to acquire the values their parents hold or think are appropriate to children in their position: there is little doubt that many private schools teach *noblesse oblige* to the children of the *nouveau riche* as well as reinforcing it in the children of "old families."

Privilege and responsibility are linked to *achievement* in the private school system. In many cases only a small fraction of the sons and daughters could surpass their father's financial success in his field. This necessitates placing a strong emphasis on the quality of the achievement and not on financial success alone. Responsibility is thus linked to privilege in one generation and achievement in the next and provides continuity and motivation where otherwise the child might well choose to live off the family's reputation and financial assets. This emphasis on responsibility results in an emphasis on humanism and an emphasis on the whole person which emerges in the curriculum and school activities. Charitable work and service, interpersonal and group responsibility are stressed in sports and physical education, music and cultural activities and in the running of the school itself. The stress on these features is far stronger than in the average high school and is linked to the future leadership responsibilities anticipated for the participants.

The schools regard their students as the potential leaders in the major facets of Canadian life. Since their parents have exercised power in the corporate, bureaucratic, and political elite, and in the professions, the expectations the school holds for its students are formulated on the basis that the student will hold similar power in the future. Leadership then becomes a component of the ideology of the school, and many of the professions involved in the socialization process at the school see themselves as influencing society by training a more humanitarian elite for the next generation. While we have stressed responsibility up to this point, leadership raises the question of individualism. Most schools stress the importance of the individual and pay careful attention to each student's abilities and aspiration, and to limitations as well. The result is a sort of nineteenth century humanitarian liberalism which functions well within the small scale structure of the school and which is not in conflict with the values of parents. Such an ideology permits the more progressive teachers to hope for change and the more conservative parents to believe that it will not occur, or only gradually. For the student the system stresses responsibility and individual contribution and appears to liberate the student from many of the "worst" peer-group and organization pressures found in many public high schools. While the ideology provides a unifying influence for a diversity of structural segments and values in and outside the schools it also tolerates a range of ideological differences and thereby maintains conflict within manageable limits.

One of the problems of change is related to the growing tendency among the girls' schools to regard their role as facilitating the entry of their graduates into the same achievement path as males while clinging to the traditional role model for upper class women. In the traditional model the woman was to maintain her social position through her selection of a husband and to demonstrate her social responsibility through participation in the higher levels of the cultural and charitable milieu in which such women found "careers." The past decade has seen a significant increase in the percentage of "old girls" who are in the labour force or pursuing professional degrees. Weinberg (1967: 22), Maxwell (1970: 147) and Weinsweig (1970: 135) all suggest that the high academic standards of these private schools attempt to make the children of privilege achievement-oriented and for some time the girls' schools have been becoming more academically oriented. At the present time most private school females can usually surpass their mother's occupational achievements although they may find themselves in the same bind as their male counterparts with respect to their father's record. Although their achievements may surpass their mother's they may not place them in key positions of power in the society. As we stated elsewhere (1975), forsaking the traditional upper class role for women may mean that these females exercise less power and responsibility than their mothers who, despite the fact that they were not caught up in the occupational struggle, wielded considerable influence. The ideologies of the schools have, with certain strains, legitimated both philanthropic and employment roles for women. As the larger culture changes, and women attending private schools accept the current ideas about achievement for women, certain strains are emerging.

ACADEMIC EDUCATION AS A PROCESS

The value of academic achievement is fostered through the recruitment process itself as well as by the staff and an elaborate system of rewards for academic progress and distinction. Many of the schools have "progress marks" and count the academic averages of house members in the system of inter-house competition. Public recognition of achievement in the academic sphere is given at the annual "Prizegiving Ceremony" attended by parents and alumni and plaques are prominently displayed in the corridors of the schools with the names of those who have achieved academic honours inscribed thereon. The reward for academic achievement is epitomized in the "senior student" prefectship — the office awarded to the Grade XIII (Ontario) student with the highest academic standing in Grade XII. This student participates in the governing of the school along with the other prefects and symbolizes the importance of academic excellence in the ideology of the system.

Most schools and their clientele do not regard private school attendance as merely an end in itself but as an environment for preparing virtually all students for university attendance. While some students who failed to live up to their early academic promise are guided towards non-university courses, the schools have a long tradition of sending a high percentage of their graduates to prominent universities such as the University of Toronto, Queen's, McGill and the University of British Columbia. Parents and staff often cite the individual attention given each student and the excellent student-staff ratio as contributing to the environment which fosters academic achievement. The small size of the schools linked with these other factors creates an environment which fosters the concern of staff for the individual student and a high level of individual and collective responsibility among students. Parents frequently refer to the large depersonalized, bureaucratic, urban high school in underscoring the advantages of private schools. The size of the schools and their enriched academic, athletic and cultural programs which seek to maximize participation obviously do stand in sharp contrast to these perceived negative characteristics.

Another factor cited by parents as contributing to the process of academic education is the absence of the distraction of students of the opposite sex. Both Maxwell and Weinsweig (1970) have pointed out that neither sex has to defer to the other academically in single-sexed schools; that is, they are not influenced by peer group norms often found in co-educational institutions that girls should under-perform boys, or that boys should seek achievement in non-academic pursuits which are defined as strictly masculine.

MORAL EDUCATION AS A PROCESS

Responsibility is emphasized along with achievement in the academic process of education but these themes emerge more clearly in the process of moral education. It should be pointed out, however, that in the schools themselves these processes are fused to create a wide variety of opportunities and the development of accomplishments which create the well-rounded individual and the potential leader. The plurality of opportunities with their accompanying systems of rewards including comprehensive and compulsory sports programs for both teams and individuals outrank the opportunities in the public school system. This is particularly true of the more prestigious schools. Weinsweig (1970) found eight annual socio-cultural events, 26 clubs and 30 athletic activities. The wide range of activities available to students increases choice and involvement and hence provides a strong basis for the development of loyalty and identification as well as aiding the schools in obtaining outside support. Throughout the diversified and compulsory sports programs the norms of competition and "fair play" which embody the values of achievement and responsibility, are reinforced on a daily basis. Since these activities are organized through the "house system," primary group loyalties, norms of inter-group competition and opportunities for leadership and leadership training are provided for all. While the role of competitive games in the socializing process are being questioned, there is little doubt that these programs at the schools prepare the students for the world in which their parents and the school expect them to function. On the other hand, it is apparent that the wide variety of activities gives opportunities to all and that many of the demoralizing aspects of competition are avoided, although obviously not the ideology it engenders.

Religion is a significant element in the ethos of the schools. Most schools start the academic day with an assembly for prayers led by the principal, senior staff and prefects. Weekly scripture classes often given by the principal or clergy, Sunday attendance at church, visits of the clergy and scripture awards on prize day link the authority structure of the school to religious ideals and practices. Several schools possess their own chapels where graduates return for weddings and the baptism of their children. The relationship between the formal status of religion in these schools and the beliefs and practices of students in a secular age is difficult to assess. As in the case of many of the activities and beliefs of the schools what is thought to be most appropriate to the development of the students is selected and reinforced. Religion is not ignored.

The teaching of religious beliefs and the conduct of religious activity is maintained because of its traditional role and its historical importance for "character building." *Character building* is a word commonly used to describe the overarching goal of private school education. The term "character" embraces several qualities, the most salient of which, are: loyalty to the school and house system, a desire and ability to cooperate with and assist one's peers, setting high personal goals (need achievement), a sense of duty and self-discipline involving role-performance in the school and elsewhere, an ability and desire to exercise leadership in connection with this responsibility, a desire to help those less fortunate than oneself, and a type of conformity in social situations which permits the individual to influence decisions and assume leadership roles. Linked to this and legitimating the expectations is the importance attached to upholding the ritual and traditions of the schools. Many of the schools give a major annual public award which is a "character medal" clearly identifying the role model which embodies these beliefs, values and behaviour.

Entailed in the process of character-building in the schools are certain themes and values which the school espouses and attempts to inculcate in its students. These are linked to the central theme of achievement and responsibility we discussed previously. *Loyalty* is probably the value most strongly and extensively extolled and rewarded. It involves a high affective commitment and identification with the various aspects of the school and the "traditions" or standards of behaviour, practices and values which are perceived to adhere to the historical community. The term "spirit" is used to connote group loyalty and group morale and it involves an embracing commitment to the social system of the school as a whole. In the mystique surrounding spirit and loyalty it is argued everyone can and should have spirit regardless of the level of their individual accomplishments in the realm of academics, athletics and leadership. In reality, the variety of activities in the school enable sufficiently high levels of participation that most people can develop a base of activities which enables them to live up to the expectations involved in the mystique. "Spirit" pins and "spirit" cups give tangible recognition to performance in this rather diffuse and intangible dimension. What loyalty and spirit seem to symbolize is a "willingness to try" in the various areas of achievement and responsibility which the schools emphasize. In separating this spirit and loyalty from the actual outcomes in the dimensions of responsibility and authority the schools are emphasizing the importance of commitment and conformity as a self-rewarding process and internalizing the normative structure as it relates to achievement and responsibility apart from the rewards attached directly to them. What is being created is yet another sphere of behaviour in which the school can offer rewards and gain commitment.

Tradition is another unifying force which plays a major role in the ethos of the subculture of the private school world. Tradition emphasizes the past and the importance of the past as a guide for the present and the future. As a legitimating force, the "accumulated wisdom" emphasizes the values of continuity and stability. Weinsweig expresses it aptly:

> As a mode of organizing school behaviour, tradition is the *sine qua non* of social control because it provides adolescent students with an overriding, easily acquired and emotionally tinged basis for group identification and conformity. Tradition is the essence of the *conscience collective* which insinuates itself into the moral structure of student obligations. (1970: 128)

The major mechanism for the transmission of tradition as a mode of legitimation and identification is ritual. In most schools there is an annual cycle of ceremonies which reinforce the ties with the past and the value of continuity — the installation of prefects, the annual prize giving and the preparations surrounding social occasions as well as the regular visits of certain dignitaries to the school. The annual cycle is supplemented by less regular occurrences such as the installation of principals, the dedication of communion vessels, the dedication of new buildings and the like. At these gatherings the values of achievement and responsibility, self discipline and service, etiquette and aesthetics are linked to the past, the present and the future. The occasions are rich in symbolism as well as ritual. The singing of the school songs by students wearing the full regalia of membership and office, house and school symbols, emblems and crests invoke the complex ties that students not only have with the school but with the past and the tradition of the school. In addition some personage of note (usually closely connected with the school) articulates the values which the ritual ceremony and dress symbolize at a less conscious level. In the case of Havergal College, Toronto (1894) the school song emphasizes the value of striving for individual but particularly collective goals to the best of one's ability using as its symbol the carrying of the torch in ancient Greece. The seven stanzas of the song contain nine phrases clearly expressing a need achievement theme. Supernatural validation of this value is clearly evoked in the last verse in a prayer in which God is addressed as "Great Captain" and requested to support the school endeavours; the last verse has additional significance since the three senior prefects at the school are Captains. Within the course of the song, achievement and responsibility are tied to the traditions of ancient Greece and the Christian religion and related to the social structure of the school itself.

For some schools the links between the symbolic element are themselves personalistic and part of the school. Ridley College's coat of arms which features bishop's mitres and the motto *Terar Deum Prosium* (May I Be Consumed in Service) is linked to the martyrdom of Bishop Ridley, after whom the school was named. However the choice of school colours (orange and black) made by the first principal was prompted by a romantic attraction to a young woman who had worn a gown of these colours to a party. She subsequently became his wife (Gossage, 1977: 40). In this case tradition became a fusion of the other worldly and the highly personal; it is essentially through this combination, the linking of the personal to the value system that tradition works to bind students to the moral values of the school.

Finally, the idea of *service to others* is one of the most prominent and reinforced aspects of the ethos of the schools as demonstrated by the Ridley motto. The obligation denoted by *noblesse oblige* is nothing other than the service entailed by elitist position. The idea that privilege entails responsibility limits the exploitation of elitist positions and legitimates in the eyes of the elite their privileged position. The notion of service is equally emphasized in the boys and girls schools although the outlets for its expression vary somewhat. For the boys, military and political service have traditionally been extolled whereas for girls service in voluntary and charitable organizations or mission work have been emphasized. Many of the girls' schools have annual bazaars which give training in the administrative roles in charitable work in fund raising and involve decision-making on the allocation of funds. The effort made and the funds raised are by no means token; one girls' school raised over $6,000 in its three hour annual bazaar in 1976. Through such undertakings, students are inducted into and trained in the philanthropic role, traditionally upheld for women of the upper classes.

Linked to service, tradition and loyalty is the idea of doing things the right way. Good manners and appropriate comportment especially in public are linked with the image of both the school and the student's family. Non-conformity is interpreted to the students as "letting the school down" which is another way of saying one is disloyal. Whereas in earlier years the niceties of class socialization could be taught for themselves, today these aesthetic aspects are increasingly linked to other dimensions of responsibility and loyalty.

SUMMARY AND CONCLUSIONS

These elite private schools (together with their counterparts in French Canada) play a strategic role in maintaining the stratification system in

Canadian society. While not all the children of the members of the various elites and "old" families go to these schools, a significant percentage do. In terms of whom they recruit and the culture and values of the schools, they can accurately be described as institutions of the upper classes. They serve to preserve elitist norms and values and reinforce these through the socialization process.

Despite the rivalry among the schools, their association with each other facilitates bonds between students of the same sex, and intermarriage with the opposite sex. The result is an upper class endogamy which reinforces the socialization process and provides intergenerational continuity of upper-class culture and structure. The private schools facilitate the kinship and associational links of the various elites in Canada, and because of the lack of private universities they are particularly crucial in this regard.

The most distinctive aspect of the socialization process in these schools is the *care* which is taken in the management of the process. Responsibility and achievement, loyalty and tradition are values which are orchestrated with the utmost care in relation to the individual student. While the ritual and symbolism have been carefully worked out over the years it is not just the social aspects of these which are attended to. The student, whose selection was a matter of concern, is constantly assessed as to his or her individual adjustment and achievement in the environment of the school. In an era where there are many complaints that secondary schools are impersonal bureaucracies, this individual concern makes a significant difference. When such concern is directed to the already privileged it undoubtedly compounds the advantages which have already accrued.

Footnotes

1. *The statistics presented above were obtained from the following sources: Canada, Statistics Canada, Education in Canada: a Statistical Review for 1974-75 and 1975-76, (Ottawa: Statistics Canada, July 1977) See Table 2 and Table 23. Canada, Statistics Canada, Private Elementary and Secondary Schools, 1975-76, Ottawa: Statistics Canada, December 1976), Table 12. Great Britain, Her Majesty's Stationary Office, Social Trends, Number 6, 1975, Edited by Eric J. Thompson and Christopher Lewis, (London: Central Statistical Office, 1975). See Table 8.1 United States, Statistical Abstract of the United States, 1976, (Washington: US Department of Commerce, Bureau of the Census, 1976). See Table 187. Australia, Australian Bureau of Statistics, Canberra, January 1976. Reference No. 13.4.*
2. *Houses are ascriptive, associational units containing members from all grades, or at least beyond grade five. Intramural competitions and sports as well as other activities are organized through these groups. While they are not residential units, except in the few schools which accept only boarders, they serve as vertically integrated units of primary group identification and socialization. This is in contrast to the horizontally integrated grade system.*

References

Canada
1972   *Canada Year Book, 1972*: Ottawa, Information Canada.

Canada
1976   Statistics Canada: "Private Elementary and Secondary Schools: 1975-76", Ottawa, Statistics Canada.

Card, B.Y.
1976   "The State of Sociology of Education in Canada — A Further Look", *Canadian Journal of Education*, Vol. 1, No. 4.

Clark, S.D.
         "The American Takeover of Canadian Sociology: Myth or Reality?" in *Dalhousie Review*, Summer, Vol. 53, No. 2, pp. 205-218.

Clement, Wallace
1975   *The Canadian Corporate Elite: An Analysis of Economic Power*, Toronto, McClelland and Stewart.

Etzioni, A.
1961   *Complex Organizations*, New York, The Free Press.

Gossage, Carolyn
1977   *A Question of Privilege*, Toronto, Peter Martin.

Hall, Oswald
1948   "The Stages of a Medical Career" in *American Journal of Sociology*, Vol. 53, March 1948, pp. 327-336.

Homans, G.C.
1950   *The Human Group*, New York, Harcourt Brace.

Lamont, Katharine
1972   *The Canadian Association of Head-Mistresses — A History* (1932-1972), Montreal.

Maxwell, Mary Percival
1970   "Social Structure, Socialization and Social Class in a Canadian Private School for Girls", unpublished Ph.D. thesis, Cornell University, 1970.

Maxwell, Mary Percival and James D. Maxwell
1971   "Boarding School: Social Control, Space and Identity", pp. 157-164 in Davies, D.I. and Kathleen Herman (eds.): *Social Space: Canadian Perspectives*, Toronto, New Press.

Maxwell, Mary Percival and James D. Maxwell
1975   "Women, Religion and Achievement Aspirations: A Study of

Private School Females" in Pike, R.M. and E. Zureik (eds.): *Socialization and Values in Canadian Society*, Vol. II, Toronto, McClelland and Stewart, pp. 104-128.

McArthur, Charles
1954   "Personalities of Public and Private School Boys" in *The Harvard Educational Review, Vol. XXIV*, No. 4 (Fall), pp. 256-62.

Newman, Peter C.
1975   *The Canadian Establishment, Vol. I*, Toronto, McClelland and Stewart.

Ollerenshaw, Kathleen
1967   *The Girls' Schools*, London, Faber and Faber.

Podmore, C.J.
1976   "Private Schooling in English Canada", unpublished Ph.D. thesis, McMaster University.

Parsons, Talcott
1960   *Structure and Process in Modern Societies*, Glencoe, The Free Press.

Penton, D.S.
1972   *Non Nobis Solum*, Montreal, Corporation of Lower Canada College.

Pike, Robert M.
1970   *Who Doesn't Get to University — and Why*, Ottawa, Association of Universities and Colleges of Canada.

Porter, John
1965   *The Vertical Mosaic*, Toronto, University of Toronto Press.

Porter, M.R., Porter, J. and Blishen, B.R.
1973   *Does Money Matter? Prospects for Higher Education*, Toronto, York University, Institute for Behavioral Research.

Simmonds, T.
         "A Place to Stand and a Place to Grow", Toronto, Deposited in the library of Upper Canada College, (Mimeo).

Sowby, Cedric W.
1971   *A Family Writ Large: Memoirs of a Former Headmaster*, Toronto, Longman.

Steele, Catherine
1971   *Havergal College: A Brief Historical Sketch*, Toronto, The York Pioneer and Historical Society.

Swan, Susan
 1977 "Are Girls' Schools Good for Girls?", *Chatelaine*, Vol. 50, No. 9, September, p. 46ff.

Wakeford, J.
 1969 *The Cloistered Elite: A Sociological Analysis of the English Public School,* London, Macmillan.

Weinberg, Ian
 1967 *The English Public Schools: The Sociology of Elite Education,* New York, Atherton Press.

Weinberg, Ian
 1968 "Some Methodological and Field Problems of Social Research in Elite Secondary Schools" in *Sociology of Education,* Spring, Vol. 41, No. 2, pp. 141-155.

Weinsweig, Paul
 1970 "Socialization and Subculture in Elite Education", unpublished Ph.D. thesis, University of Toronto.

Weinsweig, Paul
 1977 "Socialization in Canadian Private Schools: A Case Study" in Carlton, R.A., Louise A. Colley and N.J. MacKinnon (eds.): *Education, Change and Society: A Sociology of Canadian Education,* Toronto, Gage.

Wilkinson, R.H.
 1964 *The Prefects: British Leadership and the Public School Tradition,* London, Oxford University Press.

The Adoption of Oral Contraceptives Among Adolescent Females: Reference Group Influence

EDWARD S. HEROLD, PH.D.
MARILYN R. GOODWIN, M.S.C.
Department of Family Studies
University of Guelph

The objective of this study was to determine the influence of reference groups on the adoption of oral contraceptives among young single females. While there has been considerable research done in the United States on the use of contraceptives among adolescents there has been little research done on this topic in Canada especially with regard to the role of reference groups.

Data from the United States suggests that the incidence of premarital intercourse is increasing and the age of first intercourse is declining (Bell and Chaskes, 1970; Kantner and Zelnick, 1973). Also, many adolescents take unnecessary risks by not using any form of contraception or by using unreliable contraception, such as rhythm or withdrawal (Goldsmith et al, 1972; Kantner and Zelnick, 1973).

Adolescents form a distinctive group in terms of contraceptive usage patterns with most waiting until after they are sexually active before beginning to use contraceptives (Akpom et al, 1976). Thus, many are at risk of unwanted pregnancy.

In Canada, the incidence of therapeutic abortions, especially among youth, is increasing. Women 15 to 24 years old account for approximately one-half of the therapeutic abortions performed in Canada (Statistics Canada, 1973). The incidence of illegitimate births is also increasing (Health and Welfare Canada, 1975).

Adolescent pregnancy and childbirth are associated with infant and maternal mortality, suicide, failure to finish high school, welfare dependence, forced marriage and early divorce (Furstenberg, 1976). The consequences of adolescent pregnancy and childbearing warrant greater attention to the prevention of unplanned pregnancy among teenagers. It is important to understand the determinants of contraceptive use among adolescents in order to develop effective preventative programs.

There is a large body of literature on adolescent contraception and premarital pregnancy, but few studies have any theoretical explanation as to why some females do and others do not seek effective contraception. Bardwick (1973) comments that the psychological literature on oral contraceptives reveals a research area still searching for the important variables. Rogers (1973) suggests that family planning studies need to include more of an emphasis on communication and social relationships following the approach of the Classical Diffusion Model.

The model describes the process by which an innovation is communicated via certain channels over time to members of a social system. A fundamental component of the Classical Diffusion Model is the innovative-decision process. This is a mental process through which an individual passes from first knowledge of an innovation to a decision to adopt or reject and to confirmation of this decision.

It is difficult to measure progression in the adoption process over time. Most researchers study the characteristics of early versus late adopters of innovations and factors influencing the innovativeness of individuals.

One of the key factors in the adoption process is reference group influence (Rogers, 1973).

REFERENCE GROUPS

A reference group is that group whose standpoint is being used as the frame of reference by the individual. Merton (1957) distinguishes between two major types of reference groups, namely, normative reference group and comparison reference group. The normative reference group sets and maintains standards for the individual, and is a source of values. The comparison reference group provides a frame of comparison relative to which the individual evaluates himself and others. However these two types of reference groups are only analytically distinct, since the same reference group can serve both functions.

Different reference groups are relevant for differing kinds of behavior. Parents, peers and the dating partner are highly salient reference groups influencing young women's contraceptive roles (Jaccard and Davidson, 1972). However, the peer group and the dating partner generally have a stronger influence than parents over the teenage girl's contraceptive behavior (Clayton, 1972; Walsh et al, 1976).

Objectives

To further understand the role of reference groups in contraceptive adoption among young single females, the specific objectives of this research were to determine

      1.   the influence of reference groups in the stages of oral contraceptive adoption

      2.   the significance of reference groups in the innovativeness or timing of the adoption of oral contraceptives.

The focus of this study was on the adoption of oral contraceptives because they are one of the most effective birth control methods as well as being the most commonly used method among single females (Dryfoods, 1976).

METHOD

Subjects
Data were collected over a five month period (September, 1976-January, 1977) from adolescent females attending ten birth control and counselling centres in southern Ontario. Clinics were selected to represent both urban and rural communities.

Only single females attending a birth control clinic for the first time to obtain oral contraceptives were included. Females who had not yet experienced intercourse were not included in the analysis because this would have required focusing on a different set of independent variables (Reiss et al, 1975). Of 245 females attending the clinic to adopt oral contraceptives, 20% or 48 had not experienced intercourse. Thus, included in the sample were 197 single, sexually experienced females, 20 years of age and under, who were coming to a birth control clinic for the first time to adopt oral contraceptives.

Procedures
The data were obtained by means of a closed-ended questionnaire. The questionnaire was administered when the subject arrived at the clinic and before she attended a counselling session or medical examination. Participation was voluntary and anonymous. Almost all of the women who were asked to complete the questionnaire did so.

Measurement of reference group variables
To determine reference group influence on the adoption of oral contraceptives, respondents were asked: 1) how they found out about the birth control clinic; 2) who influenced them to attend the clinic; 3) who their sources of information about contraception were; and 4) from whom they had learned about side effects of oral contraceptives.

Additionally, for each of mother, father, peers, and boyfriends, subjects were asked if: 1) that person(s) would be upset to be told the subject was using birth control pills; 2) if that person(s) had encouraged the subject's use of birth control pills; and 3) how often the subject had discussed using that method with these people. For the purposes of hypothesis testing, these items for each reference group were factor analyzed and three item indexes were formed using factor-score coefficients (see Table 1). Reliability tests were performed using Cronbach's alpha coefficient.

These questionnaire items were based upon research done in the United States which found that contraceptive usage among teenagers was influenced by the extent to which parents, peers and boyfriends were approving of and encouraging of the use of contraception (Jaccard and Davidson, 1972; Venham, 1973; Akpom et al, 1976; Furstenberg, 1976).

As shown in Table 1, the reliability coefficients for the indexes of reference group support for oral contraceptive usage were mother, .76; father, .68; peers, .68 and boyfriend, .49. Because the reliability coefficient for the boyfriend support index was low, we arbitrarily decided to replace this index with the single item "My dating partner has encouraged my use of birth control pills." Harvey (1974) found that among university females at the University of Alberta one of the important reasons for contraceptive non-use was "Needs a guy's encouragement to start using the pill."

The dating partner's role in contraceptive practice has been found to be strongly related to type of dating relationship with contraceptives being used more often in relationships having high dyadic commitment (Reiss et al, 1975; Akpom et al, 1976). Couples in stable relationships

TABLE 1
REFERENCE GROUP MEASURES

Reference group variables	Measures	Scale construction
Mother's support of oral contraceptive usage	My mother would be upset if I told her I was using birth control pills. My mother has encouraged my use of birth control pills. How often have you discussed with your mother whether you should use that method?	The items were summed using the respective factor-score coefficients of .35, .36 and .36. The reliability coefficient was .76.

Reference group variables	Measures	Scale construction
Father's support of oral contraceptive usage	My father would be upset if I told him I was using birth control pills.	The items were summed using the respective factor-score coefficients of .41, .43 and .38. The reliability coefficient was .68.
	My father has encouraged my use of birth control pills.	
	How often have you discussed with your father whether you should use that method?	
Peer's support of oral contraceptive usage	My girlfriends would be upset if I told them I was using birth control pills.	The items were summed using the respective factor-score coefficients of .31, .41 and .44. The reliability coefficient was .68.
	My girlfriends have encouraged my use of birth control pills.	
	How often have you discussed with your girlfriends whether you should use that method?	
Frequency of communication with peers before first intercourse	*Before* you had first intercourse how often did you discuss with your girlfriends whether you should use birth control pills?	Single item score
Partner's encouragement to use oral contraceptives	My dating partner has encouraged my use of birth control pills.	Single item score

Reference group variables	Measures	Scale construction
Frequency of communication with partner about oral contraceptive usage before first inter- course	*Before* you had first intercourse how often did you discuss with your dating partner whether you should use birth control pills?	Single item score
Dyadic commitment	What is your present dating status?	Single item score

Note *Items were scored on a 5 point Likert scale of agreement-disagree- ment.*

might be less involved in risk taking behaviour because of their concern for one another. They are also more aware that intercourse is likely to occur and can plan ahead of time to use contraception.

Because we anticipated that the time of communication about birth control might be an important variable we also asked respondents how frequently they had discussed use of birth control pills with girlfriends or their boyfriend *before having first intercourse.*

MEASUREMENT OF INNOVATIVENESS OF ORAL CONTRACEPTIVE ADOPTION

Innovativeness of oral contraceptive adoption was conceptually defined as the degree to which a female adopts oral contraceptives relatively early after her first experience of sexual intercourse.

Technically speaking, oral contraceptives are not an innovation in that they are known by almost everyone. Nevertheless, the concept is useful in distinguishing between those who adopt oral contraceptives at the time of first intercourse and those who use oral contraceptives considerably later in their sexual history.

Oral contraceptive adoption was operationally defined as attendance at a birth control clinic for the first time to obtain oral contraceptives. Innovativeness of oral contraceptive adoption was operationally defined as the number of times a female had experienced sexual intercourse before attending a birth control clinic for the first time to adopt oral contraceptives. This was measured by the item, "How many times have you had intercourse?" The response alternatives were, (1) once (2) 2-3 times (3) 4-5 times (4) 6-10 times (5) 11-25 times (6) 26-50 times (7) 51-75 times (8) 76-100 times (9) more than 100 times.[1]

TABLE 2
CATEGORIES OF ORAL CONTRACEPTIVE ADOPTERS
ACCORDING TO THE NUMBER OF TIMES INTERCOURSE HAD
BEEN EXPERIENCED

Adopter Categories	Score Assigned	Absolute Frequency	Relative Frequency
Innovators (1-3 times)	1	33	16.8
Early Adopters (4-10 times)	2	50	25.4
Early Majority (11-25 times)	3	43	21.8
Late Majority (26-75 times)	4	45	22.8
Laggards (75 or more times)	5	26	13.2
Total		197	100.0

Following the classification system of Rogers (1973), five categories were constructed by collapsing the original nine categories (see Table 2). Thus, the subjects were distributed along a continuum on the basis of the relative earliness or lateness with which they adopted oral contraceptives. Approximately 20% of the subjects were in each adopter category, with slightly fewer in the two extreme categories.

Adoption diffusion studies generally use a time dimension for measuring an individual's innovativeness. A time dimension measure was originally considered for this study, namely, the length of time between first intercourse and attendance at a birth control clinic for the first time to adopt oral contraceptives. However, it was decided that a more appropriate measure was the number of times a woman experienced intercourse before adopting oral contraceptives. It was assumed that this is a more critical variable influencing pregnancy than is the time dimension, particularly because most young women have intercourse on an infrequent basis.

HYPOTHESIS

The hypothesis was that there would be a positive relationship between reference group support and innovativeness or oral contraceptive adoption. The Pearsonian correlation coefficient ($p < .05$) was used to test this hypothesis.

CHARACTERISTICS OF THE SAMPLE

Demographic

The mean age of the sample was 17 with 13% being 15 years old or younger and 54% being 15 or 16. Seventy-seven percent were still attending school and 81% were living in the parental home.

About one-half of the respondents' parents had completed high school or at least some college education. Twelve percent of the mothers and 16% of the fathers had completed university. A comparison with 1971 Census data shows that the level of parental education of the sample was higher than the level of education of Ontario residents who were 35 to 54 years.[2]

Fifty-six percent of the subjects were Protestant, 20% Catholic, 2% Jewish and 10% stated no religion. Although the sample was not chosen on a random basis, the religious affiliation of the sample was proportionately similar to that of the Ontario population as a whole.[3]

Dating

Most of the respondents (64%) were dating 3 or 4 times a week or more and 90% were dating at least once a week. Eighty percent were involved in a committed relationship, either a steady relationship with one person or engaged or living with someone.

Sexual attitudes and behavior

The teenagers were highly in favor of premarital intercourse under certain conditions. While 88% approved of premarital intercourse if they felt strong affection for their partner, only 12% approved of premarital intercourse with someone they had just met and whom they found physically appealing. Almost one-half (46%) felt guilty after first intercourse. However, with sexual experience, guilt diminished as only 10% of the subjects currently felt guilty about engaging in intercourse. Thirty-four percent of the adolescents became sexually active by the age of 15 and 81% by the age of 17. They had generally limited their sexual partners, with 56% having had intercourse with only one person. Only 12% had more than three sexual partners.

Attitude toward pregnancy

Other studies have reported that one of the common reasons for non-use of contraception is the belief that one could not become pregnant (Goldsmith et al, 1972; Kantner and Zelnick, 1973). However, in this sample 89% said they were aware at the time of first intercourse that pregnancy could happen to them. Almost all of the respondents had a concerned attitude regarding the possibility of pregnancy with 93% agreeing that they would be upset if they were to become pregnant at this time in their life. This is not surprising considering that the sample consisted of young women who were planning to use the birth control pill.

There was considerable worry over the possibility of pregnancy with 43% beginning to worry about becoming pregnant at the time of first intercourse. Within one month after first intercourse 86% had worried about a possible pregnancy. Additionally, three-quarters of the teenagers have worried that they might be pregnant because they have had a late period. Very few (2%) had ever experienced a pregnancy.

Contraceptive practices

Thirty-one percent of the respondents did not use a contraceptive method at first intercourse. One of the main reasons for not using contraception at first intercourse is that first intercourse is generally not expected or planned. For example, 62% reported that they did not expect first intercourse to occur when it did. The most common methods used at first intercourse were condom (39%) and withdrawal (27%). Few used the rhythm method (3%) or foam (1%).[4]

Compared with first intercourse, there was a slight increase in the use of contraceptive method or procedure at last intercourse. However, 29% were not using a method and 38% were using the less effective methods of withdrawal or rhythm. Significant age differences (p < .05) were found with those aged 17 or older being more likely to have used the condom at last intercourse, whereas, those younger than age 17 were more likely to have used rhythm or withdrawal. Also, only 20% reported using a contraceptive device every time they had intercourse. Thus, prior to clinic attendance a considerable proportion of these girls were at risk of pregnancy because of poor contraceptive practices.

Embarrassment about obtaining the birth control pill

Women must usually undergo a pelvic examination in order to obtain a prescription for the birth control pill. Thirty-eight percent of the girls reported that they were embarrassed about having an internal physical examination. A similar study in San Francisco (Urban and Rural Systems Associates, 1976) found a major obstacle to obtaining the birth control pill was the apprehension of teenagers about the pelvic examination. The young women were afraid the examination would hurt or that they would be embarrassed. Many were unaware of the purpose and procedures of the examination. Also, in the San Francisco study, many teenagers preferred a female physician because the female physicans talked to their patients more, acknowledged their fears of pain and explained the results of the examination (Urban and Rural Systems Associates, 1976).

After the prescription for the birth control pill is obtained, the pills are usually purchased at a pharmacy. One-half of the subjects in this study were embarrassed about obtaining birth control pills from a pharmacy close to where their parents lived. Considerably fewer (15%) were embarrassed about obtaining pills from a pharmacy distant from where their parents live. This further illustrates the great concern teenagers have about parental discovery of contraceptive usage.

Knowledge of side effects of the birth control pill

Almost all (83%) of the girls had heard about birth control pills having side effects. Weight gain was by far the most commonly known side effect with 41% of the teenagers having heard that birth control pills cause weight gain. This is an important finding because fear of weight gain may constitute a significant barrier to pill usage among teenagers who are generally concerned with personal attractiveness.

Most of the respondents had learned of side effects from female sources with 48% indicating girlfriends and 16% indicating mothers as sources of information. Only three percent learned of side effects from boyfriends. Other information sources were magazines or newspaper articles (20%), sex education classes at school (8%) and physicians (1%). While few of the teenagers (5%) believed that side effects outweighed the advantages of using the birth control pill, about one-third were undecided.

PERCENTAGE FINDINGS FOR REFERENCE GROUP INFLUENCE

Influence on clinic attendance

Peers were the most important source of information about the clinic, with 86% of the teenagers reporting they found out about the clinic from girlfriends. Additionally, 52% reported that their friends directly influenced their decision to come to the clinic. Settlage et al (1973) also found that most females are referred to a clinic by their friends. The adoption of oral contraceptives is often perceived by teenagers as involving great difficulty and risk. Becker (1970) suggests that where an innovation entails greater difficulty and risk in its adoption, the reinforcement and support provided through friendship channels take on increased importance.

While few (2%) of the respondents learned about the clinic from their boyfriends, 40% reported their boyfriends influenced the decision to come to the clinic. Five percent found out about the clinic from school while 3% noticed the clinic when they walked by it. Fewer than 1% learned about the clinic from parents. Other sources of information were Planned Parenthood, telephone book, mass media and physicians. Some respondents indicated they were self-referred.

The respondents were asked why they had come to the clinic instead of their family physician. Three-quarters reported that they did not want their parents to find out, while one-fifth reported that they could not talk freely with their family physician. Many were concerned that the family physician would not keep the request for birth control confidential or that he would not prescribe the birth control pill without parental consent.

When the respondents were asked if they would be embarrassed to ask their family physician for a prescription for the birth control pill, 68% said they would be embarrassed, whereas only 19% said they were embarrased about coming to the clinic.

Sources of birth control education
As shown in Table 3, girlfriends were the most important source of information about contraception, with 67% of the teenagers reporting that they had received information about contraception from their girlfriends. Sixty percent received birth control information in school and 52% from reading material. Boyfriends were the fourth most important source of information, with 24% of the subjects receiving birth control information from their boyfriends. Only 11% received birth control information from mothers and hardly any (2%) received information from fathers. Six percent reported receiving information from their family physician. In comparison, in a national population survey of Canadian women, Badgley et al (1977, p. 368) found that almost one-half of the women (46%) said their major source of information about contraception was from physicians and only 7% reported that school was their major source of information. The findings of this study indicate that for teenagers the school is a more important source of information than family physicians. Nevertheless, only 36% of the sample agreed that the education about birth control they received in school was adequate for their needs.

Pill adoption
The dating partner and peers played significant roles in the decision to adopt oral contraceptives, as 79% of the respondents had been encouraged by their boyfriends to use birth control pills, and 66% had been encouraged by their girlfriends. Additionally, 93% of the teenagers indi-

TABLE 3
SOURCES OF INFORMATION ABOUT CONTRACEPTION

| Source | Information Given | | |
	Yes %	No %	Total %
Girlfriends	67	33	100
Boyfriend	24	76	100
Mother	11	89	100
Father	2	98	100
School	60	40	100
Family doctor	6	94	100
Reading on own	52	48	100

N = 197

cated that one or more of their girlfriends were using birth control pills. On the other hand, few parents (10% of mothers and 6% of fathers) had encouraged their daughter's use of birth control pills.

There was considerable discussion with girlfriends and the boyfriend about using the birth control pill. Ninety-one percent of the teenage women had discussed this with both girlfriends and boyfriends. However, before first intercourse had occurred, 36% had not discussed using the birth control pill with their friends and 41% had not discussed it with their boyfriend.

Seventy-six percent of teenagers had never discussed the idea of pill usage with their mother, while 93% had never discussed this with their father. Similarly, 88% of the teenagers had not told either parent that they were engaging in sexual intercourse. Most of the teenagers believed that while their friends were approving of their sexual activity their parents were not. Only 13% thought their girlfriends would disapprove of their having intercourse, whereas, 72% believed their mothers would disapprove, and 78% believed their fathers would disapprove.

Communication with one's parents about sexual and contraceptive matters has been found to be related to the likelihood of contraceptive usage. In particular, the mother's participation in discussions about sex and contraception with her daughter has been related to consistent use of reliable contraception (Akpom et al, 1976; Furstenberg, 1976).

If the mother provides her daughter with specific instruction on contraceptive usage the adolescent is more likely to use contraceptives. However, if contraceptive instruction is vague, its effect on the adolescent's behavior is hardly greater than that of no instruction (Furstenberg, 1976).

Furstenberg (1976) suggests that in addition to imparting specific information, parents promote their daughter's contraceptive usage by simply raising the issue of contraception and revealing their explicit awareness that she is or may be having sexual relations. The adolescent is thus allowed to acknowledge her own sexuality and may regard sex less as a spontaneous and uncontrollable act and more as an activity subject to planning and regulation.

Hypothesis testing: reference groups and innovativeness
As shown in Table 4, no signficant relationships with the innovativeness of pill adoption variable were found for the reference group variables of mother's support of oral contraceptive usage, father's support of oral contraceptive usage, peer's support of oral contraceptive usage, partner's encouragement of oral contraceptive usage, frequency of communication with partner about oral contraceptive usage before first intercourse and dyadic commitment. Frequency of communication with peers about oral contraceptive usage before first intercourse did have a significant correlation ($r = .29$) with the dependent variable in

TABLE 4
ZERO-ORDER CORRELATIONS BETWEEN THE REFERENCE GROUP VARIABLES AND THE DEPENDENT VARIABLE, INNOVATIVENESS OF PILL ADOPTION

Reference group variables	Innovativeness of pill adoption
Mother's support of pill usage	.03
Father's support of pill usage	−.12
Peer's support of pill usage	.03
Frequency of communication with peers about pill use before first intercourse	.29*
Perception of peers as pill users	.05
Partner's encouragement of pill usage	−.01
Frequency of communication with partner about pill use before first intercourse	.03
Dyadic commitment	−.12

N = 197
* (p < .01)

the expected direction. Females who frequently discussed oral contraceptive usage with peers before first intercourse tended to be earlier adopters of oral contraceptives.

DISCUSSION

Interpersonal communication is associated with the diffusion of innovations in at least three ways. Firstly, communication provides the individual with information. Secondly, the knowledge that others have accepted the innovation provides the individual with legitimization and support for his own adoption of it. Finally, the individual is exposed to deliberate attempts to influence his acceptance or rejection of the innovation (Becker, 1970). The findings from this study support Becker's interpretation of the function of interpersonal communication in promoting the adoption of innovations.

With the pill adopter sample, peer communication provided information, legitimization and support. Peers were the most important source of information about the birth control pill as well as the clinic. Almost all of the teenage girls planning to use the birth control pill had one or more friends who were currently using oral contraceptives, and two-thirds received direct encouragement from their friends to use that method.

Partner influence was in the nature of providing support and encouragement rather than providing information. While most of the young women had discussed the birth control pill with their partner, few had acquired information either about the birth control pill or about the clinic from him.

The adolescents had received almost no information about birth control from their parents. Because they believed their parents would disapprove of their sexual activity, few of the girls had informed them of the decision to begin taking oral contraceptives.

The lack of a relationship between the reference group variables and innovativeness could be a result of the nature of the sample which consisted entirely of oral contraceptive adopters. Different results might have been obtained if the adopter sample had been compared with a sample of non-adopters as has been done by other researchers.

Also, as both early and late adopters are currently receiving the same amount of reference group support, the main difference appears to be in the timing of this support. This is indicated by the finding that frequency of communication with peers before first intercourse was significantly related to innovativeness. That frequency of communication with partner before first intercourse was not significantly related to the dependent variable suggests that the peer group is more important in the early adoption of oral contraceptives than is the dating partner.

In conclusion, the peer group is a major source of both information and support for the adolescent who is planning to use the birth control pill. The role of the dating partner is important in providing encouragement and support, but not information. Parents, for the most part, provide neither information nor legitimization and are generally by-passed in this decision-making process.

The reference group variables appear equally important for both early and late adopters of oral contraceptives with the exception that early adopters have more peer support prior to first intercourse than do late adopters.

Footnotes

1.   *This variable had 21 missing cases. The major reason for the missing cases appeared to be difficulty in recalling the number of times intercourse had been experienced. This seemed to be especially true for those who had experienced intercourse several times. To maintain sample size, the missing cases from the time dimension variable, "When did you first have intercourse?" were used. This was done as a reasonably high correlation of .63 existed between the two items.*

2.   *The 1971 Census of Canda reported that 33% of both female and male Ontario residents who were 35 to 54 years old had completed high school. Three percent of females and 8% of males who were 35 to 54 years old had a university degree. Information on level of schooling in the Province of Ontario was obtained from Statistics Canada, 1971 Census of Canada: Labour Force Activity-Work Experience Vol. III, Part 7, April 1975 pp. 1-13.*

3. Information on religious affiliation of Ontario residents was obtained from the 1971 Census of Canada in Ontario Statistics 1976 Vol. 1 Social Series p. 75.
4. The reader should note that excluded from this analysis are the 20% of pill adopters who have not yet experienced intercourse. If these females had been included then 20% would be reported as having used the birth control pill at first intercourse.

REFERENCES

Akpom, Amechi, Kathy Akpom and Marianne Davies
1976 Prior sexual behavior of teenagers attending rap sessions for the first time. Family Planning Perspectives 8: 203-206.

Badgley, Robin, Marion Powell and Denyse Karon
1977 Report of the Committee on the Operation of the Abortion Law. Ministry of Supply and Services, Ottawa, Canada.

Bardwick, Judith
1973 Psychological factors in the acceptance and use of oral contraceptives, p. 274-305. In J.T. Fawcett, (ed.) *Psychological Perspectives on Population.* Basic Books, New York, New York.

Becker, Marshall H.
1970 Sociometric location and innovativeness: reformation and extension of the diffusion model. American Sociological Review 35: 267-282.

Bell, R. and J.B. Chaskes
1970 Premarital sexual experience among coeds, 1958 and 1968. Journal of Marriage and the Family 32: 81-84.

Clayton, Richard
1972 Premarital sexual intercourse: a substantive test of the contingent consistency model. Journal of Marriage and the Family 34: 273-281.

Dryfoods, Joy G.
1976 The United States national family planning program 1968-1974. Studies in Family Planning 7: 80-92.

Furstenberg, Frank F. Jr.
1976 The social consequences of teenage parenthood. Family Planning Perspectives 8: 148-164.

Goldsmith, Sadja, M. Gabrielson, I. Gabrielson, V. Matthews and L. Potts
1972 Teenagers, sex and contraception. Family Planning Perspectives 4: 32-38.

Harvey, Ann L.
1974   Coed contraception: use and nonuse. Paper presented at the Alberta Council on Family Relations Annual Meeting, 1974, Edmonton, Alberta.

Health and Welfare Canada
1975   *Family Planning a Resource Manual for Nurses.* Information Canada, Ottawa.

Jaccard, James and Andrew Davidson
1972   Toward an understanding of family planning behavior: an initial investigation. Journal of Applied Social Psychology 2: 228-235.

Kantner, John and Melvin Zelnick
1972   Contraception and pregnancy: experience of young married women in the U.S.A. Family Planning Perspectives 5: 21-35.

Merton, Robert K.
1957   *Social Theory and Social Structure.* The Free Press, Glencoe, Illinois.

Reiss, Ira L., Albert Banwart and Harry Foreman
1975   Premarital contraceptive usage: a study of some theoretical exploration. Journal of Marriage and the Family 37: 619-632.

Rogers, Everett
1973   *Communication Strategies for Family Planning.* The Free Press, New York, New York.

Settlage, Dianne, S. Baroff and D. Cooper
1973   Sexual experience of younger teenage girls seeking contraceptive assistance for the first time. Family Planning Perspectives 5: 223-226.

Statistics Canada
1973   Therapeutic Abortions, 1973. Cat. No. CA1 BS82 C211.

Urban and Rural Systems Associates
1976   *Improving Family Planning Services for Teenagers.* Report published by Department of Health, Education and Welfare, Washington, D.C.

Venham, Lois
1973   Coeds and contraception: an examination of self image and significant other influence. Paper presented at the National Council on Family Relations, 1974, Toronto, Ontario.

Walsh, Robert H., Mary Z. Ferrell and William L. Tolone
1976   Selection of reference group, perceived reference group per-

missiveness and personal permissiveness, attitudes and behavior: a study of two consecutive panels (1967-1971; 1970-1974). Journal of Marriage and the Family 38: 495-509.

The Transition From School to Work: Growing up Working Class in Early 20th Century Hamilton, Ontario

JANE SYNGE
Dept. of Sociology
McMaster University

INTRODUCTION

One approach to studying the movement of youth into adulthood is the examination of the nature and the timing of the various transitions — leaving school, starting work, entering courtship and marrying.[1] This paper deals with the transition from school to work among working-class youth in the early 20th century in the metal working and textile producing city of Hamilton, Ontario.[2] We focus in particular on the earning capacities of working-class adolescents and explore the implications of wage-earning for adolescents' relationships with their parents.

We use early 20th century census data to show the substantial economic contributions made by working children, and material from life-history interviews to explore the implications of earning for family relationships. Contemporary research on relationships between generations provides few insights into these issues.[3] The primary role of the adolescent is now that of student. Adolescents are no longer expected to work from their early teens and contribute to the parents' household. The idea of considerable parental control over the earnings and private lives of grown children is alien to the contemporary middle class, despite the fact that the extended education of middle-class youth does in reality constitute an important element of control by the older generation.[4] There are various reasons why adolescents now have little or no financial responsibility for their families. The responsibility of the young for the old, is lessened by the institution of compulsory secondary education and the development of social welfare schemes (such as pensions, unemployment compensation, and disability payments). Also, the decrease in family size has led to a decrease in responsibility for younger siblings. With the rise of the two child family, the extension of formal schooling and the emphasis on youth-oriented consumption, adolescents had, by the mid 20th century, become expensive dependants, and it is now the wife, rather than the adolescent child, who is the secondary wage earner.[5] From the perspective of the family economy, the recent entry of married women to the paid employment must be seen in part as a response to the withdrawal of teenage children from the labour market.

Comparisons with the present day are implicit in this research, but contemporary research has not focussed on the transition from school to work. Our data show that the primary role of the working-class adolescent in the early 20th century was that of wage-earner and contributor to the family income. The primary role of the adolescent in the last quarter of the 20th century is that of student and few parents expect that children will contribute the bulk of their earnings to the family until they marry.

RESEARCH MATERIALS

The first section of the paper, drawing on census data, shows the extent of the earnings of children. The second part deals with the uses of children's earnings and with family relationships. This latter section draws on analyses of structured tape recorded interviews with forty Hamilton-reared men and women, born to Anglo-Canadian working-class parents before 1908. Hamilton was, in 1911, a city of some seventy-seven thousand population, dominated by metalworking industries and by textiles. Women accounted for over one-fifth of the paid labour force, and the great majority of these working women were young and unmarried.[6] The early twentieth century was a period of heavy immigration and about one-third of Hamilton's population had recently arrived from Britain. Many of the native-born Canadians in the city had themselves grown up on farms and migrated to the city. Immigrants from Continental Europe, particularly single men, were beginning to arrive in substantial numbers and by 1911 this group, consisting disproportionately of single men, constituted one-twentieth of the population.[7]

The respondents were chosen in such a manner that the families in which the respondents grew up are representative (in terms of occupation of father and of religion) of Anglo-Canadian working-class households in Hamilton, Ontario in the early 20th century. Father's main occupation during the respondents' childhood was used to determine socioeconomic status. Material was collected on the occupational his-

TABLE 1
OCCUPATIONS OF HAMILTON MEN AND WOMEN IN PAID EMPLOYMENT, 1911

	Men %	Women %
Agriculture	1.3	0.1
Building	13.7	0.2
Domestic and other Service Occupations	3.9	23.7
Civil Service	4.1	0.4
Manufacturing	51.5	47.8
Mining	0.4	—
Professions	2.7	10.6
Trade, Commerce	14.7	14.5
Transport	7.7	1.9
Total	100.0%	100.0%
Total Number:	29,496	7,932

Of the 3,815 Hamilton women employed in manufacturing in 1911 the great majority were in clothing and textiles industries.

	%
Clothing and allied products	52.0
Textiles	14.6
Office workers in manufacturing plants	7.2
Factory operatives	7.0
Food and allied products	5.0
Other	14.2
Total	100.0%
Total number	3,815

Source: Census of 1911
Table VI, pp. 316-325. Ottawa: Dominion Bureau of Statistics.

tories of mothers. Whether a mother was, in her youth, a farm daughter who helped at home or a milliner's apprentice certainly relates to the climate of values in the home. However, the occupation of the father more closely reflects the economic level of the household. This group of interviews is drawn from a broader study that includes material on middle class, Continental European immigrant and agricultural households, all in Hamilton and in its rural environs. Respondents from entrepreneurial and professional families and those of Continental European origin experienced different conditions and family cultures. The children of Canadians of British stock and those of British immigrant parents experienced strikingly similar economic conditions and cultures.[8] The major difference between the Canadian and British immigrant groups was the greater religious observance among native Canadians. Immigrant British who might have been lax in church attendance in the old country were soon aware that to be accepted socially they had to become active church members.

Many of our respondents first started to work during World War I. In Hamilton, a major effect of the war was to stimulate a munitions industry (developing from the existing metalworking industries) and to give rise to uniform production (again developing from the existing textile and garmentmaking industries).[9] From the perspective of adolescents, the main impact of the war in Hamilton was to stimulate the overall demand for labour.

The structured interviews follow respondents from childhood through until the 1930s, by which time many were married and had children of their own. Respondents were asked detailed questions on parents' household routines, relationships with parents, and on religious, school, and early work life, views on class, leisure, courtship, and on the routines of the years of early marriage and childrearing.[10] Each interview produced, on average, three hours of recorded material, which was then coded.

There are of course, problems in the use of interview data in that respondents may be presenting the more favourable aspects of themselves and their families. The interview schedule was designed to elicit information on both facts and on attitudes, and to allow cross checks.[10] In old age, events in early life are more closely remembered than are those of middle age.

The Hamilton-reared men and women we interviewed over the period 1973-1976 were still living in the city or its environs. The city has been expanding; industries have remained and developed. While some Hamiltonians undoubtedly migrated elsewhere, perhaps to the west, or to the United States, there has been no compelling reason for population movement. These people are, therefore, probably representative of working-class sons and daughters who grew up in the city in the early 20th century.

For the sake of simplicity we use the term "working class" to describe the sons and daughters of skilled and unskilled workers, and of men with small family businesses employing no non-family labour. The children of these groups almost invariably became skilled and unskilled workers themselves. One should, however, keep in mind that most of these respondents remembered their parents thinking of themselves as "middle class", rather than "working class."

The life history interview approach is particularly useful when one is doing research on working-class life. Working people have left few records, and the household and work activities of children and women, whatever their social status, have often been seen as unimportant and not deserving of comment or investigation.[11] Moreover, much of the historical material that we have on working-class life in the past has a particular class bias in that it stems from upper-class concern with specific social problems.

ECONOMIC CONTRIBUTIONS OF CHILDREN

Social historians have pointed out that for many working-class families the period during which unmarried children in their teens and twenties were working and contributing to the household was the only time of relative prosperity. This cycle was described by Rowntree in his studies in York, England, and by Terry Copp for early 20th century Montreal.[12] In early 20th century Hamilton sons could often earn more than their fathers, especially if the fathers had been trained in some declining trade, were immigrants, or were manual workers experiencing the physical decline of middle and old age.

Despite the fact that the wages of men were about twice those of women, working-class daughters also made substantial financial contributions to their parents' households. Women generally worked from their early or mid-teens until marriage in the early or mid-twenties, that is, for a period of about eight to ten years. In 1921 the average age of first marriage for women was 25.5 years, for men, 29.9 years.[13]

The potential contributions of dutiful children to their parents' households were, therefore, substantial. Table 2 shows that in 1911 there were in the city nearly eleven thousand male "heads of households" and over five thousand working children. The average yearly earnings of male heads of households stood at $714.40, those of co-resident children, at $372.40. Even if we estimate that the level of female children's earnings was about half that for male children, note working sons and working daughters would earn, on average, $493.60 and $246.80 respectively per year.[14] If one assumes that at least half of this money was contributed directly to the parents' household — and our interviews suggest that this might be a reasonable estimate — one sees that the period when grown children were working must indeed have been a period of relative prosperity for the family. Using these averages, one sees that one working son and one working daughter could, together, bring to the household the same income as could, on average,

TABLE 2
AVERAGE YEARLY EARNINGS OF MALE HEADS OF
HOUSEHOLDS AND CO-RESIDENT CHILDREN IN THE CITY OF
HAMILTON, 1911

	Number	Earnings
Total Number of Male Heads of Households	10,921	
Average Yearly Earnings of Male Heads of Households		$714.4
Total Children	21,852	
Children 15 and older	6,967	
Total Children Earning	5,256	
Average Yearly Earnings of Children		$372.4
Estimated Average Yearly Earnings of Female Children		$246.8
Estimated Average Yearly Earnings of Male Children		$493.6*
Average Yearly Family Earnings		$892.6

*These average yearly earnings of co-resident male and female children are computed under the assumptions that (1) male and female children worked in equal numbers (as is suggested by the fact that 5,256 of the 6,967 children over 15 were employed) and that (2) female wage rates were about half the level of male wage rates. (This relationship between male and female rates is shown in various government reports of the period. See footnote 14.)
Source: Census of Canada 1911
Dominion Bureau of Statistics, Ottawa
Unpublished tables
"Statistics of families showing family population, earnings, educational efficiency classified by occupation followed by supporting head in cities and towns of 4,000 population and over."

the male head of household himself. In the poorer groups, as Table 2 shows, the relative contribution of grown children was especially high.

Table 3 shows the average annual income of fathers in selected occupations. We see that managers, professionals, and administrators generally earned over $1,000 a year while labourers of various types earned about $500 per annum. Skilled workers and men employed in manufacturing generally earned between $600 and $800 per annum.

TABLE 3

FAMILIES WITH FATHERS IN SELECTED OCCUPATIONS, SHOWING AVERAGE ANNUAL INCOME OF FATHERS, PERCENTAGE OF FAMILY INCOME CONTRIBUTED BY CO-RESIDENT CHILDREN, AVERAGE NUMBER OF CO-RESIDENT CHILDREN OVER 7 YEARS, NOT AT SCHOOL, AND AVERAGE NUMBER OF CHILDREN PER HOUSEHOLD

Occupation	Number in Occupation	Average Annual Income of Father $	% of Family Income Contributed by Working Children	Average Income of Co-Resident Children Above 7 years *not* at School $	Estimated number of children of working age—Average number of co-resident children above 7 years *not at school*	Average number of children per household (all ages)
Bank Managers	18	3,563	3.4%	147	0.8	1.7
Managers, various (not bank or store)	100	1,510	8.6%	258	0.5	1.6
Clergymen	47	1,468	9.4%	468	0.3	2.8
Store managers	56	1,416	11.7%	240	0.7	1.6
Superintendents	35	1,355	12.3%	253	0.7	2.0
Plasterers	48	1,232	18.7%	299	0.8	2.4
Plumbers & Steamfitters	84	1,176	12.7%	185	0.8	1.8
Officials of Steam Railroad	44	1,060	14.9%	288	0.5	1.7
Accountants & Bookkeepers	200	1,037	11.7%	246	0.5	1.5
Other Office Clerks	170	965	15.0%	425	0.3	1.5
Civil Service (non-manual)	157	955	17.9%	209	0.8	1.6
Trainmen	158	862	13.3%	229	0.5	1.0
Model Pattern Makers	50	782	21.3%	225	0.7	1.7
Iron & Steel Workers (gen)	660	697	24.2%	277	0.6	2.1
Machinists	717	689	19.2%	285	0.5	1.7
Moulder	349	668	32.7%	236	0.7	2.3

TABLE 3 (cont'd)

FAMILIES WITH FATHERS IN SELECTED OCCUPATIONS, SHOWING AVERAGE ANNUAL INCOME OF FATHERS, PERCENTAGE OF FAMILY INCOME CONTRIBUTED BY CO-RESIDENT CHILDREN, AVERAGE NUMBER OF CO-RESIDENT CHILDREN OVER 7 YEARS, NOT AT SCHOOL, AND AVERAGE NUMBER OF CHILDREN PER HOUSEHOLD

Occupation	Number in Occupation	Average Annual Income of Father $	% of Family Income Contributed by Working Children	Average Income of Co-Resident Children Above 7 years *not* at School $	Estimated number of children of working age —Average number of co-resident children above 7 years *not* at school	Average number of children per household (all ages)
Carpenter	551	652	32.3%	280	0.8	2.0
Worker in leather or rubber manufacturing	100	608	39.7%	295	0.8	2.2
Steam Railroad Labourer	98	557	52.2%	324	0.9	0.9
Drivers & Expressmen	159	556	21.7%	240	0.5	1.9
Teamster	246	528	35.1%	264	0.7	2.2
Labourers in Manu-facturing	1,041	505	37.0%	266	0.7	2.2
Salesmen	265	487	26.3%	235	0.3	1.6
General Labourers	1,024	485	44.2%	273	0.8	2.3

Source: Census of 1911. Unpublished tables. "Statistics of Families, showing family population, earnings, educational efficiency classified according to occupation, followed by supporting head, in cities and towns of 4,000 population and over". Ottawa: Dominion Bureau of Statistics.
Note: Unfortunately the census does not distinguish between male and female children.

The table also shows the percentage of family income contributed by co-resident children. The contributions of children amounted to less than one-fifth of family income in the upper socioeconomic groups, rising to a third or more among families with fathers in labouring and unskilled occupations. These differences are not wholly accounted for by variations in the number of children of working age in the family. It is true, however, that men in the least well paid occupations tended to have more children aged 14 and under in the household. This would undoubtedly have placed greater pressure on those children of 14 and over to contribute to the parents' household.

The majority of working-class children entered paid employment by the age of fourteen. At this time children could leave school at fourteen: parents who could show proof of need for their children's earnings could send their children out to work at the age of 12.[15] Children who worked full-time before reaching the age of fourteen were generally from families in financial difficulties. The father had perhaps died or he was a recent immigrant having trouble in establishing himself in a job.

Several respondents described how family troubles led them to work before they reached the age of 14. One woman who was born in Hamilton in 1891, lost her father and described how she started work in the cotton mills in 1901, when she was 10 years old.

> I started to work at 10 in the cotton mill. By the time I got through after a 12 hour day I was tired . . . . I was a dolfer. You have a cart with a box in the middle to put reels in . . . . You had to run at your work. It was terrible — these long hours. It was $3.60 every two weeks we got there.
> (Case Number WCW08, woman born in Canada in 1891)

Another woman, born in England in 1898, helped to support her family at the age of 12 when her father, a recent immigrant from Britain, could not find work.

> We came here in 1910 — I would be 12. Before December Dad wasn't working . . . and I went out with Dad . . . . He was going to the factories looking for work. So we got down to the Imperial Cotton Mill, down on Sherman Avenue, and he goes to the office. The man says, "We've got nothing for you, but we can fix the little girl up if you want". He looks at me and says, "Do you want to!" "Yes". So he gives me his lunch and I started in to work.
> (Case Number WB07, woman born in England 1898, arrived in Canada 1910)

Tables 4 and 5 show the proportions of Hamilton men and women in the different age groups who were at work in 1911 and in 1921. The majority of men worked from the time they were in their mid-teens until they died. The proportion of women working was in 1921 a little

TABLE 4
AGE DISTRIBUTION OF MALE AND FEMALE WORKERS IN THE CITY OF HAMILTON IN 1911 AND 1921

Age Group	1911 Male Workers		1911 Female Workers		1921 Male Workers		1921 Female Workers	
	Number	%	Number	%	Number	%	Number	%
10-14	194	0.7	141	1.8	195	0.5	94	0.8
15-19					3,121	8.5	2,772	25.3
	7,992	27.1	4,079	51.4				
20-24					4,012	10.9	2,716	24.8
25-64	20,530	69.6	3,641	45.9	28,286	76.6	5,242	47.8
65 & over	789	2.7	71	0.9	1,313	3.6	145	1.3
Total	29,496		7,932		36,927		10,969	
		100.1%		100%		100.1%		100%

Source: Adapted from the Census of 1911, Table VI, pp. 306-307, and the Census of 1921, Table 5, pp. 400-401. Dominion Bureau of Statistics.

over half for these between their mid-teens and mid-twenties, and this proportion fell to less than one in five for the age group 25 to 64. Women's earnings were about half those of men. As Table 4 has shown women workers of the early 20th century were predominantly young, working for ten years or so from the mid-teens until marriage in the mid-twenties. The census of 1911 records less than 1% of all married women in the city as being in paid employment.[16] The relative importance of the employer taboo on the hiring of married women and the strength of social custom is unclear.[17] Where female labour is badly needed, married women have always come to be accepted as employees.

Norms relating to the disposal of earnings
It seems that most working-class parents felt that children should work full-time as soon as they were able to do so.

> The sole intention with their kids was to get them out to work as soon as possible, so that there were a few more dollars coming in the place.
> (Case Number MB10, man born in England 1901, arrived in Canada, 1902)

> As soon as you got the rudiments of schooling, it was up to you to start working.
> (Case Number MCW02, man born in Canada in 1905)

As we have described, an illness or death in the family was often the occasion for an older child to start work full-time.

TABLE 5
SONS' AND DAUGHTERS' FINANCIAL CONTRIBUTIONS TO PARENTAL HOUSEHOLD AMONG ANGLO-CANADIAN WORKING CLASS

Contribution to parental household	Men	Women	Total
	%	%	%
Was sole support of widowed mother, etc.	—	1(5)	1(5)
Paid most or all of wages to mother	11(55)	9(45)	20(50)
Paid most or all of wages to father	1(5)	1(5)	2(5)
Paid board	4(20)	5(25)	9(23)
Made no contribution	—	—	—
Independent, not living at home*	4(20)	—	4(10)
Never worked because required at home — invalid, mother, care of sibs, helped in the shop, early marriage, etc.	—	2(10)	2(5)
Never worked for other reasons	—	—	—
No answer	—	2(10)	2(5)
	N = 20 (100%)	N = 20 (100%)	N = 40 (100%)

*This category includes some respondents who came as lone immigrants in their late teens.

As table 5 shows, working-class children were expected to turn their wages over to the family, that is to their mothers, when they started working. While some respondents probably exaggerated the extent of their giving, it is clear that giving was the norm.

> I was getting to the age where I would be expected to work and everybody had to bring home their share of the bacon, no matter what family they belonged to. If you could afford more or less it made no difference, you had at a certain age go off and earn your living.
> (Case Number MCW07, man born in Canada, 1902)

> You didn't keep your money. You took it home in the envelope. You didn't even open it . . . . And you got spending money.
> (Case Number MB01, man born in England 1900, arrived in Canada 1909)

And at thirteen years of age I was out working. I quit my first job where I worked possibly forty hours a week for $4.00 a week, and went to work for another company for $4.50 a week, sixty hours a week, just to get another fifty cents to give to my mother. Every cent I earned my mother got.

(Case Number MB10, man born in England in 1901, arrived in Canada 1902)

I turned it all over, except I saved a little.

(Case Number MB04, man born in England in 1899, arrived in Canada in 1907)

Many respondents viewed the giving of their wages to their mothers as representing some return to her for the care they had been given in childhood.

I always had to give everything. I'd go home with my pay envelope without opening it and then I'd get 25¢ or 50¢. That money was to pay my board, pay for the clothes that I'd been wearing for so many years previous, pay for the camphorated oil that was rubbed on my chest when I had a cold.

(Case Number MCW07, man born in Canada in 1902)

Unfortunately the question on disposal of earnings was only posed once, for the period of adolescence. We cannot, therefore tabulate patterns of disposal at, let us say, age 21. However, we did ask whether respondents saved for marriage and found that in most families children were expected to give the bulk of their earnings to their mothers right up till the time they married, and had, therefore, no savings.

When I started work I gave all my money in until six months before I married (at the age of 26).

(Case Number MB12, man born in England 1901, arrived in Canada 1908)

Very few had saved anything, despite lengthy engagements.

Interviewer: Did you save up before you were married?
Respondent: No, not much. I couldn't save much on army pay because my mother got all I could give her. I just had enough to buy a few coffees and something like that. Of course, that stopped as soon as I was married. My separation allowance and assigned pay went to my mother, and as soon as I was married it came to my wife.

(Case Number MB11, man born in England 1895, arrived in Canada 1912)

Several respondents criticized grownup brothers and sisters for not contributing enough to the household.

My brother next to me used to stay with a bunch of his friends down at the beach for a week at a time (in the summer). He'd come home on Sundays and bring three or four shirts and have a good meal. One Sunday I asked him if he was coming back the next Sunday. He said, "I guess I am." I said, "Are you going to bring any more shirts with you?" He said, "I guess so." So I said, "When you bring them up, take them to the China-man's — let him wash them. And if you are going to eat up here every Sunday, you are going to pay for it . . . ." He wasn't giving my mother a cent.

(Case Number MC08, man born in Canada in 1902)

However, the more the family had, the more likely was the grown son and daughter or daughters to have generous spending money.

The way I worked, and the way my mother worked I could always spend more than the average boy.

(Case Number MB01, man born in Britain 1900, arrived in Canada 1909)

In only a very few prosperous working-class households, with only one or perhaps two children in the family, was the son or daughter allowed to keep most of his or her earnings.

Aging parents had, of course, an interest in not exacting too much from their children. One man recalled how his fiancée had been ill-treated by her mother. The mother had refused to give the girl adequate money for clothing, had treated her unkindly at home, and had taken a great dislike to her boyfriend. This mother was clearly jeopardizing her chances of living out her old age comfortably in her daughter's home, and had it not been for the exceptional kindness of her son-in-law, she and her husband might well have ended their lives in dire poverty or in an institution.

. . . her mother was tough on her though. She had nothing in life. Her mother used to take all the money. I told her, "You see on the pay enve-lope, the amount's only put on there in pencil, you can rub it out and put in any amount you want to put in and give it to your mother." So she took out what she was making more than when she was packing and gave the rest to her mother . . . . The old lady wouldn't look at me. She didn't want anybody to take her mealticket away.

(Case Number MCW07, man born in Canada in 1902)

Another fear was that a grownup son, if he did not find conditions at home to his liking, would leave the household, taking his earnings with him. Daughters found it less easy to escape. One man remembered being told to treat his older brother better.

I hear my mother talking to my father. "You know, you've got to talk to that laddie. If he keeps bugging his brother like that, you know he is going to leave home. Ben (the brother) has a tendency to roam." Dad — "He's going to leave home if he don't get all his own way?" So I went in, and I says, "You know, mother, there is a possibility I could leave home too." That really startled her — you see, the impudence . . . . (Dad said), "I don't know Nellie, there's a lot of truth in what he says. He could leave home."

(Case Number MB01, man born in Britain in 1900, arrived in Canada 1909)

One might ask why it was that children were, apparently, so willing to hand over substantial portions of their earnings. In families in which the money was badly needed, in which there were many young children, or in which the father was disabled or not present, respondents talked with enthusiasm of the satisfaction of contributing to the household.

> I turned it mostly all over to her (mother) because you needed every cent you could get.
>
> (Case Number WB01 woman born in Britain in 1894, arrived in Canada in 1913)

There is evidence that in Britain, also, until the early 20th century working-class children living at home generally gave most of their wages to their mothers and that only about the time of World War I did the working-class mother's traditional control of family finances and children's wages become eroded.[18] The giving of one's earnings to one's mother was seen by some respondents as the natural way of repaying one's mother for having given one a happy childhood. Some clearly saw giving to one's mother as being an important symbolic gesture and others talked spontaneously of the presents they had bought their mothers with their first pocket money allowed them from their wages.

The very fact that satisfactory pension schemes, unemployment compensation and sickness and injury insurance did not exist must have forced working-class children to be particularly aware of how they could help their parents,[19] although some, of course, found the pressures at home to be so great that they deserted. Parents would sometimes try to buy houses during this short period of relative prosperity. Should the father be forced to retire, he and his wife could then live on the rents. In the days before the existence of organized pension schemes a working man would hope that he could continue to work, at least in a light job such as caretaking, until he died. Table 4 shows that half the men of 65 and over were employed. The only alternatives were to live as a dependent in the household of a son or daughter, or to enter the "poor house."

As we have pointed out, respondents probably did exaggerate their financial contributions. Nonetheless, their responses do show that giving the bulk of one's earnings to one's mother until marriage was accepted and approved behaviour among the Anglo-Canadian working class.

THE TRANSITION — SCHOOLGOER TO WORKER

Despite the considerable importance of children's work to the family economy, there were no formal rites of passage associated with becoming a full-time worker. The transition was, however, sharper for girls

TABLE 6
QUESTION (13a)
"WHILE YOU WERE AT SCHOOL, DID YOU HAVE A PART-TIME JOB OR ANY MEANS OF EARNING A LITTLE REGULAR MONEY?"

	Anglo-Canadian Working Class		
	Men	Women	Total
	%	%	%
Had some year round paid part-time work (with perhaps additional work in the summer-time)	13(87)	2(12)	15(47)
Had unpaid part-time work	—	—	—
Summer paid work only	—	4(24)	4(13)
Had no part-time work	1(7)	11(65)	12(37)
Not asked	1(7)	—	1(3)
Sub-Total	15(101%)	17(101%)	32(100%)
Came to Canada late in Childhood	5	3	8
Total Cases	20	20	40

than it was for boys. As Table 6 shows, working-class girls rarely worked outside the home until they entered the mill or the shop in their early teens. As one man said of his sisters,

The girls were handy in the house.
(Case Number MCW03, man born in Canada in 1904)

For working-class girls, starting full time paid work did involve a change in status in the home in that, with the 10-12 hour working day, they now had no time to do chores about the house. These tasks now fell to younger sisters or back to the mother.

Working-class boys rarely did anything other than outside chores. As Table 6 shows they had generally had part-time work while in school. Working-class boys were to be found delivering groceries, serving in restaurants, helping in shops, and, of course, selling newspapers.

When I was going to school, I worked for a pickle man. I used to go there at seven in the morning till eight thirty, and from four to six, and all day Saturday. So I didn't get much time to play around.
(Case Number MB12, man born in Britain in 1901, arrived in Canada in 1908)

> I had paper routes from the time I was about 8 or 9 years old until I was quite a big boy — I guess I must have been almost 15. So that took up a fair amount of time — about two hours.
> (Case Number MCW06, man born in Canada in 1898)

Home delivery absorbed a great deal of boy labour. Before the days of cars most stores would deliver free of charge.

> If you said "deliver" it was delivered to you — free of charge . . . . They'd make up the order and deliver. There was no payments, not till the end of the week.
> (Case Number MB01, man born in Britain in 1900, arrived in Canada 1909)

Restauranteurs and shop-keepers would sometimes feed their boy workers, cutting the numbers to be fed at home. Many boys, and a few girls also, took full-time jobs in the summertime, either in factories or harvesting in the countryside. One man described his yearly cycle.

> I did errands for grocers and butchers, bicycle deliveries for a drug store — things of that nature. And then during the summer holidays — July and August — I worked at Penningtons in Dundas, making ammunition boxes for 18-pounder shells. Assembling them. Then I went back to school, of course.
> (Case Number MCW07, man born in Canada in 1902)

However, few boys spent more than a few years in these service occupations. By the time they reached their mid-teens they could command higher wages in factory work. Where fathers were self-employed, sons were expected to help out their fathers. The son of a gardener helped his father with garden work.

> He (father) had to keep the lawns watered. When I came home from school, I had a whole schedule of lawns to go and turn on the water. And mow them, and turn them off at night . . . And in the winter time, go and shovel snow.
> (Case Number MCW03, man born in Canada in 1903)

A number of respondents, male and female, described periods during which they did not attend school regularly. They were helping mother with a new baby, they were working until it was discovered that they were under age, or they were simply staying away, either with or without their parents' consent. One suspects that not attending school was, for a variety of reasons, more readily tolerated in the early 20th century than it is today.[20] In the early 20th century school urban attendance rates were only moderate. In 1909 about three quarters of the Hamilton children enrolled in school, were actually attending on any particular day. In rural areas the attendance rate stood at about fifty percent.[21] One imagines that in a society in which mothers were invariably at home, in which girls were expected to do housework, and in which a certain amount of part-time work was common among working-class boys, non-attendance was more easily tolerated than it is today.

Our data show that working-class boys experienced a gradual movement out of school and into work, and that becoming a full-time worker did not involve any formal change in status at home. Since food was plentiful in Canada there was no pattern of feeding wage-earners better food, as was common in early 20th century Britain.[22] Despite the fact that boys' earnings might be high, they were still regarded as boys, and dressed in short knickerbockers until the age of 16 or 17. Girls, while at school, led far more restricted lives, spending much of their out of school time helping at home. For them, entry to full-time work meant being excused home chores (they simply had no time for these) and meeting a wider circle of people. Working-class girls often met their husbands through work. But for girls, as for boys, starting work did not involve any major formal change in status. For example, it was the parents who decided at what age — 14, 15, or 16 — a daughter should be allowed to start going out to dances on Saturday evening.

CONCLUSION

Historians of pre-industrial society have often characterized the stage prior to marriage as one of dependency or semi-dependency. Working on the family farm, serving an apprenticeship, doing domestic work in one's parent's or someone else's household all involve dependence. In an industrial town, however, young adulthood became a period of considerable independence. For about ten years, from the early or mid-teens until some time in the twenties, working-class sons and daughters would be employed, generally living at home, and often excused from household chores. They would participate both in family social occasions and in all the social and church activities of their young co-workers and neighbours. For women this active public life ceased abruptly on marriage, when women would confine themselves to the family circle and perhaps to a few charitable activities.

It was the emergence of cities and industrial work and the concomitant decline in the institutions of domestic service and apprenticeship that allowed increased numbers of young working men and women to live with their own parents until they married.[23] The mid-twentieth century has, however, seen a reversal of that trend towards co-residence of grown children as numbers of young unmarried people now establish single person households or spend extended periods in post-secondary education.

Our data show that in the early 20th century city working-class adolescents were important contributors to their families. A parent might hope that a dutiful working child would contribute substantial portions of his or her earnings until marriage, for a period of perhaps ten years or more. Children might, of course, defect, but, nonetheless, a parent could at least hope for (if not actually receive) substantial support. At that time elderly parents were completely dependent on their children should the aging father become unable to work. The only alternative was charity. The having of children, especially children whose spouses were also willing to take one in, had an important insurance function for parents.

Let us now consider the situation from the perspective of the adolescent son or daughter. Working-class children were quite aware of household income and outgoings — the accounting was often done by the mother, who divided up the notes and the coins after supper on the kitchen table. Children knew that should the father be unable to work, the family depended on their earnings. The very fact that, in the working classes, young men and women started working in their early teens, several years before they dressed as, or were accepted as adults, must surely have encouraged them to see their work as helping the family rather than the individual.

It is significant that for working-class adolescents there was no stage before marriage at which they experienced a formal rite of passage. For example, there was no public and ceremonial marking of a change in the status of working-class children's entry to work. They left school in their early teens as children, and did not graduate from high school or college. They had no coming out parties. They had no major religious ceremonies that marked entry to adulthood. For them the most important, and the only formally celebrated change in status, came at marriage, when the primary economic obligation shifted from family of origin to marriage partner. Entry to work was not viewed as a major transition point in life partly because the transition was smooth for boys, if not for girls, and partly because entry to work involved no change in the primary loyalty to the family that parents so encouraged.

Footnotes

1. This approach is discussed by Modell and others. Modell, J., F. Fursenberg and T. Hershberg. 1976. "Social Change and Transition to Adulthood in Historical Perspective." Journal of Family History. 1 Autumn, 1976, pp. 7-33.
2. Discussion of the social structure of mid-19th century Hamilton, then a commercial rather than an industrial city, is to be found in M.B. Katz, 1975. The People of Hamilton, Canada West: Family and Class in a Mid-Nineteenth Century City, Cambridge Mass.: Harvard University Press.
3. The most useful collection of contemporary research in this area is to be found in Social Structure and Family: Generational Relations, edited by E. Shanas and G.F. Streib. 1965. Englewood Cliffs, N.J.: Prentice Hall.

4. The significance of contemporary education as a form of control is discussed by Michael Zuckerman in his article "Dr. Spock: The Confidence Man" in The Family in History edited by Charles E. Rosenberg, University of Pennsylvania Press, Philadelphia, 1975.
5. Armstrong H. and P. Armstrong, 1975. "The Segregated Participation of Women in the Canadian Labour Force, 1941-1971," Canadian Review of Sociology and Anthropology, Vol. 12, No. 4, pp. 370-384. November 1975.
6. The extent and nature of the employment of women has depended on the nature of local industry and cultural traditions. A study of working women in Montreal, 1844-1901, showed that a substantial number of married French-Canadian women did work, but that among the more prosperous Protestants population married women appear to have worked only when deserted or widowed.

    Cross, D. Suzanne. 1973. "The Neglected Majority: The Changing Role of Women in 19th Century Montreal." Paper presented at the 52nd annual meeting of the Canadian Historical Association, Kingston, Ontario, June, 1973. (Also published in Social History — Histoire Sociale). The relationship between the local economy and female employment patterns in the U.S.A. is discussed by Kleinberg. Kleinberg, Susan J. 1975. "The Systematic Study of Urban Women," Historical Methods Newsletter, Vol. 9, No. 1, Dec. 1975, pp. 14-25.
7. The following tables, drawn from the 1911 census, show that the city population was largely Canadian or British-born. British immigrants constituted nearly one third of the population and there were a substantial number of Continental European immigrants in the city. The countryside was largely peopled by Canadians of British stock.

Hamilton Population by Place of Birth, 1911

	Male	Female
Canada	25,065	26,979
Britain	12,141	9,860
Other Europe	3,019	1,254
U.S.A.	1,479	1,563
Asia	343	21

Hamilton Population by Religion, 1911

	%
Anglican	27.9
Methodist	21.2
Presbyterian	20.9
Roman Catholic	15.9
Baptist	6.0
Jewish	2.1
Lutheran	1.5
Congregationalist	0.9
Salvation Army	0.7
	100.0%

8. Our group of respondents comprises the following: Men: 8 born in Canada; 7 arrived in Canada at or before the age of 8; 5 arrived in Canada

after age 8; Women: 12 born in Canada; 4 arrived in Canada at or before the age of 8; 4 arrived in Canada after age 8.

Research on British immigrants to the United States in the 19th century has shown that there were relatively few cultural differences and that this group of immigrants was rapidly absorbed, leaving no long-lived community organizations or literature. Erickson, C. 1972. Invisible Immigrants: The Adaptation of English and Scottish Immigrants in Nineteenth Century North America. London: Weidenfeld and Nicholson.

9. The two world wars did, of course, affect employment patterns. There were increases in the employment of married women. See, Pierson, Ruth. 1976. "Women's Emancipation and the Recruitment of Women into the Labour Force in World War II." (especially pp. 4-5). Unpublished paper presented at the Canadian Historical Association Annual Meeting, Laval, Quebec, June, 1976. Ramkhalawansingh, Ceta. 1974. "Women During the Great War" in Women at Work: Ontario 1850-1930. Edited and published by the Canadian Women's Educational Press, Toronto.

Another effect of World War I was to bring Continental European workers into positions previously reserved for Anglo-Canadians. See, Avery, D. 1975. "Continental European Immigrant Workers in Canada, 1896-1919: From Stalwart Peasants to Radical Proletariat." Canadian Review of Sociology and Anthropology, 12: 1, (Feb. 1975), pp. 53-64.

10. Useful discussions of the interview method and problems of analysis in social history are to be found in the following: Thompson, P. 1975, The Edwardians: The Remaking of British Society, London: Weidenfeld and Nicolson, pp. 5-8; and Thompson, P. 1973. "Problems of Method in Oral History" Oral History, No. 1, Vol. 4, pp. 1-47, Colchester: University of Essex; and Evans, G.E., 1973. "Approaches to Interviewing" Oral History, No. 1, Vol. 4, pp. 56-71, Colchester: University of Essex.

11. For a discussion of these issues as they relate to women, see Lerner, Gerda. 1975. "Placing Women in History: Definitions and Challenges," Feminist Studies III, No. 3/4, 1975. Reprinted in Liberating Women's History, edited by Bernice Carroll, Urbana, University of Illinois Press, 1976.

12. Copp, T. 1974. The Anatomy of Poverty: The Condition of the Working Class in Montreal. Toronto: McClelland & Stewart. See, also, Rowntree's study of York. Rowntree, B.S. 1914. Poverty: A Study of Town Life. London: pp. 152-172. The same pattern of poverty in old age and, to some extent, in the years of childrearing, still exists today. For example, the Royal Commission on the Status of Women documents the extreme poverty of many elderly women. Report of the Royal Commission on the Status of Women. 1970. Ottawa: Information Canada. Pp. 312-332.

13. Vital Statistics, Canada, Annual Reports, 1941. Ottawa: Dominion Bureau of Statistics.

14. These estimates are suggested by the data below.

Average Weekly earnings of males and females in selected occupations in 1921

	SEX	
	Male	Female
Biscuit and Confectionery Makers	22.00	10.71
Office Clerks	24.36	15.25
Clothing Factory Employees	25.27	11.84
Teachers	—	21.09

Educationalists	44.11	—
Labourers	19.77	—
Nurses and Nurses-in training	—	9.84
Salesmen/Saleswomen	24.29	11.81
Tailoresses	—	14.41

Source: Census of Canada, 1921. *Ottawa: Dominion Bureau of Statistics. Table 39, pp. 152-154.*
    Analysis of material from the annual Wages and Hours of Labour, *a report of the Federal Department of Labour, also confirms our estimates.* Wages and Hours of Labour, *Department of Labour, 1914, pp. 27-28.*

15. Material on the development of legislation affecting children is to be found in the following book:
    Sutherland, N. 1977. Children in English Canadian Society, 1880-1920. Toronto: University of Toronto Press.
16. Census of 1911. Unpublished tables. "Statistics of Families, showing family earnings, educational efficiency, classified by occupation followed by supporting head in cities and towns of 4,000 population and over." Ottawa: Dominion Bureau of Statistics.
17. Bohen, Linda S. 1973. "Women Workers in Ontario: A Socio-Legal History" University of Toronto: Faculty of Law Review. Vol. 31, 1973, pp. 45-74.
18. See Stearns, P. for example, "Working Class Women in Britain, 1890-1914." PP. 110-116, in Suffer and Be Still: Women in the Victorian Age edited by Martha Vicunus. 1972. Bloomington: University of Indiana Press. Social Order. "Population Changes and the Status of the Young." London: Routledge and Kegan Paul.
19. Pension schemes were beginning to be institutionalized by the state in the late 1920's, and these schemes affected only a small portion of workers. For an account see Bryden, K. 1974. Old Age Pensions and Policy Making in Canada. Montreal: McGill-Queens University press. The first Workmen's Compensation act in Ontario was passed in 1914.
20. Various researchers have pointed to truancy legislation as a means for the social control of working class boys. Girls, confined as they generally were to the house and the immediate neighbourhood, were seen as less of a threat. For example, see A. Prentice, 1977, Education and Social Class in Mid-Nineteenth Century Upper Canada. Toronto: McClelland and Stewart, Chapters 3-6.
21. Ontario Sessional Papers, 1910, Report of the Department of Education. Toronto. Pp. 3-4.
22. The issue of status within the family and level of nutrition is raised in the following article. Oren, Laura. "The Welfare of Women in Labouring Families, 1860-1950" in Clio's Consciousness Raised: New Perspectives on the History of Women, edited by M. Hartman and L. Banner. 1974. New York: Harper Torchbacks.
23. The evidence regarding this long term trend is discussed by Katz in The People of Hamilton, Canada West, pp. 292-308.

SOCIAL STRUCTURE AND
SOCIALIZATION

A Social Ecological Model of Development

BRIAN R. LITTLE
THOMAS J. RYAN
Department of Psychology
Carleton University

This paper provides a framework for a new perspective on the well-being of Canadian children. It proposes an approach based upon an emerging social ecological perspective (Moos, 1976; Moos & Insel, 1974; Little, 1975). Within such a model, the interdependency between children and their environments is emphasized. The paper presents ten propositions which define the social ecological approach to human development. An attempt is made to further develop each proposition by deriving implications for research policy and analysis.

A DECLARATION OF INTERDEPENDENCE

My name is Guy and I's 13 years old. What makes me suffer most is not having a house, having to live in a shack where it's always cold and too small for all the family. There are nine of us. The seven children all sleep together in two 36" wide beds — pushed together in winter for more heat since we don't have enough blankets. We have an old broken-down stove. In the winter we push the beds near the stove but it's dangerous. Autumn isn't very much fun either. It's cold also, and the rats come in — you have to watch so they won't bite the smaller children. This week they chewed off part of the pump so we have no water and the neighbours tell us their well is low, so we do without water.

Based in part upon a research essay prepared under contract to Department of National Health & Welfare, Canada, June 30, 1978. We wish to acknowledge the critical and useful help from the following individuals: (a) our colleagues at the Long Range Planning Branch of National Health & Welfare, particularly Julyan Reid; (b) our colleagues in the Dept. of Psychology: D. Berkson; G. Brown; R. Doyle; R.M. Knights; J. Mitchell; A.R. Moffitt; T. Palys; R. Wells.

We're not always clean when we go to school (National Council of Welfare, 1975).

I'm Lisa and I'm ten. What I'd like to change about myself is first my hair colour, second my room and thirdly our filter system so that our pool would work again! I like sailing, and hiking, and going to the museum. Daddy is hoping to get a bigger sail boat this summer so that we can sail to Vancouver whenever we want! I don't have any brothers or sisters, but my cousin stays with us often and we get along well with each other (except she pinches me).

Proposition 1: Interdependence

Human development comprises a series of interdependent adaptations between children and their environments, involving both contemporaneous and delayed effects.

Proposition 1 embodies the basic postulate that children and their environments are indivisible, and that scientific research and public policy must reflect this fundamental interdependence.

Elaboration of Proposition 1

Traditional models of development stressing the potency of environmental factors conceive of the influence process as unidirectional. The child in such a model is seen as molded by the context, but the context is not influenced by the child. Thus, the personalities, abilities, goals and fears of Guy and Lisa are the direct effects of their environments.

Guy lives in rural Northern New Brunswick where his milieu is one of grinding poverty. Lisa lives in an affluent suburb of a pleasant coastal city in British Columbia. Were an educational or psychological consultant to prepare a standard report on these two children it would not be surprising to find a marked difference between them, particularly in their basic verbal and mathematical skills. The traditional model would account for such differences in terms of both contemporaneous and delayed effects. An example of contemporaneous effects would be Guy's inability to prepare for a school test because of inadequate lighting, or Lisa's greater motor coordination in gym classes due to the regular use of the family swimming pool. Delayed effects would be exemplified by Guy and Lisa's attitudes towards material security and employment five or ten years from now. For Guy a job washing dishes at a local restaurant will likely be seized as a chance of at least temporary respite from poverty; the same job for Lisa might be viewed as a fun diversion from school and some extra money for a trip to Switzerland.

Although this one-way model encompasses a wide variety of environmental effects it is inadequate in accounting for the dynamic effects of children in context. Evidence has been accumulating which indicates a substantial impact of the child on the environment (Bell, 1968). A particularly interesting example is that of individual differences in temperament at birth influencing the style of socialization adopted by the parents. Some children, for example, from the early days of post-natal life show irregularity in biological functions, slowness of adapting to change, negative response to new stimuli, and a prevailing mood of intense negativity (Thomas, Chess & Birch, 1968). Such children, sometimes referred to as "mother killers" place a heavy demand on the caretaker and many parents respond with inappropriate child-rearing techniques, (for example "random" beating of the child), which simply exacerbate the problem. Less dramatic but nonetheless pervasive effects of children on their environments include individual differences in such areas as activity level, sociability, and responsiveness to reward and punishment.

Child impact upon the environment also involves delayed effects. Just how aversive or supportive an atmosphere will characterize Guy's shack in five years will depend in large part upon his own tolerance, noisiness, nurturance to the younger children and capacity for helping his parents at the present time. Similarly, had Lisa been born with congenital brain damage how different would be the poolside atmosphere of her teenage life, if indeed there was a pool.

In contrast to both the environment centered and child centered views of human development, the social ecological model assumes bidirectional causality and that mutual adaptations occur between children and their environments. By adaptation we mean that the relationship between child and context have become routinized at certain levels and that the levels of functioning of child and environment are interdependent. The notion of a reciprocal interdependent model appeared when it was noted that the everyday environments of Guy and Lisa were determined in part by their own characteristics. The social ecological model takes this one step further to complete the cycle of mutual influence — Guy and Lisa are now influenced and shaped by environments which they themselves have shaped.

We assume that both child and environment are subject to constant change, generated both internally and externally. The child, for example, will be influenced by hormonal changes in adolescence to which the environment must accommodate in order to maintain its own integrity. Conversely, evidence exists to show that increased levels of environmental stimulation can increase neurotransmitter activity in cortex, an example of organismic change to environmental influence (Rosenweig & Bennett, 1972, 1976). Continual change of children and their environments poses repeated demands for adaptive response. It is thus a series of interdependent adaptations which we see as the most basic characteristic of human development.

Implications for Research and Policy Analysis
There are important implications of the Interdependence Proposition for scientific research and policy analysis. For example, most of the

current studies in developmental psychology journals are based on research designs that contravene the basic assumption of Proposition 1 resulting in a serious applicability gap between the research studies on child development and the activities of those charged with responsibility for developing public policy (Bronfenbrenner, 1974, 1976). With the recent emergence of statistical and mathematical models designed to examine the interdependent causal networks, the use of more realistic, multicausal research strategies will likely be facilitated. The development of research programs on child-environment relations explicitly designed to examine the longitudinal mutual impacts of child and context should receive very high priority.

Perhaps the major policy issues raised by the Interdependency Proposition is the warning it sounds about formulating policy on children or their environments without recognition of the other half of the interactive equation. Global psychological recommendations about the needs of children, bereft of reference to particular contexts, foster false hopes of simple solutions to problems in human development.

Given that children determine in part the flow and consequence of the environments which they inhabit, a more radical derivation from Proposition 1 would be to propose that long term planning in agencies creating and monitoring the environments of children, including schools, domestic housing, public transportation, hospitals, as well as neighbourhood and community design, must take into account the contribution to those environments made by children. Conversely, child welfare planning, acting in isolation from regional and urban planning, would risk the implementation of policies that might be systemically sabotaged by the kind of housing in which the children will be living. Consider a child care policy which attempts to increase cooperation and interdependence between groups in order to combat destructive competition between teenagers. Such a policy would be frustrated if, at the same time as children were being schooled in the advantages of cooperative sports, they were living in neighbourhoods that fostered an intense individualism by the mere structure of the separate dwellings.

In short, the chief implication of the interdependency of child and milieu is the need for similar interdependency between those who study and serve children as well as those who study and serve their environments.

MOLAR IMPERATIVES: THE NATURE OF CHILDREN'S ENVIRONMENTS

Proposition 2: Environment
Environments comprise social and material objects, events and resources which individually, and as interacting systems (e.g., biologi-

cal, social, cultural and physical-environment) influence human development.

Elaboration of Proposition 2

Proposition 2 represents an elaboration of "the environment" and serves to direct attention to the diversity of sources of influence which impinge upon and are influenced by the developing child. Traditional conceptions of environments seem unduly limited, in part as a result of the strictures demanded by classical experimental research design. A social ecological perspective shifts attention away from abstract, environmental variables analyzed at the molecular level to more concrete, ecologically representative environmental units studied at a more molar level. While the terms *objects* and *events* are self-explanatory, the term *resources* should be noted as representing an eco-system view of child and milieu. To examine a child-environment unit as a resource in the manner of ecologists or wild life biologists, for example, is to raise issues not normally encountered from a psychological perspective such as resource availability, substitutability, integrity and sharing.

To illustrate the Environment Proposition we can look at a psychological variable, spatial ability, that has been examined from each of the major systems comprising children's environments. Spatial ability, the capacity to discern shape and form, to differentiate focal objects from backgrounds, and to hold and mentally manipulate visual images has been studied from each of the four systems we posit as impinging on children. From the biological perspective, for example, there is evidence suggesting that sex-linked hormonal differences in early development account for the frequently reported superiority of boys to girls in the spatial area (Hutt, 1972). Psychologists working within the personality and social psychology areas have argued that general social orientations may influence the extent to which a child "tunes" himself to scanning the perceptual field, suggesting that social factors moderate the expression of spatial ability (Berry, 1977; Berry & Annis, 1974). Anthropologically oriented psychologists have presented striking evidence that ability to solve spatial and perceptual problems is intimately related to the type of economic subsistence system operating in the culture. Thus an Inuit child for whom the successful discrimination of spatial form is necessary for successful hunting will show greater acuity than a child living in a food gathering culture in Sierra Leone, where such a visual discrimination is less necessary. A closely related approach falls primarily within the environmental systems area, but also exemplifies the interaction of physical environment with social systems stressed in Proposition 2. This approach looks at the free range latitude given to children in their neighbourhoods as a determinant of later spatial skill. Studies have shown, for example, that boys are given more free reign to explore outside of their own yard than are girls. It is hypothesized that such rambling about the neighbourhood enables the pre-school boy to learn spatial orientation and form more rapidly than his sister (Hart, 1977).

Implications for Research and Policy Analysis

The Environmental Proposition can be seen as an elaboration of the basic postulate contained in the Interdependence Proposition. One implication is that studies which use abstract, easily manipulable environmental stimuli or variables can contribute little to knowledge about child-environment relationships. Representative sampling of environmental elements, as well as children is seldom carried out in policy-related research and very rarely indeed in pure research. A social ecological focus on child development would make the use of real (or simulated) everyday, molar-level environmental objects a necessary condition for research claiming relevance to policy concerns.

Given the multi-system membership of most molar objects in a child's environment it can be postulated that such objects have differential claim upon the child according to the number of such systems to which the object belongs. Take the mother as a social object, for example. In early infancy she functions as a pivotal element in the biological system (provider of necessary nutrition), the social system (providing social reinforcement, smiling, contact comfort), cultural system (early language training) and environmental system (arranging physical safety of house). Using total system involvement as a criterion, then, primary caretakers are essential resources to the child. Less obvious examples might be close neighbours who satisfy basic system functions for the children next door (recall, for example, Guy's reliance on his neighbour when the well pump fails).

Finally, while Proposition 1 implied a need for greater interdisciplinary research between child investigators and environmental researchers, Proposition 2 indicates a need for more integrative research within the different environmental sciences. The problems associated with interdisciplinary research are very great and this difficulty constitutes one of the major blockages to a strong research base bearing on the health and well-being of children (Brunswick, 1956; Overton & Reese, 1977).

CHILDREN AND CHANNELS: THE INTEGRATIVE ROLE OF PERSONAL SYSTEMS

Proposition 3: Channelization

Children constitute personal systems, whose processes and development are channelized by the environmental systems impinging upon them, and whose prime function is the integration of such systems.

Elaboration of the Channelization Proposition

Children can be examined from innumerable perspectives, each serving a particular purpose. As viewed by a myopic sociobiologist, for example, a child is simply a gene's way of creating more genes. Viewed from her mother's perspective, Lisa may be the very reason for living. The concept of personal systems provides a conception of children which, while sufficient to capture their complexity and idiosyncracies, stops short of mere sentimentality (Little, 1972, 1976). Personal systems are open and serve as the point of conjunction of biological, social, cultural, physical-environmental and other external systems. Closely related to the concept of personality, personal systems are less encumbered by the tradition of individualism and presumed cross-situational consistency associated with the older term (Argyle & Little, 1972; Mischel, 1968; Partington, 1976).

The process of channelization is critical to our social ecological perspective. It is adapted from personal construct theory where it refers to the selective structuring of human action:

> We conceive a person's processes as operating through a network of pathways rather than as fluttering about in a vast emptiness. The network is flexible and is frequently modified, but it is structured and it both facilitates and restricts a person's range of action. (Kelly, 1955)

The first part of Proposition 3 postulates that children's development is structured by the biological, social, cultural and physical environmental influences impinging on them. Guy's feelings and thoughts about himself and his town will be channelized by factors such as his height and health (biosystem), the fact that he comes from a large and poor family (social), and lives in a French Canadian area of Northern New Brunswick (cultural) and by the crowding and cold of his dwelling (physical environment). The child's particular status on these factors determines in part the degrees of freedom open to the child's development. They partially define the child's options for living.

But if the child's personal system is channelized by the various integrated systems of influence impinging upon it, it also in large part determines the net impact that each system will eventually have. This integrating function, the second half of Proposition 3, is also critical for understanding the resolution of factors influencing the developing child. We do not see children, then, as passive recipients of the impinging systems at whose intersect they stand, but rather as active, personal systems of influence themselves, who seek to balance, resolve and integrate the disparate sources of influence which channelize their actions. The critical function of personal systems is the executive control and integration of the diverse systems of influence which impinge upon it. The means by which such integration takes place will vary considerably as a function of age. The integrative centrality of the personal system as schematically represented below, has been dealt with in more detail elsewhere (Little, 1976).

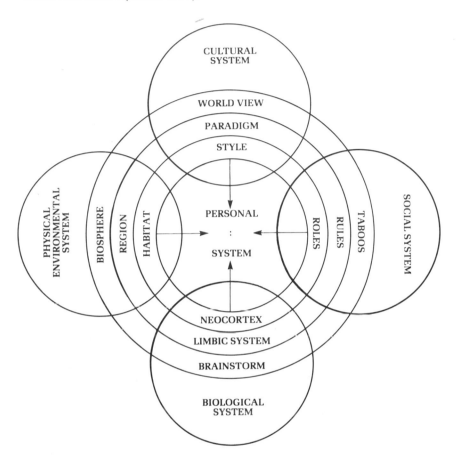

Implications for Research and Policy Analysis

Proposition 3 asserts that the child's processes are channelized by the environmental systems impinging upon him, and that this process is critical to understanding the practical implications of the Proposition. For example, there is a need for research to detect and classify the patterns of stimulation which, in fact, impinge upon children. Such research has already begun in several domains, particularly in the physical-environmental system (Price & Blashfield, 1975; Sells, 1974; Stokols, 1978).

A corollary to the Channelization Proposition would specify that the means whereby personal systems achieve integration of their varied environmental systems is through the development of appropriate orientations and competencies. One important practical aspect of this Proposition is the need for children to be both formally and informally appraised not on the basis of abstract intellectual abilities such as I.Q., but in terms of the competencies necessary to meet the demands placed upon them by the eco-systems in which they are embedded (Uzgiris & Weizmann, 1977). Note that the broader intellectual and personality dimensions such as intelligence, creativity, and adaptability may be appropriate dimensions for evaluating the children who are likely to be shifting between eco-systems. For appropriate assessment of children in their present contexts, however, ecologically appropriate measures are necessary. Take, for example, a child living in a high density, low income area of Toronto. The environmental demands upon this child are more likely to make toughness, large muscle dexterity and verbal dominance more ecologically appropriate than nurturance, small muscle skills, and verbal complexity. The latter behaviours would, however, be regarded as ecologically adaptive, relevant competencies, in some of the more gracious and spatious settings in West Vancouver.

CHILDREN AS MEDIATORS: THE TRANSFORMED ENVIRONMENT

Proposition 4: Mediation
The transactions between children and their environments are mediated by their sensory, cognitive, affective and behavioural processes.

Elaboration of the Mediation Proposition
The mutual influence processes or transactions between children and their environments are typically not direct, but are mediated by intervening systems of representation. One consequence of such mediation is the creation of an area of selectivity or choice between the "raw" environment and the adaptive response of the child to it, an area that provides for increased "degrees of freedom" with development. Each of the four process areas that are hypothesized as mediating between children and their environments constitutes a major area of psychological research and only highly selective examples of the mediational nature of each will be given.

Sensory processes set limits upon the capacity of the child to adapt to the different patterns of stimulation discussed in Proposition 3. The importance of environmental complexity, such as richness of visual stimulation, is mediated by the extent of development of the child's sensory apparatus. Young organisms respond positively to heightened stimulational complexity; conversely, sensory deprivation at younger ages is likely to show more deleterious effects than if these extremes were experienced by the child later in life.

The cognitive or thinking processes also mediate the impact of the environment and the nature of the child's adaptive actions back upon the environment. The impact of a particular kind of teaching program, for example, will be mediated by the level of conceptual complexity of the child. More complex children will learn better from programs that allow for discovery of principles, rather than rote learning of rules. Conceptually less complex children show the opposite pattern of response. They perform more adequately under relatively structured conditions (Hunt, 1971, 1976).

By children's affective processes we refer to their interest in and orientations towards aspects of themselves and their surrounding systems, together with the corresponding subjective feelings such as love, fear, or hate. A child's affective state or level of development will mediate the impact of a given pattern of environmental stimulation. There is evidence, for example, that high anxiety levels in children will interfere with their ability to respond to complex patterns of stimulation. Children with moderate levels of anxiety perform better on tasks requiring attention than either those who are very high or very low on anxiety (Sarason, Davidson, Lighthall, Waite & Ruebach, 1960).

By a child's behavioural processes we refer to an extremely wide range of actions by the child upon the surrounding environment, particularly in the sense of motor action upon it. An example of the Mediation Proposition in the behavioural domain can be given by referring again to the area of sensory stimulation. There is evidence that organisms will only benefit from the effects of sensorially enriched environments to the extent that they are actively engaged in motoric exploration of that environment. Being moved passively around the same area will not lead to the same benefits as active exploration (Held & Heim, 1965). A child who gets bused from home to school every day, in other words, will benefit less than one who rides her bike or walks even though they travel the same route.

Implications for Research and Policy Analysis

The transformation of environmental influences by the mediation of the child's developing processes has important implications for the design of programs for enhancing the quality of life of children. It must be understood that there can be no general propositions regarding the benefits or costs of environmental systems without specification of the characteristics of the target group of children for whom programs are being planned. Grand and global prescriptions on what constitutes high quality environments for children, therefore, represent a misleadingly simple picture of the child in context (Endler & Magnusson, 1975).

Furthermore, as cognitive processes play an increasing role in mediating environmental transactions in later stages of development, there is a need to develop measures of children's subjective judgments of their contexts, and for policy to be developed in the light of the knowledge gained from such measurements. An excellent example of the possible dangers that can derive from ignoring the child's subjective construing of environmental objects is the discovery that many Canadian children do not read the skull and crossbones symbol on bottles as "Danger" but rather as "Pirate Food!" The switch from the old, inappropriate symbol to the stamping of a green-faced "Mr. Yuk" on poisons represents a small but potent example of the practical implications of the Mediation Proposition.

A number of research programs in the environmental psychology field relate to children's images of their cities and their subjective representations of what their social ecologies comprise (Ittelson, Proshansky, Rivlin & Winkel, 1974; Lynch, 1960). One program is the development of objective taxonomies of the pattern of stimulation generated by the child's development and use of subjective measures taken from the child's perspective. The development of a detailed, objective classification of the environmental context within which Guy or Lisa was raised might place a heavy weight on the objective indices of economic status, state of physical repair of the house, number of siblings, and physical health of parents. What we might miss in the inventory of everyday influences on the lives of these children would be the importance of Guy's dog, with whom the problems of making do during the dark winters are shared, and with whom he romps through the woods in the spring where, for a brief time, life is green and fun. We might also miss mentioning Lisa's tree-fort where she hides from the noise and bustle of what she sees as a "plastic patio" populated by the bikinis and Bar-B-Q's of her affluent neighbourhood.

The major manner in which children mediate their environmental transactions is through the initiation of personal projects (Little, 1972, 1978). Projects represent integrated sets of actions performed over time which can serve the needs of children and/or their environments. Thus, children start life as major projects for their parents and the channelization of resources in the direction of supporting the newborn child constitutes an extraordinary change in the social ecology of the family. As a child develops, cognitive, affective, and behavioural processes become coordinated into projects which at first are small scale (e.g., finding a hidden toy) but which grow to constitute major initiatives (e.g., planning a career).

By initiating personal projects children interact with their environments so as to recruit helpers, share resources, schedule activities and terminate commitments. Lisa's trip to Switzerland is a project that involves a large network of assistance and support. As a project her trip mediates the impact of her summer job, making it tolerable as a means to an exciting end. Guy's job, on the other hand, may in itself constitute a prepotent project: the only one in which he feels he should invest his full energy and concern. The objective patterns of stimulation coming from the restaurant kitchens in British Columbia and New Brunswick may appear similar. Whether they are construed as a blessing or a bore, however, depends on the mediation of the project systems within whose structures the meaning of environmental transactions take shape.

CROSS-IMPACT OF CHILDREN AND CONTEXTS: HELP, HINDRANCE AND HARMONY

Proposition 5: Cross-Impact
The cross-impact of children and environments may constitute helps or hindrances to the achievement of their respective goals or projects.

Elaboration of the Cross-Impact Proposition
The relationship between child and context are such that at any given moment four joint outcomes are possible, depending upon whether they help or hinder each other.

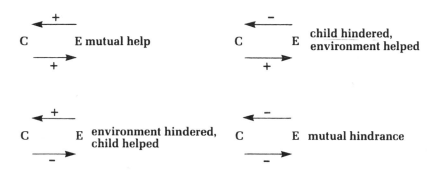

The mutual help condition is, under most conditions, the most desirable kind of relationship. An example of this would be a home where a childless couple desiring a baby, were able to adopt a child who had previously been maltreated. An example of the second situation, where the environment achieves its goals but at a cost to the child, would be one where a teenage girl is sexually abused by a parent, or a young boy is forced to work to support his mother's drug habit. The third situation is typified by homes where there is a considerable demand placed on parents by children with exceptional needs. Mutual hindrance or depletion occurs when neither the child nor the resource gains from the situation. In the example above, the child may turn against an abusing parent and refuse to fulfil the role of satisfying their particular needs.

Implications for Research and Policy Analysis
While earlier propositions stress the interdependence of child and context, Proposition 5 explicates the different forms of satisfaction and

conflict that can arise within the child-environment system. Unlike those perspectives which see enmity as the natural and inevitable relationship between the developing child and the socializing milieu, we see mutual antagonism or hindrance as only one of several states at which the child-environment ecosystem can stabilize.

A home atmosphere in which the child's personal projects were helped and supported by the environment and where the child, in turn, helped in achieving the goals of the environmental systems surrounding him should prove both more cohesive and more able to cope with threat than less mutually supportive systems.

Another example of mutual facilitation would be the relationship between a school basketball team and a 6' 10" well-coordinated newcomer to the school. Here the school's project of winning a cup for the first time in twenty years, and the boy's project of getting accepted quickly at his new school are in a pleasant state of psychological accord or congruency.

States of mutual incompatibility between children and their environments are, we propose, prime candidates for dissolution. The institution of the family in Canada today, in contrast with two hundred years ago, would appear to be in danger of dissolution due to a state of chronic mutual hindrance. In the days when Canada was first being settled, families were typically embedded in a rural, extended family, labor-intensive economy in which the child served a vital and visible role in the well-being of the family. Today, in a largely urban, nuclear-family, industrialized economy the child is often construed as a net drain on the resources of the family. The child, in turn, in attempting to become independent and self-sufficient, finds the family projects and his own to be in conflict. Under such conditions the desire to leave home as soon as economically feasible is high. We hypothesize that family systems whose cross-impacts are mutually negative will be less able to handle the everyday stresses that characterize contemporary living. Recent research, for example, has indicated a relationship between family climate characterized by mutual conflict and the incidence of problem drinking and behaviour problems in family members (Moos & Moos, 1976).

The two middle conditions of imbalance, where the goals or projects of either the child or the environment are hindered, tend to devolve into a stable state of mutual antagonism. In one sense without some form of reciprocal nurturance, resource depletion of either the child or the environment will occur. If Lisa's peer group (part of the social system impinging upon her) is unrewarding to her and frustrate her personal project of being an intellectual, we propose that there will be pressures channelizing her behaviour in the direction of frustrating her friends' projects in return. We see this as a strain towards congruency in a social ecosystem more than as an explicit attempt to "even things up." Obviously, there is a need for research to discover means of promoting positive cross-impacts between children and their environments.

DEVIANT CHILDREN: DIFFERENT, DIFFICULT OR DISCREPANT?

Proposition 6: Discrepancy
To the extent that the child's behavioural processes are construed as discrepant with normal or desired standards, attempts will be made to channelize those processes so as to reduce the discrepancy.

Elaboration of the Discrepancy Proposition
A social ecological view of deviance is construed as discrepancy from standards. Note that it is construed discrepancy, not actual discrepancy, which we hypothesize will give rise to channelization attempts (Kelly, 1955). This proposition directs attention to a number of potentially unsettling issues. Given the socially construed nature of discrepant behaviour, the question of who is construing the child's behaviour as discrepant becomes particularly important. If the people doing the construing differ from the child or the child's family in class, education, or ethnic origin, the difficulties of relativism become particularly acute (Rappaport, 1977). The ascription of discrepancy is always based on some explicitly or tacitly codified set of standards. While most typically these standards specify what is acceptable or normal conduct, they can also set criteria for excellence or social desirability for a child.

Note that we are not saying that channelization will necessarily reduce the discrepancy but only that it will create pressures to correct for deviations. We use the term "channelized" as in Proposition 3 to refer to the setting up of networks through which behaviour is both facilitated and restricted along lines pointing towards increasing congruency with the prevailing norms. Amongst the various routes through which discrepant behaviours might be rechannelized are:

(1) "transplantation": the child is removed from the ecosystem within whose normative structure the child's behaviour appears discrepant, and placed in a context where the behaviour is regarded as normal.

(2) "standard shifting": the standards upon which the child's behaviour is evaluated are shifted so that previously discrepant acts are now construed as normal.

(3) "behaviour change": perhaps the most frequent and simple means of channelizing discrepant behaviour is to simply redirect it by suggestion, modelling, coercion, and other formal or informal behaviour change techniques.

(4) "treatment": where a biological system is either directly or metaphorically used as a reference point for change attempts.

In terms of the success with which the above strategies rechannelize discrepant behaviour into normal ranges, much of the research evidence relating to self-fulfilling prophecies would seem to indicate that the mere act of *construing* a child's behaviour as discrepant may be sufficient to channelize such behaviour even more deeply along a deviant route (Rosenthal & Jacobsen, 1968).

Implications for Research and Policy Analysis

While Proposition 6 specifies what happens when normatively discrepant behaviour occurs, the following deals with what should happen as viewed from a social ecological perspective.

Active promotion of ecological competency, rather than detection and reduction of discrepancy, leads to the most effective enhancement of life quality in children.

The fundamental postulate of interdependency must always be the prime consideration when deciding upon the intervention strategy to be used when discrepancies between a child's behaviour and the relevant standards have been detected. Instead of looking only at the particular ecosystem pressures which led to the child's behaviour, the primacy of the context is assumed, as is the presumed need to redesign the child to fit that context.

The redesign of children's contexts as an alternative to reshaping their individual behaviour is consistent with activities in the areas of family therapy and community psychology. A recent example is provided by a study which attempted to promote the cognitive and social development of young children. Instead of dealing directly with the children, however, the researchers taught the parents a variety of ways for interacting with their children during the first few years of life (Ryan, 1977). A more extreme view of discrepant behaviour, particularly as it applies to the criminal practice system, has been called "radical non-intervention." The central idea here is that the labelling of a child as a delinquent may become a self-fulfilling prophecy; through the very process of labelling and exposure to criminal ecosystem (detention centres, etc.) the child's behaviour is channelized in precisely the wrong direction. It is proposed that non-intervention, while a radical step, may actually decrease the frequency of discrepant behaviour. While the conditions under which this alternative is effective are not clear at present, it does serve as an appropriate alternative to consider under those conditions where intervention into a given ecosystem will only exacerbate, not eliminate, a problem. It might be mentioned that projects attempting to increase the intellectual skills of native Indian children might benefit from serious consideration of radical non-intervention (Milton, 1971).

To the extent that discrepant processes in a child impinge upon the standards of competency of a diversity of systems of influence, we see the direct intervention into changing those processes as high priority. This proposition attenuates, in some respects, the tendency of the social ecological perspective to look to the rather more easily manipulable systems in the social and physical environmental domains rather than to the biological systems more uniquely associated with the child's personal system. But if, through brain damage, for example, a child is unable to meet normative standards in the areas of language acquisition, peer interaction, and self-control, we see such transystem incompetency as an important criterion for direct (e.g., surgical, neuro-psychological therapy) intervention into the system primarily responsible for the deviancy. While such an approach is readily justifiable in cases where clear evidence for the causal primacy of the biosystem exists, an area of particular sensitivity arises where the "medical model" has been extrapolated into a working metaphor for the analysis of personal or social problems (Szasz, 1961). Broad tolerance for discrepancies and attempts to match such discrepancies with accommodating social structures would seem to be the prevailing orientation required of a social ecological approach to deviancy (Rappaport, 1977).

WHO HELPS AND HOW?: EFFECTIVENESS, EMBEDDEDNESS AND ECOSYSTEMS

Proposition 7: Embeddedness
The effectiveness of the primary caretakers in providing needed resources to the child is channelized by the larger ecosystems within which the caretakers are embedded.

Elaboration of the Embeddedness Proposition
The social ecological model placed substantial emphasis upon seeing the primary caretaker-child relationship as one embedded in larger ecosystems which vary in scale from the housing they occupy, to the neighbourhood in which they are located, the city and region in which they live, and the whole biosphere within which all our families are embedded (Bronfenbrenner, 1977; Brim, 1975; Porteus, 1977). The ecological context refers to those patterns of cultural and social beliefs and customs, including religious, commercial-economic, and other formal systems of influence that surround the family and which shape and are shaped by their lives (Leff, 1978).

The following description would serve to exemplify Proposition 7. A single parent finds it impossible to get someone to baby sit at her remote cottage for an occasional Thursday evening break, and she takes out her frustration the next morning on her six-month old infant. Here, that aspect of the ecosystem channelizing her behaviour is spatial (long distances preventing access of help) and social-demographic (loss of extended family and high frequency of separated and single-family parent families leading to loss of availability of alternative care-takers for children) (Garbarino, 1977).

Another example of the impact of the ecosystem within which the child-caretaker unit is embedded can be seen in a recent study, which indicated a significant relationship between the ambient noise level in apartments (which varied with height from street level) and difficulties in reading skills in children. Given some suggestive evidence that early muscle pattern movements in children are closely synchronized with the voice interaction patterns of parents, the simple ecological fact of living in a noisy environment may mask sound patterns that are funda-mental in preparing the infant for the acquisition of speech (Cohen, Glass & Singer, 1973).

The Embeddedness Proposition formalizes the assumption that children and their primary caretakers represent just the first two layers of an increasingly inclusive set of contexts, and that how successful the child's needs are met is determined in part by the pressures, problems and historical progressions of that larger milieu within which the child care system is located.

Implications for Research and Policy Analysis

With the division of labour and specialization that accompanied the industrial revolution and with the continued proliferation of specialists catering to the particular needs of our children (teachers, physicians, orthodontists, child psychologists) it is becoming decreasingly likely that the parent will be the direct provider of materials and services to the child. Given this specialized society within which most Canadians live, it is not so much the direct provision of goods, services and experi-ences that must be carried out by the primary caretaker so much as it is the provision of resources (which includes, but is not restricted to, direct provision). The parent must know when, how, and where to pro-vide the child with satisfaction of primary needs, appropriate educa-tional experiences, and socialization into the normative framework of the society. It is difficult to conceive of achieving this state of affairs, unless we undertake to prepare individuals for parenting by teaching them, at least the rudiments of human development.

From the social ecological perspective the most critical functions are those of joint monitoring and integrating of the child's needs and the resources available in the surrounding ecosystem. This function requires intensive scrutiny of the child in a variety of situations, the accurate reading of the child's needs, moods, and subjective feelings, and an abiding concern with the total well-being of the child.

In conjunction with providing the monitoring and integrating role, the primary caretaker also needs to transfer those monitoring and inte-grating skills to the child in order that independence can eventually be achieved. To the extent that children are unaware of the means of access to the people and institutions necessary to their well-being, their needs are likely to be frustrated later in life.

Critical to the success of the parent in providing the child with executive management of the ecosystem as well as training the child in these areas, is the access the parent has to information generally. It has been recently suggested that inequities in access to information is greater than inequity in the financial resources of families (Brim, 1975).

Associated with access to information is the availability of and access to natural helping resources, which we regard as those individuals (e.g., grandmas, neighbourly neighbours), groups and institutions who provide a resource for a given child-care ecosystem without explicit payment or professional status. (Institutions such as churches and schools may also serve other explicit needs in a professional way.) Given the demographic conditions discussed in earlier sections, where families are increasingly set apart from each other, the frequency and potency of such natural helping resources is likely diminishing (Gottlieb, 1977).

Where there are no natural helping resources accessible to a child-care system, or where one cannot be created, steps should be taken to create functional equivalents of natural resources. Examples of this would be the growth of Foster Grandparents, Meals on Wheels, and other attempts to recreate what, in earlier periods, would have been the functions of the village or extended families. However, it is necessary to look first at the surrounding ecosystem to make sure that natural support systems are not already in place, if only as potential resources.

Direct intervention into children's lives, whereby the child is brought face to face with socializing and correctional agents without the mediation of the parent, is actively discouraged, as the result would be to frustrate rather than facilitate the provision of needed resources to the children. Examples would be medical visits where the parents are excluded and direct handling of a delinquent child in correctional institutions without the intermediary of family courts. A less obvious example, but having equal capacity to frustrate the needs of the child would be the case of a pre-school child being sent to an after-school enrichment program, about which the parents understand little (Ryan, 1972).

Among some of the difficulties posed by direct intervention of the professional are systematic undoing of the expert work by the intact family system once the child returns to it, the inability of the professional worker to break through the problem area which has its locus in the primary facility relationships, and the turning away from a potentially helpful role by natural groups within the child's milieu because they assume they aren't expert enough to help (Gottlieb, 1976).

There is need, then, to direct energies towards detecting, encouraging, aiding and consolidating those natural helping systems currently available to the child. It will likely be necessary to undo the considerable public relations job of professionals in order to convince families that there are alternative, and frequently better, resources nearby.

THE TORN WEB: TRANSITIONS, STRESS, AND SYSTEM INTEGRITY

Proposition 8: Limits
There are demand limits to the adaptational competencies of children and their environments beyond which the integrity of the affected systems is sacrificed.

Elaboration of the Limits Proposition
In social ecological systems, as in any natural ecosystem, the reciprocal adaptations between individuals and their milieu give rise to a fairly stable share in which the normal circuits of interdependent actions are carried out uneventfully. But this natural "web of life" can be stretched and torn by rapid changes in the states of its constituent members. If the pressures or demands upon either the child or the environments become too great, that particular system will sacrifice its integrity, by which we mean that its responses will no longer be in accord with its long term goals or values.

A series of recent studies on the psychological costs of adaptation to environmental stressors exemplifies this proposition. The basic paradigm involves subjecting an individual to a noxious stimulation, typically loud noise, during performance of a laboratory task requiring concentration. The standard progression of responses to the environmental stressor includes initial alarm and arousal, followed by apparent adaptation and levelling off of the autonomic functions. This apparent adaptation to stress, however, is illusory in that when subjects who have gone through the process of being stressed are subsequently asked to complete a set of clerical exercises their performance is impaired. Compared to a control group who are at the same level of arousal but who have not had to adapt to the environmental stress, the experimental subjects proved to be less efficient and more socially aggressive (Glass & Singer, 1972).

An example of such a pattern occurring in the child's social environment can be seen in a father who, having apparently adapted during a Saturday morning of babysitting, copes well until after the children are in bed, when he snaps at his wife. The pattern is seen in children, raised in an overly stimulating home atmosphere where there is overcrowding and poor insulation, who appear to adapt to the stimulational demands in the home environment but are irritable and confused at school. In both of these cases the cost of adaptation to an overdemanding milieu is the loss of integrity of those processes with which we cope with the more mundane pressures of everyday life.

Implications for Research and Policy Analysis

We hypothesize that acute shifts, either qualitatively or quantitatively, in the normal activity patterns and psychological processes of child and/or context pose threats to the adaptive integrity of the systems affected. Note this suggests the threat can occur both to the subsystem that has changed rapidly and to the subsystem that has not reciprocated the change. We also assume (Proposition 5) that the child-caretaker ecosystem as a whole may break down under those circumstances.

This hypothesis suggests that it is during periods of rapid change that vulnerability of the child in context is highest. Among some of the more readily discernible transition points would be the immediate post-partum period, children leaving for pre-school for the first time, the mother starting an outside job (or finishing one). Each of these transition periods involves either a rapid quantitative or qualitative change in the daily patterns of behaviour. As discussed above, if the pace is fast, and unpredictable, adaptation will occur, but the costs may be high. This strongly implies the need for families to know when such transition points are about to arrive, if that is possible, so that steps beyond the normal can be taken to offset them.

To the extent that there are buffer resources, which are construed as extra sources of support or help not normally available, but which can be drawn upon during periods of transition and other troubling occasions, children and their contexts will cope better with the accompanying stress. With respect to children, we can talk about internal resources and external resources for coping with transition period stress. By internal resources we refer to stress coping mechanisms which would include such competencies and dispositions as flexibility, and complexity (Uzgiris & Weizmann, 1977). Coping resources that are virtually unexplored in children are their sense of humour and general life values and how they bear upon problems during transition periods. Examples of external buffer resources are special friends and relatives not normally accessible but who can be made available during emergencies, and a whole range of distress services such as emergency telephone lines at community health centres, and twenty-four hour counselling services related to child abuse, depression, and suicide.

ON SCALE AND SERENITY: COMPETENCY, CONTROL AND CONSTRAINTS

Proposition 9: Control

The adaptational competencies of children will be enhanced to the extent they have developed a sense of perceived control over their environments that is based on an accurate reading of ecosystem constraints.

Elaboration of the Control Proposition

Considerable evidence has been accumulating over the past decade indicating the critical role played by an individual's perceived control over the events in his/her life. Research has demonstrated that having perceived control over the source of noxious stimulation both increases the speed of adaptation to the stress and reduces the cost experienced later (Glass & Singer, 1972). Relatedly, in a major study of factors enhancing success in schools, the best predictor of success was the sense of perceived control that the individual experienced vis-a-vis the school setting (Coleman, 1966).

Accurate reading of ecosystem constraints is regarded as a critical moderator of the effectiveness of perceived control and adaptational consequence. By reading we mean the acquisition of knowledge about events and relationships in the interacting systems of influence affecting the child. Only if the ecosystem constraints within which the individual is embedded make the expectation of control realistic will such perception increase the adaptational competencies of the child. Consider, for example, a ghetto child who has been told that he's no good and that chances are he'll never amount to anything. Such a child will likely have an unrealistically low sense of perceived control and would likely fail to attempt to succeed in a milieu where trying might yield at least a modest step up out of poverty. He would not, therefore, be enhancing his adaptational competencies but would be foreclosing on them. Another child, however, in the same ghetto may have been led to believe that if she wishes to be a Montreal neurosurgeon she can be one — without any change in the contexts in which she lives. To the extent that the odds are ecologically stacked against such a child entering this profession, a very high sense of perceived control may actually be maladaptive for her. As soon as the realities of ghetto life are met, feelings of perceived control will be diminished or even extinguished. It can be suggested that an ecologically unrealistic sense of perceived control can generate sudden drops in motivation to succeed that leads to even more serious consequences then to perceived helplessness. One study, for example, showed that residents of an old people's home who had control over when college students visited them, fared very well when the "visiting experiment" was being carried out, in comparison with another group who were visited at the whim of the students. However, after the experiment was completed and no visitors came to either group, it was the ecologically unrealistic group, the perceived control residents, who literally suffered most. Incidence of sudden health decline and even death were significantly higher in this group (Shultz, 1975).

Inequities, then, in access to realistic information upon the environment can attenuate the positive effects of perceived control. In the final analysis, what seems to be needed is less of an increase in perceived impact and more genuine impact. If realistic impact can be achieved, the child can accept the equally realistic constraints with the serenity which derives from an intimate knowledge of the ecosystem.

Implications for Research and Policy Analysis
The scale and structure of children's everyday environments can facilitate or frustrate their perceived control and sense of competency. The beneficial impact of small scale behaviour settings on children has been amply documented in studies which have shown that children attending small schools benefit from increased instruction, sense of competency, and complexity, and greater identification perceived impact on the school (Moos & Insel, 1974).

One of the critical features of the structure of children's environments relates to the extent to which the areas they inhabit are legible — easy to comprehend spatially. Children raised in areas that are formless and imageless are less likely to engage in active exploration, and thus not likely to enhance their perceptual skills (Lynch, 1972).

An interesting feature of behaviour settings which can increase the child's sense of control and competency is the extent to which the various behaviour settings in which the child participates daily can be linked together with mental paths. There is research evidence to suggest that behaviour problems in school are higher in children who are bused or driven to school compared to those who walk or bike. The latter children, it is suggested, are able to form social-spatial schemata which connect their disparate settings together (Ittelson et al, 1974).

Social or physical environments which are either unresponsive or negatively responsive to the action of a child will block the development of a sense of perceived control. Conversely, environments which are positively responsive to the actions of the child facilitate the growth of a sense of control. In the social domain, it can be seen that the child's perspective has come to play an important role in family decision-making. In fact, it has been shown that infants only a few days old will respond enthusiastically to responsive environments. On the physical side, it can be seen that the field of architecture has been influenced by research in environmental psychology and has become increasingly responsive to the psychological-spatial needs of future residents.

THE TENSION OF INTEGRITY: CONGRUENCY, CREATIVITY AND CHILDREN'S UTOPIAS

Proposition 10: Integrity
To the extent that the component systems of a child-environment ecosystem are in a state of optimal congruency, the integrity of that ecosystem is enhanced.

Elaboration of the Integrity Proposition

An important principle which seems to characterize a broad range of system relationships within complex environments has been termed intersystems congruency (Michelson, 1970). This formulation sees a strain towards congruency between social customs and physical milieu, or between personal life style and housing preference. The assumption underlying the theory is that pressures to change incongruous subsystems will be mounted and that environmental and social planning should attempt to prevent mismatches before they take a toll on human lives. The appropriation of this principle as a central proposition of a social ecological model seems warranted, though we wish to add an important qualification to the general formulation that congruency is the desired end state of the interacting systems that constitute the child in context, namely, the term optimal.

We assume that mere congruency or matching between a child's personal system and the surrounding social and physical systems may lead eventually to a happy but habituated homeostasis in which change, variety and the convivial annoyances of living systems are theoretically absent and environmentally designed out. We would thus define optimal congruency as that state of congruence between any two aspects of the child-environment ecosystem in which the positive gains of harmony, shared goals, convergence of means, etc., are achieved without the loss entailed by lack of stimulation. Thus minimal deviations from complete congruency would be posited as more optimal than either large or zero discrepancies, a hypothesis for which considerable empirical support has been amassed (Wohlwill, 1973).

We see the total child-environment resource unit as an ecosystem at risk: the integrity of the child in the final analysis is limited by the integrity of the total ecosystem of which the child is but one critical component.

Implications for Research and Policy Analysis

Children must be socialized into a supportive orientation towards their environment, or, to be more precise, they must not be socialized along routes that will destroy the integrity of their environments. We are not advocating automatic conformity with one's context. While such conformity might perpetuate a state of affairs with long term catastrophic consequences for the environment and hence for the child, it might also aid in establishing congruency between the personality and social systems. In other words, it is entirely possible that children, by revolting against the environment, be it the family, the school, or the large economic system in which they are embedded, may increase the integrity of that larger system by achieving a shift away from mere congruency, and pushing towards higher levels of integration.

Techniques for training children in environmentally supportive roles have appeared recently (Leff, 1978). Particularly promising are attempts to develop techniques and programs for increasing interdependency and cooperation between children. Such a notion is in contrast to the tradition of rewarding competition between individuals and groups. Research programs are developing games involving cooperative enjoyment and exercise in pursuit of a common goal. These have very clear implications for fostering ecological orientations of the sort needed for enhancing the integrity of the larger ecosystem in which we participate.

Throughout this paper, we have proposed that the child is interdependent with its immediate context and its context, in turn, is interdependent with the larger ecosystem. The eventual limits to the quality of life are met in the biosphere, the encircling layer of nurturance that supports earth's biotic life. The revolt against environment or the pursuit of a higher ecological integrity reaches its limit at the biosphere — where there exists a non-negotiable relationship of interdependence that, in recent history, and continuing to present day, has been jeopardized (Leff, 1978). Thus we endorse the shift from examining children in the Canadian context, to examining children in their universal context, where the ultimate limits to their well-being will be met.

The ability of children to rechannelize their own context is, in essence, a creative act, and recent attempts to develop innovative thinking skills appear very promising as stimulants to creativity. One particularly interesting line of inquiry for social ecological researchers would be the systematic examination of children's views of utopia. Here, at an age of relative innocence, we can see glimpses of alternative environments and trace the genesis of changes that lead to the demise of dreams.

References

Argyle, M., & Little, B.R.
  1972   Do personality traits apply to social behavior? *Journal for the Theory of Social Behavior, 2,* 1-35.

Bell, R.Q.
  1968   A Reinterpretation of the Direction of Effects in Studies of Socialization. *Psychological Review, 73,* 81-95.

Berry, J.W.
  1977   An ecological approach to cross cultural psychology. *Man-Environment Systems, 4,* 365-383.

Berry J.W., & Annis, R.C.
  1974   Ecology, culture and psychological differentiation. *International Journal of Psychology, 9,* 173-193.

Brim, O.G.
  1975 Macro-structural influences on child development and the need for childhood social indicators. *American Journal of Orthopsychiatry,* 45, 516-525.

Bronfenbrenner, U.
  1974 Developmental research, public policy and the ecology of childhood. *Child Development,* 45, 1-5.

Bronfenbrenner, U.
  1977 Toward an experimental ecology of human development. *American Psychologist,* 32, 513-531.

Bronfenbrenner, U.
  1976 The Experimental Ecology of Education. *Teachers College Record,* 78, 157-204.

Brunswick, E.
  1956 *Perception and the Representative Design of Psychological Experiments.* Berkeley: University of California Press.

Cohen, S., Glass, D.C. & Singer, J.E.
  1973 Apartment noise, auditory discrimination and reading ability in children. *Journal of Experimental Social Psychology,* 9, 407.

Coleman, J.S. et al.
  1966 *Equality of Educational Opportunity.* Washington, D.C.: U.S. Department of Health, Education and Welfare.

Endler, N., & Magnussen, D. (Eds.)
  1975 *Interactional psychology and personality.* New York: Halstead Press.

Garbarino, J.
  1977 The human ecology of child maltreatment: A conceptual model for research. *Journal of Marriage and the Family,* 39(4), 721-735.

Glass, D., & Singer, J.
  1972 *Urban stress.* New York: Academic Press.

Gottlieb, B.H.
  1977 The primary group as supportive milieu: Application to community psychology. Symposium, APA.

Hart, R.
  1977 Comparing the outdoor opportunities of girls and boys. In B. Sprung (Ed.), *Non-sexist curricula for pre-school children.* New York: Teachers College Press.

Held, R., & Heim, A.
1963   Movement-produced stimulation in the development of usually guided behavior. *Journal of Comparative and Physiological Psychology*, 56, 872-876.

Hunt, D.
1976   Teacher's adaptation: 'Reading' and 'flexing' to students. *Journal of Teacher Education*, XXVII, 268-275.

Hunt, D.E.
1971   *Matching Models in Education: The coordination of teach methods with student characteristics.* Toronto: Ontario Institute for studies in Education.

Hutt, C.
1972   *Male and female.* Baltimore: Penguin.

Ittelson, W.H.
1974   Proshansky, H.M., Rivlin, L.G. & Winkel, G. *An Introduction to Environmental Psychology.* New York: Holt, Rinehart and Winston.

Kelly, G.A.
1955   *The Psychology of Personal Constructs*, Vol. 1. New York: Norton.

Leff, H.
1978   *Experience, environment, and human potentials.* New York: Oxford University Press.

Little, B.R.
1978   *Personal projects: A rationale and method for investigation.* Unpublished manuscript, Carleton University, Department of Psychology.

Little, B.R.
1978   *Environmental psychology and the evaluation of change.* Invited address, Conference on the Evaluation of Change, Edmonton, Alberta.

Little, B.R.
1972   Psychological man as a scientist, humanist and specialist. *Journal of Experimental Research in Personality*, 6, 95-118.

Little, B.R.
1976   Specialization and the varieties of environmental experience: Empirical studies within the personality paradigm. *Experiencing the Environment.* New York: Plenum Press, 81-116.

Lynch, K.
1960 *The Image of the City.* Cambridge, Mass.: MIT Press.

Michelson, W.
1970 *Man and his urban environment: A sociological approach.* Reading, Massachusetts: Addison-Wesley.

Milton, G.A.
1971 *Familial and cultural patterns in the underachievement of west coast Canadian children.* Symposium of Canadian Psychological Association meetings, St. John's.

Mischel, W.
1968 *Personality Assessment.* New York: John Wiley & Sons.

Moos, R.
1976 *The human context.* New York: John Wiley and Sons.

Moos, R., & Insel, R.
1974 *Issues in social ecology.* Palo Alto, California: National Press Books.

Moos, R., & Moos, B.
1976 A typology of family social environments. *Family Process, 19,* 351-371.

National Council of Welfare on Children in Poverty in Canada
1975 *Poor kids.* Ottawa: National Council of Welfare.

Overton, W.F., & Reese, H.W.
1977 General models for man-environment relations. In H. McGurk (Ed.), *Ecological factors in human development.* New York: North Holland Publishing Company.

Partington, J.T.
1976 The Interdependent Mode of Personality Causality. In L.H. Strickland, F.E. Aboud & K.J. Gergen (Eds.). *Social Psychology in Transition.* New York: Plenum.

Porteous, J.D.
1977 *Environment and behavior: Planning and everyday urban life.* Reading, Massachusetts: Addison-Wesley.

Price, R., & Blashfield, R.H.
1975 Explorations in the taxonomy of behavioral settings: Analysis of dimensions and classifications of settings. *American Journal of Community Psychology, 3,* 335-351.

Rappaport, J.
1977 *Community psychology.* Chicago: Holt, Rinehart and Winston.

Rosenthal, R., & Jacobson, L.
1968   *Pygmalion in the Classroom.* New York: Holt, Reinhart and Winston.

Rosenweig, M.R., & Bennett, E.L.
1972   Cerebral changes in rats exposed individually to an enriched environment. *Journal of Comparative and Physiological Psychology, 80,* 304-313.

Rosenweig, M.R. & Bennett, E.L.
1976   Enriched environments: Facts, factors and fantasies. In J.L. McGaugh & L. Petrinovich (Eds.), *Knowing, thinking and believing.* New York: Plenum.

Ryan, T.J.
1976   Promoting child development through a program of home visiting. *Canadian Journal of Behavioural Science, 8,* 102-105.

Ryan, T.J.
1972   *Poverty and the child: A Canadian study.* Toronto: McGraw-Hill Ryerson Ltd..

Sarason, S., Davidson, K., Lighthall, F., Waite, R., & Ruebush, B.
1960   *Anxiety in elementary school children.* New York: John Wiley and Sons.

Schultz, R.
1975   *Some life and death consequences of perceived control.* Paper presented at Twelfth Carnegie Symposium on Cognition.

Sells, S.B.
1974   An interactionist looks at the environment. In R.H. Moos & P.M. Insel (Eds.), *Issues in Social Ecology.* Palo Alto: National Press Books.

Stokols, D.
1978   Environmental Psychology. *Annual Review of Psychology, 29,* 253-95.

Szasz, T.S.
1961   *The Myth of Mental Illness: Foundations of a Theory of Personal Conduct.* New York: Hoeber & Harper.

Thomas, A., Chess, S. & Birch, M.G.
1968   *Temperament and behavior disorders in children.* New York: University Press.

Uzgiris, I.C., & Weizmann, F.
1977   *The structuring of experience.* New York: Plenum.

Wohlwill, J.
1973   *The study of behavioral development.* New York: Academic Press.

Television and The Changing Cultures of Childhood

THELMA McCORMACK
York University

THE NEW AND OLD CULTURES OF CHILDHOOD

Television is so much a part of the culture of childhood in North America that some people think it *is* the culture of childhood, a world unto itself, so complete and satisfying that children may, like Peter Pan, never grow up. Others, however, have suggested that television is destroying the culture of childhood by encroaching upon it with adult versions of reality, catapaulting children too quickly into the world of hostage-taking, homicidal psychopaths and corrupt politicians; introducing them to complex adult relationships before they can understand or cope with them emotionally (Klapper, 1961); conditioning them to instant, shallow interpretations of events (Cirino, 1977); standardizing their minds and stereotyping their imaginations (Gomberg, 1964).

Marshall McLuhan (1964) believes television is a radical break in the history of Western civilization, a technological revolution altering our modes of perception from the old, print-linear thinking to the new, electronic-holistic thinking. Thus, the generation gap between adults who are pre-television and children who are post-television is unbridgeable. Bronfenbrenner (1970) with a more gradualist sense of history sees television as "the unmaking of the American child," a result of structural rather than technological trends that have changed the nature of community and parental authority. TV, for Bronfenbrenner, fills a social vacuum which it did not in, or of itself, create.

Only one thing is certain: no subject in modern times has ever been more over-discussed and under-researched than children and television. The various discussions are interesting in themselves because they reveal many of the deeper ideological ambiguities we have inherited and share in the twentieth century. Our conceptions of childhood, often nostalgic and romanticized; our ambivalences about leisure and consummatory values, or about highbrow art and lowbrow entertainment; our fears of being manipulated by super powers; our conflicts about a duty to discipline and a need to be loved by our children — all of these and others are in the background of discussions, and account for the disproportionate feeling these discussions generate.

Nor are they confined to North America alone. The Soviets, for example, are fearful that television compromises artistic quality for program popularity, that children's natural spontaneity and creativity are being replaced by sedentary spectatorism, that an appreciation for fine literature is being eroded. Young children, they say, are exposed to too much conflict, sex, and violence (Soviet, 1975) sounding very much like ourselves. And their television writers, like ours, have their professional pride, protesting against pressures to produce programs that are all sweetness and light. In short, discussions of television bring out the latent concerns we have about the processes of modernization, the democratization of culture, and the interdependencies of everyday life in large scale, complex societies.

Television has not created a new culture of childhood, but it has come to symbolize it. The traditional culture of childhood with its fairy stories, leisurely pace, trial-and-error learning, identification with parental models has not vanished any more than the rural village or extended family have disappeared from history. But they no longer set the tone of the society. Those who cherish memories of the old culture and deplore the changes are apt to use television as the whipping boy, seeing in it only the frenetic pace of Saturday morning cartoon programs, the television gun slinger as larger than life hero, the disrespect for marital fidelity and the debasement of language. These and other similar invidious descriptions often obscure the banality of much children's literature and art in the past, the high rates of illiteracy, the exploitation of children in factories and on farms, the punitive methods of education that broke body and spirit. The truth is that the transformation from traditional to modern cultures of childhood began long before television, and the *Gemeinschaft* world left behind and so fondly recollected is, in many respects, better forgotten.

Television is just the tip of the modern iceberg, and typically, we make the mistake of confusing it with the whole. Television is highly visible and unprotected. It lacks the prestige of the church, the professional mystique of educational systems, and the power of business and governments. Everyone is an "expert" on television; everyone feels free to criticize it. The networks are considered fair game; and the Canadian Broadcasting Corporation, because it is a public system, more so.

But the fallacy most commonly made by the public is to treat television as a form of technology rather than a social institution or a means of communication; to assume that technology comes into existence from out of nowhere and is accountable to no one, exerting an unnatural force over our minds without our consent or cooperation. The direction of the influence is determined by the technology itself.

Technological determinism is a beguiling theory, but bad sociology, pontificating and asserting what needs to be demonstrated and proved; that is, how cultures create and use, or fail to use, any new type of technology whether it is television, dishwashers, farm equipment or airplanes.

In the comments that follow, we will suggest an alternative and broader perspective to technological determinism. Briefly, we will suggest that we can best understand how television impinges on the lives of children by placing television in the larger social contexts of their lives, by examining how different classes of children use it, its meaning for them, and by drawing on our growing knowledge of the communication processes.

THE STATE OF RESEARCH

In the quarter of a century that has passed since television was introduced into Canada, the U.S. and Britain, only two comprehensive studies have been carried out, one in Britain (Himmelweit, Oppenheim and Vince, 1958) and one in the U.S. which included some Canadian material (Schramm, Lyle and Parker, 1961). Both were conducted in the late 1950s when television was still a fascinating novelty, a status symbol that sat in the middle of the living room, and constituted an evening's entertainment for the family and for curious guests.

Both studies reflect the questions of the day. What kinds of activities did TV displace? Were children becoming TV addicts? Would schoolwork suffer? Was TV "kitsch" a further assault on traditional authority? Would television abuse the open minds of children and bring us one step closer to mass society? Would television narrow the gap between rich and poor, bright children and slow learners, the in-groups and the out-groups by providing us all with a common culture? Would television bring families together, and would the new togetherness be silent members of a family sitting dazed in front of television without any interaction between them, a proximity rather than social cohesion?

Looking back on these two pioneering studies, one can appreciate their achievement in cooling-out some of the apprehensions and enthusiasms which parents and educators expressed at the time. But they are insufficient for several reasons. First, although they examine a wide array of problems, they still treat television apart from the larger culture of childhood, and, in so doing become studies of a cultural technology rather than studies of a technological culture.

Second, the findings cover a period in the 1950s when television was still new and set ownership selective. In part, then, what they were observing was the sociology of innovation and diffusion. Third, television has itself changed. In Britain there are now both public and private systems; in Canada, cable has given audiences more channels and more access to U.S. television; and, in the U.S. television production has become more expensive (due to colour), more dependent on advertising, and more slick.

Finally, the composition and organization of audiences have changed. Nowadays almost everyone has a television set so that the audiences are more representative of the population as a whole. In addition, more and more homes have second and third sets so that families are no longer required to view together in order to view at all. Moreover, young audiences today are the children of parents who grew up with television. At the time these studies were done there was no adult generation that had been steadily exposed to television. Last, but not least, family life is changing. Many mothers who would have been at home and who took the initiative in turning on the set during morning hours when pre-schoolers were at home are at work, their children in day-care centres.

In spite of these weaknesses, the two studies remain our most important sources of information. Neither has been replicated on the same scale. Subsequent studies have focussed on specific problems such as the effects of TV violence, and many of the studies are nothing more than straight market research.

Almost all of the research has been carried out in the U.S. where television is a business enterprise, and programming decisions are made with an eye on ratings and commercial success in market areas. Unlike education, television cannot count on captive audiences. School goes on despite the boredom of pupils and their short spans of attention; American television does not. It is difficult to imagine either Canadian or American networks giving prime evening time to a bedtime program for young children as they do in Eastern Europe.

Nor should we make the mistake of assuming that when popular American children's programs like Sesame Street are imported into Canada and other countries that research on these programs in the U.S. will apply equally well elsewhere. Research is not culturally interchangeable the way the parts of a car might be.

And finally, we cannot expect American researchers will provide answers to our uniquely Canadian question about the effects of U.S. television on our sense of national identity.

PATTERNS OF TELEVISION CONSUMPTION

Bearing in mind these reservations we can review the material at hand. Contrary to the view that television would disrupt family life, the findings suggest that it was quickly accommodated into existing patterns. After the first shock wore off, families went back to customary ways. Bedtimes were only slightly pushed back; homework was done (Japanese findings do not bear this out), and families in the habit of regular mealtimes resumed them.

Himmelweit, et. al. (1958) found that the time spent watching television was disposable time that would have been spent "doing nothing." If any activities were curtailed, they were apt to be "equivalents" such as radio listening (Abrams, 1956) and comic book reading. But a recent study in Scotland (Brown, Crammond and Wilde, 1974) found a decrease in outdoor activity. The effects of television viewing on serious reading are still not clear; whether children are reading more or less than they did; whether children's reading tastes are influenced by television or their television tastes influenced by literature, or both by some other factor. But McLuhanesque prophecies that reading would become obsolete have not proved true, and the larger fact is that children, like adults, are multi-media users.

Children start watching TV when barely out of the crib. They do this with the blessings of parents who approve of television and believe their children can learn from it (Steiner, 1963). This belief may be based on their own experiences as adults, for young children learn very little from television (most of them are unable to follow the plots) and retain less even when the programs are intended to teach. Parents are often deceived by the ease with which children pick up a TV vocabulary or the idioms of commercials into thinking there is also comprehension.

It is hard to know what there is about television that young children enjoy so much although the fact that they are watching it does not necessarily mean that they are either enjoying it or concentrating on it. Often they are frightened by it, yet list the programs that frighten them among their favourites. Television producers seem to think that what children want is fresh material and new characters, but the evidence is that what they really like are old characters and familiar materials (Noble, 1970).

Whatever the source of pleasure, it is strong enough for parents to recognize and use it as a form of discipline. But, in general, parents set up few rules about TV viewing, and when they do the rules concerning program choices tend to be negative — what cannot be seen — rather than positive suggestions about programs which should be seen. Whether this reflects parental indifference or merely acquiescence probably varies with family structure. However, the overall impression is that parents think they ought to supervise TV viewing more, but do, in fact, very little. Perhaps it is too much to expect parents to supervise television viewing in the late afternoon and early evening when both parents are preoccupied with other more compelling demands on their time.

As more young mothers remain in, or return to, the labour force, and pre-school children are placed in day care centres or "head start" programs, the pattern of pre-school activity may change. More organized, more didactic and more traditional activities such as story telling may displace television, especially during the morning hours. But for the present and for children at home, television viewing starts during the pre-school years increasing and peaking during the school years.

As we noted earlier, it is not just television viewing that increases, but other forms of media consumption as well. During adolescence, the pattern changes with television and books declining and movies, radio, records and newspaper reading increasing. These are media which can be enjoyed privately, which help to create mood, and strengthen peer group bonds apart from the family better than television does.

Canadian teenagers show the same pattern but not as clearly as in the U.S. (CBC, 1973). Does this reflect a difference in socialization patterns between the two countries, or is it a difference in Canadian television programming? Or is it a sign of things to come when multiple set ownership is widespread with teenagers having their own sets, and channel choices increased and specialized? Speculating about the future, television may become more like present day radio with its disc jockeys and calculated appeals to the teenage market.

The significance of the change in viewing habits during adolescence cannot be emphasized strongly enough. First, it illustrates how the social and psychological needs in children's social development shape the habit more than the habit shapes the social and psychological needs of children. Second, it suggests that television viewing should be seen as part of a larger pattern of media consumption, and that it is the pattern of media consumption that changes. We might, therefore, understand more about what television means to children by examining what television has in common with other media that might be technologically quite different such as newspapers and records, but sociologically alike or closely related. Finally, it suggests that television viewing is not as addictive as was thought. Children are habit makers, but television is not habituating.

The myth of TV addiction, however, dies hard. It is sustained in part by the fact that school age children, unlike younger or older ones, are regular and devoted viewers, that they are old enough to understand much of what they see, and tend to be more selective about what they see. In other words, they are not just viewers; they are "fans"; some of them, as we shall see later, highly critical "fans."

CHARACTERISTICS OF HEAVY AND LIGHT VIEWERS

Among this age group, a distinction can be made between heavy and light viewers. Heavy viewers tend to be children whose family lives are characterized by tension (Maccoby, 1954) and an authoritarian structure (McLeod, O'Keefe, 1972). They have fewer closer friends (Riley and Riley, 1951). Among high school students and older children, the heavy viewers tend to be young persons with weak peer group ties (Johnstone, 1971). Heavy viewing is more common among lower income groups (Greenberg and Dervin, 1970).

Heavy viewing, then, is related to either a disadvantaged social status or some failure in inter-personal relationships. Taken together these associations imply that heavy TV viewing is in some way symptomatic, a form of social deviance, and further, that television compensates for the bad luck or personal misfortunes of reality. Happy, well-adjusted, middle-class children who have friends and a rich assortment of diversions are predictably light or lighter viewers.

Or is this an anti-television bias? Some of the so-called heavy viewers may be closer to the statistical average than some of the light viewers, but since the latter have not been studied in any detail we know less about them. Is heavy viewing indicative of some personal or social cross to bear, or is *any* extreme deviation from the norm in either direction the proper measure of deviance?

The plausibility of the latter hypothesis is supported by studies which relate TV viewing and intelligence. In the early research, especially the British, there seemed to be a connection between high I.Q. and low viewing. This may have disguised a social fact; namely, that highly educated parents were often very snobbish about television in its early days and were themselves light viewers. More recent research (Roberts, 1973) indicates that bright children and, perhaps, more importantly, children with a strong sense of personal efficacy tend to be heavy viewers. These children tend to do everything more including television viewing. Carrying this one step further, these children may be the precursors of adult opinion and taste leaders (Katz and Lazarsfeld, 1955); that is, people who set the pace and style of their respective groups.

I.Q., then, may not be as important as informal leadership qualities or the sense of personal efficacy, but there appears to be no contradiction between intelligence and heavy viewing. The more challenging intellectual activities are not displaced by television, and bright children may experience television in a more sophisticated way. As indicated earlier television has acquired more intellectual respectability among a new generation of parents from whom children take their cues about viewing (Abel, 1976). Finally, we need to examine the hypothesis that opinion and taste leaders, regardless of intelligence or socio-economic status are heavy viewers. Television, having become so much more a part of the lifestyles of children, the opinion leaders define what is "in" and become opinion leaders by knowing what is "in."

Whatever the correlations turn out to be, the larger fact remains that there are variations in viewing patterns among individuals, among groups, and among social classes. As we shall see later, the same holds true for program preferences. The conclusion to be drawn is the same, that television viewing is more influenced than influencing; it is subject to the predispositions, social and psychological, which audiences bring to it.

The age variations are more telling than anything else, for they suggest that different stages in the life cycle create different needs and different expectations which television may satisfy more or less well (McLeod, O'Keefe, 1972). Thus, the term "television habit" is misleading for it implies an autonomous and obsessional quality that is insulated from either new experiences from outside or social development from within. An alternative model would distinguish between the routinization of viewing — regular after-school and Saturday morning viewing — and habit, dropping the latter in favour of a model which assumes that television viewing is always a new experience being tested by its viewers at successive stages in their social development. If it persists, it is not because of inertia or compulsion, but rather because it has met the new or developing needs of children.

PROGRAM PREFERENCES

Just as children start to choose among friends and school subjects, so too they start to have preferences among television programs. This selectivity should be borne in mind when newspaper stories count up the number of acts of violence that one could possibly see in an average week or month of TV viewing. These statistics are intended to shock and would, indeed, do so if we could assume that children watch indiscriminately.

All of the evidence points to the fact that children are not only selective among programs but within a given program as well. Their own classifications of programs do not necessarily correspond to those of adults (Harper, Munro and Himmelweit, 1970). For example, to a very young child an adult Western may be about horses and classified with other animal programs. Or to take another example, children in the U.S.S.R., like children in Canada, prefer war and detective programs over educational ones. Is the salient dimension violence or is it action?

Program preferences are difficult to interpret, for what people say they like and what they view may be different. Families who view together make compromises, or some members defer to others so that the real viewing choices may not be one's first choice. Still, program preferences are not random, and many are so predictable that they are hardly worth mentioning except to illustrate the point. Girls, for example, prefer romance and drama to sports programs and comedy, while boys reverse this order. As sex roles go, so go television program preferences.

Hardly less predictable is the finding that children's preferences taken as a whole parallel those of their parents, so that far from creating dissonance between generations television is one of the many threads connecting them. Particular incidents, then, where there is discord should not conceal the extent to which television is part of the socialization process by which the value configuration of one generation is passed on to the next.

If television is a conservative force contributing to the maintenance of the social order and to an orderly passage from generation to generation, it is often perceived otherwise, as a stranger rather than a close relative in the household, an exogenous and rival authority for the perpetuation of social norms. The answer may lie in the fact that we project and objectify what we are often unwilling to recognize in ourselves. Violence is a case in point. Parents who use corporal punishment with their children, teachers who believe in the strap, adults who favour the death penalty, hockey fans who believe fights are part of the game — are shocked, they say, by the violence on television. In other words, the very social norms we accept in reality appear repugnant to us in the mirror of television, and we seek to disassociate ourselves from, not the norms, but the mirror.

Children's Preferences for Adult Programming

Starting from kindergarten age, children prefer adult programs, becoming less and less interested in programs intended for their age group (Schramm, et al. 1961). Earlier studies of radio showed the same precocity (Herzog, 1941).

Children's programs may not be sufficiently engaging. In the U.S.S.R. they appear to have had more success with their children's programs by using formats that are participatory. Children are encouraged to write letters, send in drawings which are later analyzed on a popular art program, and generally become active partners in production. Children's programs may also be pitched below levels of cognitive development. Television typically underestimates the intelligence of its adult audiences; it may be doing the same for its youthful ones.

Still another explanation examines the social structure. The early interest of children in adult programs can be understood as a reaction on their part to their exclusion from adult experiences. "The child wants to be 'in' on the exciting world of adult life," writes Shayon (1951). "We put him into cocoons, set him apart in school. . . delay, as long as possible, his full membership in adulthood's private club." Thus, one of the unanticipated consequences of our age segregated society is to create a countervailing pressure among growing children whom it is intended to protect.

Finally, if we look at the total culture of children — the games they play, the riddles they tell, the songs they sing — a curious pattern of dual citizenship emerges. Children participate actively in two cultures, their own and the world of adult television. Now, as in the past, children bounce balls while chanting rhymes centuries old and passed on from one generation to the next through a hidden network of children (Opie, 1959).

The two worlds children live in have a dialectical relationship to each other. One is "folk," the other, modern; one is subversive, the other respectable. Clapping in a circle, children ritually poison the teacher, while sitting in front of television, teachers are friendly and human, victims themselves of officious principals. On the surface, these two worlds are contradictory, but on a deeper level of psychological growth they are complementary.

Fantasy vs. Reality

Another set of findings that are problematic concerns a distinction between fantasy/entertainment programs and realism/information programs. Many studies indicate that children who are poor or lonely or have home environments that are rejecting prefer fantasy and tinsel-town entertainment, while middle and high income groups or children who have good relationships with other children or who come from warm, supportive family environments are drawn to the reality type of programming.

Implicit in this is the notion that television entertainment has an escapist function for children who are economically and/or emotionally deprived. Yet, in several ways this is a middle-class perspective which emphasizes mastery of the environment, achievement, future planning, and what David Riesman has called "other directedness" (1950). In the eyes of middle-class parents, a child without a great many friends is a lonely, unhappy, failed child, too moody and introspective for his or her own good; the day-dreaming child is an idle child wasting time that could be spent more constructively in learning about the real world or acquiring social skills for dealing with it.

But Bruno Bettelheim (1976) in a study of children's fairy tales has argued that excessive realism retards and distorts personality development in children. Without the rich symbolism of fantasy and without periodic withdrawals from reality, children remain emotionally stunted, growing older but not up. Bettelheim is critical of middle-class parents' distrust of imagination and their demand that children confront a world of cause and effect rather than be misguided by a world governed by magic and surprise. Bettelheim, then, is critical of the pejorative use of terms like "fantasy" and "escapism" when applied to children.

Bettelheim's notion of fantasy and Walt Disney's are different aesthetically, but he would understand at once why children are attracted to Saturday morning animated cartoons where the little mouse triumphs over the predatory car, an analogy of power relationships in the family.

Still, if we accept the idea that realism is desirable, and that children use television to discover the world as it is and to prepare themselves for it, anticipatory socialization (Mendelsohn, 1966), distortions can be dysfunctional for the individual and for the social class. There is, then, a certain pathos and political tragedy in statistics showing that working-class children avoid the realism of "news" and other informational programs.

Reality, however, is not the same for all classes. In a stratified society there are different realities, as different as the private room in an exclusive hospital is from a crowded ward in a public institution. What they have in common is less than what they do not. Within the boundaries set by class, we live by a version of reality, one that is credible to us. For children growing up in the slums, the world of "news" with its emphasis on the powerful, the decision makers is less credible than the world of victims portrayed in police dramas, hospital series and soap operas. Entertainment which stars Black teachers, Black detectives, Black nurses, Black entrepreneurs have a credibility for Black children (Greenberg, 1972) although their exact surroundings are different. These programs are more realistic than public affairs programs where Blacks and working-class people generally are invisible.

Finally, the impression given in these studies is that children from working- and lower-class backgrounds turn to television and an entertainment type of television in particular because their lives are culturally impoverished. Books, music, toys, crayons and recreational spaces that middle-class children have within reach are missing from the homes and neighbourhoods of the poor. Bored, restless, lacking privacy, these children turn to the dream worlds of television drama and situation comedy.

Recent anthropological studies on "the culture of poverty," however, suggests that this too may be a biased, middle-class perception of poverty. Talley's corner and "street corner society" are alive with activity; the poor have their own patterns of leisure and recreation which we are only beginning to study. Poverty is a different culture but not necessarily an alienated or deprived one. Before concluding, then, that the preference for "fantasy" or entertainment programming among low income viewers is a consequence of their poverty, the absence of other leisure resources and the failure to develop leisure skills, it is necessary to look at the totality of working-class culture.

To summarize, the program preferences of children are important if only to illustrate that children do have preferences, and that they are not empty recipients of what is available. This is sometimes frustrating for parents who see their children turning away from "good" children's programs to adult "junk," but the general pattern is that preferences run through families, and family preferences run through social classes. Thus, the lines of social differentiation are maintained through time.

Beyond this our knowledge of program preferences is limited by the fact that adults set up the typologies based on criteria that are not those of the children themselves. The error is compounded by larger distinctions such as "news" and "entertainment" which are equated with "realism" and "fantasy." This particular dichotomy has been used to develop the thesis that in a society of social inequality, the "have-nots" withdraw into a world of wish fulfillment and make-believe. While this might be a fair observation to make about adults, it is not necessarily the case for children. Alternately, we have suggested that a model, based on symbolic interactionist theory, in which we presume that all persons are in search of meaning, of interpretive scenarios that orient them to their reality. Since many of the programs labeled as "fantasy," — as indeed, they are from a middle-class perspective — have more credibility to the underclass than those described as "realism," it is not surprising that they appeal to the poor; it would be more surprising and more irrational if they did not.

COMPREHENSION

How much do children understand of what they see on television? How much do they believe, and how much do they discount?

Adults are often poor judges of what children understand or how they interpret what they read or see. One study is particularly interesting because the children themselves were asked, and because the study in question concerned children's comprehension of commercials (Robertson and Rossiter, 1974). Using "attribution theory" (a method which asks subjects to account for their behaviour and takes these accounts at face value) the investigators found that by the time children have reached Grade V, they not only can and do differentiate between programs and advertising, but are thoroughly wised-up about commercials, aware of their purposes, and negative in their attitudes toward them.

Another study examined comprehension by comparing viewing contexts (McCormack, 1962). A program designed for educational television by the Canadian Broadcasting Corporation and using National Film Board footage on the building of an igloo was shown twice on the same day; first in the early afternoon when children in Grades II and III saw it in their classrooms; and second, in the late afternoon when children saw it at home. On the following day, children were interviewed about the program. Those who had seen it in school recalled primarily information about the construction of the igloo; that is, factual material which teachers, they thought, would expect them to learn. Children who had seen it at home recalled normative information; that is, knowledge about the Inuit and their social behaviour. When the children were asked how long it took to build an igloo, the errors again reflected the context. Children who had seen the program in school speeded it up, while children who had seen it at home slowed it down.

Comprehension, then, is a function of both audience and context; the cognitive development of the child and the normative structure of the viewing environment.

COMMUNICATION THEORY AND THE PROBLEMS OF EFFECTS

The studies of children and television discussed thus far have emphasized the strategic importance of studying the audience and some of the intervening, mediating factors. One way or another these studies all minimize the direct influence television has on an audience, rejecting alarmist images of television as a sinister force manipulating its audiences at will, the "seduction of the innocent," as Fredric Wertham (1954) once described it. What these studies are all saying is that exposure to television is meaningless, that the viewer has to cooperate for anything to happen, and that the viewers set their own terms for cooperation.

Yet even without these data, one would have hypothesized that television could have only slight impact, if, indeed it has any at all. Under ideal conditions of social learning, children offer strong resistances to learning through misinterpretation or inattention. Television is far from ideal. Its programming is fixed and cannot be adjusted to the individual needs of children, as a teacher might do in a small classroom. The program schedule is rigid and cannot be altered to meet a child's readiness to learn. Television has, then, the worst features of a textbook and none of the flexibility of good face-to-face teaching.

In addition, the punishment and reward mechanisms are missing. Television does not award prizes, give grades or reproach its viewers; it neither approves nor disapproves of their behaviour. And, finally, to the extent that children learn by doing, correcting themselves as experiential feedback indicates a wrong turn, television offers no such learning opportunity. Whatever learning theory one favours, the answers are the same: television is a weak, inefficient influence, one that is cancelled nine times out of ten.

This is one reason why social scientists are sceptical of studies which attempt to show television's effects. Many of them would prefer not to use the term "effects" at all for it implies (1) an audience that is passive, malleable, vulnerable to any stimulus; (2) that we can predict specific effects from specific content; (3) that audiences are homogeneous rather than a multiplicity of smaller audiences; and (4) that communication is a one-way process, from set to viewer.

By contrast, a communication model starts from the premise that communication is an interactional process of give and take in which information is transmitted and meaning is created. Like two parties in a conversation both are active and reactive, but at times one may be more influential than the other in a process which moves toward or away from consensual validation. This model leaves open for inquiry the nature of media effects, whether they reinforce or alter behaviour, and the conditions under which various effects might occur. Hypotheses about media effects may be derived from studying either the audiences or media content, but their verification require looking at both in an interactional process.

In a static society, the media have little influence on individuals beyond providing them with a sense of collective identity, just as religion does. But under conditions of social change, conventional sources of learning may be inadequate and, more importantly, discredited. Given these circumstances the media may have a significant in-put (McCormack, 1964).

Modern and modernizing societies have a high rate of social change, so that there is a constant of receptivity built into them. The relevant world, the "significant other" is always larger than the world experienced at first hand, and the future is always to some degree ambiguous. A learning readiness, then, exists, greater for some groups than others. But it is also in the modern and modernizing world that the media are perceived as unreliable, biased, the voice of government, in the case of totalitarian countries; the voice of business interests, in the case of capitalist countries. The more untrustworthy the media are in the eyes of their beholders, the less influence they have despite the readiness of people to be influenced.

MEDIA VIOLENCE

In recent years the public has been concerned about violence in society — inter-personal violence, political violence and social violence. Violence is a complex social phenomenon, and the theories about it range from a Hobbesian view that we are all violent in the state of nature to a Rousseauian view that we are peaceful in the state of nature but made violent by society. Between these are many theories to account for both the type and rates of violence. None of them, however, attribute much importance to media violence. Overall, poverty and racial discrimination are better predictors of violence than media exposure, but no single factor can provide an explanation of anything as complex as violence. Slightly more attention and weight have been given to the media as contributing to the rapid spread or escalation of certain forms of collective violence such as riots and demonstrations, but the violence in these is usually the violence of the police or other agents of law enforcement.

Nevertheless, not everyone has been satisfied that television violence is harmless. Cases of children carrying out bizarre acts of violence imitating something seen on television suggest a potential danger. And many people are concerned with the possible desensitization to violence that comes from constant and repeated exposure to media violence either in the news or drama.

Several investigations of media or television violence have been conducted, the most extensive by the U.S. Surgeon General (1972); the most recent, the Ontario Royal Commission on Violence in the Media Industries, the LaMarsh Commission (Ontario, 1977). Prior to either of these was the work done by the U.S. National Commission on the Causes and Prevention of Violence (Baker and Ball, 1969).

The results are inconclusive in part because the effects studied are not violence, but aggression, and only a fraction of violence in the modern world is motivated by aggression. Moreover, aggression does not always or necessarily take the forms of violence since learning to cope with aggressive feelings or aggressive arousal is a normal part of growing up. Finally, aggression itself may not always be undesirable. Apathy is certainly as much a problem in the modern world as aggression. In a social world of "rising expectations" and blocked opportunities, consensus and the avoidance of conflict are not always possible.

But it is the contention of a number of psychologists that exposure to media violence can produce aggression both in the short run and long run; not just among abnormal children but among children who are stable and whose mental state is not in question.

One group of studies examined immediate consequences of exposure to televised violence. (Most of these studies are experimental laboratory studies, and what children were viewing, either as experimentals or controls, were specially prepared films.) The specific hypothesis examined was a theory of catharsis, a theory going back to Aristotle. Very simply, it postulates that we discharge our aggression through the vicarious experience of art. Thus the effects of viewing televised violence should be to lower aggression. These were the findings in a number of studies (Feshbach, 1955, 1961, 1969; Singer, 1968). This notion was challenged by Berkowitz and his associates who were able to demonstrate just the opposite, that exposure to film violence increased aggression.

A second group of studies looked at long range effects. Based on a theory of modelling, Bandura and associates (Bandura et. al. 1963) demonstrated that children learn patterns of aggression from role models in the media. Having learned it, Bandura claims, it becomes a permanent part of our repertoire of responses which may be activated at any time in the future with only the slightest provocation. The first part of this is easier to prove than the second, but one longitudinal study indicates that young children who prefer programs with violence are considered to be more aggressive than others ten years later (Lefkowitz, et. al. 1972). But studies of adolescent delinquents do not support relationships between television viewing and real incidents of anti-social behaviour (McIntyre and Teevan, 1972), while Milgram and Shotland (1973) demonstrate the presence of self-inhibiting mechanisms, and Hyman (1974) has suggested that children may also learn sympathy and cooperative behaviour from media violence.

All of these studies, pro and con, have been criticized on methodological grounds, but the impasse is more conceptual than methodological. At the present juncture, then, one chooses not on the basis of conclusive evidence, but on the basis of a theory of human nature, a theory of childhood socialization, and a theory of communication.

CHILDREN AND MEDIA POLICY

Children are not the tractable victims of television, as we have seen, but the media have a responsibility to children. For many, this responsibility involves some form of censorship, especially of television which comes into the home where very young children are attracted to it at an age when they are unable to distinguish fiction from fact, and when their sense of right and wrong, good and bad is still not developed. Others are prepared to take the risk on the grounds that it is neither possible nor desirable to protect children from experiencing aggression.

Still others say that if television can teach anti-social behaviour, it can teach pro-social behaviour as well. But the pro-social behaviour they have in mind tends to be middle-class virtues which have not always served the poor or the socially stigmatized minorities well. Social engineering through television also raises certain ethical questions.

More research is needed, especially of how television enters the various cultures of childhood, the rich and the poor. If the issue of media violence is to be pursued further, new models are needed; and, in particular, we need to know more about why media violence has credibility to some children and not others; more fundamentally, whether credibility of media violence is related to children's experience of violence in their homes and classrooms and neighbourhoods.

In addition the media can assign their best creative talent to developing new programming for very young children with a view not to influencing behaviour, but taste. Children might also be given more access to the media, preparing and participating in programs.

Above all, the media can accept the fact that they are not parents nor teachers, but rather companions of children exploring the human condition.

References

Abel, John D.
1976 "The Family and Child, Television Viewing," *Journal of Marriage and the Family,* May. 331-335.

Abrams, Mark
"Child Audiences for Television in Great Britain," *Journalism Quarterly,* 33, (1) 35-41.

Baker, Robert K. and Ball, Sandra J.
1969 *Violence And the Media.* Vol. IX, A Report to the National Commission on the Causes and Prevention of Violence. U.S. Government Printing Office. Washington, D.C.

Bandura, Albert; Ross, Dorthea and Ross, Sheila A.
1963 "Imitation of Film-Mediated Aggressive Models," *Journal of Abnormal and Social Psychology,* 66, 1. 3-11.
1963 "Vicarious Reinforcement and Imitative Learning," *Journal of Abnormal and Social Psychology,* 67, No. 6, 601-607.

Berkowitz, Leonard
1962 *Aggression,* New York, McGraw-Hill.
1964 "The Effects of Observing Violence," *Scientific American* 21, No. 2, 35-41.
1965 "The Concept of Aggressive Crime: Some Additional Considerations," in Leonard Berkowitz, ed. *Roots of Aggression,* New York, Atherton.

Bettelheim, Bruno
1976 *The Uses of Enchantment,* New York, Knopf.

Bronfenbrenner, Urie
1970 *Two Worlds of Childhood.* New York. Russell Sage Foundation.

Brown, J.R.; Cramond, J.K. and Wilde, R.J.
1974 "Displacement Effects of Television and the Child's Functional Orientation to Media," in Jay Blumler and Elihu Katz, eds. *The Uses of Mass Communication.* Beverly Hills, Sage.

Canadian Broadcasting Corporation
1973 *Patterns of Television Viewing in Canada.* Ottawa.

Cirino, Robert
1977   *We're Being More than Entertained.* Lighthouse Press, Honolulu, Hawaii.

Feshbach, Seymour
1955   "The Drive-Reducing Function of Fantasy Behavior," *Journal of Abnormal and Social Psychology,* 50, 3-11.
1961   "The stimulating Versus Cathartic Effect of Vicarious Aggressive Activity," *Journal of Abnormal and Social Psychology,* 63, 381-385.
1969   "The Catharsis Effect: Research and Another View," Commission on the Causes and Prevention of Violence, Vol. 9, 461-472. U.S. Government Printing Office.

Gomberg, Adeline
1964   "The Working-Class Child of Four and Television," in Arthur B. Shostak and William Gomberg eds. *Blue Collar World.* Englewood Cliffs, New Jersey. Prentice-Hall.

Goranson, Richard E.
1970   "Media Violence and Aggressive Behavior," in Leonard Berkowitz, ed. *Advances in Experimental Social Psychology,* Vol. 5, 1970, 1-31.

Greenberg, Bradley S.
1972   "Children's Reactions to TV Blacks," *Journalism Quarterly* Spring. 5-14.

Harper, D. Munro, Joan and Himmelweit, Hilde T.
1970   "Social and Personality Factors Associated with Children's Tastes in Television Viewing," in Tunstall, Jeremy Ed. *Media Sociology,* U. of Illinois. Urbana.

Herzog, Herta
1941   *Children's Radio Listening.* Office of Radio Research. Columbia University. New York.

Himmelweit, Hilde; Oppenheim, A.N. and Vince, Pamela
1958   *Television and the Child.* London. Oxford.

Hyman, Herbert H.
1974   "Mass Communication and Socialization," in W. Phillips Davison and Frederic T.S. Yu eds. *Mass Communication Research,* New York. Praeger.

Johnstone, John W.C.
1974   "Social Integration and Mass Media Use Among Adolescents: A Case Study," in Jay Blumler and Elihu Katz, eds. *The Uses of Mass Communications,* Beverly Hills. Sage.

Katz, Elihu and Lazarsfeld, Paul F.
1955   *Personal Influence*. Glencoe, Illinois. Free Press.

Klapper, Joseph T.
1960   *The Effects of Mass Communication*. Glencoe, Illinois. Free Press.

Lefkowitz, M; Eron, L.; Walder, L. Huesmann, L.R.
1971   "Television Violence and Child Aggression: A Follow-up Study", Surgeon General's Report. Vol. 3. Television and Adolescent Aggression. Government Printing Office. Washington, D.C.

Maccoby, Eleanor
1951   "Television: Its Impact on School Children," *Public Opinion Quarterly*, 15, No. 3, Fall. 421-444.

McCormack, Thelma
1962   "The Context Hypothesis and TV Learning," *Studies in Public Communication*, No. 4. Autumn, 111-125.
1964   "Social Change and the Mass Media," *Canadian Review of Sociology and Anthropology*, Vol. 1, No. 1. 49-61.

McIntyre, J. and Teevan, J.
1971   "Television and Deviant Behavior," in Surgeon General's Report. Vol. 3 Television and Adolescent Aggression. Government Printing Office. Washington, D.C.

McLeod, Jack M. and O'Keefe, Garrett J. Jr.
1972   "The Socialization Perspective and Communication Behavior," in F. Gerald Kline and Phillip J. Tichenor, eds. *Current Perspectives in Mass Communication Research*, Beverly Hills, Sage.

McLuhan, Marshall
1964   *Understanding Media*. New York. McGraw-Hill.

Mendelsohn, Harold
1966   *Mass Entertainment*, New Haven, Conn. College and University Press.

Milgram, S. and Shotland, R.L.
1973   *Television and Antisocial Behavior*. New York. Academic.

Noble, Grant
1970   "Concepts of Order and Balance in a Children's TV Program," *Journal Quarterly*, 47, 101-108.

Ontario
1977   Royal Commission on Violence in the Communications Industry. Final Report.

Opie, Iona and Opie, Peter
1951   *The Lore and Language of Schoolchildren*. London. Oxford.

Riesman, David
1953   *The Lonely Crowd*. New York. Doubleday, Anchor.

Riley, Matilda White and Riley, John W., Jr.
1951   "A Sociological Approach to Communications Research," *Public Opinion Quarterly*, 15, 444-460.

Roberts, Donald F.
1973   "Communication and Children: A Developmental Approach," in Ithiel de Sola Pool and Wilbur Schramm, eds. *Handbook of Communication*, Chicago. Rand, McNally.

Schramm, Wilbur; Lyle, Jack and Parker, Edwin B.
1961   *Television in the Lives of our Children*. Toronto. University of Toronto Press.

Shayon, Robert Lewis
1951   *Television and Our Children*. New York. Longmans, Green.

Singer, David
1968   "Aggression Arousal, Hostile Humor, Catharsis," *Journal of Personality and Social Psychology*. Monograph Supplement, Vol. 8, No. 1, Part 2, 1-14.

Steiner, Gary A.
1963   *The People Look at Television*. New York. Knopf.

Soviet
1975   "Children's Television in the USSR," in *Soviet Education*, Oct. Vol. XVII, No. 12.

Serious Thieves: Lower-class Adolescent Males in a Short-term Deviant Occupation[1]

W. GORDON WEST
Ontario Institute for Studies in Education

INTRODUCTION

Studies of deviant behaviour have occupied a deservedly central place in sociology, both because they are considered useful to society, and because they are relevant to the central theoretical issue in sociology — the nature of social order. Of the various forms of deviance, theft would seem to be a prime topic, being of material concern to the authorities, and challenging the legitimacy of distribution of property and the social relationships incumbent upon property. Official statistics (e.g. Statistics Canada, 1969; Bell-Rowbotham, and Boydell, 1972: 110) indicate that about 80% of the specified violations of the criminal code in Canada involve theft. Of those thieves successfully prosecuted, about 40% are juvenile, the modal age is 15-17 years, most are working class in origin, and the great majority are males. Yet there are very few studies of theft or thieves, and almost no studies of those Canadian thieves who figure so prominently in the official statistics.

Besides being scanty, the existing literature has a number of methodological drawbacks and weaknesses. Official statistics have been shown to be unreliable indicators of crime in the population (e.g. Box, 1971), and can best serve as measures of the behaviour of the organizations which produce them (Kitsuse and Cicourel, 1963), or as clues for further investigation (e.g. Normandeau, 1971; Chimbos, 1973). In addition, they tell little of thieves or theft themselves, being raw aggregate data. Self-report studies (e.g. Vaz, 1965; Byles, 1969) seem to give much better information on the distribution of criminal activities, but also do not reveal much about how the activities are carried out, and rely on reports of behaviour rather than actual observations. Case studies (e.g. Sutherland and Conwell, 1937; King and Chambliss, 1972; Miller and

Helwig, 1972; Pollock, 1973; Jackson, 1969) give good analyses of the phenomenal worlds of thieves, but are often of unknown representativeness, or clearly do not describe the type of thief most often appearing in courts. Extensive interview studies of a number of thieves resolve this issue more adequately, but access has typically been sought through prison populations, and hence leaves some doubt about the representativeness and validity of the data, as well as lacking observational checks (e.g. Denys, 1969; Irwin, 1970; Letkemann, 1973; Cressey, 1953; Shover, 1973; Lemert, 1967a, 1967b).

In addition to these methodological problems, research on thieves has had a peculiar focus substantively. Subjects in case studies and intensive interview research are usually rare professional thieves, who are interesting as extreme cases, but hardly typical of the thieves who are of most concern to the police (Klein, 1974). Alternatively, self-report surveys probably gather data more indicative of petty theft activities, which almost everyone seems to have committed — but which are of minor concern to the police. The large group of more-than-amateur but less-than-professional thieves are left unstudied, although they are of considerable concern socially.

In adapting a symbolic interactionist perspective, I hope to avoid some of the theoretical misconceptions which have plagued earlier studies. Assumptions about social consensus (e.g. Merton, 1938), a deterministic view of human action (cf. Box, 1971), and a simplistic assumption that social categories self-evidently refer to behaviour (Nettler, 1974; cf. Becker, 1974) are to be avoided.

Legally, a thief is one who is convicted of taking another's property without his permission.

(1) Everyone commits theft who fraudulently and without colour of right takes or fraudulently and without colour of right converts to his use or to the use of any other person, anything whether animate or inanimate, with intent,

(a) to deprive, temporarily or absolutely, the owner of it or a person who has special property or interest in it, of the thing, or of his property or interest in it,

(b) to pledge it or deposit it as security,

(c) to part with it under condition with respect to its return that the person who parts with it may be unable to perform, or

(d) to deal with it in such manner that it cannot be restored in the condition in which it was at the time it was taken or converted.

(2) A person commits theft when, with intent to steal anything, he moves it or causes it to move or to be moved, or begins to cause it to become moveable.

(3) A taking or conversion of anything may be fraudulent notwithstanding that it is effected without secrecy or attempt at concealment.

(4) For the purposes of this Act, the question whether anything that is converted is taken for the purpose of conversion, or whether it is, at the

time it is converted, in the lawful possession of the person who converts it is not material.

(Martin, *et al.*, 1972: Section 283)

My concern is focussed on actors labelled as thieves rather than acts labelled as theft (Lemert, 1967d). Using a "sensitizing concept" approach (Blumer, 1969), I have operationally defined "serious thieves" as those persons having all the following characteristics: (a) being recognized and labelled by themselves as thieves, (b) being recognized and labelled by their peers as thieves, (c) having been officially convicted by courts or labelled by police as thieves, and (d) having gained at least $500 in profit from theft within a two-year period or less, making at least $100 or at least one third of their total income from theft during any single month in which they were actively thieving. These criteria distinguish the subjects from petty or amateur thieves. In addition, serious thieves are distinguished from professional thieves: (e) they do not have as highly developed skills, such as safe-cracking, confidence racketeering, pickpocketing, or counterfeiting, (f) serious thieves are non-migratory, (g) serious thieves can rarely "patch" ("fix") cases that come to the attention of the police, (h) as a result, serious thieves spend two-thirds to three-quarters of their time locked up (compared with one-quarter to one-third of professionals' time) if they continue thieving for more than a couple of years, and (i) serious thieves make much less money, talking of "scores" of hundreds rather than thousands of dollars.

METHOD

In carrying out this research, I used participant observation methods (e.g. McCall and Simmons, 1969; Schatzman and Strauss, 1973; Becker, 1970.) Since there is no defined population of serious thieves, random sampling was not feasible. I gained access to 200-300 lower and working-class delinquent Toronto boys through camp counselling, boys' club work and detached youth work between 1963 and 1969. In 1971, formal research began and I "mapped" this population and gained multiple entry to six main groupings in one area of town. Trading on personal relationships, I adopted the classic participant observer role of casually associating with 2 of the most delinquent of these groupings, participating in political, family, "work," and leisure time activities (e.g. pool, dances, drinking, etc.), initially emphasizing observation. Living in the neighbourhood over 12 months (in 1969 and 1972), my contacts expanded, allowing me to conduct theoretical sampling as the analysis evolved, explicitly searching for negative evidence to modify or refute hypotheses (Robinson, 1951; Turner, 1953). Data were collected by observation on 143 days during the 13 months of intensive research, and on 40 additional days during the following year which was devoted mainly to analysis and writing. In addition, some four months after beginning the research, I began formal structured in-depth interviews with 40 serious thieves, 2 non-thieving peers, 2 professional thieves and 4 "fences." Almost all were interviewed at least twice during sessions of from 90 to 120 minutes. Notes were generally recorded immediately after leaving the field; overall, some 750 pages of single-spaced typed notes were accumulated.[2]

Generally, a process of analytic induction was used to develop "grounded theory" (Glaser and Strauss, 1967). On first entering the field, I had only a general topic of delinquency and adolescent peer groups in mind. After doing a few interviews, it became evident that many of the youths to whom I had access were heavily involved in theft, and I focussed on this, using studies of occupations (e.g. Hughes, 1971) as well as deviance to guide the research questions. After each interview or field observation, I elaborated the evolving analysis, and checked that the new data corroborated it; negative evidence was incorporated in revised hypotheses. By re-checking old notes, and seeking negative cases, the sampling design was elaborated. Reliability was established by retesting hypotheses, and cross-checking interview, observational and documentary data. In learning to live in the neighbourhood and participate in the everyday lives of thieves, I continually tested my understanding in a pragmatic sense. Seven informants read reports and drafts, suggested modifications and offered new information; one became a veritable "Doc" (cf. Whyte, 1955) upon his enrolling in sociology courses on returning to school at an "open-door" college. This method does not clearly address statements regarding the probability of such a social type as "serious thief" in various populations, but it does allow theoretical and empirical analysis of the type (see Zeldich, 1969; Sieber, 1973).

Background

In describing background factors of the thieves studied, I am able to elaborate some antecedent or concommitant "causes" of becoming a "serious thief," not "causes" of "thieving." All thieves in the sample lived in or grew up in a lower- and working-class area of Toronto (see Garner, 1971; Mann, 1968; Butler, 1970.) The neighbourhood has a high density of population, large families, and 55-60% of the household heads are unemployed. Twenty-eight to forty-five per cent of the families in the area are headed by females (see Lorimer and Phillips, 1971). The neighbourhood youths associated in loose peer clusterings (e.g. Lerman, 1967; Rogers, 1945), but these groups are not the highly structured gangs described in many American studies (e.g., Short and Strodtbeck, 1965). Although the area is known to the police as a high-crime district, the theft ratio when compared with a middle-class suburb falls from 5:1 in official statistics to 1½:1 in Byles' self-report questionnaire study (1969). This study will address the puzzle implied by such data: that although everyone seems to steal, it is generally working-class youths who become occupants of the status "thief."

The families of the 40 thieves intensively interviewed are socially and economically handicapped, preventing their full participation in urban Toronto (cf. Lodhi and Tilly, 1973): only 14 of the 40 have both parents who were native-born, urban raised, and English speaking. Almost all, however, are Anglo-Saxon or French Canadian. The families of all 40 thieves are working-class or lower-class in occupational ranking, and half are single-parent families.

The thieves themselves are disadvantaged in numerous ways. Their mean number of school years completed was only 8.4, and all but 6 were dropouts at the time of interviewing. Thirty-six of the 40 had been in low non-academic school streams. Thirty-three of the 40 had committed petty theft as juveniles, 35 had been charged as juveniles (27 with theft offences), and 8 were incarcerated. The thieves who had left school had spent an average of 40-45% of their time unemployed by the time of the interviews, and 91% of them were unemployed at least 20% of this time. The jobs they obtained were low-paying (averaging $65-70/week in 1971) and low status menial ones, such as printers' helpers, delivery-boys, etc. They had difficulty maintaining employment, averaging 7.5 months per first job, and 3.9 jobs in the average time of 3 years between school-leaving and interviewing. In sum, they all had economic problems. All thieves studied were male, and averaged 18.8 years at the time of the interviews, ranging from 15 to 23 years. These characteristics of the sample closely approximate those of official thieves as indicated in police and court data.

The Occupational Perspective
Serious thieves hold an occupational perspective on thieving, which I conceptualize as a major concommitant variable accompanying the status. Thieving is organized, or rationalized in Weber's sense (1964), so that it takes on the qualities of an occupation.

Occupations link individuals to the larger society by providing them with a regular income of disposable resources in return for providing a service in economic production or distribution.

> A perspective is. . .a coordinated set of ideas and actions a person uses in dealing with some problematic situation, . . . a person's ordinary way of thinking and feeling about and acting in such a situation. These thoughts and actions are coordinated in the sense that the actions flow reasonably, from the actor's perspective, from the ideas contained in the perspective. Similarly, the ideas can be seen by an observer to be one of the possible sets of ideas which might form the underlying rationale for the person's actions and are seen by the actor as providing a justification for acting as he does.
>
> (Becker, et al., 1961: 34)

For thieves to hold an occupational perspective, they must organize their activities efficiently and rationally; goals must be sought on the basis of an "objective" assessment of pros and cons. Practitioners must develop a sensitive appreciation of potential opportunities for business. Risks peculiar to the occupation are collectively minimized; in an illegal job, practitioners disguise the crime and their identities as perpetrators. Routines are developed. In a distributing or marketing job such as theft, customers who are trustworthy, pay well, and handle quantities of goods are preferred. Sufficient income must be obtained to maintain one's life-style.

"Irrational" thefts, thefts without a reasonable expectation of monetary gain, thefts committed primarily to incite a reaction, thefts committed to hurt the former owner or to destroy property, thefts where the gains are donated to a revolutionary group — all these constitute negative evidence for the establishment of my hypothesis. Such characteristics would suggest other explanations of theft such as mental illness or kleptomania (e.g. Eysenck, 1964) thrill seeking (e.g. Cohen, 1955), idiosyncrasies or revolutionary aims (e.g., Hobsbawm, 1959), assertion of self-hood (e.g., Matza, 1964) or perverse values (e.g., Cloward and Ohlin, 1960). These alternative explanations may be satisfactory explanations of certain kinds of theft, but they are inadequate for the population studied.

The thieves studied practice six specialized ways of stealing.

1.   Shoplifting consists of legitimately entering a commercial goods outlet and stealing goods by removing them without payment (cf. Cameron, 1964). It is often done surreptitiously by hiding the items sought in clothing, shopping bags, etc., leaving the proprietor in a state of double ignorance: neither the offender nor the offence is known (at least until inventory). An alternative method is known as "snatch-and-grab," whereby the "boost" is executed by simply running from the store after the item is procured. Clothing and electrical appliances are favoured items. Obviously, many "scores" have to be "pulled" since each item is of no great value. Partners are often used to "keep six" (watch) in shoplifting.

2.   Houseburglary consists of breaking-and-entering a home and stealing goods or money. Times are selected when the owner is absent or asleep. Entry skills are crucial, as the burglar does not gain access legitimately. Among the thieves studied, however, such skills are only crudely developed, and usually consist of breaking windows or forcing doors or locks. A few thieves develop enough skill to pick locks, or cultivate contacts who obtain master keys for them. Expensive electrical goods, clothing, and money are the usual items stolen. Again, partners are often used to "keep six" and maintain morale.

3.   Commercial burglary is also carried out surreptitiously by breaking-and-entering a store, warehouse, or factory and stealing

expensive items or cash. Times are again selected when proprietors are absent, usually at night. Entry skills become more important as most establishments make formal attempts to prevent burglary. As with houses, windows are broken and doors forced or locks picked; not infrequently, inside employees "set up" the job for an "end" (or "cut") by failing to lock up properly, etc. Higher gains of $100-300 per thief per "score" reward the more extended effort. Some thieves specialize further by "hitting" only certain types of stores or sites, e.g., copper pipe is stolen from buildings being demolished. Partners assist each other.

4. "Clouting" consists of stealing goods in transit. Delivery vans are followed, then unloaded while drivers are absent or distracted; warehouses are entered and goods loaded onto legitimate-looking carriers. If well done, with a good "front" (performance in disguise), the victim is unaware of his loss as well as the identity of the criminal. As with commercial burglary, "inside" information helps, as otherwise the packages stolen are of unknown value. Partners are common.

5. Vehicle theft consists of stealing expensive bicycles or cars, which are usually the most valuable single items possessed by individuals (other than houses). High skills (such as "hot-wiring") are unnecessary, since many downtown lots require car owners to leave their keys in the cars in order to repark them bumper-to-bumper. The thieves merely drive cars off the lots without paying, or wait until after closing hours, when the attendents must place the keys back into the car for their owners. The cars are then "stripped down" for parts or searched for goods; no thieves I knew sold the cars whole. As with shoplifting, a number of cars must be stolen to make a profit comparable to burglary, as each car only averages about $10-20 profit. Car-theft is often practiced alone.

6. Fraud and forgery are the least practiced specialties among these thieves. Basically, schemes are elaborated whereby someone else's signature or worthless paper is exchanged for money or goods. Bogus cheques, stolen identification cards, "scams" on returning merchandise, etc., are endlessly elaborated. Only 6 of the thieves interviewed practice this solitary specialty, as it seems to require middle-class skills and appearances which few can emulate (cf. Lemert, 1967c; Denys, 1969; Cressey, 1953; Jackson, 1969).

All 40 thieves practiced at least two of these specialities, and all recognized practitioners of other specialties as thieves. There is little prestige differentiation, but the most successful thieves (in terms of profit) practice a greater number of specialties. This further indicates the low, non-professional level of mechanical skill.

In the acquisition of goods, all these types of thieves require some highly developed definitional skills which provide evidence of their holding an occupational perspective. Activities are rationally calculated in an ends-means fashion to produce a profit, a net gain of goods acquired to those expended. This requires skill at perceiving "set-ups," "capers," "scores," or "jobs" — situations which one can turn into a money-making theft proposition. There is a never-ending search for the "weak points" in the property institution. Consequences are carefully calculated. Since the thief cannot legally enforce his "alternative definition" of property relations, and since his "alternative definition" is invariably opposed by property owners, he must resort to stealth and deception. He thus disguises (a) the crime itself and (b) himself as the perpetrator (Goffman, 1959). The thief attempts to appear as such for the shortest time possible, and tries to avoid face-to-face confrontations with owners. Cash or easily sold goods are most desirable.

If discovered, the thief can resort to a number of routine moves, whereas his victim usually finds the situation to be an emergency one. The thief may simply withdraw if the action has not proceeded too far, thereby avoiding having the situation defined as a "theft." This is often done in combination with a claim that an absent-minded "innocent" mistake has been done by entering the wrong car, house, etc. On some occasions, the thief may feign indignation, asking to see the manager, etc. — in effect, "upping the ante" and daring his accuser to pursue the accusation. The thief may cause confusion, e.g., by upsetting a counter of goods, making time for his escape. He may threaten violence, especially if accompanied by fellows who temporarily outnumber the forces of law. Finally, the suspected thief may flee, an eventuality for which he is always ready. If caught, he may confess or give a "sob-story" on a lesser offence (e.g. trespassing), and if he is young or innocent-looking, be released.

When interacting with victims the thief must surreptitiously impose his definition on the situation, but with customers there is a mutually acceptable common understanding of events. Motives other than occupational ones (e.g., kleptomania, thrill-seeking, perverse values expression, idiosyncrasies) would not require the exchange of stolen goods for money, since the act of theft itself would presumably be intrinsically satisfying. Although their methods, job sites, hours of business, etc. vary, serious thieves are all left with a common problem: they must ultimately dispose of at least some stolen goods and convert them into money or material that is personally desired. Their use of regular distribution methods for such exchanges provides further evidence that such thieves hold an occupational perspective.

These thieves used three main types of customers. Legitimate merchants in pawn shops or small stores handle considerable quantities of goods, although the variety is limited (e.g., cigarettes, car parts, electronic equipment, bicycles, etc.). However, they pay very little (only about 10-20% of the retail value), and are somewhat untrustworthy as they are not thoroughly integrated into institutionalized theft, and are often checked by the police. Under pressure, they might "fink out" and betray thieves.

Much more trustworthy are consumers of "hot goods" who use the merchandise themselves or sell small quantities of it to friends and family, as they are known personally to thieves and usually are neighbours. In addition, they pay about 33-50% of the retail value. Since any particular customer buys only small quantities, a large number of consumers are needed to provide a thief with a livable income.

The ideal customer is the fence or regular buyer of stolen merchandise (Messinger, 1966; Klockars, 1974; Leonard, 1974; Hall, 1952). Fences all have a "front" or legitimate activity (e.g., storekeeping, janitoring, etc.) which provides a cover for their activities and "explains" their handling of quantities of goods. A few fences merely act as "connections," middle-men who act as salesmen for a price. Fences pay 20-30% of the retail value and are trustworthy as much of their livelihood depends on theft, and they are usually ex-thieves themselves. Each fence has contact with 10 to 30 thieves, 3 to 10 bulk buyers, and 10 to 100 individual consumers. (A few are also involved in "dealing dope" or marketing drugs such as "quick" (amphetamines), "grass" (marijuana), "junk" (heroin), etc.).

During the couple of years preceding 1971, the thieves studied averaged approximately $50 profit from their activities during a work week of 2-25 hours, an income comparable to that from their full-time legal jobs. Nonetheless, their overall profit (10-50% of retail value) collectively amounted to about $250,000 by their estimates, an average of some $7,000 each during their careers. The biggest single "score" was $3,500 from a store burglary, but the usual amount varied from nothing to $400.

There is overwhelming evidence in support of the basic claim that serious thieves hold an occupational perspective.

The four items of data indicating others held an occupational perspective refer to incidents where non-thief peers accompanied thieves, or are from interviews with professionals, who not unexpectedly view

TABLE 1[3]
EVIDENCE FOR THE OCCUPATIONAL PERSPECTIVE AMONG
SERIOUS THIEVES

	Social Status	
	Serious Thief	Other
Occupational Perspective	302	4
Other Perspective	11	24

their activity similarly to serious thieves. There are also 11 items of data which are truly negative, where serious thieves abandon the occupational perspective and reverted, in most cases, to "theft-as-a-lark" (frivolous thefts).

Careers

Not all persons who come from the same background as the sample become thieves. Access (recruitment, training, and colleagues) is required in order to perform as a serious thief and it may be conceived as an intervening variable. Some persons who have access remain constrained by conventional commitments (such as a spouse, a good job, or their self-concept). Serious thieves all lack these commitments, although they may later acquire them and stop thieving. Shifting situations and commitments (Becker, 1970) make serious theft a very short-term occupation.

Recruitment is a crucial intervening variable which is necessary before anyone can become a serious thief. Thieving must exist as an on-going activity (with routines, "fences," etc.); it must be visible to potential recruits; and such recruits must be able to join the activity before they can themselves perform. All these conditions were present in the neighbourhood; from an early age most residents become aware of theft activity on an informal basis. By adolescence the exploits of peers become fairly common knowledge, especially as the formation of peer groups around recreational pursuits means that different members are in different occupations (both legal and illegal). There are no restrictive formal requirements to becoming a thief, as there are to many legal jobs.

Although the technical skills required by these thieves are generally quite unsophisticated, some training is required, especially in social and perceptual skills. A few youths learn techniques such as lock-picking, car-driving, use of "shims" (flexible metal slides used to slip locks), etc. All of them learn to redefine the "normal" world of non-thieves into potential "job-sites" to carry out their trade. They are constantly "casing" sites. In addition, they learn how to differentiate potential colleagues and contacts. These are required to offer "tips," accompany one on jobs, and purchase "hot" goods. As with recruitment, much of this training occurred while the youths were children or young adolescents, associated with peers. Comparatively light penalties for juvenile thieves allow a period of grace in this training.

These thieves practice their trade with colleagues. Colleagues offer emotional support and companionship and provide recruitment and technical training. These contacts are developed over a number of years in a geographical community, where reputations are developed and known by word of mouth. An elementary division of labour is apparent on most "scores" (e.g., in being the "heavy" or "muscle-man," the "brains" or planner, and in "keeping six" or watching). Much cooperation exists between specialists, e.g., burglars sell stolen identification papers to fraud artists, car-thieves rent "hot" cars to burglars or shoplifters, etc.

Although I have no comparable data on middle-class youths, it is unlikely that they become serious thieves as described here (although they steal almost as frequently while they are juveniles) (Byles, 1969; Vaz, 1965). Because of their background and upbringing, middle-class youths are likely to find conventional activities more attractive than theft. Studies of middle-class communities (e.g., Seeley, et al., 1956) do not report the presence of access factors. In any case, these access factors are necessary and not sufficient "causes."[4]

Should a person take advantage of this access to serious thieving, he will attempt to solve his economic difficulties by organizing his stealing into an occupation. Almost inevitably, however, he will commit critical mistakes which will precipitate a career crisis within two or three years. Economic success is only moderate among these thieves (although comparable to their legitimate jobs). Partly because of low skill levels, any one "score" offers only a minimal profit, and committing an increasing number of infractions eventually results in arrest.

Frequent contact with the police allows these thieves to develop routine relations and ploys with them. Quite often the police know about illegalities without being able to press charges and secure a conviction in court. Although these thieves are able to work with the police and courts to their advantage, they are not able to "lay a patch" or "fix" cases as are professional thieves (e.g. Sutherland and Conwell, 1937). When a charge is laid, these thieves generally have recourse only to those ploys available to the ordinary citizen (legal aid, bargaining on pleas, presenting extenuating circumstances, etc.). The main exceptions occur when they are able to coerce local neighbourhood witnesses, or when they (rarely) are able to trade information ("rat out") for a lesser charge. Interestingly, few of these thieves perceive the courts and the police as grossly unfair.

First and second convictions usually result in probation or short sentences of a couple of months. Incarceration serves as a forced holiday, as well as a "business convention" among colleagues. In addition, it confirms a previously ambiguous identity, and a "state licence" which is recognized both by colleagues and the public.

As his arrest record accumulates, the sentences grow dramatically longer, and precipitate a career crisis for the thief. If he continues in the occupation, he almost certainly will spend most of his time incarcerated. Three main options are open to him: continuation, resulting in a life as a convict; moving to a safer illegal "scam"; or "going straight."

Two of my forty interviewees have become "jailbirds." Although they continue to perform as serious thieves when released, it seems more sensible to characterize their primary status as convict since they spend about three quarters of their time incarcerated. Neither of these youths has a wife or stable female friendship, a job they recognize as satisfactory, or a self-concept inimical to being a prisoner.

Five of my interviewees have abandoned serious theft to take up another safer illegal occupation. Most of these are "service industry" crimes (e.g., "bootlegging," "bookmaking," "dope dealing," "fencing") which are difficult to prosecute since all parties immediately involved approve of the activity, and there are no complainants. A few become low-level workers in more elaborate organized crime such as fraud rackets, confidence games, and "shady" business practices. However, the opportunity to gain entry to such activities is limited in Toronto; the thieves I know have such weak contacts with professionals that they are generally unable to provide me with access for research purposes.[5]

Twenty-one of my interviewees "went straight" by the summer of 1973. Most became involved with a woman; this required that they support their partner and any children and necessitated a larger income than serious theft provides. Most have sought and obtained better jobs, partly from having gained more experience, being older, and having contacts pay off. A few are on welfare or job-retaining programmes which provide at least partial support. Only 3 have reformed without a spouse or good job. All 21 of these youths eschew being a "jailbird"; their self-concept is such that they explicitly couldn't "shake good time" (bear being incarcerated).

The data corroborate control theory explanations of deviance and survey research on recidivism (e.g., Box, 1971), which postulate that restraining "sidebets" are required to prevent persons from breaking the law. The same three factors which "insulate" (Reckless and Dinitz,

TABLE 2
CONVENTIONAL COMMITMENTS AND CRIMINALITY

	Active Criminals		Reformed Criminals	
	N	%	N	%
Without Commitments				
(Woman, Job, School Plan)	17	89	3	14
With Commitments				
(Woman, Job, School Plan)	2	11	18	86
Total	19	100	21	100

1967) a person from becoming a serious thief are also associated with abandoning crime as a life-style.[6] "Going straight" does not mean that a person will never commit another crime as an isolated act, but rather that he will no longer occupy the status of criminal (secondary deviant). Indeed, it is only the desires of "good citizens" to satisfy their own wants and their willingness to aid criminals (by placing illegal bets, buying "hot goods," "setting up" their factories for break-ins, etc.) that allow crime to persist.

Situational adjustment seems a useful concept in explaining this process of personal change. The thieves studied lacked social advantages and had problems from an early age in dealing with formal organizations such as schools and police. Their age, background, and upbringing specifically made it difficult for them to earn a living legally. Their community provided recruitment, training, and colleagues required to be a serious thief. However, when their situations change, and accumulated arrests, suitable jobs, and conventional marital relationships make being a thief less attractive, they abandon the status.

Trust

Serious thieves experience some peculiar problems in carrying on their activities because of their illegal nature. Social officials and many ordinary citizens seek to eliminate thieves, who thus experience a severe problem of integrating their actions with others, and constantly face the threat of betrayal ("ratting" or "finking"). Also, like other businessmen, serious thieves face the crucial problem of enforcing contracts, but do not have the usual recourse to the law and police as ultimate sanctions.

One obvious strategy to meet these difficulties is to operate covertly, expose oneself as little as possible, and minimize the opportunities for "burning" (breaching agreements). I have already described precautions taken in acquiring goods; it is noteworthy that serious thieves also restrict the distribution of any incriminating information among themselves. They keep "hot goods" for a minimum amount of time. But serious thieves such as those studied must reveal themselves at least occasionally to others, not only in acquiring but also in distributing stolen property. They need colleagues for recruitment, training, and support, and customers to buy their goods. A second type of strategy, then, is to deal only with *trustworthy* people.[7]

Trust exists "where an actor has offered a definition of himself and the audience is willing to interact with the actor on the basis of that definition. . ." (Henslin, 1968: 140). For serious thieves, persons are deemed trustworthy when they have "sidebets" (Becker, 1970) which commit them to being faithful. In institutionalized theft, these sidebets consist of (1) direct personal gain, (2) the necessity of maintaining personal ties through maintenance of a community reputation as trustworthy, (3) vulnerability to retaliatory violence if trust is betrayed, and (4) the holding of an ideological viewpoint supportive of theft.

If a person stands to make a direct personal gain, he is more trustworthy. Customers and colleagues fall explicitly into this category, whereby long-run material considerations result in informal but socially institutionalized behaviour. Although they find it very difficult to implicate the police in this network, serious thieves are able to construct the sidebets of many neighbourhood citizens so that the latter at least tacitly support this system of "hidden transfer payments."

A person's involvement in a community network of friends, relatives, and acquaintances also makes him or her more trustworthy. Contacts vouch for each other in a complex "grapevine." The transformation of dyadic exchange relationships into at least triadic ones obligates the transacting parties to a community which persists independent of their personal interactions (Simmel, 1950). Although professional thieves rely on a similar network of occupational contacts, the serious thieves studied remain more tightly integrated within their geographical community.

Persons who are vulnerable to violent retaliation are more trustworthy. Just as legitimate businessmen seldom resort to coercion although it is available if needed, illegitimate businessmen seldom use violence. Since the police cannot be used for this purpose by thieves, "heavies" ("muscle-men," or persons specializing in violence or force) are available if needed. Although their actions can legally be prosecuted, their neighbourhood presence and the relative inability of the police fully to protect someone being assiduously sought allow this informal method of social control to operate effectively.

Finally, sharing ideological legitimations of theft makes one more trustworthy. Such worldviews may actively encourage or support theft, or simply not actively disapprove of it for others. Poor people are especially likely to harbour resentments against those who have more material possessions, almost everyone knows of some "graft and corruption" in normal business practices, and "necessity knows no law." Relative isolation within a community which accepts and supports institutionalized theft protects persons from conflicting ideologies, and makes it increasingly difficult to conceive of other ways of acting. Thus social relationships attain a more persistent stability (Berger and Luckmann, 1967: 103, 108).

It should now be evident that secrecy and trust are essential for the operations of serious thieves. Without these two factors, they cannot routinize their activities within a community, part of which seeks their elimination. Such trust is granted only when at least one (and preferably more) of the four conditions outlined above are present. Without the construction of these sidebets, trust is not granted, and serious theft becomes untenable as an on-going enterprise. The ten cases of negative

TABLE 3
TRUST IS ASSOCIATED WITH SIDEBETS

	Trust	Non-Trust
Sidebets Present	355	10
Sidebets Absent	0	25

evidence in the table are instances where individuals "finked" under extreme police pressure, or "burned" fellows (sometimes under the influence of amphetamines).

CONCLUSIONS

I have attempted to illuminate the phenomenon of deviance by studying theft, which is an important type of illegal deviance. Using participant observation methods and analytic induction, I have specifically focussed on "serious thieves," who seem to be the most numerous thieves of material consequence, rather than petty amateurs or rare professionals.

I have tried to understand theft from its practitioners' viewpoint, and to understand how the activity is integrated into the community, and institutionalized. Longitudinal data were gathered on the social process of becoming and renouncing being a thief. By integrating the research with survey and official data on the subject, I have discussed the place of such thieves in the wider society. Finally, in adopting a framework suggested by Matza (1969), I have depicted the subjects as actors who create their own world by exercising will within situations of external constraints.

Although an important social type, serious thieves have not been well studied before. They clearly differ from amateurs in their larger profits, the occupational organization of their activities, and the development of a community support system. In locating major precipitating factors in the economic situation of these youths, the study lends partial support to Marxist analyses of crime (e.g., Taylor, Walton, and Young, 1973); it also denies the utility of other popular explanations of theft (e.g., psychological ones).

Yet serious thieves also differ from professionals, and not only in the relative lack of sophisticated techniques and organization of their job. Serious theft is a short-term occupation. By showing that such thieves quit their status when conventional commitments are acquired, the study corroborates control theory (e.g., Durkheim, 1951; Hirschi, 1969; and Box, 1971). This modifies "vulgar" Marxist analysis by incorporating other social factors, such as attachments to spouses.

It also requires crude statements of labelling theory (e.g., Nettler, 1974: 202 ff.) which claim that mere labelling causes behaviour; in this study, multiple convictions are more likely to result in abandonment of the deviant status, especially when conventional commitments are present (cf., Bordua, 1967). Jail acts as a deterrent in interaction with these restraining sidebets. Nonetheless, it should be clear that an interaction perspective on deviance has been central to the analysis (see, e.g., Becker, 1974). The fact that most of these thieves "cool out" further refutes "psychological" or "type of person" explanations of the activity, in favour of a social situational one.

This exodus from the status suggests that crime in Canada, or more specifically Toronto, may differ from illegal activities practiced elsewhere. Since Toronto has comparatively uncorrupted police and little "organized" professional crime, there is less access to professional adult criminal statuses for serious thieves. The peer group structure is markedly different from that discussed in American accounts of gangs (e.g., Short and Strodtbeck, 1965; Cloward and Ohlin, 1960). Situational adjustments in later life seem more readily available, perhaps because of the lack of ethnic barriers for these youths (most are white Anglo-Saxon or French Canadian). Nonetheless, the enduring structural disadvantages of this age, sex, and socio-economic group (see, e.g., Committe on Youth, 1971; Ross, 1975; Greenberg, 1975) suggest that the status of "serious thief" will remain attractive to new younger recruits.

Serious theft exists as an ongoing activity through its integration with the community. Serious thieves rely on the legal system and commodity market system to provide them with a livelihood. They rely on community demand for services in creating a bastard institution (Hughes, 1971). All of this is enacted within a negotiated social order (rather than a consensual one) which relies on trust for its perpetuation.

Footnotes

1. *This article is based on my Ph.D. dissertation of the same title, Northwestern University, Evanston, Ill., U.S.A., 1974. My thanks to Ms. Marie Scott for typing assistance, and Howard S. Becker, John I. Kitsuse, Allan Schnaiberg, Ed Vaz, and Abdul Lodhi for their comments on earlier drafts.*

2. *Two interviews were tape recorded as a validity check, and compared with notes recorded from memory for the same interviews; recall was better than 90% (by space) for relevant data. This reassurance encouraged me to continue not using the recorder, as it threatened to interfere with rapport.*

3. *This table and table 3 are constructed by counting items of information found in the field notes relevant to the hypotheses. It thus provides a quasi-statistical indication of the weight of data supporting the hypotheses as stated. See Becker, et al., (1961) for further examples and elaboration.*

4. My sampling procedure — working "backwards" from a sample of thieves — does not allow me to estimate probabilities that persons with these characteristics or situations become serious thieves.
5. This difficulty experienced initially as a research problem of access seems to me good evidence of a substantive finding. My couple of contacts through other sources with professional thieves involved with organized crime indicate that organized criminals are as likely to be of middle-class as lower-class origins, especially as small-business skills are usually required in greater degree than most working-class people have developed.
6. Considerations of causality become intriguing here. The empirical evidence indicates that it is unlikely that either stopping being a thief or marrying/working routinely precedes the other. I could not, for instance, tease from the data support for the claim that merely having a job must be perceived by the actor as "good" both in the sense of providing adequate pay and being worthwhile retaining. Different actors go through different sequences of weighing the factors in their minds as they change the meanings of terms (e.g., marriage) for themselves. I take this as a paradigmatic example of Blumer's concern with interpretive practices in his arguments against "variable analysis" (Blumer, 1969).
7. This problem and concept became apparent to me some six months into the research, when I was struck by the openness with which information was being shared with me, by my inclusion in "job" plans, etc. As in footnote #5, a methodological problem provided evidence for a substantive issue.

References

Becker, H.S.
1961   et al., Boys in White. Chicago: University of Chicago Press.

Becker, H.S.
1974   Outsiders. Toronto: Collier-Macmillan, revised edition.
       Sociological Work. Chicago: Aldine, 1970.

Bell-Rowbotham B., and C.L. Boydell
1972   "Crime in Canada: A Distributional Analysis," in C.L. Boydell, et al., Deviance and Societal Reaction in Canada. Toronto: Holt, Rinehart, and Winston.

Berger P. and T. Luckmann
1967   The Social Construction of Reality. New York: Doubleday-Anchor.

Blumer, H.
1969   "The Methodological Position of Symbolic Interactionism," in his Symbolic Interactionism. Toronto: Prentice-Hall.

Bordua, D.
1967   "Recent Trends: Deviant Behavior and Social Control," Annals of The American Academy of Political and Social Science. 369 (Jan.) 149-63.

Box, S.
1971 *Deviance, Reality, and Society.* Toronto: Holt, Rinehart, and Winston.

Butler, J.
1970 *Cabbagetown Diary.* Toronto: Peter Martin.

Byles, J.
1969 *Alienation, Deviance, and Social Control.* Toronto: Interim Research Project on Unreached Youth.

Cameron, M.O.
1964 *The Booster and The Switch.* Toronto: Collier-Macmillan.

Chimbos, P.D.
1973 "A Study of Break-and-Enter Offences in Northern City, Ontario," *Canadian Journal of Criminology and Corrections,* XV, 3 (July) 316-25.

Cloward, R. and L. Ohlin
1960 *Delinquency and Opportunity.* Toronto: Collier-Macmillan.

Cohen, A.K.
1955 *Delinquent Boys: The Culture of the Gang.* Toronto: Collier-Macmillan.
Committee on Youth. *It's Your Turn. . .* Ottawa: Information Canada, 1971.

Cressey, D.R.
1953 *Other People's Money.* Toronto: Collier-Macmillan.

Denys, R.G.
1969 "Lady Paperhangers," *Canadian Journal of Corrections and Criminology,* XI, 165-192.

Durkheim, E.
1951 *Suicide.* Toronto: Collier-Macmillan.

Eysenck, H.K.
1964 *Crime and Personality.* London: Routledge and Kegan Paul.

Garner, H.
1971 *Cabbagetown.* Richmond Hill, Ontario: Simon and Schuster.

Glaser, B. and A. Strauss.
1967 *The Discovery of Grounded Theory.* Chicago: Aldine.

Goffman, E.
1959 *The Presentation of Self in Everyday Life.* New York: Doubleday-Anchor.

Greenberg, D.
1975   "Coming of Age in Delinquency: A Theoretical Synthesis" Unpublished M.S., Sociology Dept., New York University.

Hall, J.
1952   *Theft, Law, & Society.* Chicago: Bobbs-Merrill.

Henslin, J.
1968   "Trust and The Cab-Driver," in M. Truzzi, ed., *Sociology and Everyday Life.* Toronto: Prentice-Hall.

Hirchi, T.
1969   *Causes of Delinquency.* Berkeley: University of California Press.

Hobsbawm, E.J.
1959   *Primitive Rebels.* New York: Norton.

Hughes, E.C.
1971   *The Sociological Eye.* Chicago: Aldine.

Irwin, J.
1970   *The Felon.* Toronto: Prentice-Hall.

Jackson, B.
1969   *A Thief's Primer.* Toronto: Collier-Macmillan.

King, H., and W. Chambliss
1972   *Box Man: A Professional Thief's Journey.* Toronto: Harper (Fitzhenry and Whiteside).

Kitsuse, J.I. and A.V. Cicourel
1963   "A Note on The Uses of Official Statistics," *Social Problems,* XI, 608-14.

Klein, J.F.
1974   "Professional Theft: The Utility of a Concept," *Canadian Journal of Criminology and Corrections.* XVI, 2, 133-144.

Kockars, C.
1974   *The Professional Fence.* Toronto: Collier-Macmillan.

Lemert, E.
1967a   "The Behavior of the Systematic Check Forger," in his *Human Deviance, Social Problems, and Social Control.* Toronto: Prentice-Hall.
1967b   "Role Enactment, Self, and Identity in the Systematic Check Forger," *ibid.*
1967c   "An Isolation and Closure Theory of Naive Check Forgery," *ibid.*
1967d   "The Concept of Secondary Deviation," *ibid.*

Leonard, H.B.
1974   "The Fence: Alive and Well," *Criminology Made in Canada*, II, 1, 13-28.

Lerman, P.
1967   "Gangs, Networks, and Subcultural Delinquency", *American Journal of Sociology*, LXXIII, (July) 63-72.

Letkemann, P.
1973   *Crime as Work*. Toronto: Prentice-Hall.

Lodhi, A. and **C. Tilly**
1973   "Urbanization, Crime, and Collective Violence in Nineteenth Century France." *American Journal of Sociology*. LXXIX, 2 (Sept.).

Lorimer, J. and **M. Phillips**
1971   *Working People*. Toronto: James Lewis and Samuel.

Mann, W.E.
1968   "The Social System of a Slum: The Lower Ward, Toronto" in his *Deviant Behaviour in Canada*. Toronto: Social Science Publishers.

Martin, J.C.
1973   *et al. Martin's Annual Criminal Code*. Agincourt, Ont.: Canada Law Book Ltd.

Matza, D.
1964   *Delinquency and Drift*. New York: John Wiley and Sons.
1969   *Becoming Deviant*. Toronto: Prentice-Hall.

McCall, G., and **J. Simmons**
1969   *Issues in Participant Observation*. Don Mills, Ont.: Addison-Wesley.

Merton, R.K.
1938   "Social Structure and Anomie," *American Sociological Review*, III (October).

Messinger, S.
1966   "Some Reflections on 'Professional Crime' in West City." mimeo.

Miller, B. and **D. Helwig**
1972   *A Book About Billie* (retitled *Inside and Outside*) Ottawa: Oberron.

Nettler, G.
1974   *Explaining Crime*. Toronto: McGraw-Hill-Ryerson.

Normandeau, A.
1971 "Quelque faits sur le vol dans les grands magasins à Mont-réal," *Canadian Journal of Criminology and Corrections*, XIII, 251-65.

Pollock, D.
1973 *Call me a Good Thief.* Montreal: Transformation Information Centre.

Reckless, W.C. and S. Dinitz
1967 "Pioneering with Self-Concept as a Vulnerability Factor in Delinquency," *Journal of Criminal Law, Criminology, and Police Science*, LVIII, 4.

Robinson, W.S.
1951 "The Logical Structure of Analytic Induction," *American Sociological Review*, XVI, 6 (December).

Rogers, K.
1945 *Streetgangs of Toronto.* Toronto: Ryerson.

Ross, M.
1975 "Economic Conditions and Crime — Metropolitan Toronto 1965-72," *Criminology: Made in Canada*, II, 2, 27-41.

Schatzman, L., and A. Strauss
1973 *Field Research.* Toronto: Prentice-Hall.

Seeley, J.
1956 *et al., Crestwood Heights.* Toronto: University of Toronto Press.

Short, J. and F. Strodtbeck
1965 *Group Process and Gang Delinquency.* Chicago: University of Chicago Press.

Shover, N.
1973 "The Social Organization of Burglary," *Social Problems*, XX, 4, 499-514.

Sieber, S.
1973 "The Integration of Fieldwork and Survey Methods," *American Journal of Sociology*, LXXXIX (May).

Simmel, G.
1950 *The Sociology of Georg Simmel*, ed., K. Wolff. Toronto: Collier-Macmillan.

Statistics Canada
Census #93-609. Ottawa: Information Canada, 1969.

Sutherland, E. and C. Conwell
1937   *The Professional Thief.* Chicago: University of Chicago Press.

Taylor, I.P., P. Walton, J. Young
1973   *The New Criminology.* London: Routledge & Kegan Paul.

Turner, R.
1953   "The Quest for Universals in Sociological Research," *American Sociological Review*, XVIII.

Vaz, E.
1965   "Middle-Class Adolescents: Self-Reported Delinquency and Youth Culture Activities," *Candian Review of Sociology and Anthropology*, II, 1 (February).

Weber, M.
1964   *The Theory of Social and Economic Organization*, Toronto: Collier-Macmillan.

Whyte, W.F.
1955   *Streetcorner Society.* Chicago: University of Chicago Press.

Zelditch, M.
1969   "Some Methodological Problems of Field Studies," in G. McCall and J. Simmons, eds., *Issues In Participant Observation.* Don Mills, Ont.: Addison-Wesley.

Childhood and Adolescent Socialization Among Hutterites[1]

KARL A. PETER

Simon Fraser University

HUTTERITE SOCIALIZATION: SOME THEORETICAL CONSIDERATIONS

The main characteristic of the Hutterite socialization process, a characteristic which seems to distinguish Hutterite socialization processes from similar processes found in Western societies, is found in the communal orientation of the group. The Hutterite systems of communal property ownership, redistribution of goods and allocation of work are without question inseparable from the processes of socialization which prepare individuals for participation in these institutions. As such they must be recognized as forces giving direction and focus to socialization processes.

But Hutterites as a distinct socio-cultural group which, despite their interdependence with their respective host society, remain institutionally complete, face an incomparably more important and difficult socializing task than mere preparation of its members for participation in institutions practicing communal property relations.

For more than four and a half centuries Hutterites have maintained a religious-ideological and behavioral alternative relative to those societal conformities which have characterized Hutterite host societies. To keep this alternative credible, attractive and dynamic such that the great majority of Hutterites choose to remain members even when they have an opportunity to leave, constitutes the major socializing task of Hutterites.

The Problem of Separation

It should be remembered, that Hutterites have chosen a mode of existence which continuously demands separation from their respective host society. "Separation from the World" originally was a conscious religious choice designed to separate the believer from the unbeliever and to protect the believer from the contagious influence of a sinful world. The "chosen people" the "community of saints" were to stand out in a world of sin and spiritual corruption by being radically and visibly different.

Such sentiments of course are frequently found in social movements particularly during their vigorous early stages. A critical stage however is reached when the social movement becomes institutionalized. The creation of permanent and enduring institutions on the part of the social movement requires the establishment of mutually agreeable relations between the movement and its host. In the face of such requirements the initial anti-societal sentiments of the movement must be modified and replaced by a sense of coexistence and cooperation, however limited. The contacts established in this way make it more and more difficult for the movement to truly remain "separate" from its host. The more intense these contacts are, the longer they last and the greater the number of social contacts there are, the more difficult it is for the movement to remain separate. Separation in the sociological sense here refers to the ability of a socio-cultural group to be predominantly socially and culturally self determinate despite relations of interdependence with outside socio-cultural forces.

What distinguishes the Hutterite group from all other groups which are either religiously similar or communally similar, is their ability to maintain this separation and self determination in an institutionalized form even after the religious justification for separation has lost much of its original fervor.

The Effects of Isolation

The argument is being made, that social isolation is the major force that insures degrees of self determinate development for Hutterites. The fallacy with this argument is that social isolation is seen as a cause while in reality it is an effect. The maintenance of social isolation in itself is problematic for Hutterites and far from being a cause of their self determination; it is, rather the active ongoing dynamic toward self determination which produces social isolation. There is no question that social isolation facilitates self determination; it creates conditions under which self determination is more probable than under any other conditions, but it is not the cause of it.

Hutterites have not withdrawn from contacts with the wider society; rather, they present to their membership an active, living and viable alternative which stands in contrast to the values and institutions of their host society.

This alternative must continuously be of such a nature that it can endure comparisons relative to the prevalent ideological and behavioral conformities of contemporary society and command the loyalty and allegiance of its members in spite of this evaluation.

On these accounts Hutterites seem to succeed splendidly.

The Functional Aspects of the Hutterite Alternative

To state the fact that they do succeed is not to say that they succeed easily. To appreciate the nature of this task and the way in which the task is translated into processes of socialization one must be aware of some fundamental conditions.

The viability of the Hutterite alternative consists of maintaining a religious worldview in the face of a modern scientifically colored, individualistically oriented, secular, materialistic ideology.

This religious worldview among Hutterites, as elsewhere, serves three basic social and psychological functions. In the first instance religion serves as a systematic symbolic universe which assigns meaning to the religious group and the world in which it exists. It explains the origin of material things and human life and as such is able to make definitive statements about the meaning of the world, of life and human existence.

To the extent that any systematic view of the above nature includes a definition of man and his place in the world, the second basic function of religion consists of making definitive statements in regard to the imperatives of human behavior. Laws and norms, cults, rituals, taboos, and folkways constitute systematically selected and ethically consistent forms of behavior which are perpetuated in processes of socialization, suggestion, education, example and tradition.

The third basic function is of a psychological nature. It is designed to overcome the helplessness of man in the face of existential problems of being and non-being, of existential anxieties derived from failure, suffering, accidents and death.

These existential anxieties are the least susceptible to rational scientific manipulation. Their alleviation seems to require some sort of supernatural legitimacy, something science, as a man made imperfect, incomplete and fragmented body of knowledge, is unable to provide. Religion, in contrast, organizes man's life energies, his drives, and basic needs into meaning, outlook, hope and optimism designed to overcome, or at least endure without despair, failure, suffering, and death.

The Hutterite socializing task is to maintain the unity of these three religious functions in spite of the challenge of science to the first and the challenge of individualism (and materialism) to the second. Depending on the outcome of these two challenges the third function will follow suit. Whether an individual consults his priest or his psychiatrist when plagued by existential anxieties depends into which ideological system he is integrated.

Contradictory Trends among Hutterites

The particular Hutterite attempt to preserve the unity of these three religious functions is problematic due to two apparently contradictory orientations in Hutterite culture. As is the case in most religious sectarian movements, the Hutterite challenge toward the conformities of the times turned conservatively inward as the larger society turned indifferent or became tolerant of non-conformism. Religious indifference or toleration relieved the sect from the necessity of developing and maintaining an intellectual elite whose task was the continuous reformulation of the sect's position in the struggle with contemporary conformist ideologies. Religious persecution was emminently suited to do this, yet religiously mindless persecution due to the ravages of war oriented the group toward physical survival. By the middle of the Seventeenth century Hutterite religious scholarship had come to a standstill. With the exception of a flurry of revival activities during the middle of the Eighteenth century this is still the case today. As a result the Hutterite religious worldview is not only extremely conservative but in many respects outright archaic. Moreover it has no culturally accepted and legitimized mechanism to update it.

The difficulties to maintain an archaic worldview are compounded in a fast changing modern world due to progressive Hutterite attitudes toward the production of goods. The economic sentiments of the sect were and still are essentially anti-capitalistic. The concept of supply and demand as market regulating forces drew nothing but scathing condemnations from Hutterites. An entirely different attitude however prevailed in regard to the mode of production. The sect proved highly inventive in relation to the organization of work and the rationalization of production. In a rudimentary form it introduced semi-industrial productive methods 150 years before the emergence of the first truly industrial plant in England at the beginning of the Eighteenth century. The sect has retained this ability to organize its mode of production rationally and in accord with the latest technological principles throughout its history. The Hutterites broke through the anti-technological bias of the Guild system. They updated their skills and crafts with most modern, often imported, techniques which they actively sought out in foreign countries. They adapted to agriculture when the industrial revolution put many of their crafts out of business and they finally adapted industrial techniques to agriculture. In each instance Hutterites proved to be very progressive in structuring their productive processes in a most modern, science oriented way.

It follows that a main part of the socializing task in Hutterite culture is designed to overcome the contradictory influence between an archaic religious worldview which denies to science any valid explanatory or causal function and yet allows for technological orientations and encourages creativity in the field of productive technologies.

Hutterites are in need of a basic personality structure which is prepared to practice science for technological purposes, yet at the same time refuses to regard science as an explanatory system regarding the nature of man and the world he lives in. Such a personality structure in addition should not resort to individualism as a criteria of judging the validity of behavioral norms and traditions.

How is such a personality constructed and what are the processes by which it is obtained?

The Hutterite Personality Structure

Only a preliminary answer to these questions is possible at this time without referring to a great number of empirical data. The key elements in the construction of the Hutterite personality is the isomorphism between the Hutterite view of the nature of human nature and the Hutterite view of the real world. Both of these views are dualistic, postulating opposing forces who are in constant struggle with each other.

As will be explained in more detail later, the Hutterite view of the nature of human nature contains the opposites of the spirit contra the flesh. The first is directed toward God, the latter to sin. The first leads to eternal life, the latter to eternal death.

The Hutterite view of the real world contains the opposites of the community of believers contra to the world of the unbelievers. The first consists of the Hutterite community, the second consists of the rest of the world. The community of believers incorporates the spirit of God; it constitutes a "forecourt of heaven," (Vorhof des Himmels) the assurance of life. The bad, the ungodly, the flesh, the morally depraved inhabit the world where people are awaiting eternal death.

One of the consequences of this view is the de-legitimation of the world and its contemporary manifestations. The causal and explanatory forces of this world are manifestly untrue. War, genocide, crime, poverty, human arrogance and ignorance are evident everywhere in the world and determine its course.

The Hutterite individual is socialized to be deeply suspicious of the motifs and attitudes of those raised in the image of the world. Since the final outcome of the world — eternal death — is known to him, he can have no desire to participate in it.

While the de-legitimation of the world is caused by its own refusal to accept the true meaning of God's spirit, Hutterites see no reason to reject the technological processes of the world as long as these processes are used in the spirit of God. That is to say for the good of the community and the spirit it stands for. Hutterites might become wealthy but they are not to use wealth for enjoyment. They might be skillful but they are not allowed to develop false pride or arrogance because of it.

The physical world with all its attractions, successes and failures really cannot touch the truly spiritual man. Earthly existence demands that he works and produces for himself and for others. But worldly attractions, successes and failures in the end are of no consequence to him spiritually. The term "Gelassenheit" denotes a feeling of self-surrender to God's guidance; the forsaking of all concerns for personal property or pride. It defines a feeling of freedom from the anxieties and pains of the world by rendering the affairs of the world meaningless and trivial. But the extraordinary capacity of Hutterites to denigrate the predominant secular ideologies would be of relatively little consequence if it were not backed up by an extraordinary communal-behavioral system. It is of greatest importance to realize that Hutterites have remained a small group society despite their numerical growth during the last 100 years from a few hundred to 23,500. There are good economic and socio-cultural reasons for not letting a community grow beyond a membership of 140.

Hutterites grow up in a primary group and never experience any socialization into a secondary group. It is the secondary socialization which brings to bear different points of view on the individual's personality development, something Hutterites have little opportunity to experience.

The Unity of Belief and Behavior
There is furthermore the extraordinary consistency between the behavioral expressions in the community and the basic religious tenets. The communal validation of religious beliefs is behaviorally visible; it is direct and forms the basic life experience of Hutterite children. Life long primary interaction congruent with religious views elicit extremely strong habitual forms of behavior on the part of Hutterite members.

There is no possibility for a Hutterite to doubt because he lacks even the language in which doubt can be expressed, not to speak of the logic necessary to organize an expression of doubt. Hutterites make no converts, although there was some recent reconciliation with the "society of Brothers" and the establishment of a Hutterite colony in Japan; for all practical purposes no adult educated converts have joined the group and remained part of it during the last 200 years. When Hutterites purposefully were sent to educational institutions to become doctors or teachers and when these members expressed opinions contrary to accepted Hutterite views or violated behavioral norms they were expelled. The same fate awaits any member who seriously dares to act in a similar way. The possibility of expelling members is an effective mechanism to maintain Hutterite conservatism. The existence of a number of expelled ex-Hutterite groups in Western Canada testifies to the determination of the sect to get rid of internal dissenters.

To understand Hutterite socialization is to understand first the dynamics by which the sect keeps itself apart from the rest of society. In the second instance it requires an understanding of the effects which a primary group has on individuals when this group engages in a behavioral system fully integrated, validated and legitimized with its religious beliefs.

THE STRUCTURAL COMPONENTS OF THE HUTTERITE SOCIALIZATION PROCESS

Child socialization and adolescent education among Hutterites is a responsibility shared by the Hutterite family and the Hutterite community in various proportions depending on the age of the child. For the first two years of its life, a child is exclusively cared for within the extended family where it receives a great amount of attention and affection from all family members regardless of sex. While female Hutterites traditionally cater to the physical and emotional needs of children, males care little about physical needs but tend to show a great deal of affection and warmth toward children without making too much of a distinction regarding the closeness of kinship ties.

It is not uncommon that mothers having twins or having had two children within a very short space of time, will give one of the children to a sister or another relative to care for. This arrangement might last for a number of years until the mother feels able to carry the burden of an additional child. The exchange of these children is totally unproblematic mainly due to the fact that the environments are very similar.

In addition, Hutterites tend to blend the personalities the child is exposed to by having relatives accompany the child which changes its environment. The foster mother for example who has raised the child for two or three years accompanies the child when it goes back to its biological family for up to six weeks.

Adult Orientation of Hutterite Culture

Hutterite culture is an adult, not a child, oriented culture. While there are many children to be found in every community due to the high birth rate of the sect, children are subordinate to adult activities, adult values and adult expectations. The imposition of the community values and expectations begins at the third birthday of the child when it enters the "little school." In this, what is essentially a kindergarten environment, the child is exposed for the first time to the two important structural components of Hutterite society — age and sex division.

Exposure to Communal Stratification

Separated by sex and stratified by age the children sit at their tables and even sleep in their bunk beds during the day. This age and sex differentiation will remain a lifelong feature for the Hutterite to the extent that all activities in the community in one way or another will take these criteria into account. Hutterite women who are taking turns in acting as kindergarten nurses let the children play but do not play themselves nor do they assume the role of a child to initiate children's responses.

Children are seen as lovable creatures, saved by God due to their innocence and ignorance; yet they carry in themselves the germ of Adam's sin, which if allowed to develop, will push them into carnal desires. As will be shown later in this article, the Hutterite ideal of man is that kind of man who knows about God; knows about his carnal nature; is able to suppress his carnal nature; has acquired faith and consequently is able to live according to the will of God.

Hutterite Perception of Children

Since adult Hutterites are supposed to have reached this stage, children by necessity are being looked at, not as inferiors, but as incompletes. They are seen as needing the help and assistance of adults in reaching the full stage of spiritual maturity. Therefore, there can be no question of adults assigning value and importance to children's games and plays. Nor do they regard these as means to develop child personalities.

From these religious convictions it follows, that personalities are developed through the knowledge of God, the suppression of man's carnal nature and the acquisition of faith.

The Structure of the Socialization Process

The socialization process is therefore structured in accord with these convictions. For the "little school" this means that the kindergarten nurses teach the word of God to the young by having them learn and recite bible quotations, songs, moral tenets and other religious material until they know them "by heart." Other elements of socialization which are seen as important are discipline, modesty, respect for elders, sensitivity toward others, pacifism, sense of duty and obediency.

Despite these stern demands Hutterites do not maintain a socialization environment that favors insensitivities. The primary group environment, the family and the peer group act as social modifiers through which the above mentioned demands are reduced to endurable human levels.

The Facilitation of Socialization through the Primary Group

A sympathetic understanding for human failings accompanies the demand for self discipline. Patience, forgiving and forgetting are as much a part of the process as is corporal punishment and exposure to communal shame.

The peer group in particular is the place where individuality is allowed to develop within the limitations of sex and age role prescriptions. Competitions and rivalries are by no means absent in the peer group.

The family on the other hand influences the socialization process of the school through the status which it maintains in the community. While Hutterites pride themselves in saying that the communal socialization process recognizes no family ties, these nevertheless reassert themselves in very subtle ways.

Individual Differentiation

It may be the small amount of extra care or attention which a child receives in a higher status family which might make a large difference in its performance in the socialization process. It might be an attitude of greater expectations for social mobility which influences a child from a higher status family. But there is also the recognition of talent, intelligence and adaptability independent of a family background which is capable of propelling one child further than another.

Promotion through Age

With its sixth birthday, the Hutterite child enters its next stage of development by joining the group of 6 to 15-year-olds. This group is usually referred to as the "large school" since it falls within the years during which the requirements of public education are satisfied.

By special arrangements with provincial governments Hutterites maintain public schools in their communities. While the building is publicly owned, the school grounds are made available by the community. The teachers are appointed by the local board and teach the provincial curriculum, but restrictions regarding the use of radios, television and other devices are usually entered into between the school board and the community.

The Change from Female to Male Responsibility

This group of adolescents incorporates the same age and sex division as outlined earlier. It is significant to note that the responsibility for socialization now passes from female into male hands. The rotating kindergarten nurses are replaced by the German school teacher who is a member of the council of elders and therefore one of the six persons responsible for the administration of the community. This move brings the socialization process much closer to the central interest of the community. As a result, the discipline and the general demands are much stricter. The children have to care for their own dining room. They set the table, wash the dishes and dispense the food with the aid of the teacher's wife. Table manners are enforced, by the strap if necessary. Permission for any unusual activity must be obtained from the teacher whose jurisdiction is not confined to the school hours but extends to the waking hours of the children.

German school is held once a day for about one hour. The memorization of religious texts continues, to which is added the writing and reading of Gothic-German. Since all of the Hutterite religious literature is handwritten, the ability to read and write this type of German is essential for the understanding of Hutterite religion.

Hutterites do not like to interfere with the appointed school teacher who conducts public school. If there are no objections on their part as to a "too worldly" exposure of their children they like to leave the public teachers alone, oft times developing respectful, if not friend-ly, relations with them.

Social Mobility and the School

The Hutterite child who enters public school at the age of six is most likely unable to speak an adequate English, therefore losing a year or two before normal progress can resume. Since the child, however, is taken out of school at the earliest permissable age, usually when it reaches its 15th birthday, few Hutterite children attain the ninth grade.

Hutterite parents tend to be rather indifferent about the grade their children reach in school. The one-room school environment makes the attainment of grades somewhat academic in the first place and since the Hutterite child is not required to enter the public job market, the certification of any educational attainment is superfluous.

While still in school, usually at the age of 12 years, Hutterite chil-dren slowly begin to participate in the communal work patterns. Females begin to help their female relatives in their rotating tasks, while male children begin to attach themselves to some older male rel-ative who happens to be one of the many bosses. These work patterns intensify particularly during the school holidays.

Initiation to Adult Status

On its 15th birthday, the child is taken out of school. At the same time it leaves the children's dining room and takes its place in the adult din-ing room. This event is of greatest significance since it signifies the attainment of an adult status. Where children are not allowed to leave school at such an age, they are known to have developed temporal emotional disorders. A number of Hutterite communities were fined and one or two Hutterite parents even went to jail because they insisted in taking their children out of school.

The 15th birthday marks the day of social promotion from child to adult status. A person still required to attend school, has this promo-tion nullified throwing it into an ambiguous in-between position which, in the highly status conscious Hutterite community, is very painful to endure.

Entrance into the Workforce

At the same time the Hutterite adolescent enters his respective division of labor. Young females and young males form a group of unspecial-ized laborers which can quickly be moved from one work pattern to another.

Much of the hard manual labor that is left in the communities is done by these young males. The females participate in the typical work reserved for women, e.g. cooking, baking, gardening, canning, dish-washing, sewing, cleaning, washing, and child supervision. Some of these activities are conducted within and supervised by the family, like cleaning, washing and sewing. Most others are communal activities organized and supervised by the females of the community.

Apprentice Adults

The status of adolescents over 15 years and up to baptism is something of an apprenticeship for adult roles. While they are allowed to dine with the adults and are part of the adult age and sex division, as unbaptised members they nevertheless have not achieved full religious-spiritual status.

Certain privileges which are gradually bestowed on them, like the issuing of a cloth chest for girls, the inclusion in the distribution circle of wine and honey and wool, slowly draws the adolescent closer and closer into the adult environment.

This is particularly true in the economic field where adolescents might develop special interests and skills which are needed and valued in the community.

Individuality in the Labor Force

A young boy, for example, may specialize in the wiring of electric motors. Although this is not a crucial skill for the community nor a full time occupation, it is a handy skill to have should the occasion arise.

Young girls might corner certain occupations for themselves like cleaning eggs or even copying religious books should their handwriting be good enough to be entrusted with such a job.

On the other hand, Hutterites call these adolescent years "the foolish years." They expect and, in fact, experience a lot of difficulties with their adolescents who find the world beyond the confines of the community too tempting.

Deviant Behavior

Smoking, drinking, the possession of radios and musical instruments are the most common transgressions. Young males particularly are prone to leave the communities for periods of time and "give the world a try." Most of them return eventually and become loyal members, but a small number nevertheless leave the communities and never return.

The Hutterite community deals with this type of deviancy with a great deal of patience and wisdom. Hutterites try to avoid making a complete break with the deviant member always hoping that he or she might change their minds. All too often this is exactly what happens.

A boy might find life on the outside a little too much to deal with or he dearly misses the support and assistance of relatives and friends in the community.

Permissiveness with a Difference

The deviant is always taken back into the community but that does not mean that he is fully accepted. Through his behavior he must show that what he had done was wrong. He must in fact convince the community members that he has learned he has done the wrong thing. He must show remorse for having done so and must be willing to repent.

If the community members are convinced that all this is the case he will be forgiven and the case will be forgotten. But to convince all members of the community of the seriousness of one's attitudes is rather difficult and those who try to fake their good intentions will find that doing so successfully is impossible.

Consequently, the offender is faced either with making a whole-hearted commitment to the community and becoming a full and loyal member, or to exist on the fringes living a shadow existence and being neither a full member of the community nor a non-member.

The latter alternatives are extremely painful. The sight of an alcoholic having been excommunicated from the community years ago yet begging the preacher to be reinstated is indeed a tragic experience. Needless to say that no one will be reinstated unless he has convinced his fellow members through his behavior not through his verbalizations that he deserves it.

Baptism and Marriage

Baptism and marriage mark the final stages in the socialization process of Hutterites. While the first of these designates full spiritual maturity, the second marks the attainment of social maturity. Baptism takes place between the ages of 19 and 21 and in many cases is followed by marriage within six months to a year. There is a trend however, to postpone marriage until the middle 20s.

The married man and woman are recognized as the fundamental unit of the community. Men who remain unmarried are not eligible for high status positions which has the effect that the opportunity structure is closed to them and social mobility is impossible.

The married couple is recognized in terms of the redistribution of goods, e.g. housing, clothing, etc., but also acknowledged in the division of labor. As stated already, married men are looking forward to social promotion, which often is accompanied by a parallel promotion of the wife. The manager's wife often becomes the head cook who is in charge of all food supplies, storage, canning, etc. An unmarried woman may be able to carve out a private career for herself; she might choose to care for her ailing father or mother; these roles are not socially rewarding in the long run.

There is no discrimination toward men or women who happen to be widowed nor is there any discrimination toward a childless couple. Children are expected to be born at the appropriate time after marriage and women who do not seem to be able to produce children are subject to sympathetic understanding.

Baptism, The final stage toward Conversion

Baptism is a highly ritualized procedure. The applicant has to memorize a long list of questions and answers designed to test his religious knowledge. The elders who are requested by the applicant to help him in getting baptized, also subject him to rigorous questionings regarding his former and future life, his personal weaknesses, past failings and future good intentions.

In accordance with the Hutterite worldview, the applicant has to demonstrate that he has gone through the cycle of seeking and obtaining the spirit of God, followed by adherence to the narrow path of righteousness for the future. Baptism is the final stage of the conversion experience which begins when the child learns that it is endowed with a carnal nature and ends with the secure knowledge of being saved by God for all eternity.

THE RELIGIOUS CONTENT OF THE HUTTERITE
SOCIALIZATION PROCESS AND ITS SOCIO-CULTURAL EFFECTS

Childhood and adolescent socialization among Hutterites follows a "Bildungsideal," an image of what Hutterites consider to be a fully developed and matured person of the Hutterite faith. The formulation of such a "Bildungsideal" is extremely difficult, if not impossible, in complex societies due to ideological and social diversities. The ideological and socio-cultural homogeneity of Hutterites and the relatively uniform demands which the Hutterite Gemeinschaft makes on the individual in contrast tends to favor the formulation and the maintenance of a "Bildungsideal" as a guide for processes of education and socialization.

This is not to say that the Hutterite "Bildungsideal" is a simple matter. On the contrary, the concept contains a number of historical, socio-cultural, religious and minority elements whose relation to each other have greatly changed from the founding days of the Hutterite sect to the present.

The exploration of the Hutterite "Bildungsideal" must begin with the principle religious doctrines of the sect and at the same time must attempt to account for the changes that occurred during the last 450 years in the socio-cultural perceptions of these doctrines. Socialization of their children was for Hutterites only second in importance to the religious education of adults which, after all, aimed at the attainment of the goal of salvation. The literature on child socialization and education therefore goes back to the early 16th century when the sect was still in the social movement stage.[2] Two radically new religious concepts, those of adult baptism, and the communal upbringing of children, were among the religious cornerstones of the sect and drew the attention and the inventiveness of the Brethren toward forms of child socialization different from anything practiced in Europe at the time.

Communal versus Kinship Ties

Children were removed from their parents shortly after birth and reared as communal wards. Parent-children relationships were discouraged in favor of adult-children relations thereby de-emphasizing kinship ties in favor of communal ties.

The practice of adult baptism was based on the assumption that only a fully matured person could understand the teachings of God and experience the gift of faith which would draw it toward God as symbolized by the act of baptism.

These religious convictions not only put the community in place of the family as the main socializing agent, but also altered the child's societal role. While child baptism among Catholics and Protestants continued to constitute the child's entry into the civil and spiritual community, independent of the child's wishes, Hutterites emphasized voluntarism on the part of the individual capable of making a choice.

As a result, Hutterite teachings were seen as being destructive not only of civil society but of the religious communities as well. In response to such accusations the sect devoted great care to develop and to justify a system of socialization and education sufficiently sophisticated to refute their critics and persecutors.

The Hutterite Worldview

A shorthand version of the Hutterite worldview is contained in Codex Braitmichel[3] written in 1566 and containing a collection of treatises by various Anabaptist writers of the previous forty years. It is this worldview which gives rise to the Hutterite "Bildungsideal" and assigns meaning to Hutterite institutions.

Reading clockwise from the top, it pictures man as going through a process of separation from God caused by the fall of Adam and result-

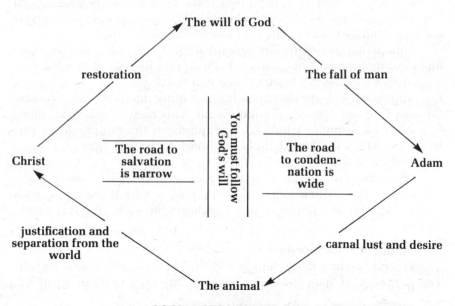

ing in man having the status of an animal. Through a process of separation from the (animal) world and justification through Christ can man be restored to the will of God again.

It is the fate of every individual to go through this cycle during his lifetime. Burdened with original sin, man has the tendency to cater to carnal lust and animal desires.

Only through the separation from the world, which is hopelessly lost to the carnal practices of man and through the sacrifice of Christ can man be restored to act again according to the will of God. Hutterite social institutions are designed to help man in his efforts to suppress the animal desires in himself and attain restoration to the will of God.

The Meaning of Hutterite Institutions
The community of goods, for example, is designed to suppress man's most dangerous desire — the lust for private property and power.

The community of faith, that is the Hutterite religious community, is designed to bring about the restoration of man through communal teachings and mutual assistance in the acquisition of religious knowledge and faith. As the members of a community are obliged to help each other and to "watch over each other," so are the adults of every community obliged to aid all of their children in reaching the goal of eternal life.

There are a number of elements contained in this worldview which highlight the understanding of Hutterite socialization processes.

The will of God is seen as the supreme authority for everything that is good and desirable. God is the source of power (faith) and goodness (grace).

A Hutterite therefore perceives these qualities as being situated outside himself but obtainable to himself through appropriate behavior accompanied by the acquisition of knowledge and faith.

This perception of power sources outside the individual requires an orientation toward authority which is possible only through a proportioned lessening of human self-assertiveness.

Approved self-assertiveness on the other hand is assertiveness through God not through the individual. This raises the crucial question. When and under what circumstances can the individual be certain that whenever he attempts to assert himself it takes the form required by God?

This uncertainty acts as a factor of individual inhibition under social conditions when much of the authority which originates with God for all practical purposes now resides in the authority of the community.

The Nature of Human Nature
The second important element is a definition of man's carnal nature. The carnality of man is perceived as a universal trait of mankind.

While man can rise to come near the divine level of God, most likely (as for the world) he is bound to stay on the carnal level and therefore suffers eternal death.

For the purposes of socialization Hutterites, therefore, teach to their children and expect to find in them, elements of their carnal nature. But at the same time they also expect them to acquire the means to suppress these carnal elements.

Consequently there is no such thing in socialization as the simple acquisition of goodness for an individual who is neither born good nor bad. Hutterites must first learn that their nature is bad, followed by the suppression of badness and the final acquisition of goodness.

The Absence of Sacraments

In the process of going through this cycle, Hutterites have no sacraments save baptism to assist them. While they retain in their teachings the sinful nature of man as found among the Catholics, they eliminated the sacrament of absolution as the major instrument to alleviate the uncertainty of salvation.

Hutterite preachers do not bless people but "wish" that blessings might be bestowed on them. They do not forgive sins but "wish" that sins might be forgiven to them. In every instance, God is seen as the deciding authority and the preacher does not presume to act in his name or exercise his powers.

The Hutterite individual therefore is very much alone with his doubts and uncertainties. His preacher is only a teacher who is believed to have some gifts for teaching but does not act in the name of God. The only support, albeit a powerful one, comes from his fellow man; that is his religious community, which for all practical purposes is also his social and economic community.

In his association with the members of his community, the Hutterite individual finds the power source greater than his own, which helps him to deal with his carnal nature and assists him on the narrow path to salvation.

The Role of the Community

This association with his fellow man, although it has a rational explanation, reaches into the deeper layers of the individual's emotional equipment. Very powerful, probably biologically based feelings of primary group affiliation are being activated and directed by it.

The Hutterite community is seen as life leading to immortality. The outside world is characterized by decaying lust leading to death. The individual's participation in the community of the true believers therefore is capable of removing the individual's doubt about his eternal status and replaces it with certainties of salvation.

The Hutterite community is also the vehicle which essentially provides an institutionalized conversion experience to the individual.

From the depth of his carnal damnation the individual acquires in the community the knowledge of God.

The Importance of Faith

But knowing God is a necessary, not a sufficient, condition of salvation. The acquisition of faith which follows the knowledge of God is emminently mystical and a matter of direct discourse between God and the individual mediated by the community.

It cannot be rationally manipulated or produced and is obtainable only through a profound inner experience which the individual must undergo.

While this conversion experience is facilitated by the knowledge obtained from the teachings of preachers, its acquisition is aided by the spiritual assistance of community members whose expectations and sympathetic understandings gently lead the individual toward the emotional state when the individual feels to be in direct mystical relation with God.

Conversion for Everyone

While there were no manuals and ritualistic prescriptions for the founders of the sect who underwent such a conversion experience during the fervor of the Reformation, the established sect nevertheless came under the obligation to provide the conversion experience for all of its members.

Today, the whole process of socialization of Hutterite youth is essentially a formalized and institutionalized vehicle to obtain a conversion experience for every member of the Hutterite community provided he or she possesses the mental capacities to absorb, memorize and verbally reproduce the requirements which signify its progress.

This institutionalization of a conversion experience has retained its teaching aspects insofar as it concerns the Bible knowledge preached daily in Hutterite church sermons, but also maintains a mystical-emotional element which circulates in a non-verbal fashion among the members of the community.

The formal test of having mastered the first is provided by an examination of the young Hutterite shortly before baptism. The conviction that the latter has been attained by the young Hutterites rests with the conviction of the community, that the person in question has matured and is ready for full membership. It is derived from an intimate knowledge of the individual's personality in a primary and life long social setting.

The Nature and Role of Punishment

Hutterites use two forms of punishment for children: corporal punishment in the form of the strap, and exposure to shame. The use of corporal punishment is justified on the grounds that man's carnal nature develops much quicker in children than the knowledge and understanding of God. Shame is an advanced form of punishment in that it already requires the individual to have an understanding of right and wrong. The exposure of the deviant to the open disapproval of the community is seen as an effective learning experience rather than as a humiliating experience. Corporal punishment diminishes greatly with advancing age and ceases completely at the age of 15.

Justification of Sex Differentiation
The hierarchical structure of the Hutterite community is powerfully reinforced by religious concepts. Sex differentiation is justified by the allegory of Adam's fall. Eve, as will be remembered, gave Adam the apple to eat and therefore was instrumental in *perceiving* evil while Adam himself was only innocently duped. Women are seen therefore as being in greater need for spiritual guidance which can only be given by males. Their exclusion from religious offices and decision-making bodies is justified in this way. Male dominance is a general feature of Hutterite society.

The Intricacies of Social Status
A good indicator of Hutterite status differentiation is the privilege of saying grace at mealtime. In the usual communal setting it is always the higher status male who exercises this privilege. If, for example, a Hutterite family visits someone outside the community and if mother and son are present, the son will automatically say grace if he happens to be baptized. The mother will say grace if he is not. Any baptized member will say grace in the company of unbaptized members regardless of age and sex. The status of the young baptized male is higher than the status of the older baptized female, whose status in turn is higher than that of the young unbaptized male.

If a male and female of equal age are present, the male will say grace. If two males of unequal age are present, the older male will say grace.

The conclusion that can be derived from these examples is that sex is valued higher than age in a female — male situation when both happen to have the same religious status. The religious status (baptism) is valued higher than sex or age. Age finally is the crucial criteria for status if religious status and sex status happen to be equal.

The sex identification is of course always visible and therefore easy to apply. Baptism and age, however, are more difficult to ascertain. Hutterite males begin to grow a beard as soon as they are baptized making it easier for males strange to each other to identify their respective statuses. The age status is usually ascertained through verbal discourse if it is not obvious by sight.

The Value of Social Positions

Finally, social position in the form of a member having been elected to the all male council of elders overrules age. Any elected elder in a Hutterite community must of course be baptized and married to obtain a position in the first place. The six elders are stratified into the two preachers, the boss, the fieldboss, the German school teacher and an elder at large.

This group enjoys special privileges outside the age structure. In church, they sit as a group on a bench facing the congregation and at the dining table they occupy the head table with the boss saying grace. The two preachers have their meals separately at the home of the older preacher.

Social Expectations and Social Mobility

The existence and the functioning of this elaborate status stratification is of utmost importance in the socialization process of Hutterites. As I have shown elsewhere in greater detail[4] the population increase of Hutterites leads to a doubling of the population roughly within one generation. The result of this population growth is the need for constant expansion through the creation of new communities. Each new community is an offspring from one existing community and populated by this community.

This means, that for each generation that grows up a whole new set of status positions is being created.

Social mobility within the Hutterite community is therefore not only provided but assured. For the adolescent male Hutterite, the knowledge that social mobility is possible to him is not only an incentive but also a device which channels him into the direction of realizing certain aspirations which the community raised in him in the first place.

That is to say, that the Hutterite community raises certain social-economic and status expectations in the minds of its adolescents and proceeds to satisfy them by creating and allocating status positions in newly formed communities commensurate with its population increase.

The Hutterite community therefore provides not only a secure economic and social environment for all of its members but also a future and satisfying individual career opportunities at least for its male members.

For female members who in general marry outside their respective communities such an organized structural system of social mobility and promotion does not exist. To a large extent, females depend on the status and career opportunities of their husbands.

The Protection of the Male Hierarchy and Opportunity Structure

The smooth functioning of the male mobility structure is being protected by the patrilocal rule in marriage which requires females to reside in the community of their husbands. Since no husband makes an attempt to reside in the community of his wife, the male hierarchy of all communities is never disturbed by intruding males.

The result of this protective device is that Hutterite adolescents can fairly early calculate their career expectations relative to their peers and see them fulfilled. It is this possibility of long range individual career planning, supplemented by a centralized primary authority, which presents itself as a holistic ideological, economic, and socio-cultural unit to the adolescent, ties the Hutterite individual to his community and induces extraordinary amounts of loyalty in his behavior.

The Chosen People Syndrome

There is another extremely important factor in Hutterite socialization which influences Hutterite personality development to a great extent. References have been made to the religious demands for separation from the world. In fact, Hutterites do maintain a "chosen people" attitude which was very pronounced centuries ago and today exists in a much more muted form.

It originated in religious convictions, but in the course of the centuries some economic and socio-cultural attitudes of superiority were added to it.

For much of their history Hutterites lived in an Eastern European environment where their presence was valued because of its beneficial cultural and economic influence on the rest of the population.

Indeed, the sect takes great pride in accepting unfavorable agricultural conditions and within a few years turning things around, emerging with extraordinarily successful operations. A recent example of this type of superior agricultural craftsmanship can be observed among some communities that have settled in Saskatchewan during the last twenty years.

Hutterites know that they are successful farmers; they know that their economic system works extremely well and while their religious convictions forbid them to openly express pride, the Hutterite adolescent nevertheless is not burdened in facing the rest of society from the inferior point of view of an unsuccessful minority.

Several years ago a number of Hutterite preachers visited a large Western Canadian university. After having been shown around and being duly impressed by the facilities from medicine to agriculture, one would have expected them to be at least ambiguous toward their objections to higher education.

Hutterite Self-perception

On the contrary, while praising the work done at the university, they unashamedly asserted in private that they knew all the things that were done at the university. In a different way they claimed, but equally valid and originating from a better authority, namely God.

There was more in this assertion than a simple defence against an overwhelming amount of scientific knowledge. In a very self-confident manner these preachers compared their society with the outside world and felt they came out on top.

Indeed, from the Hutterite point of view, the world daily gives countless examples of its follies, false pride, vanity and immorality that it becomes unnecessary to point out that the Hutterite way of life is immeasurably better.

The Role of Biblical Analoguing

To see the world in biblical analogues as Hutterites do, provides them with a ready explanation of any current event. The American and Russian space programs are seen in the same light as building the tower of Babel. An expression of the vanity of man and totally useless for man's temporal and eternal existence.

The young Hutterite therefore is presented with a worldview that does not allow him to compare himself with the rest of the world in unfavorable terms. If he does not laugh at the world, after all, there are many things in this world which are rather good, he nevertheless is convinced that his own culture and community is incomparably better than the strife and crime-ridden society in which his own community forms an oasis of peace.

Cultural Self-esteem

Self-confidence and self-esteem about the validity of his own culture sustains the Hutterite personality in the face of the complex demonstrations of an industrial society. That he must engage in intellectual limitations to maintain the validity of his culture can be favorable compared to those dreadful conditions, created when man's mind is allowed to develop freely.

From its inception, Hutterite culture developed as an alternative to the "world." The fact that this alternative survived for nearly 450 years remaining steadfast during periods of most cruel persecution and suffering, is regarded as evidence of the righteousness of the Hutterite way of life.

References

1. The paper is based on extensive field work conducted over a number of years in various Hutterite communities. Hutterite religious and historical writings were extensively used as sources of data in regard to the religious and historical content elaborated on in this paper.
2. Robert Friedmann unter Mitarbeit von Adolf Mais, Die Schriften der Huterischen Taeufergemeinschaften, Gesamtkatalog ihrer Manuskript-

buecher, ihrer Schreiber and ihrer Literatur 1529-1667 (Hermann Boeh-laus Nachf. Graz-Wien-Koeln 1965) pg. 172.
3. Ibid., pg. 136. See also: Robert Friedmann, Hutterite Studies, (Mennonite Historical Society, Goshen, Indiana 1961) pg. 296.
4. Karl Peter, The Dynamics of Open Social Systems, in Social Process and Institution, James E. Gallagher and Robert D. Lambert editors, (Holt, Rinehart and Winston of Canada Ltd., Toronto, Montreal 1971) pg. 164 ff.

Political Socialization Among Youth: A Comparative Study of English-Canadian and American School Children

RONALD G. LANDES
Saint Mary's University

The rapid growth in the field of Comparative Politics in the past decade and a half has not only resulted in a major increase in the amount of comparative data available, but, perhaps more significantly, it has also produced a growing concern with and attention to the methodology of comparative political analysis (see, for example, Scarrow, 1969; Holt and Turner, 1970; Przeworski and Teune, 1970; Mayer, 1972). Unfortunately, the connection between these two elements has not always been immediate. While we would agree with Blondel (1972: 5) that "any analysis of government is, in the deepest reality, either implicitly or explicitly comparative," much of what passes for comparative research seems to be of the implicit genre. This criticism is particularly true, we feel, of the literature which purports to compare various segments of the Canadian and American political systems. While the comparative literature on these two systems spans three decades, it appears that few definitive answers are supported by empirical research (Arnold and Tigert, 1974: 68).

Such a perspective is particularly evident in relation to the possible comparative studies between Canada and the United States in the political socialization area. To this point such research is almost nonexistent. While several research collections on the political socialization process in Canada are now becoming available (Zureik and Pike, 1975; Whittington and Pammett, 1976), the only article that seeks

---

By permission, E-J. Brill, Leiden, Holland

to provide a comparative analysis of the process in Canada and the United States is the work of Jon Pammett (1971). However, even this article could be classified in the implicit genre in that the focus of Pammett's (1967: 12) study of Kingston, Ontario was an attempt to discover "the effect the factor of religion has in producing differential patterns of political socialization in children." His original purpose (Pammett, 1967: 21) was not to make a comparative study of Canadian and American children, although in his later article (Pammett, 1971: 139-140) he does suggest some interesting, speculative hypotheses about the similarities and differences between the United States and Canada in the political socialization area.

Thus, the following article is a brief summary of some of the major findings from the first explicitly comparative study of the political socialization process in Canada and the United States (Landes, 1973). Using a purposive sample of approximately 600 children in grades four through eight in both Belleville, Ontario and Watertown, New York,[1] the following areas will be investigated in this comparative analysis: the child's affective response to government, the child's cognitive perception of the political structure, the development of political knowledge, the acquisition of partisan orientations, and the perception of similarity between Canadians and Americans.

THE CHILD'S AFFECTIVE RESPONSE TO GOVERNMENT

In considering the child's developing perception of the political system, one of the first problems encountered by the analyst is the focus of the child's attention on the political world. In an early and important article in the political socialization field, David Easton and Jack Dennis (1965: 42) suggested that it is "through the idea of government itself that the child seems able to reach out and at a very early age to establish contact both with the authorities and with certain aspects of the regime." In investigating the child's developing affective image of the policy in the American system, Easton and Dennis (1965: 55) came to the conclusion that the child "begins with deep sympathy for government, and this early aura of approval is likely to remain at the base of his acceptance of the government. . ."

In reviewing the comparative literature on Canada and the United States, several major themes of their respective political cultures led us to expect that the level of political affect expressed for government in Canada would be higher than that found in the United States (Lipset, 1967; Hartz, 1955; Presthus, 1973). In particular the significance of the factor of elitism, among others, was the basis for John Meisel's (1975: 244-245) conclusion that "the total effect . . . has been to make Canadians less deferential than the British, and more so than the Americans." In a significant comparative study of interest groups in Canada and the

United States, Robert Presthus (1974: 3-39) also suggests that certain elements of Canada's political culture (i.e. the mosaic philosophy of acculturation, a corporatist theory of society, deferential patterns of authority, and a quasi-participative politics) may help to explain the "differential perceptions of legitimacy regarding government in each society." Particularly the greater role of government in the economic sphere in Canada than in the United States, such that nearly 40% of the Gross National Product was spent by all governments in Canada in 1971 (Van Loon and Whittington, 1976: 1), would provide a basis for inferring that acceptance of government, and thus a more positive view of government, would perhaps characterize Canadian rather than American attitudes. An additional line of reasoning which supports this interpretation is the work of Paul Abramson and Ronald Inglehart (1970), in which they argue that the idealization of political authority should be higher in democracies which are also monarchies than in democracies with only elected political figures.

In considering the child's affective response to government, three indicators of the child's perception of the image of government will be investigated in this comparative study: benevolence ("Would want to help me if I needed it"), dependability ("Makes mistakes"), and leadership ("Makes important decisions").[2] By first of all analyzing the "don't know" alternative we can see to what extent the children in both cities are at least vaguely aware of the concept of "government." Only in grade four do a significant number of children indicate that they do not know what the word "government" means (17 and 18% in Belleville and Watertown, respectively). These percentages drop to 7 and 3%, respectively, by grade five and to 2% by the grade eight level in both cities. Thus, on these data, it is apparent that over 90% of the children by the grade five level have an early recognition of the concept of the government, with nearly total recognition (98%) by the time they reach junior high school.

In relation to our first indicator regarding the benevolence of government (Table 1), the "high" benevolence rating is equal in grade four in Belleville and Watertown (37%), and although there is some fluctuation over the grade span, the percent of Canadian children in the "high" category remains relatively stable, except for grade six, while the percentage of American children declines noticeably in grades six through eight. Thus, by the grade eight level, nearly twice as many Canadian children (38%) than American children (20%) feel a "high" level of benevolence toward their government.

Perhaps even more significant is the pattern of development for the "low" benevolence comparison in Table 1. For both the Canadian and American children the view of government as benevolent declines sharply over the grade span. In other words, the percentages in the "low" columns for both cities nearly double between grades four and eight, such that one-fifth of the Canadian students and over one-third of the American students feel that government would only "seldom" or "not usually" want to help them if they needed it. Such comparisons as these based on Table 1 are consistent with our view expressed above that the level of political affect would be higher in Canada than in the United States.

TABLE 1
THE BENEVOLENCE OF GOVERNMENT "WOULD WANT TO HELP ME IF I NEEDED IT" (PERCENT AGREEING)

Grade	High Benevolence "Always" and "Almost Always"			Medium Benevolence "Usually" and "Sometimes"			Low Benevolence "Seldom" and "Not Usually"		
	Can.	Amer.	E & D	Can.	Amer.	E & D	Can.	Amer.	E & D
4	37	37	57	34	25	36	12	18	7
5	40	37	48	40	35	44	12	26	8
6	27	21	48	47	44	44	17	32	7
7	45	17	45	32	50	47	22	33	9
8	38	20	43	37	41	48	21	36	9

In Table 1 we have also included the results from the Easton and Dennis (1969) study, so that a comparison of the image of government among American children using data collected a decade apart could be presented.[3] In contrast to our data from Watertown, the Easton and Dennis work found a very large segment of children scoring in the "high" benevolence column (57% in grade four, which declines to 43% in grade eight) and very few children ranking "low" in their perception of governmental benevolence. The comparison of these two sets of data is striking and significant, in that by the grade eight level four times as many students in Watertown (36%) expressed a "low" level of benevolence than did the students studied a decade earlier (9%).

Our second indicator for comparing the children's view of government concerned the dependability of government in relation to how often it was perceived as making mistakes. In Table 2 we see that while relatively few of either the Canadian or American children view government as ranking "low" on the dependability rating, the Canadian children do give a much larger response to this item in terms of perceiving their government as ranking "high" in terms of "almost never or rarely" making mistakes. For example, by the grade eight level nearly twice as many Canadian students (37%) as American students (20%) ranked government "high" on the dependability evaluation. While in both groups of children there is an increasing pattern of viewing the government as "sometimes and often" making mistakes, such an image begins slightly higher in the American sample and increases at a faster rate across the grade span than in the Canadian sample (i.e. the "medium" category in Table 2). Again this pattern is congruent with our expectations concerning the image of government between these two countries.

TABLE 2
THE DEPENDABILITY OF GOVERNMENT "MAKES MISTAKES"
(PERCENT AGREEING)

Grade	High Dependability "Always" Never and "Rarely"			Medium Dependability "Sometimes" and "Often"			Low Dependability "Usually" and "Almost Always"		
	Can.	Amer.	E & D	Can.	Amer.	E & D	Can.	Amer.	E & D
4	44	35	73	37	40	26	3	6	2
5	52	35	70	33	54	30	7	9	0
6	43	25	70	47	63	29	2	7	1
7	45	24	66	50	72	34	2	3	0
8	37	20	59	60	72	40	3	6	0

In comparing the American data from Watertown with the Easton and Dennis study, we are again struck by the large differences in the results of the studies conducted a decade apart. For example, by grade eight nearly three times as many students (59%) in the Easton and Dennis study ranked government as highly dependable than did the American students in Watertown (20%). A plausible explanation, we suggest, for these differences on our first two indicators is that the turmoil of American politics in the 1960's, both in foreign and domestic affairs, is reflected in the later data from Watertown. Such an interpretation would be consistent with recent studies on American adults which have found, for example, that "there has been a significant growth in mistrust of government and in pessimism over the ability of government and political leaders to cope with current problems and issues" (Dawson, 1973: 50; see also Dahl, 1976: 111; Miller, 1974).

A third and related factor in the child's image of government is what we have labeled the leadership of government in terms of making important decisions. As indicated above, the greater role of government in Canada would lead us to expect that it would be perceived as making more important decisions than the American government, despite, we suggest, the greater significance of the role played by the United States in world affairs. The results in Table 3 do indeed confirm our expectations. While very few students in either city rank government in the "low" category on the leadership rating, the Canadian children, particularly in the later grades, rate government more highly than their American counterparts. For example, in grade eight 89% of the children in Belleville and 73% of the children in Watertown rate government as making important decisions "all and a lot of the time." Correspondingly, more of the American children rank their government as the "medium dependable" category than is true for the Canadian students. As with our previous two indicators these findings were consistent with our prediction that the child's affective response to government would be greater in Canada than in the United States.

TABLE 3
THE LEADERSHIP OF GOVERNMENT "MAKES IMPORTANT DECISIONS" (PERCENT AGREEING)

Grade	High Leadership "All" and "A Lot of the Time"			Medium Leadership "Sometimes" and "Seldom"			Low Leadership "Almost Never" and "Never"		
	Can.	Amer.	E & D	Can.	Amer.	E & D	Can.	Amer.	E & D
4	53	50	83	25	22	16	4	7	1
5	69	56	86	20	38	14	4	4	0
6	73	50	88	18	36	11	2	8	0
7	89	76	89	7	22	10	3	1	0
8	89	73	93	8	19	7	2	5	0

The comparison of the Watertown and the Easton and Dennis data in Table 3 also shows the pattern evident on our other two indicators. The level of "high" leadership in Watertown is significantly below that of the earlier study (73 versus 93%, respectively, at the grade eight level). Once again these data probably reflect the political conflict and vast changes which took place in the American political system between the Easton and Dennis survey (1961-1962) and the Watertown data collected in January, 1972.

In concluding our discussion of the child's affective response to government in these two communities, several major points should be emphasized. First, as previous research led us to expect, the political affect expressed for government by children in these two cities is higher in Canada than in the United States for our three indicators of benevolence, dependability, and leadership.[4] Secondly, in comparing our American data from Watertown with the American data collected a decade earlier by Easton and Dennis, we have witnessed significant differences in the child's image of American government. The lower scores on the rating of governmental qualities by the American children in 1972 than in 1962 could be explained, we suggested, by the conflict and turmoil evident in the American political system throughout the period between the two surveys. As a result of the pre-Watergate data from Watertown, we would suggest a need for a possible revision in the conclusion that "in the United States a positively supportive image of the general structure of authority is being widely and regularly reproduced for young new members" (Easton and Dennis, 1969: 138).

THE CHILD'S PERCEPTION OF THE POLITICAL STRUCTURE: A PRESIDENTIAL AND A PARLIAMENTARY SYSTEM

The rating items discussed in the previous section provided us with an indication of the level of affect felt by the child for the general political structure in the Canadian and American systems. However, the child relates to his political system not only on an affective basis, but also in relation to his developing cognitive perceptions of the specific structures of the policy. In other words, the developing recognition by the child of the more detailed aspects of the political system is a key ingredient of what Easton and Dennis (1969: 288) have called the institutionalization of political authority. Therefore, our concern in this section will be twofold: first, to consider the extent of the institutionalization of a political authority and secondly, to compare the effects that a presidential or a parliamentary structure has on the child's perception of the polity. These effects will be judged by the responses to two questions: "Who makes the laws?" and "Who does the most to run the country?"

In Table 4 we see the Canadian children's responses to the lawmaking question. The "don't know" category is revealing in that approximately 20 to 25% of the students at all grade levels admit that they cannot select the political institution that is responsible for making the laws of the country. More importantly, the data in Table 4 clearly reveal the early personalization of the political system by the Canadian children and the growing institutionalization of political authority as the children mature. For example, note the pre-dominance of the Prime Minister and the Queen, the two faces of the divided political executive in Canada, at the grade four level and their subsequent and large decline across the grade span in relation to the lawmaking function. Correspondingly, across the grade span the House of Commons increases sharply in the child's view of the political system, from 16% in grade four to 46% in grade eight. Here we have some initial evidence that the process of the institutionalization of political authority is applicable to the Canadian as well as to the American political system.

The data for the American children are also presented in Table 4. The patterns found in the Watertown data are similar to those previously reported by Easton and Dennis (1969: 118-121). For example, although the President dominates at the youngest grade level, he is quickly overtaken in the lawmaking function by the House of Representatives in grade five and even by the Senate in grade six. While in the Easton and Dennis study, 44% of the children in grade four viewed the President as the chief lawmaker, a percentage which declined to 5 by the grade eight level, in our Watertown findings the corresponding percentages are 39% in grade four and 8% in grade eight. These findings in Table 4 support the Easton and Dennis view that as children mature there is an increasing institutionalization of political authority.

TABLE 4
AWARENESS OF CHIEF LAWMAKER ("WHO MAKES THE LAWS?")

Grade	Don't Know	Percent of Canadian children selecting				
		Queen	Prime Minister	House of Commons	Senate	Cabinet
4	20	24	39	16	1	1
5	17	18	27	28	4	5
6	19	10	26	33	2	8
7	26	13	15	36	4	6
8	25	6	5	46	6	11

Grade	Don't Know	Percent of American children selecting				
		Supreme Court	President	House of Representatives	Senate	Cabinet
4	26	16	39	12	4	2
5	23	17	20	34	6	0
6	19	34	9	22	13	4
7	19	13	14	20	27	8
8	16	6	8	38	23	9

Our second major theme in this section, the effects of the parliamentary or presidential structure on the child's perception of the political system, can be investigated by comparing the two sections of Table 4. In relation to the Cabinet, the impact of the political structure in these two systems appears to be beyond the view of our sample children in grades four through eight. While important differences exist in the role of the Cabinets in these two systems, such distinctions are not yet an element of the child's cognitive perception of the political system. However, some interesting differences are evident regarding the structures responsible for the lawmaking function. For example, the difference in the role of the Senate in both systems is quite apparent, with the American children perceiving their Senate as an important part of the lawmaking function, while the Canadian children attach little importance to their own Senate.

Probably more significant is the difference in the view of the role of the executive and legislative branches in the lawmaking function evident in Table 4. For example, the executive branch (Prime Minister and Queen) dominates among the younger Canadian children, but is replaced by the legislative branch (House of Commons plus the Senate) by the grade seven level. Likewise, the American executive (President) is seen as the chief lawmaker in grade four, but is overtaken in this role by the legislature (House of Representatives plus the Senate) in grade five. Thus, in the American presidential system the lawmaking function is more readily transferred to the legislative branch at an earlier age than in the Canadian parliamentary system. This pattern is perhaps a reflection of the fusion of executive and legislative power in a parliamentary political system.

Having considered the child's perception of the lawmaking function in both political systems, we now turn to our second indicator respecting the child's perception of who runs the country (Table 5). While the American children selected the President about 63% of the time (except for grades five and seven), the Canadian children chose the Prime Minister as running the country in grade four 54% of the time, a figure which declines to 24% by the grade eight level. Conversely, the choice of Parliament increases from 13% in grade four to 54% in grade eight among the Canadian children while the legislature (Congress) is selected by 15% of the American children in grade four, a figure which only increases modestly to 24% by the grade eight level. The effects of the presidential-parliamentary structure are clear, we feel, in the data in Table 5. The American President totally dominates in regard to running the country, a view which has a basis in political reality.[5] By contrast, in the Canadian parliamentary system, the Prime Minister does not dominate (except in grade four) and is displaced by Parliament in the child's view by the grade seven level.

TABLE 5
AWARENESS OF WHO RUNS THE COUNTRY

| Grade | ("Who does most to run the country?") Percent of Canadian children selecting | | | |
	Don't Know	Parliament	Prime Minister	Supreme Court
4	18	13	54	15
5	11	33	42	13
6	14	33	43	10
7	16	40	31	12
8	11	54	24	9

| Grade | Percent of American children selecting | | | |
	Don't Know	Congress	President	Supreme Court
4	12	15	63	7
5	7	13	76	4
6	4	30	62	4
7	7	32	57	4
8	9	24	63	3

In regard to both of our indicators, therefore, the structure of the political system, whether a presidential or a parliamentary setup, does appear to have an impact on the child's developing perception of the polity. In both systems a developmental pattern of the institutionalization of political authority was evident across the grade span. Also, the children increasingly associate the legislative structures with the law-making function. However, there were also some differences between the two systems in relation to lawmaking: for example, the different ratings given to the two Senates.

With regard to our second indicator ("Who runs the country?"), in the American system the children view the President as the one who runs the country, while in Canada the older children view Parliament as both making the laws and running the country. Such findings as those presented above are congruent, we feel, with the distinction between the presidential structure of the American system and the parliamentary structure of the Canadian system. These results also seem to suggest that future research in the political socialization area should deal more explicitly with how differences in political structure (i.e. whether it is presidential or parliamentary, federal or unitary) influence the child's developing perception of his polity.

THE DEVELOPMENT OF POLITICAL KNOWLEDGE

The third major area of analysis in this comparative study is the development of political knowledge among the students in our Canadian and American samples. Our concern will be twofold: first, with the level of political information acquired by the children and secondly, with the developmental pattern of political learning, in particular, the age at which political knowledge is acquired. As an indicator for the level of political information we will use the child's ability to name particular political figures. Of course, our indicator is a low level abstraction for the more sophisticated concept of political information. However, given the age of our respondents, we feel that knowledge about political leaders is a suitable indicator for this comparison.

In Table 6 we present our data concerning the acquisition of knowledge about the major political leader at each level of government for both the Canadian and American children. In both groups the level of political information, as expected, shows a marked and steady increase across the grade span. For example, among the Canadian children in grade four 26, 13, and 37% can correctly name the Mayor, Premier, and Prime Minister, respectively, while in grade eight the corresponding percentages have increased to 68, 73, and 94%. It is evident in these data that the Prime Minister is the most salient in the child's perception of these three political authority figures. At all grade levels the Prime Minister is the leader that is correctly named the most often. Except in grade four, the children can correctly name the Mayor and Premier about the same percent of the time at all grade levels.

A similar pattern of results is also apparent in the American data summarized in Table 6. The predominance of the President in the

American political system is evident. At grade four 79% of the children in Watertown can correctly name the President, and this correct perception becomes virtually complete by grade seven. This predominance is especially noticeable at the younger grade levels, where only 21 and 16% of the children in grade four can correctly name the Governor and Mayor, respectively. In grades four through six more children can correctly name the Governor than the Mayor, but this pattern reverses itself among the older children.

TABLE 6
THE DEVELOPMENT OF POLITICAL INFORMATION

Percent of Canadian Children Correctly Naming Political Leaders		
Grade	Mayor of City	Premier of Ontario	Prime Minister of Canada
4	26	13	37
5	47	45	66
6	66	56	79
7	69	69	82
8	68	73	94

Percent of American Children Correctly Naming Political Leaders		
Grade	Mayor of City	Governor of New York	President of the United States
4	16	21	79
5	32	50	90
6	42	52	96
7	72	67	99
8	85	74	99

In comparing the levels of political information evident in our Canadian and American data in Table 6, we can see that the active head of the national government, particularly among the younger children in both systems, predominates over other authority figures in the child's developing cognitive image of the political system. Moreover, in a comparison of the political leaders at the same level of government, it is apparent that the level of knowledge about the American President is greater at each grade level than the knowledge Canadian students have of their Prime Minister. This knowledge differential is particularly striking among the younger students.

The comparison regarding local and state or provincial leaders shows a mixed pattern of responses. The American children can more often name their Governor in grades four and five than the Canadian children who can name their Premier. In the later grades the children in both cities are about equal in their ability to name their state or provincial political leader. For the local level of government the younger

Canadian children can more often name their Mayor, but by grades seven and eight the older American children have a higher level of correct information.

On the basis of the kind of data presented in Table 6, we would have to conclude that the levels of political information acquired by the Canadian and American children in these two cities are quite similar. Only on the Prime Minister-President comparison is there a large and persistent difference across the entire grade span. This particular finding is not surprising, considering the presidential *versus* parliamentary structure of the American and Canadian political systems discussed in the previous section of this paper. However, in relation to our two other indicators of political knowledge, the comparisons show a mixed pattern of responses. On a number of possible comparisons concerning the levels of political information between the Canadian and American children, (data not presented here), the differences are either small or show a mixed pattern, as with the data in Table 6.

Our second major focus in relation to political information concerns the age at which political orientations are acquired. For example, Jon Pammett (1971: 140), on the basis of his study of Kingston, Ontario, suggested the following hypothesis:

> The socialization of political orientations in many Canadian children takes place in adolescence rather than at earlier stages of development. In the United States, for comparison, many more political orientations are learned in pre-adolescence.

Previous research has suggested some support for Pammett's view. In comparing the political socialization patterns of legislators in Canada and the United States, Allan Kornberg and his colleagues (1969: 87) came to the conclusion that Canadians "seem to go through the same general process as do Americans, but that for the former the events take place somewhat later in life." Although isolated findings, such as the children's ability to name their chief executives at the early grade levels, support such an hypothesis, the majority of our data do not show that the Canadian children in Belleville acquire their orientations at any later date than their American counterparts in Watertown. Whether in terms of political information and knowledge, willingness to rate authority figures on various characteristics such as benevolence, ability to perceive and rate the levels of government in their federal system, and partisan attachment,[6] the Canadian and American children are very similar in the extent and age at which political orientations develop. If our data are representative they indicate that the patterns of political learning may not be very different for English-Canadians and Americans in the early 1970's, a conclusion which is contrary to Pammett's hypothesis and much of the conventional wisdom about the political socialization process in Canada. Such a conclusion, we feel, points to the significance and need for additional comparative research conducted in both systems at the same point in time.

THE ACQUISITION OF PARTISAN ORIENTATIONS

In comparing the child's acquisition and development of political orientations in Belleville and Watertown, it is not unreasonable to expect that such a key component of a system's political culture as political party identification might differ considerably in nature and extent. While previous research has usually indicated a high level of partisan identification in American children (Greenstein, 1965: 64-84), it has often been suggested that Canadians do not exhibit such an early attachment to political parties (Pammett, 1971: 140). In assessing these ideas we will analyze both the total level of party identification and the apparent continuity in the transmission of party identification between the parent and child. Table 7 presents a comparison between the levels of party identification for the various grades in Belleville and Watertown, along with similar data from previous research. These results are all based on a question similar to the one we used: "If you could vote, what would you be?"

TABLE 7
COMPARATIVE PARTY INFORMATION

Sample location	Grade 4 5 6 7 8 (% with a partisan preference)				
(1) Belleville, Ontario (Dec., 1971)	33	55	63	62	48
(2) Watertown, New York (Jan., 1972)	20	31	34	42	43
(3) Kingston, Ontario (1966)*					
(a) Public Schools	25	27	44	42	46
(b) Separate Schools	35	29	53	54	54
(4) National American Sample (1961-1962)*	49	55	57	56	53
(5) New Haven, Connecticut (1958)*					
(a) Upper SES	63	66	61	71	49
(b) Lower SES	63	56	56	67	61

*The data are taken from the following sources: (1) Kingston, Ontario: Jon H. Pammett, "The Development of Political Orientations in Canadian School Children," Canadian Journal of Political Science, 4 (March, 1971) pp. 132-141; (2) National American Sample: Robert D. Hess and Judith V. Torney, The Development of Political Attitudes in Children (Chicago: Aldine Publishing Company, 1967); (3) New Haven, Connecticut: Fred I. Greenstein, Children and Politics (New Haven, Connecticut: Yale University Press, 1965).

Contrary to our expectations based on previous research, the data for the Canadian children indicate a higher level of partisan identification in all grades than for the American children in Watertown (row 1 versus row 2). In grade four 33% of the children in Belleville identify with a political party, while only 20% of the children in Watertown make such a selection. By grade eight 48% of the Canadian compared to 43% of the American children express a partisan affiliation. Comparison of these data with previous research also shows some interesting deviations from the expected pattern. Our data (row 1) tends to show, particularly in grades 4 through 6, a higher level of party identification than Pammett found in Kingston (rows 3a and 3b). Such evidence, we feel, should prevent the easy acceptance of the view that the level of party identification is lower in Canadian than in American children.

The American data (row 2) for Watertown also exhibit important differences from previously reported research (rows 4 and 5). Particularly at the younger grade levels, the children in Watertown show a very low level of partisan attachment. For example, only 20% of the children in grade four in Watertown identify with a political party, while in the Hess and Torney data (row 4) 49% and in the Greenstein study (rows 5a and 5b) 63% indicate such an attachment. The levels of identification in grades seven and eight in Watertown (42 and 43%, respectively) are still less than the identifications of children in grade four in the Hess and Torney and in the Greenstein study (49 and 63%, respectively). In addition our data from Belleville (row 1) are very similar to the American sample of Hess and Torney (row 4). Given these data we feel that it would be unwise to conclude that the development of party identifications among Canadian children are learned less frequently and later in life than their American counterparts.[7]

A usual corollary of the view that partisan identification is lower in Canadian than American children (an interpretation which our data questions) is the idea that a possible explanation of such a pattern might be the lack of continuity in many Canadian children of the partisan orientations of their parents. Again our data do not seem to support such an inference.

Table 8 presents the results of crosstabulating the child's party preference with his perception of his parent's party affiliation. Because of the small N's for the minor parties in Canada, we include only the results for the major parties in each system. The evidence of parent-child congruence in party identification is undeniable. For example, of the Canadian children who indicate that they would vote for the Conservatives, 68% say their parents are also Conservatives. Similarly, 62% of the children who select the Liberals also say their parents are identified with the Liberal party. A corresponding pattern is also apparent in the American data.

TABLE 8
CROSSTABULATION OF THE CHILD'S PARTY PREFERENCE
WITH KNOWLEDGE OF HIS PARENT'S PREFERENCE

	American Sample		
	Child's Perception of Parental Preference		
Child's Party Preference	Don't Know	Republican	Democrat
Republican	32	61	2
Democrat	20	8	70
Sometimes One and Sometimes Another	50	25	20
Don't Know	81	8	8
Don't Know What These Words Mean	92	2	4

	Canadian Sample		
	Child's Perception of Parental Preference		
Child's Party Preference	Don't Know	Conservative	Liberal
Conservative	18	68	10
Liberal	28	6	62
Sometimes One and Sometimes Another	58	16	15
Don't Know	78	5	7
Don't Know What These Words Mean	89	4	6

This pattern of parental-child congruence is also seen in the various "don't know" categories. For example, of the Canadian children who say they would sometimes vote for one or another party, 58% do not know the party affiliations of their parents. Also, 78% of the children who answer "don't know" for their own voting preference indicate they "don't know" their parents identification either.

Of course we must stress that these data are based on the child's perception of his parent's political affiliation. We have no way of knowing whether or not the child is correct in his information. However, the data in Table 8 would at least question the view that the apparent transmission of partisan preference from parent to child is low in Canada. In addition, the level of parent-child congruence in partisan preference, as perceived by the child, is very similar in Belleville and Watertown.

PERCEPTION OF SIMILARITY BETWEEN CANADIANS AND AMERICANS

As a final point of comparison the children in Belleville and Watertown were asked whether or not they thought that Canadians and Americans were alike or different in most ways (Table 9). About 55% of

TABLE 9
SIMILARITY OF CANADIANS AND AMERICANS

| | | Belleville, Ontario | |
Grade	I'm not Sure	Alike in Most Ways	Different in Most Ways
4	24	55	22
5	18	58	23
6	18	58	23
7	16	55	28
8	12	58	29

| | | Watertown, New York | |
Grade	I'm not Sure	Alike in Most Ways	Different in Most Ways
4	41	43	16
5	23	60	16
6	28	70	3
7	19	70	11
8	28	65	8

the Canadian children at all grades indicate that they are similar to the Americans in most ways. Only 22% of the Canadian children in grade four and 29% in grade eight feel that there is much difference. For the American children 43% in grade four and 65% in grade eight feel that they are like Canadians in most ways. In contrast to the Canadian children, the older the American children are, the more they feel they are like the Canadians. While the Canadian children increasingly perceive themselves to be different from the Americans over the grade span, the Americans see themselves as more like the Canadians in the later grades. By grade eight 29% of the Canadian children, but only 8% of the American children, perceive a difference between themselves.

It is interesting to compare the Canadian data in Table 9 with the earlier study by John C. Johnstone (1969: 22-36) which was conducted among a national sample of adolescents in 1965. In response to whether or not Americans and Canadians were generally the same, Johnstone found that among the English-speaking adolescents 79% thought they were alike in most ways and 18% thought they were different. These findings are much higher than the ones found in Belleville. For the children in Belleville around 55% of all grade levels thought that the Americans and Canadians were alike, while an increasing number of the older children (29% by grade eight) perceived a difference. Also, in Belleville anywhere from 12 to 24% selected the "I'm not sure" category, while only 3% did so in Johnstone's Survey.

In comparing Johnstone's findings with our own, we can speculate on the discrepancies apparent in the results. We would offer as a possible explanation the recent and growing emphasis in the Canadian system on its distinctiveness in relation to its American neighbor. Particularly revealing is the small but steady trend among the older Canadian children to see a greater difference between themselves and the Americans. In contrast to the adolescents surveyed in 1965, the children in Belleville in late 1971 were perhaps expressing a growing awareness of their own Canadian identity.

CONCLUSION

Using a purposive sample of approximately 600 children in grades 4 through 8 in both Belleville, Ontario and Watertown, New York, we have sought in this article to summarize some of the major findings from the first explicitly comparative study of the political socialization process in Canada and the United States. Several major conclusions seem to be warranted by the data. First, many of the differences we expected to find between the Canadian and American children simply were not evident in our results. On many indicators (for example, the development of partisan preferences) our findings ran counter to those of previous research. Moreover, in several important areas, the similarities in the patterns of political learning are very apparent for the Canadian and American children. A second major finding was that there were in specific areas (i.e. the child's affective response to government, the effects of the political structure on the institutionalization of political authority) important differences in the development of political orientations between the Canadian and American students. In addition to these findings based on the comparisons between the students in Belleville and Watertown, we also sought to relate our findings to previous research, in particular the work of Easton and Dennis for the American system and Jon Pammett for the Canadian system. Here again major discrepancies were apparent between the various data sets (for example, the American child's affective response to government).

Given the nature of our data (i.e. that our sample was limited to one city in both countries), it would perhaps be unwise to assert that the patterns found in these two cities are definitive for all other areas in these two systems. However, such data as presented above at least make us reluctant to accept the conclusions of previous research and thus, they clearly demonstrate the need for and importance of additional comparative research on the political socialization process in Canada and the United States.

Footnotes

1.   The assumption underlying the city selection process for this comparative analysis was the idea of choosing two cities which were reasonably similar on a number of important economic and social characteristics. In other words, we followed the "most similar systems" method of compari-

son which seeks to minimize the effects of such variables as town size, geographical setting, occupational makeup, and ethnic-racial composition in our data. Using general classification schemes and census data comparisons, Belleville, Ontario and Watertown, New York were viewed as appropriate cities for such a comparison.

The sample utilized can be described as one of "purposive" design selected from the children in grades four through eight in Belleville and Watertown. In consultation with the schoolboards and principals we chose schools which were "representative" of each city and comparable between cities. Schools from several sections of each town and from both the separate and public school systems were included. Approximately 600 questionnaires were administered in each city in late 1971 and early 1972.

2. The indicators utilized were taken from those developed by David Easton and Jack Dennis (1969: 168). Of their original 14 indicators, 5 were selected, on the basis of a pretest, for inclusion in the final format for the students in Belleville and Watertown. Due to space limitations only 3 of these items are presented in this particular analysis.

Each item originally contained six possible answers, plus a "don't know" alternative. For Tables One through Three, we have collapsed the six answer categories down to three, producing a high, medium, and low split for each variable. The "don't know" column is not included in the Tables. In addition, a "no answer" column was eliminated from the Tables, and this, along with rounding errors, accounts for the fact that the row percentages may not add up to 100%.

3. The data from the Easton and Dennis study (1969: 132-133) were also collapsed into our 3 groupings for the purposes of comparison. The Easton and Dennis study is referred to as the E & D column in Tables One through Three.

4. If the mean scores on these indicators are compared by grade level, using a difference of means test, the Canadian children have lower scores (higher affect) in all 15 cases, 13 of which are statistically significant at the .05 level using a one-tailed test.

5. The data from Watertown on this indicator are very similar to the Easton and Dennis (1969: 120) results. For example, in grade five 72% and in grade eight 58% of the children in the Easton and Dennis study viewed the President as the one who runs the country, while the corresponding figures in Watertown are 76% in grade five and 63% in grade eight.

6. Only a part of the data on which this conclusion is based has been presented in this article. For a fuller treatment of the many possible comparisons see the original thesis text (Landes, 1973).

7. The nature and extent of partisan identification among Canadian adults has produced a number of conflicting interpretations. For an example of the recent arguments both pro and con regarding the concept of party identification, consult the following sources: Meisel (1975), Jacek (1975), Jenson (1975), and Sniderman et al. (1974).

References

Abramson, Paul R, and Ronald Inglehart
  1970   "The Development of Systemic Support in Four Western Democracies," *Comparative Political Studies* II (January), 419-442.

Arnold, Stephen J. and Douglas J. Tigert
1974 "Canadians and Americans: A Comparative Analysis," *International Journal of Comparative Sociology* XV (March-June), 68-83.

Blondel, Jean
1972 *Comparing Political Systems.* New York: Praeger Publishers.

Dahl, Robert A.
1976 *Democracy in the United States: Promise and Performance,* third edition. Chicago: Rand McNally and Company.

Dawson, Richard E.
1973 *Public Opinion and Contemporary Disarray.* New York: Harper and Row.

Easton, David and Jack Dennis
1969 *Children in the Political System: Origins of Political Legitimacy.* New York: McGraw-Hill.
1965 "The Child's Image of Government," in Roberta Sigel (ed.), *Political Socialization, Annals of the Academy of Political and Social Science* (September), 40-57.

Greenstein, Fred I.
1965 *Children and Politics.* New Haven: Yale University Press.

Hartz, Louis
1955 *The Liberal Tradition in America.* New York: Harcourt, Brace, and World.

Hess, Robert D. and Judith V. Torney
1967 *The Development of Political Attitudes in Children.* Chicago: Aldine Publishing Co.

Holt, Robert T, and John Turner (eds.)
1970 *The Methodology of Comparative Research.* New York: The Free Press.

Jacek, Henry J.
1975 "Party Loyalty and Electoral Volatility: A Comment on the Study of the Canadian Party System," *Canadian Journal of Political Science* VIII (March), 144-145.

Jenson, Jane
1976 "Party Strategy and Party Identification: Some Patterns of Partisan Allegiance," *Canadian Journal of Political Science* IX (March), 27-48.
1975 "Party Loyalty in Canada: The Question of Party Identification," *Canadian Journal of Political Science* VIII (December), 543-553.

Johnstone, John C.
1969   Young People's Images of Canadian Society. Ottawa: Queen's Printer.

Kornberg, Allan, et al.
1969   "Some Differences in the Political Socialization Patterns of Canadian and American Party Officials: A Preliminary Report," Canadian Journal of Political Science II (March), 64-88.

Landes, Ronald G.
1973   Socialization to Political Culture: A Comparative Study of English-Canadian and American Schoolchildren. Toronto, Ontario: Ph.D. Dissertation, Political Science Department, York University.

Lipset, Seymour Martin
1967   The First New Nation. New York: Anchor Books.

Mayer, Lawrence C.
1972   Comparative Political Inquiry: A Methodological Survey. Homewood, Illinois: The Dorsey Press.

Meisel, John
1975   Working Papers on Canadian Politics, second enlarged edition. Montreal: McGill-Queen's University Press.

Miller, Arthur H.
1974   "Political Issues and Trust in Government: 1964-1970," American Political Science Review LXVIII (September), 951-972.

Pammett, Jon H.
1971   "The Development of Political Orientations in Canadian School Children," Canadian Journal of Political Science IV (March), 132-140.
1967   Political Orientations in Public and Separate School Children. Kingston, Ontario: M.A. Thesis, Political Science Department, Queen's University.

Presthus, Robert
1974   Elites in the Policy Process. New York: Cambridge University Press.
1973   Elite Accommodation in Canadian Politics. Toronto: Macmillan of Canada.

Przeworski, Adam and Henry Teune
1970   The Logic of Comparative Social Inquiry. New York: John Wiley Interscience.

Scarrow, Howard
1969 *Comparative Political Analysis: An Introduction.* New York: Harper and Row.

Sniderman, Paul M., *et al.*
1974 "Party Loyalty and Electoral Volatility: A Study of the Canadian Party System," *Canadian Journal of Political Science* VII (June), 268-288.

Van Loon, Richard J. and Michael S. Whittington
1976 *The Canadian Political System*, second edition. Toronto: McGraw-Hill Ryerson Limited.

Whittington, Michael S. and Jon H. Pammett
1976 *Foundations of Political Culture: Political Socialization in Canada.* Toronto: Macmillan of Canada.

Zureik, Elia and Robert M. Pike (eds.)
1975 *Socialization and Values in Canadian Society.* Volume One: *Political Socialization.* Toronto: McClelland and Stewart.